This book is concerned with the conflict between the goals of justice and economic efficiency in the allocation of risk, especially risk pertaining to safety.

The author approaches his subject from the premise that the market is central to liberal political, moral, and legal theory. In the first part of the book, he rejects traditional "rational choice" liberalism in favor of the view that the market operates as a rational way of fostering stable relationships and institutions within communities of individuals with broadly divergent conceptions of the good. Markets are needed most where they are most difficult to create and sustain, however, and one way to understand contract law in liberal legal theory, according to Professor Coleman, is as an institution designed to reduce uncertainty and thereby make markets possible. Another target of this book is the prevalent view that tort law helps rectify market failures when transaction costs are too high to permit contracting. The author argues instead that tort law should be understood as a way of rectifying wrongful losses, not inefficient exchanges.

Risks and wrongs

Cambridge Studies in Philosophy and Law

GENERAL EDITOR: JULES COLEMAN (YALE LAW SCHOOL)

ADVISORY BOARD

David Gauthier (University of Pittsburgh)

David Lyons (Cornell University)

Richard Posner (Judge in the Seventh Circuit Court of Appeals, Chicago)

Martin Shapiro (University of California, Berkeley)

This series reflects and fosters the most original research currently taking place in the study of law and legal theory by publishing the most adventurous monographs in the field as well as rigorously edited collections of essays. It is a specific aim of the series to traverse the boundaries between disciplines and to form bridges between traditional studies of law and many other areas of the human sciences. Books in the series will be of interest not only to philosophers and legal theorists but also to political scientists, sociologists, economists, psychologists, and criminologists.

Other books in the series

Jeffrie G. Murphy and Jean Hampton: *Forgiveness and mercy*

Stephen R. Munzer: *A theory of property*

R.G. Frey and Christopher W. Morris (eds.): *Liability and responsibility: Essays in law and morals*

Robert F. Schopp: *Automatism, insanity, and the psychology of criminal responsibility*

Steven J. Burton: *Judging in good faith*

Risks
and wrongs

JULES L. COLEMAN
YALE LAW SCHOOL

CAMBRIDGE
UNIVERSITY PRESS

Published by the Press Syndicate of the University of Cambridge
The Pitt Building, Trumpington Street, Cambridge CB2 1RP
40 West 20th Street, New York, NY 10011–4211, USA
10 Stamford Road, Oakleigh, Victoria 3166, Australia

First published 1992

Printed in the United States of America

Library of Congress Cataloging-in-Publication Data
Coleman, Jules L.
Risks and wrongs / Jules L. Coleman.
p. cm. – (Cambridge studies in philosopy and law)
Includes index.
ISBN 0–521–32950–7 (hardback) ISBN 0–521–42861–0 (pbk.)
1. Law – Philosophy.   2. Torts – Economic aspects.   3. Contracts –
Economic aspects.   4. Liability (Law)   5. Justice.   6. Risk.
7. Social choice.   I. Title.   II. Series.
K230.C64R57   1992
340′.1–dc20   91–37630
                                                                                    CIP

A catalog record for this book is available from the British Library.

ISBN 0-521-32950–7 hardback
ISBN 0-521-42861–0 paperback

To my children
JESSE, JEREMY, and LAURA

Contents

Contents

Preface

In the early 1980s I wrote a series of articles on the moral foundations of the economic analysis of law in response to Richard Posner's laudable efforts to defend efficiency as a moral ideal. Although these articles succeeded in calling into question the prevailing account of the normative foundations of economic analysis, I was never very pleased with them. My problems were of two sorts. If others like Posner did not have the intellectual integrity to see that efficiency needed a defense and the courage to provide one, there would have been no Coleman essays on the subject. However sound and well-received my arguments may have been, they were almost entirely negative, critical, and counterpunching in nature. Second, since my own philosophical training and instincts included a fair bit of rational choice theory, I felt a bit inconsistent about criticizing economic analysis while at the same time committed to a form of rational choice social science. The connection between economic analysis and rational choice theory is too close for this dichotomy to be psychologically, let alone philosophically, sustained.

Eventually, in the mid 1980s, I set out to provide a defense of economic analysis that would not be subject to the objections I and others had raised. Instead of grounding economic analysis in utilitarianism, as classical economists had, or deontic moral theory, as Posner sought to do, I sought to defend it as an implication of a kind of rational choice contractarian political theory. Rational choice contractarian political theory could itself be derived from a more abstract approach to social and moral sciences I came to refer to as the market paradigm. Part I of this book develops in a compressed form that conception of the market paradigm that would have provided the defense of economic analysis Posner had unsuccessfully pursued. Part I also contains the arguments that led me ultimately to reject the market paradigm and to abandon my efforts to defend conventional law and economics. In its place, Part I also presents the political theory I believe can ground a more limited defense of a different kind of law and economics scholarship. I call this theory *rational choice liberalism*. One feature of rational choice liberalism is the importance it attributes to markets as against efficiency as such. Part I sets out my defense of markets, not economic efficiency as a property of social states. The kind of economic analysis I defend, then, will not provide solace for most contemporary law and economics scholars. The remainder of the book develops the scope and limitations of this kind of approach to legal interpretation. Although many of the topics I discuss here are familiar from my previous work, my views have changed significantly. The argument in Part III in particular replaces all previous claims I have made about tort law and the allocation of safety related risks.

I have tried to present a coherent and unified argument from beginning to end. No doubt I have failed. In some places, the ungenerous reader may feel that I have not provided arguments at all, although in certain circles the failure to provide an argument is a sign of intellectual strength, not weakness. It is unlikely, however, that philosophers who adopt this post-modern approach to argument will be among the readers of this book. I have tried to identify places where arguments are incomplete or otherwise needed. I have no desire to fool anyone.

Because the book includes materials drawn from economics, law, and philosophy, the most difficult task for me (other than making the argument plausible) has been trying to determine the reader to whom the argument is addressed. Economists are not likely to be deeply enlightened by what I have to say about the foundations of rational choice theory.

I am, after all, much more a consumer of rational choice theory than a producer of it. What I have tried to do is present philosophical arguments. My hope is that these arguments are not only good ones, but accessible to lawyers and economists who are interested in the questions this book addresses. At the same time, I hope that the problems I pose and seek to resolve interest philosophers sufficiently to encourage others to take up similar problems in other areas of the law and political theory. In the end, my hope for this book is that those who read it take it to be good evidence for the research program I suggest in Part I, namely a unified, but not a reductionist, social and moral science.

Acknowledgments

Many individuals have read and commented upon various sections of this manuscript. I am especially indebted to John Ferejohn, Jean Hampton, David Gauthier, David Schmidtz, Steven Croley, Jeffrey Lange, and Ned McClennen for comments on Part I. Bob Cooter, Alan Schwartz, Randy Barnett, and Bob Scott were very helpful in clarifying the arguments of Part II, with which all of them no doubt disagree, but for different reasons. That section is drawn from an article I wrote with Douglas Heckathorn and Steven Maser, and they deserve equal credit (but full blame) for it.

Many individuals had input into the argument in Part III. Larry Alexander and Jacob Adler commented on an earlier version of significant sections of it. Heidi Hurd and Anita Allen commented on more recent versions. France Kamm read the central chapters on two different occasions, and her comments were especially insightful and helpful both times. Bruce Ackerman forced me to consider the extent to which my views in Parts II and III could be reconciled. Jody Kraus helped me formulate some of the basic arguments about rights, and spent many months trying to convince me that everything else I had to say on the subject of tort liability was wrong. In contrast, Carl Wellman spent some time trying to convince me that what I had to say about rights was wrong. Although they have not read the manuscript, the influence of both Richard Epstein and George Fletcher is apparent.

Three individuals had an especially strong impact on the shape of argument in Part III. Ernest Weinrib has engaged me in debate on these topics for nearly a decade. Our friendship and respect for one another survives the fact that he thinks my views are roughly as mistaken as I think his are. For years, he has pressed against me the view that my theory of corrective justice has nothing to do with corrective justice. At first, I understood him to be arguing only that my view had nothing in common with Aristotle's view of corrective justice. Since I studied philosophy at Rockefeller University, I thought that the very earliest philosopher was Frege, so I was unimpressed by this argument. Indeed, I looked everywhere in Frege's work, but could find no useful reference to corrective justice. Ultimately, however, Weinrib won me over, but not so far over as to embrace his views.

Like anyone working in analytic jurisprudence, I have followed the work of Joseph Raz. But I did not learn until the summer of 1990 that Raz had been teaching and thinking about my views on torts for years. While in Oxford during that summer, I was fortunate enough to spend time with Raz, during which he pressed a variety of criticisms against me, the force of which were too obvious to miss. In 1991 I returned to Oxford, where I again discussed my newly developing ideas with Raz, especially on the relationship between corrective justice and other legal and political institutions for allocating loss. In a few short hours, Raz led me to see things clearly that had been, until then, fuzzy at best. Everyone should have the opportunity to discuss his work with someone like Joseph Raz. I know of no person more sympathetic, thoughtful, decent, and concerned with bringing out the best in the work of others. He's the sort of professional each of us should aspire to become.

Above all others, however, I owe a special debt of gratitude to Stephen Perry. Stephen has worked over my materials for years and probably knows more about my views on torts than I do. In a paper he presented at Oxford commenting on my thesis, he advanced a series of sustained objections that made it literally impossible for me to defend the views with which I had grown so accustomed to being associated. From that moment on, we forged a close friendship and working relationship. We discussed every change in the overall argument that I contemplated making. In fact, any mistakes that remain are probably his doing.

On January 31 and February 1, a conference was held at the University of San Diego Law School in which a penultimate draft of this book was discussed. I am grateful to Dean Kristine Strachan for funding the conference. I am especially indebted to Larry Alexander for organizing it and making it successful. Several of the arguments herein have been sharpened as a result of comments made by participants. The distinction I draw in the book between top-down and middle-level theory grows out of the contributions at the conference of David Gauthier and Jean Hampton. Chapter 21 attempts to bring the arguments in Parts I, II, and III together. The need for it grew out of comments made by Gauthier, Hampton, and Peggy Radin as well as many earlier discussions with Bruce Ackerman.

Stephen Perry's criticism of my analysis of the necessity cases has shaken my confidence in the argument presented in Chapter 15. Objections to the argument in Part II by Richard Craswell, Alan Schwartz, and Randy Barnett have forced me to clarify the argument and emphasize its connection to Part I in ways I previously had failed to do. The papers by Ken Simons and Emily Sherwin led me to develop further the relationship between corrective justice and the norms it sustains. Papers by Steven Walt and David Gauthier also required me to state more carefully the argument against the market paradigm and its consequences. Though I have tried to respond to the main objections that were raised, I doubt that I will have satisfied these or other critics completely. The papers are collected in a forthcoming issue of the *Harvard Journal of Law and Public Policy* and readers of this book are directed to that issue.

Dean Guido Calabresi of the Yale Law School provided me with research support and time off to complete the manuscript, which was begun during a sabbatical funded in part by the Guggenheim Foundation in 1989–90. Along with Joel Feinberg, Calabresi is responsible for my having an interest in these topics in the first place. He taught me both law-and-economics and tort law. Many of the ideas developed here first came to my attention upon reading his *The Costs of Accidents*. There is every reason to believe, however, that he continues to disagree with me at nearly every turn.

In late March, 1992, I was informed by Cambridge University Press that the only existing completely copyedited version of my manuscript had been stolen. My immediate thought was that the book was so good that some potential author could not resist the temptation to steal it and publish it under his own name. Apparently, this has happened to others. My next thought was that someone was so anxious to read it that he could not await its publication. Unfortunately, my hopes were dashed. My manuscript was merely coincidental to the crime, not its object.

The loss of the manuscript, however, set me back substantially. I was forced to reconstruct the text from previous, unedited drafts and notes. Had it not been for the support of my family and the help of Steven Hetcher and Trish DiMicco, I doubt that I would have had the energy to pursue its completion.

Several students at Yale in addition to Steven Hetcher have worked as research assistants at earlier stages on this project. I am grateful to Steven Croley, Anthony Sebok, Tim Lytton, and Christopher Gilkerson for their help. In addition to doing all of the copyediting work on this final draft and reviewing the copyediting of earlier drafts, Steven Hetcher has influenced the discussion of the relationship between corrective justice and conventions in Part II. I owe a large debt to Trish DiMicco for putting the manuscript together more times than either of us wanted and for enduring my obsessive personality.

I am one of the people in philosophy who does not feel underappreciated or undervalued – except on rare occasions, and then only by a few people. I have had wonderful colleagues and great friends in the professions with which I am associated. What more can one ask for (other than a good

Acknowledgments

salary and generous retirement and dental plans)? Each in his or her own way has made it possible for me to undertake and complete this project (twice). I have also been lucky in love. My wife, Mimsie, has guided me through this project in the way in which she has guided me through our life together: with strength, understanding, and laughter. I want to acknowledge the contribution to this manuscript of my three children: Jesse, Jeremy, and Laura. Without them, I would have completed it years ago and everything I would have argued for then I would now be in the position of denouncing or apologizing for. Whether this is something I end up doing a few years from now remains to be seen. Finally I want to thank Donald Fagan, Lou Reed, Neil Young, Graham Parker, and Van Morrison. Without them I could not have made it from the late sixties at Berkeley to the early nineties at Yale.

Introduction

This is a book in liberal political, moral, and legal theory. It is impossible to characterize liberalism in either a comprehensive or an uncontroversial fashion. Sometimes liberalism is thought to identify a set of political or moral *values*, for example, autonomy, equality, or neutrality. Other times liberalism is identified with concrete political *rights* of the sort conferred on individuals in the U.S. Constitution: especially, freedom of expression, religion, and association. Yet other times it is thought to articulate a form or family of political *justifications* or constraints on justificatory strategies, for example, the claim that political authority must be justified to those individuals against whom the coercive powers of the state are to be deployed.

Characterizing liberalism is further complicated by the conceptions of it that have been offered by its communitarian critics. Some of these critics identify liberalism with a metaphysically thin or empty conception of the person or with a form of normative atomism. Other communitarian critics associate liberalism, not with basic political rights and moral values, but with concrete political and economic institutions, including the private law of property and contract and, most importantly, the market.

Liberalism does not require commitment to the market as a scheme of economic organization, nor must an argument for the market proceed from liberal premises only. The liberal ideal of rational autonomous agency among persons can be given institutional expression in forms of social organiza-

1

tion other than the market. In that case property and contract may be less important to liberalism than its communitarian critics suppose. Having said that, it remains true that the market has traditionally played an important role both in the characterization of liberalism and in its implementation in concrete political institutions. Different forms of liberal theory are likely to express the centrality of the market in different ways, however.

THEMES

In the first part of this book I explore a form of liberal theory that treats the market as the cornerstone in its interpretation of important liberal political, legal, and moral practices. I call this conception of liberalism the *market paradigm*. The market paradigm as such is not a theory advanced by any particular political, legal, or moral theorist. Rather, it is one that grounds a family of political, legal, and moral theories, each of which has been (and can be) advocated and defended independently of one another and of the market paradigm itself. Still, it is the relationship of these theories to the market paradigm and the underlying commitments of the market paradigm itself that will interest us here.

Several theories in fields as diverse as jurisprudence, political philosophy, and moral theory can be construed as instances of the market paradigm. In this book I consider three: one about the nature of law, another about the foundations of political authority, and a third about the nature and scope of morality.

Consider, first, law and economics. Under a well-known, if infrequently realized, set of conditions, resources move to their most highly valued uses without the interference of law. When these conditions are not satisfied, however, legal institutions are necessary to promote efficiency. Thus, the best interpretation of current legal institutions, especially the private law of property, contract, and tort, understands them as designed either to facilitate market exchange or to rectify market failures. The justification of legal practices, and the

2

use of coercive authority within them, depend on the relationship these institutions bear to the market and, in particular, to the efficiency of markets. Law generally, and private law in particular, are solutions to problems of market failure.

Consider next the political contractarianism often attributed to Hobbes. Political association is a response to a collective action problem that all agents face in the state of nature. The problem is that the state of nature is a *prisoner's dilemma* (henceforth P.D.). In a standard P.D., each individual's acting in self-interested but rational ways leads to an outcome that is less than optimal for each. The collective action problem can be solved by an enforceable contract among all agents. In this contract each agrees to forgo an individually rational strategy in favor of a jointly maximizing one. The contract is enforceable by a political authority that the agents authorize to compel their compliance. In Hobbesian contractarianism, political associations are established by contracts; they are schemes of rational cooperation designed to produce efficient equilibria that are unobtainable by noncooperative practices under conditions of market failure. They are cooperative alternatives to competitive failures. I call this position *rational choice contractarianism,* and its central hypothesis is that a justified political authority represents a particular kind of solution to the problem of market failure (represented by the prisoner's dilemma payoff structure of much human interaction in the state-of-nature).

Whereas rational choice contractarianism may have its roots in Hobbesian political theory, some contemporary moral theorists, for example, David Gauthier, have explored the possibility of analyzing morality as a solution to a similar problem of collective inefficiency or market failure. To be rational is to act on the basis of one's self-interest. Rational agents seek to maximize their expected utility. Morality constrains the extent to which individuals are free to act on the basis of utility-maximizing reasons. Because moral constraints restrict the extent to which individuals are free to pursue their rational interests, it is natural to ask whether, and if so, under what conditions, rational individuals would adopt moral

3

constraints. When, in other words, is it rational to constrain one's rationality? We can begin to answer this question by asking another. Under what conditions, if any, might it *not* be rational for individuals so to constrain themselves?

The First Fundamental Theorem of Welfare Economics entails that under conditions in which competitive equilibria obtain, each individual acting purely on the basis of self-interest does as well as he or she can, given the utility of others. Thus, under conditions of perfect competition, it is not rational for individuals to impose moral (or other) constraints on themselves. Under these conditions a constrained agent will do less well than she or he would do in the absence of constraint. The competitive market is, to use Gauthier's terms, "a morally free zone." It follows from the fact that morality is irrational under the conditions of competitive equilibria that moral constraints are rational only under the conditions of market failure. Moral constraints are schemes of rational cooperation for mutual advantage designed, in effect, to solve the problem of inefficiency created by the failure of the conditions of perfect competition to obtain. Morality, like law and political association more generally, is a solution to the problem of market failure.

In the market paradigm, legal, political and moral institutions are collective schemes of self-constraint and rational cooperation. They are to be understood as rational responses to the generic problem of market failure, and justified to the extent that they replicate the outcomes of competitive markets. Cooperation is a response to failed competition, inexplicable otherwise, and justified, moreover, only to the extent it mimics aspects of competition. This is the core of the market paradigm.

Chapter 1 articulates the building blocks of the market paradigm and develops their implications for moral, political and legal theory. Chapter 2 critically evaluates the market paradigm. Whereas the market paradigm treats all forms of rational cooperation as responses to failed competition, competition presupposes cooperation, and is itself incomprehensible without it. If the market paradigm does not have the place of the market in liberal political theory just right, it remains true that the market is central to liberal political theory, and we should see if we can give an account of the market's centrality that is consistent with both political liberalism and principle of rational choice with which we begin.

Markets maximize social interaction without individuals first being required to agree upon fundamental social values or to share a conception of the good or of the constitutive elements of the good life. The market is a particularly appropriate form of rational organization under certain sets of empirical circumstances, including heterogeneity of values, cultural diversity, geographic dispersion and the like. In such communities markets contribute to social stability. That is their attraction to liberal political theory. In addition, to the extent the preference for stability is itself rational in such communities, markets are a rational form of cooperation. Though based on the principle of individual rationality, the market is itself a way in which individuals give expression to a prior commitment to cooperate. It is a form of cooperation by competition, an appropriate form of social and economic organization under a wide range of empirical conditions, and its attraction to the liberal depends on those conditions being satisfied.

Markets are most attractive where individuals have broadly divergent conceptions of the good, where the relationships among individuals tend to be one-dimensional, discrete, nonrepeating, and where the benefits and burdens of cooperation are spread over persons, time, and geography. They are least necessary where interaction is repeated, where relationships are multidimensional and direct, and where there are shared conceptions of the good. Markets are most attractive where they are most difficult to establish and sustain; and they are least attractive or necessary where they are easiest to create and sustain.

Markets contribute to social stability under a set of conditions that coincide with increased uncertainty. The problem of uncertainty that makes markets attractive to the liberal also makes them difficult to implement and sustain. One way of

Introduction

creating and sustaining markets relies on having a legal institution of contract. Contract helps create and sustain markets by reducing the extent of uncertainty that exists under those conditions in which markets are most attractive. Contract law consists in exogenous transaction resources that safeguard against contract failure by reducing uncertainty. Part II of this book presents this liberal conception of contract law.

If contract is designed to facilitate exchange by providing safeguards to contract failure, tort law might then be understood as designed to promote efficient outcomes when contracting is not possible. Contracts assign risk by mutual agreement; tort law assigns risk by public norm. Contracts assign risk ex ante; tort law assigns risk ex post. If contract is designed to facilitate the market process through which individuals freely move resources to their most highly valued uses, then tort law is a set of norms that allocate costs so as to move resources to their most highly valued uses when transaction costs make it impossible for individuals to do so through conventional market processes. Tort law is designed to encourage forced (not free) efficient exchange.

Whereas the market provides a good point of departure for analyzing the process of rational contracting, this book argues that the same is not true of tort law. Whereas Part II sets out a general theory of rational contracting, Part III develops a theory of tort law that relies on the principle of corrective justice. Rather than viewing tort law as designed to rectify market failure by moving resources from one party to another in the form of "forced transfers," the chapters in Part III argue the view that on the whole tort law rectifies wrongful losses by imposing their costs on those individuals who have the duty in justice to repair them.

METHODOLOGY

I should say something about the book's methodology. Parts II and III explore aspects of existing legal practices, in particular, Part II looks at contract law and Part III seeks to provide

6

an understanding of important aspects of tort law, focusing primarily on accident law. In each case, my goal is to provide an *explanation* of those parts of the practice I discuss. In doing so, I am concerned to understand the law from the standpoint of practitioners who ask not only, "How may we carry on this practice in a way that is faithful to its inherent norms?, but rather, "How may we carry on this practice in a way that is faithful to norms that are both inherent in it and reflectively acceptable to us?"[1]

We can distinguish among at least three legitimate forms of legal theory. One of these seeks an understanding of the law that will enable individuals who live within it to *predict* the behavior of relevant officials, or the direction the law will take, and, in some cases, how others with whom they interact will behave in certain settings. Let's refer to this form of explanation as "positivist." For the positivist, explanation is normally tied to prediction, and prediction is *instrumentally* important to individuals within a practice as well as for those observers who, to use Hart's useful phrase, adopt the external point of view. This kind of explanation enables individuals within a practice to anticipate legal rulings and to conform their behavior and expectations accordingly, while it also provides external observers with a lens through which they might understand the *causes* of social behavior, if not the *reasons* for it.

Whereas there is much to be said for positive legal theory of this sort, this book makes no predictions, derives no theorems, and is generally uninterested in this form of explanation. It is interested in providing an explanation of our practices, or important parts of them, but explanations that make sense of the practice in the light of norms it claims are inherent in it, norms, moreover, that could withstand the test of rational reflection. This sort of explanation focuses on the reason-giving or normative dimension of social practices. Again, borrowing from Hart, these explanations are especially relevant to those adopting the internal point of view, as well as to outside observers who want to understand a practice not merely as convergent behavior, but as behavior regulated by norms, in which those norms figure in the explanation of convergent behavior.

We can also distinguish among at least two ways of approaching this sort of explanatory inquiry. The first kind of explanatory approach adopts what I will call a "top-down" strategy. In top-down explanations, the theorist begins with what she takes to be the set of norms that would gain our reflective acceptance, at least among those practitioners who adopt the internal point of view. Then she looks at the body of law she seeks to understand and tries to reconstruct it plausibly as exemplifying those norms. Parts of the law that fail to be plausibly reconstructed might then be identified as mistakes; suggestions for reform are made. Theorists adopting a top-down approach face two significant burdens. The first is to defend the norms identified as meeting the appropriate characterization of the test of reflective acceptance. The second is to explain the sense in which the practice exemplifies those norms.

In contrast to the top-down approach, one can work from the middle up. I call this "middle-level" theory. In middle-level theory, the theorist immerses herself in the practice itself and asks if it can be usefully organized in ways that reflect a commitment to one or more plausible principles. This approach seeks to identify the principles that are candidates and those aspects of the practice that reflect them. Other theorists might suggest other principles or a different mapping of principles to aspects of the practice. Sometimes theorists will disagree about the proper formulation of principles they otherwise agree are reflected in legal practice. Other times there will be disagreement about which principle among the set of plausible candidates provides the best understanding.

Questions about which principle provides the best understanding can be complex. One principle may have greater apparent explanatory scope of application, but be less likely to secure reflective acceptance, its scope being purchased at the price of implausibility, and so on. This, for example, is my view of the relative merits of corrective justice and economic efficiency as accounts of the structure of tort law. Eco-

nomic analysis claims a broader scope of application, but its claims rest, I believe, on an implausible account of why injurers and victims are brought together in litigation; and it is unclear that efficiency as such is the sort of norm that could secure reflective acceptance among participants in the practice.

Both top-down and middle-level theory provide accounts of the normative, or reason-giving, dimension of social practices. Practitioners of either approach face substantial obstacles and skeptical challenges. Top-down theory can be so immersed in foundational debates regarding the reflective acceptability of a set of principles that it may never descend to the level of the practice those principles are supposed to illuminate. Or the principles may descend imperialistically leading to a conceptual remaking of the practice in the light of the foundational view. More often than not, this will result in a picture of the practice that makes it all but unrecognizable to those familiar with it. Finally, top-down theorists face the skeptic's charge that the foundational principles are not really being formulated abstractly or independently of the practice, but with an eye towards the practice, making the enterprise appear viciously circular.

Middle-level theory faces similar problems. It may so engage the practice that it gets lost in it. If it becomes so nominalist and particularistic, it may fail to locate principles of sufficient generality to coherently structure and organize the practice. When organizing norms are uncovered by middle-level theory, the suspicion will often persist that the principles discovered are advanced less because they inhere in the practice than because they reflect the theorist's favored foundational view.[2] This kind of criticism, alas, is unavoidable.

This book offers a middle-level account of accident law and a top-down account of contract law. Why the difference in methodology? I do not answer this question directly until Chapter 21. Moreover, in the end, the only convincing defense will be the enterprise itself. The approach is defensible if it illuminates, otherwise it is not. Still, I want to offer two preliminary reasons for the approach I have taken.

9

In the first place, I know a lot more about torts than I do about contracts. So it is easier for me to look at contracts from the lofty position of the philosopher and more natural to look at torts from the muddled position of the torts teacher. Second, recall that my motivation in Part I is to provide a moral or political theory on which the economic analysis of law could comfortably rest. No one, least of all me, denies the predictive insights that can be gleaned from the application of economic analysis at the micro level. Some might accept its plausibility as an account of legal practice at the middle level. Other than economists and lawyer economists, however, most observers have not found the economic interpretation of our practices when taken as a whole to be persuasive. And part of the reason for that, as Dworkin and I among others have pointed out, is that efficiency is not the sort of "principle" that is reflectively acceptable on its own terms, unconnected to the role it might play in the pursuit of other values or as a dimension of other values.

Our legal practices are normative. If economic analysis is to provide a satisfactory understanding of them, economic analysis itself will require a normative grounding. To that end, I present the market paradigm. Its ambition is to provide the kind of normative defense of economic analysis Posner sought. Moreover, the market paradigm offers a top-down defense of the economic analysis of law. If in order to be justified the law must respond to problems of market failure, then the only plausible interpretation of our legal practices that honors them is an economic one. There will be no need to muddle about in middle-level theory. In Chapter 2, I reject the market paradigm, but I do not reject the idea that economic analysis can be given a normative defense. In that regard, I present rational choice liberalism. The main difference between the market paradigm and rational choice liberalism is that the former promises a defense of economic efficiency whereas the latter does not. Rational choice liberalism argues for the centrality of markets, not efficiency, in liberalism. It defends markets because they can contribute to

rational social stability under a broad range of circumstances likely to arise in liberal cultures. It therefore deemphasizes both the efficiency of markets and their laissez-faire dimensions. It is a liberal defense of the market, not an economic or a libertarian one.

Like the market paradigm, rational choice liberalism promises the possibility of a top-down approach to understanding legal practices, at least those that are essential to the creation and development of markets. Unlike the market paradigm which invites us to look at legal practices as contributing to the efficient allocation of resources, rational choice liberalism asks us to look at legal practices from the point of view of the role they might play in creating and sustaining markets. If rational choice liberalism is a defensible political theory, then it can provide a normative grounding for economic analysis, but a form of economic analysis that emphasizes the importance of markets and not the desirability of efficiency as an independent moral ideal.

Chapter 2 does not defend rational choice liberalism as a full political theory. That issue is not directly addressed until Chapter 21, where the need to tie together the normative premises of Parts I, II, and III is confronted. Chapter 2 merely makes the case for rational choice liberalism by showing that it is compatible with the initial starting points of the market paradigm – rationality and the market – without being subject to the objections that prove fatal to the market paradigm. Chapter 2 does, however, invite us to approach various legal practices from the perspective of understanding them in the light of the role they play in creating and sustaining markets. I apply this top-down approach to legal understanding in the discussion of contract law in Part II. Proponents of conventional law and economics are asked to read Part II as an invitation to reconceptualize contract in economic terms that emphasize coordination, cooperation and stability apart from efficiency. This explains the sense in which this book applies a top-down approach to contract law. It does not apply the same kind of approach to tort law. Why?

The answer is simple enough. I believe that applying rational choice liberalism to tort law will miss much that is important about the practice. Remember, the difference between rational choice liberalism and the market paradigm is that the latter sees all law entirely in terms of its role in promoting efficiency whereas the latter claims that certain parts of the law help to create and sustain the conditions under which markets can flourish and contribute to stability. My view is that tort law is not primarily an institution designed to create or sustain markets. Therefore, any approach to understanding tort law from that perspective will miss or misunderstand at least as much as it illuminates. On the other hand, if we look at tort law from the inside, we will see that at its core tort law seeks to repair wrongful losses. Tort law implements corrective justice, or so I argue. Part III works from the practice itself to the relevant principles inherent in it. In doing so the argument tries to analyze the central components of corrective justice, namely, wrongful loss and responsibility for it. Because this is a book in liberal theory, the text tries to make clear the relationship between these dimensions of corrective justice and liberal political theory.

Part I outlines a form of liberalism, rational choice liberalism to be precise. Part II applies it to contract law. Part III works from tort law to the principle of corrective justice, and from the principle of corrective justice to liberal ideals. But are the liberal ideals expressed in Part III compatible with those in Parts I and II? Parts I and II appear to emphasize stability; Part III autonomy, responsibility, and well-being. It may be that these liberal ideals are not entirely of a piece with one another. Different parts of the law may be animated by different strands of liberalism. The book concludes in Chapter 21 with a very preliminary and sketchy attempt to bring these strands of liberalism together. Fully developing the theory outlined in Chapter 21 is, thankfully, beyond the scope of the book. The argument presented there should be read as a first step along the path of developing the deeper political theory on which the normative commitments of the

various parts of this book ultimately rest. This is just a very long work in progress. But let's see what progress we can make. We begin with a formulation and development of the market paradigm.

Part I

The market paradigm

Chapter 1

Rationality and cooperation

The market paradigm is committed to two basic postulates: the first is the principle of rationality; the second is the economist's conception of the perfectly competitive market as its ideal institutional embodiment. These two premises are designed to help answer two questions. These are: Under what conditions is it rational for individually rational agents to cooperate with one another? What is the shape and content of rational cooperation? In effect, the market paradigm attempts to uncover the *motivation* for rational cooperation and its *substantive* content.

Because the market paradigm accepts only the principle of rationality, it assumes no criterion of justice or fairness that cannot itself be derived from the principle of rationality or otherwise implicated in the process of rational choice. The market paradigm does not deny that there can be a justified morality. Quite the contrary. It means to demonstrate the conditions under which a morality could be justified. In general, if the norms constitutive of a political, legal, or moral order are to be justified, if the force employed to enforce them and the disapprobation that accompanies failures to comply with them is to be warranted, then the content of the rules must follow from the principle of rationality. Justification is a matter of rationality alone.

These concerns of the rational motivation for political and moral constraint, of the ways in which the theory of rational motivation constrains the substance of a political morality, and of the way in which justification depends on the principle of rational choice all presuppose or require a conception of rationality. To which conception of rationality is the market paradigm committed?

1.1 INDIVIDUAL AND COLLECTIVE RATIONALITY

Let's begin with the economic conception of individual rationality as utility maximization. When pursuing a noncooperative strategy a rational agent seeks to maximize her utility; under conditions of uncertainty, she seeks to maximize her expected utility. What constraints does rationality so conceived impose on rational cooperation generally and on legal and political norms in particular? The obvious answer is that in order to be justified such norms must be rational. The claim that rational justification requires that political practices be rational is analytic, but it is the sort of analytic truth that can be illuminating.

We begin with the distinction between two dimensions of rationality: *individual* and *collective* rationality. Collective rationality is defined in terms of Pareto optimality and ranges over state-descriptions or social states.

> D1: A social state is collectively rational iff it is Pareto optimal.

Pareto optimality is itself defined in terms of Pareto superiority.

> D2: A social state is Pareto optimal iff there are no social states Pareto superior to it.

Pareto superiority is correctly defined in terms of individual preferences over social states.

> D3: A social state, S′ is Pareto superior to another state, S, iff no one prefers S to S′, and at least one person prefers S′ to S.

Strictly speaking, the Pareto criteria order individual preferences over social states. Though social states may be com-

18

pared with respect to a range of properties, it is common to identify Paretianism with a kind of welfarism. Thus, we might define Pareto superiority as follows:

D3': S' is Pareto superior to S iff no one is worse off in S' than in S, and at least one person is better off in S' than in S.

We can now define individual rationality.

D4: A social state is individually rational for an agent iff it leaves her no worse off than the status quo.

Though collective rationality is defined in terms of Pareto optimality which is then defined in terms of Pareto superiority, individual rationality is not itself definable in terms of Pareto superiority or optimality. An outcome can be individually rational for an agent, but not Pareto superior. Some outcomes, after all, make some agents better off than they would be in the state of mutual noncooperation only by making others worse off (and are thus not individually rational for them). Such outcomes are not Pareto superior, however rational they are for at least some individuals. The defection outcome in a P.D. has the property of being individually rational for the defector, but not Pareto superior to the status quo. That is because the defector takes advantage of the compliance of others which enables her maximally to benefit without constraint, but which forces others to absorb the costs of self-constraint without the benefits of cooperation.

This example illustrates one way in which rationality and Pareto superiority can be connected.

D5: If a social state is individually rational for all agents, then it is Pareto superior.

Or,

D6: A Pareto superior state is individually rational for all agents.

19

The market paradigm

Because there are at least these two distinct criteria of rationality, the claim that the market paradigm is committed to the principle of rationality as a basis of political justification and as a theory of human or moral psychology is ambiguous. There are significant differences among the claims that: a political (or moral) arrangement is justified iff it is collectively rational; such arrangements are justified if they are individually rational; such arrangements are justified iff they are both individually and collectively rational. To embrace collective rationality as *the* criterion of political justification is to claim that political justification is a matter of Pareto optimality only. To claim that political arrangements can be justified only if they are individually rational for all agents is to say that political arrangements must leave no one worse off than they would be in the state of mutual noncooperation. But such arrangements need not exhaust the gains from cooperation. Finally, arrangements that are both individually and collectively rational for all agents are maximally productive (collective rationality) and to each person's relative advantage (individual rationality).

These principles of rational action express aspects of a theory of human motivation as well as a theory of political justification. The rationality of a course of conduct is supposed to provide agents conceived of in a certain way with reasons for acting. Arrangements that exhaust the gains from cooperative endeavors (collective rationality) and do so in a way that makes everyone as well off as he or she might be in the state of mutual noncooperation (individual rationality) are desirable, feasible, and enforceable. Indeed, in conventional rational choice theory, individual and collective rationality provide separately necessary motivations for collective action.

The individual rationality condition imposes the constraint that legal, political and moral institutions must ultimately be weakly in each individual's interest, at least from the ex ante perspective. That is, the norms imposed by either a justified morality or political authority must weakly enhance each individual's utility, or, put slightly differently, each rational individual would agree to comply with the norms of a polit-

20

ical morality only if ex ante each perceived compliance to be at least in his or her interest.

If political norms are constraints on the pursuit of individual interest, then they can be justified only if each rational agent could understand compliance with them to be in furtherance of those interests. Rationality counsels constraint on the pursuit of individual interest only when constraint furthers those interests. This is one way in which the analytic truth that rationality counsels constraint on rationality only if doing so is rational can be illuminating.

1.2 THE PRODUCTIVE DIMENSION OF MORALITY

We might characterize this implication of the principle of rational constraint as the proposition that a justifiable political morality must have a *productive dimension*. To claim that a justified political morality must be productive implies two things, each of which corresponds to a principle of rationality. First, a political morality can be justified only if it is Pareto optimal, that is, only if it exhausts the gains from cooperation. Given a set of constraints, it must be maximally productive. Second, a political morality can be justified only if it is individually rational, that is, only if it is welfare increasing for each individual, or, at the least, only if it is welfare reducing for no individual. If political and moral principles are constraints, justifiable only if they are rational, and rational only if they are productive or welfare enhancing, it follows that a justified political morality consists in a set of *mutually advantageous constraints:* that is, such constraints must be beneficial to each individual whose compliance with their demands is rational. From the ex ante perspective at least, political, legal and moral constraints fall within the domain of mutually advantageous interaction.

We can reach the same conclusion from the opposite direction. Instead of assuming that political institutions are productive, imagine that they are unproductive. Rather than creating a larger pie, the purpose of political institutions is to redistribute shares of the same pie. In effect, we are suppos-

21

ing that political institutions are *redistributive* only, thus lacking a productive dimension. This would render political association a series of zero-sum games. In a typical zero-sum game, one player's gain is equivalent to another's loss. No gains without corresponding losses. (Importantly, no losses without corresponding gains as well.) In fact, given the costs of rent-seeking behavior, that is, the expenditure of resources for the sole purpose of redistribution, the political realm would more likely constitute a negative, rather than a zero-sum, game.

How might we represent the vision of political morality as a zero-sum game in rationality terms or in utility space? When an arrangement is collectively rational or Pareto optimal, no one's well being can be enhanced except at another's expense. When resources are allocated in a Pareto optimal fashion, only nonproductive redistributions are possible. If political, legal or moral constraints were designed to redistribute wealth, as they might be if they were designed to shift resources from one Pareto optimal state to another, then cooperation could improve someone's well-being only by making other individuals worse off. A set of political constraints of this sort, consisting in the movement of resources along the Pareto frontier, could not be individually rational for all agents. Compliance with the norms constitutive of such a cooperative scheme would not be in the interests of those whose lot would be worsened by it. Purely nonproductive cooperation is not individually rational for all agents. It follows that only productive cooperation can be rational for everyone. Justifiable schemes of political association governed by norms of a political morality are themselves mutually advantageous schemes of cooperation.[1]

1.3 THE DISTRIBUTIVE DIMENSION OF MORALITY

The analysis to this point implies that in order to be rational political cooperation must be productive. If the market paradigm followed conventional economic conceptions of rational motivation, it would be left here: to be justified, polit-

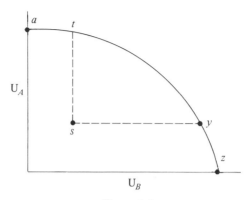

Figure 1.1

ical, moral, and legal arrangements must be exhaustively productive and mutually advantageous. But this conception of rational motivation is incomplete. Though it is true that in the absence of uncertainty and risk-aversion, rationality precludes purely redistributive schemes, all forms of rational cooperation have a distributive dimension. The distributive dimension of cooperation is also an element of its rationality. Thus, a full theory of rational motivation will conjoin principles of collective and individual rationality with what I will call a principle of *bargaining* or *distributive* rationality.[2]

Let's make the intuitive observation more precise. We have shown that rational cooperation must have a productive dimension. Therefore, rational cooperation cannot be entirely redistributive. That, in turn, means that cooperation cannot consist in moving from one Pareto optimal outcome to another. Such transfers are, by definition, redistributive only. Therefore, rational cooperation arises when individuals find themselves situated in less than Pareto optimal, that is, inefficient, circumstances.

Let S be the state of mutual noncooperation and assume that S is suboptimal. Relative to S, there exists a number of ways of improving each person's welfare that will satisfy both the individual and collective rationality conditions. In Figure 1.1 point s represents an inefficient state of the world. Points *a* through *z* are Pareto optimal or efficient. That is, any point here represents a state of the world in which further improvement of any individual's welfare or utility is possible only by reducing the welfare of others. All movement along the Pareto frontier involves wealth redistribution only. So securing everyone's rational agreement to movement from one point to another along the frontier is not possible. This is a graphic illustration in utility space of the point made earlier that for risk-neutral agents rational cooperation cannot be entirely redistributive. Cooperation can be rational only if it involves movement toward the frontier, not simply along it.

In order to be rational, cooperation must move everyone (in this simple case, *A* and *B*) from *s* toward and ultimately to some point on the Pareto frontier. Moreover, only points *t* through *y* are rational for both *A* and *B*. All states of the world represented by points between *a* and *t* make *B* worse off than he is at *s*, and all points below and to the right of *y*, for example *z*, make *A* worse off than she is at *s*. Only the points between *t* and *y* are feasible and enforceable for *A* and *B*. Still, there are a number of options available to both *A* and *B*, a number of different ways of distributing the benefits and burdens of cooperation. Thus, a number of *efficient* schemes of cooperation are available to *A* and *B*, differing from one another in their *distributive dimension*. This argument demonstrates that rational or optimal cooperative schemes differ from one another not in their relative efficiency but in the ways in which they distribute the cooperative gains. Thus, distribution is always an aspect of cooperation.

The next question is whether the distributive dimension of cooperation is part of the problem of rational choice. Is the distributive dimension of cooperation an aspect of its rationality. If the conventional economic theory of rational motivation were correct, the choice among the set of institutional arrangements collectively and individually rational could not itself be a matter of rationality. Any arrangement that is both collectively and individually rational would be equally rational and, given the theory of justification as rationality, equally justified.

Alternatively, one could adopt a theory of justification of a different sort, in which rationality played a different (and weaker) role. For example, one might argue that in order to be justified any such arrangement must be rational, but its being rational would not entail its being justified. To be justified, the benefits and burdens of cooperation must be both rationally and fairly allocated, where *fairness* is to be understood as stating some independent criterion of assessment outside the domain of rationality. In effect, any such approach treats rationality as a necessary but not a sufficient condition of political justification. Additional criteria of political justification arise outside the domain of rationality.

In both of these alternatives, the individual and collective rationality conditions jointly specify the full extent of the theory of rational justification. In one of these approaches, the entire theory of political justification is given by the theory of rational justification. In that account, all options that are individually and collectively rational are equally justifiable. In the other account, the full theory of political justification includes, but is not restricted to, the theory of rational justification. In order to be justified, political institutions must be both rational and *fair*, where fairness is on this account a criterion of assessment beyond the realm of rational choice.

Neither of these approaches is altogether satisfactory. For advocates of the market paradigm, the second alternative is not available because it permits principles outside the domain of rational choice to enter into the justification and explanation of rational cooperation. The market paradigm, however, countenances no principles of justification that cannot be grounded in the principle of rationality or otherwise implicated in the process of rational decision. If collective and individual rationality specify the full criteria of political justification, the distribution of the costs and benefits of cooperation is irrelevant to the justification of authority.

If the distribution of the benefits and burdens of cooperation is immaterial to the justification of political authority within that rational choice framework, then so much the worse for it. If the manner in which rules distribute the benefits and burdens of cooperative schemes is relevant to their justification, and if justification is entirely a matter of rationality, then the distributive feature of cooperation must be an aspect or dimension of the theory of rational choice. This is the only alternative acceptable to a rational choice theorist bent on providing a plausible interpretation and justification of our ordinary notions of political authority and of the social practices that exemplify them. The full rational choice theory of human motivation and political justification, then, consists in principles of collective, individual, and division rationality.

1.4 MORALITY AS PRODUCTIVE AND DISTRIBUTIVE

The connection between production and division in the theory of rational cooperation runs deeper still. The argument to this point invites us to reconsider the way in which the shape and content of morality ought to be conceived. Contrast the rational choice conception of morality with utilitarian and egalitarian conceptions of it. While utilitarians have rightly emphasized the productive dimension of cooperative social interaction, their critics have correctly faulted utilitarianism's disregard for its distributive aspects. Similarly, traditional accounts of social justice, for example, egalitarianism, have emphasized the distributive dimension of cooperative social interaction at the expense of its productive dimension. While utilitarianism implores us to maximize some good without regard to its distribution, egalitarianism demands that we distribute opportunities, welfare or resources without regard to incentive effects.

Sophisticated versions of these "ideal" types have been developed to make room for matters of distribution in the case of utilitarianism and incentive effects in the case of egalitarian theories: approaches that either "balance" equity and efficiency or lexicographically order one with respect to the other. Even these more sophisticated versions of the ideal types miss the central insight of the rational choice argument. For the view entailed by a rational choice approach is not that productive and distributive considerations are elements, equal or otherwise, in a theory of just social cooperation; rather it is that these elements are inextricably linked – their union is the glue that bonds us in rational cooperative endeavors.

Just as important, the connection between production and distribution gives rise to the inescapable tension between the incentives of cooperation and conflict. It is part of what makes cooperation so attractive, and, often, so difficult to secure; and once secured, so fragile, and difficult to maintain.

1.5 RATIONALITY AND RATIONAL CHOICE

So far, we have drawn the following implications from the market paradigm. First, because law, and morality are schemes of rational cooperation, they fall within the domain of mutually advantageous interaction. Second, in order to be rational, cooperation must be productive. Third, cooperation has an essential distributive dimension; thus, rational cooperation is necessarily both productive and distributive. Both are elements of rational choice.

The emphasis on rational *choice* is important because there is a distinction between a rationality and a rational choice theory of political justification. The claim that a social arrangement is justified because it is collectively rational is a rationality conception of political justification; it is not, however, a rational choice theory of justification. The reason is simple enough. Such a theory lacks the dimension of individual rational choice. In other words, such theories hold that some arrangement is justified if it is rational, not if rational individuals choose, would choose, or would have chosen it. In order for a theory to count as a rational choice theory, it must be committed to a principle in virtue of which rational individuals are presumed to *choose* among collectively rational outcomes. As we have already demonstrated, not all points along the Pareto frontier would be equally attractive to all agents. Thus, if the theory of justification is to be relative to the choices and decisions of the participants, we need to supplement the principle of collective rationality. The principle of individual rationality takes us at least part of the way toward creating a rational choice theory of political justification.

All points on the Pareto frontier are collectively rational, but not all of the points represent outcomes that could be justified within the rational choice framework. The reason is that some collectively rational outcomes are not individually rational for all participants and therefore could not surface as a feasible cooperative outcome. The best illustration of this is the defection payoff in the P.D. The defection payoff is collectively rational or Pareto optimal, and is thus represented as a point on the Pareto frontier. On the other hand, because such outcomes often render a cooperator who is exploited by her partners worse off than she would have been in the absence of her incurring the costs of constraining her rationality, rational parties cannot jointly choose the defection payoff. This is true for all agents, and it means that only the set of collectively rational outcomes on the contract curve is feasible. The collective rationality condition limits cooperative schemes to those that are Pareto optimal. The individual rationality condition further restricts cooperative solutions to the contract curve, that is, the set of mutually advantageous Pareto optimal outcomes. The principle of bargaining or division rationality limits the set of cooperative schemes still further. Each rational individual has a preference for a particular division of the gains. Rational cooperation can succeed only when differences among those preferences are resolved and a particular outcome along the contract curve is chosen.

The market paradigm is committed, therefore, to a rational choice theory of political and moral justification. This commitment to rational choice theory has additional consequences. These are of two types: methodological and substantive. The substantive implications are themselves of two sorts. First, rational choice political justification marks a kind of liberalism. Second, in the rational choice approach, the motivational aspect of the theory constrains its substantive component. The methodological implications of the theory are also of two sorts. First, rational choice liberalism suggests a form of political contractarianism as the mechanic through which the substantive principles of cooperation are to be conceived. Second, because cooperation is both productive and distributive, the most appropriate model for characterizing the contract in rational choice terms is given by the theory of rational bargaining. Let's take up each of these points in turn.

1.6 LIBERALISM AND RATIONAL CHOICE

The first claim is that the market paradigm is a form of political liberalism. The basic idea is this. In the rational choice approach, political principles must be individually rational – that is, they must be justifiable to each agent whose conduct is to be regulated by them and whose failure to comply with their dictates calls for the application of the state's coercive authority. This way of justifying power – justification to each individual against whom the authority of the state is to be deployed – exemplifies liberalism as a form of political justification.

Roughly the same point can be given a historical gloss. Liberalism stands for the demystification of authority and for the celebration of the power of reason. The rational choice approach to political justification is a form of liberalism in which reason is characterized narrowly as rational decision. For liberalism generally, to justify is to show the legitimacy of authority by an appeal to reason; for the rational choice theorist, to justify is to show the legitimacy of authority by appeal to human interest.

In fact, we can distinguish between two ways of understanding the liberal ideal of "justifying authority to each rational person." In one sense, we imagine that there exists a sound argument whose conclusion is that the relevant authority is justified. Because the argument is sound and because each agent is rational, each agent grasps the soundness of the argument. In this sense, the authority is justified to the agent and to anyone else who has adequate rational capacities. But the authority is also justified to the agent because it is justified on other grounds, in particular, on whatever grounds render the argument for it sound.

In contrast, we can imagine a justification that appeals not to each individual's rationality understood as a cognitive faculty, but to each agent's *interests* or preferences. In this sense, authority is justified to each individual if it can be shown to be in the individual's interest to comply with it. It is in this sense that the appeal to the individual rationality condition in the market paradigm constitutes a liberal justification of authority.

1.7 MOTIVATION CONSTRAINS SUBSTANCE

Next, let's consider the way in which the theory of motivation within the rational choice framework constrains the substance of a political morality. Once again the key is the individual rationality condition. The individual rationality condition renders defection payoffs infeasible for rational cooperators. Thus, rational individuals will not engage in cooperative endeavors unless they can rely on the compliance of others. No one can expect the principles of a political morality to demand more of cooperators than it is rational for them to comply with. In other words, individual rationality constrains cooperation to a set of outcomes with which individuals can comply. In that way, individual rationality as a theory of human motivation constrains the substantive demands imposed by the principles of a rational political morality.

1.8 RATIONAL CHOICE CONTRACTARIANISM

What is the extent to which the rational choice approach suggests a contractarian methodology for deriving or articulating the principles of a justified political authority? In order for cooperation to be rational, each individual must perceive compliance as being in his or her interest. In theory that means that any justifiable scheme of cooperation could secure the rational agreement of those whose conduct would be constrained and whose utility would be advanced thereby. So we might view a justifiable political morality as the outcome of a hypothetical agreement among those persons. This agreement is a scheme of self-imposed constraints by which the benefits and burdens of cooperation and the risks associated with human interaction that is animated by cooperative and conflicting interests are allocated; it is a contract.

We might make the same point in a slightly different way. In seeking an agreement all agents share an interest in having cooperation prove maximally productive; the contract that specifies the terms of cooperation should leave no potential gains unsecured. This is simply what the *collective rationality* condition requires. That common interest aside, each party seeks to maximize his or her relative share of the gains. Here the principle of *division rationality*, or, what in Chapter 5 I call the principle of *concession rationality*, is at work. At the same time each agent is concerned to guard against the defection or free riding of others. Without compliance, agreement is empty, a waste of time. This feature of rational cooperation, compliance, is expressed by the principle of *individual rationality*. Thus, the contractarian methodology of the market paradigm follows from the principles of collective, individual, and concession rationality. Collective rationality demands that all the gains from trade be exhausted; concession rationality distributes the gains from trade; and individual rationality requires that the distribution of the benefits and burdens of cooperation – its terms – be enforceable. As we shall discuss in Chapter 5, these are the fundamental elements of the rational contract.

1.9 CONTRACTING AND BARGAINING

In a divisible P.D.,[3] the choice among sets of rational constraints is a choice among alternative "contracts." Thus, the choice of rational constraints is a contract. Various contracts differ with respect to the ways in which they allocate the benefits and burdens of rational cooperation. We might view each player's interest in contracting as consisting in maximizing her share of the benefits and minimizing her share of the burdens. Cooperation requires that concessions be made, that a bargain be struck. Thus, social cooperation is plausibly understood as the result of a hypothetical *agreement or contract*, in which the contract itself is modeled as a *rational bargain:* the result of a rational process of claims and concessions from those claims.

The bargaining model is preferable to other ways of fleshing out the concept of the social contract, for example, individual rational choice under conditions of uncertainty, for at least two reasons. First, the bargaining model makes explicit both the productive and distributive dimensions of cooperation in ways that are not exactly ignored but, nevertheless, are not made explicit in the usual conception of individual choice under uncertainty. Second, the bargaining model emphasizes the interactive, dynamic aspects of contracting – the process of staking claims, and then making concessions from those claims – in ways in which individual rational choice under uncertainty does not.

Securing each individual's rational agreement requires *first* that the compliance problem be resolved. It makes no sense to commit oneself to a scheme of mutual constraint when one's cooperators are unwilling so to constrain themselves. The free riding of others need not merely return an individual to the status quo ante. If noncompliance is sufficiently widespread, it may make a compliant person worse off than she would have been in the absence of an agreement to cooperate. For a compliant person in such a case constrains herself while the defection of others thwarts the efforts of the group to gain by mutual constraint. Because a compliant person risks making herself worse off by agreeing to limit her options when others are unwilling to do the same, it is the principle of individual rationality that requires that the compliance problem be resolved before negotiations can commence.

Thus, we can say that individual rationality requires that

an agreement be enforceable. An agreement will be enforceable only if it is rational for a sufficient number of individuals, pursuing their own interests, to comply with its terms. Participants will comply with those terms only if they are consistent with the demands of individual rationality. This is yet another way of illustrating the very stark and powerful way that the theory of motivation constrains the substance of a defensible political morality within the rational choice framework.

1.10 AN ASSESSMENT

The argument to this point demonstrates the following:

1. Commitment to the individual rationality condition entails that the norms constitutive of a justified political morality must be justifiable to each agent given his or her interests.
2. This theory of justification is, in an important and prevalent sense of the term, liberal.
3. This form of liberalism itself suggests a methodology of hypothetical contractarianism as a way of deriving the substantive demands of a justifiable political morality.
4. If we model the problem of rational choice as the problem of agreeing to a contract, rationality requires first that the defection problem be resolved.
5. Because defection occurs whenever it is not rational for agents to comply with the terms of an agreement, the threat of defection affects the substantive terms of the agreement.
6. If defection is individually rational on some occasions, it is the individual rationality condition, understood as a theory of human motivation, that further constrains the substantive norms of a justifiable political morality. It does this by limiting the range of potential norms to those representing outcomes on the contract curve.

1.11 WHEN INDIVIDUAL AND COLLECTIVE RATIONALITY COLLIDE

We have explored the shape that rationality imposes on cooperative endeavors and the ways in which, methodologically and substantively, it invites us to think about political morality. However, we have only hinted at certain tensions that arise within the rational choice framework, tensions that are unavoidable once we countenance that cooperation, like contracting, has elements of both cooperation and conflict. It is time to address the sources of conflict directly.

Cooperation can be modeled as a rational contract, and a rational contract has the payoff structure of a P.D. We have mentioned the P.D. on several occasions and it may prove fruitful if we analyze it somewhat more closely at this point. A P.D. is a game that has a certain payoff structure in which certain inequalities obtain. Alternatively, it can be defined as a game in which the dominant individual strategy is defection or noncompliance. To see this consider the standard form of the P.D.

In a standard P.D. there are two players and two courses of conduct open to them, which, for convenience we can call Cooperate and Defect. Both players do better if both cooperate than if both defect. The dilemma arises in part because each does better still if she defects whenever the other cooperates and worse if she cooperates when the other defects. Thus, player 1 should play defect no matter what player 2 does. If player 2 plays defect, then by playing defect, player 1 avoids the misery of being taken advantage of by player 2's defection. If, however, player 2 pursues a cooperative strategy, then while player 1 can join in the fruits of cooperation by a similar play, she does better still by free riding and playing the defect strategy. The same is true of player 2. Thus, we say that both players have a dominant strategy. A *dominant strategy* is one that is rational to pursue regardless of the decisions of others. In the usual case, the dominant strategy for all players is to play Defect. Because both parties defect, cooperation is not possible, and the gains it would otherwise make available are unobtainable.

If the problem of rational cooperation is analyzed as an ordinary P.D., it is easy to see why the compliance problem dominates the analysis – cooperation succeeds with it, and fails without it. This preoccupation with compliance is illustrated in the work of Michael Taylor[4] and of Robert Axelrod.[5] Taylor and Axelrod agree that cooperation is impossible if the decision to cooperate is made at one time for all time. The reason is that the defection strategy will dominate. Individual rationality will dictate noncooperative plays for all actors. Thus, they invite us to reconsider the nature of cooperation.

Every instance of the decision to cooperate is a P.D., but the strategies it is rational to use may well depend on the iterated nature of the cooperative enterprise. Thus, Taylor argues in *Anarchy and Cooperation* that in an infinitely iterated version of the game, cooperation can emerge as an equilibrium strategy. In a more recent book, Taylor considers the possibility that the P.D. can be solved – or what might be a more accurate characterization of his view, that it will not arise, in what he calls communities characterized in certain ways.[6] Thus, individuals who play the same P.D. game over time may adopt cooperative strategies that would not be rational in any single play of the game. Or cooperation can emerge among individuals who live in communities characterized by certain properties that encourage compliance and reduce defection incentives. For his part, Axelrod suggests that the success of cooperation depends on adopting strategies other than pure defection or pure cooperation. In his view, tit-for-tat turns out to be a rational strategy in repeated plays of the P.D.

Whether these results turn out to be correct is not significant for our current purposes. Instead, I want to emphasize two points. First, Taylor and Axelrod show that the convergence of individual and collective rationality is necessary to render cooperation rational and feasible, and it is the divergence between them, as in the single-play P.D., that renders rational cooperation under a wide range of circumstances impossible. Their work, each in its own way, tries to find characterizations of the problem of rational cooperation that allow potential cooperators to align the demands of individual with those of collective rationality. Because cooperation is impossible without compliance, and because compliance requires convergence of the demands of individual and collective rationality, it is not surprising, that so much attention has been placed on the compliance problem, in effect, the need to align the motivation of individual rationality with the demands of collective rationality.

In a single-play P.D. the demands of collective and individual rationality diverge. In some cases, agents may want to embed their interaction in ongoing iterations of the same problem thereby changing the problem. The hope is that long-term individual interests will coincide sufficiently to allow cooperative benefits to be realized. Alternatively, individuals may seek to embed their interactions in groups or communities of, broadly speaking, like-minded individuals. This will have the effect of reducing the divergence among individual interests, thereby reducing the conflictive dimension of cooperation. Also, rational agents may look inward. Rather than focusing on the iterated nature of their interactions or the community of agents with whom they interact, rational individuals may decide that it is in their individual interests to dispose themselves to act in nonindividually maximizing ways. Just as we started by asking under what conditions is it rational for groups of individuals to impose external constraints on their individually rational strategies, we might now ask whether, and if so, under what conditions, it can be rational for particular individuals to impose internal or motivational constraints on their dispositions to behave in individually rational ways.

All of these suggestions arise once we think of cooperation as a form of contracting. Doing so invites emphasis on the P.D. structure of contracting. And once we do that, we are struck by the divergence between the demands of individual and collective rationality. Those same aspects of rational action that render cooperation attractive and desirable threaten to make it impossible. To overcome that problem, we must change the nature of the game, of the payoff structure facing the agents. And we can do that either externally or internally, by changing, in other words, the nature of the rational choice or decision problem or the nature of the motivational

36

structure of individuals confronted with the problem at hand.

Still we should not allow ourselves to be seduced by the compliance problem. For if we are seduced, we will be misled into thinking that bringing individual rationality in line with collective rationality suffices to render cooperation successful. Our attention will be diverted from other core aspects of rational cooperation, in particular, the division problem. For in order for an agreement to be rational not only must the parties to it comply with the constraints cooperation imposes, but they must also agree on a set of constraints.

Constraints differ with respect to the ways in which they allocate the benefits and burdens of cooperation. Thus, rational cooperation requires a rational division of the gains. In fact, because a rational division of the gains is necessary to devise a set of constraints designed to produce those gains, there is a sense in which the productive dimension of cooperation depends on the distributive dimension of it: no agreement on their division, no gains. Without agreement on the division of risks, responsibilities, and rights, there is no compliance problem to worry about. On the other hand, if the compliance problem is not resolved, it is irrational for individuals to consider together various possible divisions and to choose among them. And this is what makes the problem of rational cooperation so interesting and important; there is no need to consider the compliance problem if individuals cannot first agree on a division of cooperation's spoils; yet, there is no rational incentive to bargain over the cooperative surplus unless the division problem can be resolved.

1.12 THREE PROBLEMS, FOUR MODELS

If we think of an agreement to cooperate as a rational contract, we can identify three problems capable of producing contract failure:[7] identifying the opportunity to secure cooperative gains (collective rationality), dividing those gains among cooperators (division rationality), and protecting the division against rational defection (individual rationality). Failure to identify the existence of mutual gains, or to agree upon their division, or to protect a division once agreed upon will result in contract failure. Cooperation, however rational and desirable in theory, will not emerge in practice.

It is not surprising that theorists have been led to model rational cooperation in various ways, depending on which feature of the contract they view as most important and which source of contract failure they are most concerned about. If one were to emphasize the collective rationality condition, one may be led to model rational cooperation, as a *pure coordination* game. If politics is a form of rational cooperation which in turn is modeled as a pure coordination game, the legitimacy of politics will depend on its collective rationality. Politics consists in conventions that solve coordination problems. Conventions that solve pure coordination games are Nash equilibria; they are self-enforcing in the sense that no individual has an incentive to alter his or her strategy unilaterally. No explicit resolution of the bargaining or defection problems is required by the conventional approach to coordination. Some have associated Hume with the view that many important forms of rational cooperation create coordination problems resolvable by conventions. In this view, the emerging convention replaces the contract as the metaphor of rational cooperation.

Theorists like Taylor and Axelrod emphasize the individual rationality condition and the need to coordinate the demands it imposes on individual action with the aims of collective rationality. Thus, their metaphor for rational cooperation is the P.D. They recognize that ordinarily the P.D. destroys cooperation. For cooperation to succeed, the P.D. must be embedded in either iterated interactions or the structure of a community of a certain kind. Again, if politics, a form of rational cooperation, is modeled as a P.D., either single or repeat play, then its legitimacy depends on its being a solution to a P.D. This is the view commonly attributed to Hobbes.

It is also possible to model politics or morality as a *pure division game.* Egalitarian political theory may invite this characterization, and remarks by some political economists who have characterized the political realm as a zero-sum game invite it as well. Such a model emphasizes the division problem at the same time that it ignores the collective and individual rationality conditions of rational cooperation. It treats politics entirely as rent-seeking activity, which, on reflection, altogether disables us from thinking about it as a form of rational cooperation. Or, by emphasizing the uncertainty of the choice facing agents, it allows us to envision the political realm primarily as an insurance mechanism.

The "game" that captures the full complement of rationality conditions is the *divisible prisoner's dilemma.* As I make clear in Chapter 5, the divisible prisoner's dilemma has coordination, division, and defection aspects. It represents, in effect, a bargaining problem embedded within a prisoner's dilemma. The coordination aspect of the game involves the parties identifying cooperative payoffs. The division aspect is represented by the existence of a number of such payoffs, and the need for players to choose among them, to pick a contract. The defection problem is represented by the fact that the game's payoff structure is a prisoner's dilemma and that an incentive to defect always exists for all players. It represents, in effect, a bargaining problem embedded within a P.D.

The contract model is not logically entailed by the rational choice approach. On the other hand, the contract, as I have characterized it, incorporates all the features of the other approaches we have touched upon. In any circumstances in which individuals have an interest in cooperation, there is a coordination dimension. That dimension is presented by the possibility of joint gains. In utility space it is represented by the Pareto frontier. In the typical case, however, cooperation does not succeed just because the agents have identified common interests. For in all cases there is a distributive question about how the joint gains are to be allocated. Admittedly, there will be cases where the distributive question is swamped by the possibility of joint gains, and in such cases, conflict over shares may prove trivial. But even this case can be represented contractually as the case in which division problems are trivial.[8]

The market paradigm is committed to the principle of rationality and to perfect competition as its institutional embodiment. We have focused so far on the content of the principle of rationality and the shape such a principle might put on rational cooperation. Very little has been said about when rational individuals might find it necessary to cooperate, that is, to impose constraints on their individual utility-maximizing behavior. All that has been mentioned is that if these constraints are to be rational, then they must have certain properties. In other words everything I have argued so far is compatible with there never being any reason for individuals to cooperate – that is, to forgo individually rational action in favor of agreement upon and compliance with a jointly maximizing strategy. The rational choice dimension of the theory gives cooperation its shape. What gives cooperation its motivation? Here is where that other basic postulate of the market paradigm – the economist's conception of perfect competition – enters the argument.

1.13 COOPERATION AND MARKET FAILURE

Under conditions of perfect competition, each agent's acting noncooperatively, that is, each pursuing individually utility-maximizing strategies – leads to a Pareto optimal outcome. This is the basic implication of the First Fundamental Theorem of Welfare Economics: Under conditions of perfect competition, rational utility-maximizing strategies yield a Pareto optimal outcome (in the core). When the conditions of perfect competition obtain, each individual does as well as he or she might given the utility of others. No one can be made better off except at another's expense.

This theorem has two important implications. First, in the event an economy were perfectly competitive, there would be no productive role for the political (or legal) realm. There are no additional gains to be secured by and distributed through the political process. Therefore, the only role left for politics is a redistributive one. Perfect competition guarantees that the economy will reach the Pareto frontier. The only question that remains is where along the frontier it will be. This is a matter of redistribution only, which can be accomplished either by wealth transfer ex post, or by redistributing endowments ex ante.

Second, if we think of morality or law as constraints on individual self-interest, in the sense that sometimes to act on the basis of the dictates of law or morality is to act contrary to one's self-interest, then under conditions of perfect competition it is not rational for individuals voluntarily to commit to moral or political constraints. For an individual who constrains himself will necessarily do less well for himself than if he did not.[9]

Taken together, these points imply that moral, political, and legal rules cannot be individually rational under conditions of perfect competition. Such rules are constraints that are entirely redistributive, that is, nonproductive. Because they are redistributive, they will reduce the welfare of some and would, therefore, not be rational for them. Such persons could not rationally agree so to constrain themselves. Moreover, if in order to be justified, moral, political, and legal institutions must be individually as well as collectively rational, political and moral constraints are, under conditions of perfect competition, arbitrary and indefensible.[10] It follows that given this criterion of political justification, in order to be justified, moral and political, including legal, institutions must be solutions to problems of market failure. That is, law, politics, and morality are rational only if there is a productive dimension to potential cooperation; and there is a productive dimension only if the conditions of perfect competition are not satisfied – only under conditions, therefore, of market failure. In each case the particular solution to the problem of market failure that law, politics, and morality turn out to be is determined by applying the rational bargaining model.

Moral and political institutions are schemes of cooperation

designed to capture the gains created by the failure of competition. Thus, social cooperation, individual action based on the pursuit of jointly maximizing strategies, occurs just because competition under certain conditions, that is, individual action based on the pursuit of individually maximizing strategies, is inefficient or collectively suboptimal. *Rational cooperation is a solution to failed competition; otherwise it is neither explicable nor defensible.*

Under the conditions of perfect competition, individually rational strategies align with the demands of collective rationality. When these conditions do not obtain, the demands of individual and collective rationality diverge. This creates the opportunity for cooperation. The success of cooperation depends on aligning the demands of individual and collective rationality. We see this most clearly in the studies of the P.D. Aligning the demands of individual and collective rationality is necessary but not sufficient for cooperation to succeed. In addition, cooperators must agree on a division of the cooperative gains. This feature of rational cooperation has no counterpart in rational competition. In rational competition all agents are price takers; the behavior of no party can affect prices. Thus, in competition there is no bargaining and therefore no division problem for rational agents to resolve. But it is the capacity of each individual to affect the success of cooperative endeavors that makes bargaining necessary and strategic behavior likely. Because there is no counterpart to the division problem in the model of rational competition, it is not surprising that theorists of rational cooperation have often ignored it. The argument of this section is not just that ignoring the division problem renders analyses of rational cooperation incomplete. Rather, it has been that failure to countenance the centrality of the division problem is to misunderstand the nature of rational cooperation completely.

The failure under ordinary circumstances for the demands of individual and collective rationality to converge is all that we need mean by the term, market failure.[11] The usual sources or causes of market failure include externalities/public goods and social bads, extreme inequalities in bargaining strength, and imperfect information. Even a cursory glance at this list indicates that market failure is everywhere, but then so too are politics, law, and morality. That's the point. It's not that perfect competition can ever be realized in practice; it can't be. Rather, the point of the argument is conceptual; if perfect competition were possible, rational actors would have no place for law or morality, and it is just because markets fail that they do. This, then, is the basis of the rational reconstruction or interpretation of political, legal, and moral institutions. Such institutions emerge among individuals for purely instrumental reasons, to capture gains, unobtainable as a consequence of failed competition.

This is the market paradigm: Failed competition gives cooperation its rationality. Rational choice gives it its shape and content.

Chapter 2

Competition and cooperation

What justifies a morality's most fundamental claims or principles? Why ought anyone do what morality requires? These are the basic questions regarding a morality's foundation and its motivational efficacy. In the market paradigm rationality provides both the foundation and motivation of political morality. Consider first the way in which rational choice theory helps to resolve the problem of motivation, or what we might otherwise call the compliance problem. A set of moral principles must not only specify substantive standards, but it must also provide individuals with *reasons* for complying with those standards. If individuals are already disposed to act on the basis of moral reasons, the problem of motivation is reduced significantly, if not eliminated altogether. If, however, individuals need reasons for being moral, then the requirements of morality must provide those reasons connected to facts or reasonable hypotheses about human psychology and nature. If we assume that whatever else they may be, people are rational – or, to put it weakly, that well-ordered persons will not generally act to hamper their well-being, however they conceive it – to motivate their compliance with the dictates of morality, moral principles must bear some important relationship to individual rationality. In the rational choice account, moral and political principles motivate rational actors because the principles themselves are derivable from individual rationality.

Rather than saying that our fundamental commitments are mere expressions of attitudes or in some other way without foundation, the principle of rationality seeks to provide our most fundamental commitments with a grounding outside of morality, yet within reason. So it is the need to ground morality and the political in a nonnormative foundation, as well as the need to connect the demands of our normative life with facts or at least plausible hypotheses about the nature of human psychology and motivation that makes pursuing a rational choice approach plausible and potentially rewarding.

2.1 RATIONALITY AND NORMATIVE NEUTRALITY

One objection to the market paradigm, then, depends on the rejection of rationality as a basis of political justification and as a theory of human psychology. For example, if one rejects the idea that legal and moral practices require justification, then a fortiori they require no justification in terms of their ultimate rationality.[1] Alternatively, one can maintain that cooperative practices, especially those that involve coercion, require justification, but deny that rationality can provide the needed justificatory argument. Or one can accept that political and moral justification is a matter of rationality, but deny that the economic conception of rationality to which the market paradigm is committed is up to the task. Perhaps a Kantian conception of the person and of rational agency is a more appropriate place in which to embed moral practices than are the economic conceptions of rationality and the person.

Alternatively, the critic can accept in principle the claim that rationality provides one sort of foundation or grounding for morality, but deny that the relevant principles of rationality – individual, collective, and division rationality – are either normatively neutral or otherwise nonnormative. Thus, the foundation of morality that rationality provides will not reside in fact but in value instead. We can distinguish between formal and substantive principles of rationality. The *formal* principle requires that individuals act consistently with respect to a set of axioms or principles to which they are committed. Irrational action in this sense is action that is in-

45

ternally inconsistent. The defense of this principle of rationality need not rest on normative principles of a controversial sort, as they do not depend in any straightforward way on a particular conception of what individuals ought to do with their lives. On the other hand, any *substantive* principle of rationality, for example, the principle of individual utility maximization, does rest on a conception of the point of human action and is therefore not normatively neutral. And it is to such a substantive conception of rationality – rationality as utility maximization – that the market paradigm is committed.

Moreover, no substantive principle of rationality, whether Kantian or Coasean, can itself be derived from the formal principle. Thus, the choice of one rather than another substantive principle of rationality rests on normative and pragmatic considerations. These might include the principle's implication for the possibility of collective action, of acting on the basis of projects and plans, and of making and sustaining commitments. In any event, reasons of a normative sort would have to be adduced to defend one rather than another conception of practical as opposed to formal rationality; and so any defense of practical rationality as utility maximization would itself be normative. Thus, an interpretation of political morality rooted in practical rationality could not really constitute a grounding of it in fact, not value. It would not, in other words, be normatively neutral.

2.2 RATIONALITY AND HUMAN MOTIVATION

A critic of the rational choice approach might also charge rationality with being both an inaccurate and incomplete account of human psychology and motivation. Let's draw a distinction between rationality conceived of as utility maximization and reasonableness conceived of as a distinct human faculty capable of motivating action. For the sake of argument we assume that rationality requires individuals to act in their own interests, however they conceive them. A reasonable person, however, may act contrary to rationality when doing so is required by his commitment to norms that appear to conflict with his interests narrowly conceived. In that case, political justification or the substantive demands of morality must provide reasons for acting that are capable of motivating a reasonable, not necessarily a rational person. A richer conception of human psychology, of the attitudes toward actions and norms, does not affect the relationship between morality's demands and its motivational component, but it does suggest that the norms of a political morality will have a different shape if they are to provide reasons for acting adequate to motivate reasonable, not narrowly rational, agents.

2.3 RATIONALITY, JUSTIFICATION, AND MOTIVATION

Our critic objects to the market paradigm's reliance on rationality as a condition of political justification and as a theory of human motivation. With regard to rationality as a basis of political justification, the objection is that the principle of rationality is not adequately neutral. With regard to rationality as an account of human psychology, it is that individuals are not narrowly rational in the way in which rational choice theory assumes they are.

There is no reason why a defender of morality's rationality must deny the normativity of rationality. Rationality's normativity is a problem only for those proponents of a rational choice approach who make it a problem by adopting a particular metaphysics or epistemology. Further, pragmatic considerations adduced in favor of a conception of practical rationality need not undermine its claim to neutrality.[2] More importantly, it is not obvious that the sort of normative considerations that might prove necessary to defend one rather than another conception of practical rationality beg any substantive moral questions. It may be that the range of moral principles or norms compatible with the rational choice framework that begins with an admittedly normative conception of practical rationality is sufficiently broad and diverse

The market paradigm

that we ought to be skeptical of the charge that all the normative work is being done when the choice of one rather than another conception of rationality is made. It all depends on how minimal in content and broadly appealing the normative considerations adduced in favor of one rather than another conception of practical rationality are.

If reasonableness is a psychological property, then someone committed to the rational choice approach would be committed to demonstrating the rationality of acting reasonably under various circumstances. This is precisely what rational choice theorists seek to do. David Gauthier,[3] for one, defends the rationality of being a constrained utility maximizer; Edward McClennen[4] argues for the rationality of resoluteness; David Schmidtz[5] defends local optimization or satisficing on rationality grounds. In one way or another, each countenances the centrality of reasonableness, and seeks to explain that faculty in terms ultimately of its rationality.

2.4 MORALITY AND RATIONAL BARGAINING

Chapter 1 draws two fundamental conclusions about the nature of cooperation within the market paradigm. First, rational cooperation is a solution to failed competition. Second, the proper model for understanding rational cooperation is the divisible prisoner's dilemma. In the market paradigm, rational cooperation is a solution to a bargaining game embedded in a P.D. Two problems arise when applying the bargaining approach to rational cooperation: fairness and ambiguity. We can state the *fairness* problem in the following general way. The bargaining approach requires a specification of the bargaining framework. Do we assume that individuals bring to the bargaining table vastly disparate holdings, inequities that are either transmitted or exacerbated by bargaining? In that case, bargaining merely makes matters worse. How could the outcome of a bargaining process that reflects, or worse, exacerbates an unfair initial allocation of resources be said to be the proper construction through which a defensible morality or a legitimate political order is to be

48

Competition and cooperation

conceived? On the other hand, to restrict bargaining only to fair initial bargaining positions may be to presuppose a theory of fairness not itself deducible from the principle of rationality. The rhetoric of bargaining is one of "threats" and "bluffs." Is this any way to think about justice or the conditions of political legitimacy?

There is no agreement among game theorists as to the proper solution to a bargaining problem. Under well-defined conditions different theories may provide unique solutions, but there is, in general, no agreement on how to choose among the different principles of rational bargaining. If, for any solution to a bargaining game, a different bargaining theory would have given a different solution, and there are no independent grounds for choosing among bargaining solutions, then the results of applying bargaining theory to the problem are fundamentally *ambiguous*. If bargaining theory does not discriminate in a plausible way among collectively rational outcomes, what does the principle of concession rationality add to the standard economic conception of human motivation beyond unnecessary complexity and confusion? However serious the ambiguity problem is, it is not unique to bargaining theory. For example, if we tried to decide on principles of political authority by applying a voting rule, we would face a similar problem. By applying different, but equally plausible, voting rules to the very same profiles of preferences, we can get very different results.

2.5 FAIRNESS AND RATIONAL BARGAINING

Fairness is the more pressing problem of the two. The bargaining game characterization of the choice problem is a celebration both of the distributive dimension of rational cooperation and of the ways in which production and distribution are inexorably conjoined in our normative social practices. It also represents a particular method of resolving division problems, one, unfortunately, that is likely to extend or even exacerbate preexisting distributive inequities. Bargaining has two dimensions: One concerns the chips one brings to the

49

table, and the other concerns the rules by which the bargain is forged. The first is about prebargaining holdings; the second, about the ways in which those holdings affect the bargaining process. The usual analysis presupposes that prebargaining holdings are represented by an equilibrium secured noncooperatively. When this equilibrium is suboptimal, players have an incentive to cooperate. This is just another way of illustrating the claim of the market paradigm that cooperative enterprises emerge only when competitive ones fail, that is, when competition or individually rational strategies produce suboptimal outcomes.

Prebargaining holdings are either fair or not. The bargaining process itself is either fair or not fair. The fairness of the outcome of a rational bargain will depend on the mix of these two elements. Fair initial holdings can result in unfair outcomes if the process of bargaining is itself unfair. Similarly, a fair process of rational bargaining can lead to unfair outcomes if the initial holdings are unfair. Unfair initial holdings conjoined with an unfair process will also yield unfair, even if rational results. Rational bargaining yields fair outcomes only if both prebargaining holdings are fairly allocated and the process itself allocates the benefits and burdens of cooperation fairly, or if rational rectification is embedded in the theory of rational bargaining.

Absent rectification, there is nothing in the concept of rational bargaining that seems to preclude unfair outcomes. It is more likely that unfairness, either in initial holdings or in the process of bargaining itself, exists, and that bargaining can be both rational and unfair. In that case, isn't it unlikely that the rational bargain will prove to be an appropriate instrument for settling on the substantive principles of a legitimate political morality? How can the unfair outcome of any process, bargaining or voting, characterize the demands of morality? Political associations may be viewed as schemes of rational cooperation, but if they are viewed as the outcome of a process of rational bargaining what reason do we have for supposing that the terms of the association are fair enough to treat the exercise of political power as legitimate authority? The same problem applies to the claim that morality can be derived from the theory of rational bargaining.

At least three options are open to the rational bargaining theorist to meet this objection. First, the theorist can argue that because fairness is explicitly outside the rational choice framework, the unfairness of an outcome is irrelevant to its ultimate defensibility. Or the theorist can argue that rationality is all that matters, but once the problem is correctly characterized, the rational solution will have a "ring" of fairness to it – though fairness as such does not matter. Part of correctly characterizing the problem is noting that the bargaining problem is faced by agents in a state of nature. In such circumstances, considerations of rationality alone will lead all agents to adopt cooperative strategies that appear fair to those concerned about fairness, though the fairness of the outcome is irrelevant to its defensibility within the rational choice framework. Finally, our rational choice theorist might accept fairness as an external constraint on rationality, but argue that the rational bargaining solution is not unfair.

The first approach rejects fairness and contemplates that the rational may well be unfair, even in a state of nature, but is untroubled by that result. The second approach also rejects fairness, but argues that the rational bargain in a state of nature will appear fair anyway. The third approach actually accepts fairness as an external, tentative but revisable constraint on rational bargaining, and argues that the rational choice approach meets its demands. In a compressed and outline fashion, let's consider all three approaches to the fairness problem.

2.6 FORGET ABOUT FAIRNESS

In denying that fairness matters, the rational bargaining theorist hangs onto her central thesis that all and only the rational is justifiable; political and moral justification is a matter of rationality only. In effect, the theorist implores us to reconsider our pretheoretic conceptions of morality and, if necessary, to amend them in the light of the theory's implications. If an outcome is not rational, it is not moral; it's as simple as that. This bold strategy lacks intuitive appeal, but we should not reject it on those grounds alone. In fact, I recommend we simply treat it as an undeveloped version of the second approach. Both share commitment to rationality as the appropriate criterion of justification. The first contemplates that this may lead to unfairness, in which case, so much the worse for fairness. The second approach develops what rationality requires and shows that this fear is groundless.

2.7 RATIONALITY RINGS OF FAIRNESS

Like the first, the second approach to the fairness problem prohibits fairness from entering as a constraint on rational bargaining. Nevertheless, it attempts to demonstrate the intuitive attractiveness of the theory of rational bargaining in a state of nature.[6] The principle of individual rationality that stimulates the interest in cooperation under certain conditions similarly stimulates the need for compliance. Without compliance, after all, cooperation is irrational. Agents in a state of nature have reason to believe that only certain kinds of bargains will be complied with; only certain forms of cooperation will therefore be possible. Rational agents will constrain themselves from cooperating with others who take advantage of them. Thus, the only potential cooperators are those who forgo predation. The state of nature is a P.D., and because it is, all agents will have good reason to attempt to cooperate, and that implies that no agent has rational grounds for pursuing a predatory strategy. Rationality, therefore, precludes bargaining from threat advantages secured in a war of all against all. Instead, it requires bargaining from "threat advantages" secured noncooperatively among agents who view themselves and one another as potential rational cooperators. The holdings that result from this rational strategy may have a ring of fairness to them, but it is rationality alone that drives them, rationality alone that grounds them. There is no principle of fairness involved.

2.8 FAIRNESS IS A CONSTRAINT

The claim that a rational bargaining theorist can accept fairness as a constraint on the outcomes of bargaining is itself somewhat problematic. As we stated at the outset, the market paradigm accepts no principle of fairness or of impartiality external to the process of rational choice. There are no principles other than those that can be derived from rationality or otherwise implicated in the process of rational choice. What status, then, can the rational choice theorist accord fairness and impartiality as constraints on a justifiable political authority?[7]

The rational choice theorist can accept a pretheoretic or intuitive conception of fairness that stands as a criterion against which the outcomes of rational bargains are to be measured. This criterion cannot be assumed valid or defensible on other grounds. It is to be treated as a guide or a parameter to the formal analysis – a test that we may have to alter or abandon altogether, but only at some cost to the plausibility of the ultimate account, in light of the outcomes of rational bargaining. Once we adopt a revisable, pretheoretic conception of fairness, the trick is to show how a process of rational bargaining can satisfy it. If it cannot, then we may have to consider revising the conception of fairness or completely abandoning the rational choice approach.[8]

Before you and I agree to cooperate, we may have incentives to take as much from one another as we can to enhance our relative bargaining positions. Predation appears to be a rational strategy for each of us. If one of us succeeds at predation, then that person would bring to the bargaining table holdings that have been, from an intuitive point of view at least, illegitimately or wrongly obtained. From that position, we may bargain fairly. Still, the net result of our efforts will be to create constraints that are unduly burdensome for one of us – the one who, to quote the legendary Don Imus, "brings less to the table." Is this problem insurmountable?

In *Morals by Agreement*, David Gauthier argues that the problem is not insurmountable, that rational bargaining can give rise to fair outcomes.[9] I take his argument to be the following: A bargain that is not enforceable cannot be rational. This follows from the individual rationality condition. If it is rational for a contracting partner to defect from an agreement, then the agreement is unstable. Rational parties will not enter bargains that are unstable in this sense because doing so promises only to make them worse off than they currently are. If third-party enforcement mechanisms exist, they relieve much of the pressure of finding an enforceable agreement. In a state of nature no third-party mechanisms exist, and so in order to be rational a bargain must be self-enforcing. In order to be stable or self-enforcing, agreements in a state of nature *must be fair.* In that case, rational bargaining will yield fair agreements or no agreements.

In short: Bargaining is rational only if compliance is. Compliance is rational only if the bargains struck are fair ones. Fairness precludes predation. Therefore, for individuals who want to secure the gains cooperation makes available, rationality precludes predatory behavior. The compliance and fairness problems are resolved simultaneously; they are, in effect, the same problem.

Whether fair or not, bargains in a state of nature have a P.D. structure. Thus, in order for bargaining to be rational, let alone fair, sufficiently widespread compliance must be anticipated by all agents. Compliance can be achieved in a number of ways, with two general strategies distinguished: external and internal sources of compliance. *External* sources are of two sorts: political and social. Hobbes's *Leviathan* is a *political* solution. It works by changing the payoff structure of the agent's decision to cooperate. Michael Taylor's "communities" are *social* solutions. In them, individual interaction is embedded in social relationships of a deep and rich enough sort to create incentives to cooperate. Closely knit communities also act as low cost monitors capable of punishing defection through adverse reputational effects.[10]

Gauthier argues that the compliance problem can be resolved internally. In an *internal* solution, the agent does not respond to external institutions or practices that change the payoff structure of his options. Rather, he changes his evaluation of the various options. He changes his preference over them. He prefers compliance to defection. He alters, in other words, his motivation or his disposition. Doing so will be rational for him under some conditions, but not others. A disposition for compliance will be rational for an agent only if it is utility maximizing. Whether it is utility maximizing depends in turn on the extent to which such a disposition is already distributed within a community as well as on the capacity of agents to determine whether those with whom they interact are so disposed. Thus, we can imagine situations in which both the epistemic and threshold problems are resolved; in these circumstances, the internal or dispositional solution to the compliance problem can be rational for a sufficiently large number of agents to make cooperation possible.

An internal solution to the compliance problem has interdependent dimensions. Compliance is not ensured by one person's adopting a disposition toward compliance. It is solved only when a sufficiently large number of persons so dispose themselves. Whether it is rational for any person to so dispose herself will depend on what others do, and so on. Thus, it may be rational to dispose oneself toward compliance if sufficiently large numbers of others are similarly disposed, but is it ever rational for anyone so to dispose himself full stop? If not, then how are we to imagine that the threshold number of individuals disposed to cooperate has emerged in a community? How is *that* "collective action problem" resolved? This might mean that even the internal solution Gauthier offers merely postpones the collective action problems it is designed to alleviate. It simply moves the problems to a more fundamental level.[11] Let's set this particular problem aside for now.

Gauthier wants to offer not just an internal solution to the compliance problem, but also a moral solution to it: one that is not only internally generated but whose external implications are fair. That means a bargain that is fair and impartial in the appropriate sense, one that justifies a rational agent's decision to alter her or his preferences for compliance. To ensure a relationship between fairness and stability, individuals must develop a more finely honed disposition, namely, the disposition to comply with all and only fair bargains. If they develop such a disposition, then all rational bargains will be fair bargains, as only fair bargains are self-enforcing and only self-enforcing bargains are rational. So we really need two arguments: one that demonstrates the rationality of the disposition to compliance in the state of nature; the other that demonstrates the necessity of finely honing that disposition so that it requires compliance with fair bargains only.[12]

We have distinguished among three approaches one could take to the fairness problem. At bottom they each share the following argument strategy: In a state of nature, individually rational strategies will prove to be suboptimal or inefficient. Only cooperation can be optimal; only cooperation can render everyone better off. Therefore, cooperation can be rational for all agents. Cooperation can be rational to contemplate, however, only if sufficient compliance can be anticipated. Not every cooperative scheme can secure the compliance of a sufficiently large number of persons. Only those that are fair, or have a "ring" of fairness, can. Cooperation is rational if compliance is; compliance is rational, if cooperation is on fair terms (or appears to be).

Whatever its individual strengths or shortcomings, each of these arguments rests on a deep confusion about the rationality of cooperation. The problem is that in each argument, cooperation is presumed to be rational for all agents, provided compliance is rational, whereas cooperation may not in fact be rational for all agents, whether or not compliance is. It is true that in a state of nature noncooperative interaction will be suboptimal (if the state of nature is a P.D.), but it does not follow that cooperation is rational for all agents. In order to determine whether cooperation is rational for her, each agent must compare the difference between what she can obtain by being a predator who may have to forgo cooperation with what she can secure by being a cooperator who has to forgo predation. Whereas it is true that only by being a cooperator can someone secure a place on the Pareto frontier, it is not true for all agents that every point on the Pareto frontier is preferable to all points within it.[13]

Predation may be irrational for those individuals who believe both that cooperation will be a rational strategy for them, and that others will not cooperate with predators. But cooperation that requires forgoing predation may not be a rational strategy for all agents. That depends on the difference between an agent's expected holdings in a suboptimal equilibrium secured noncooperatively in which the agent is free to act as a predator and the agent's expected payoff under cooperation in which no predation occurs. It is simply false that each agent a priori will see the need ultimately to cooperate and will adjust predatory behavior accordingly. The major premise in all arguments designed to forge an alliance between fairness and rationality is unsound.

2.9 SOLVING THE FAIRNESS PROBLEM

The fairness problem is not unique to those analyses of rational cooperation that emphasize the role of rational bargaining. Indeed, fairness is a problem for all contractarian theories – but it may be tractable, nevertheless. Any contractarian theory has to specify at least three things: The *conception of the contractors:* Who are they? What are their relationships to one another? Are they merely bundles of preferences, or do they have a moral psychology? What moral faculties do they possess? The *choice problem:* Is the contract to be modeled as an individual rational decision under conditions of uncertainty, a rational bargain, a dialogue, or a social choice? The *environment of the problem:* Is the contract being consummated in a state of nature? Do we assume zero transaction costs, full information, repeat play?

Whether a fair outcome can result from a process of rational contracting may depend on our conception of the contractors and the environment of the problem. For example, if we set up the problem so that we envision contractors as disposed to cooperate on fair terms only, then rational bargaining is perfectly compatible with fair outcomes. Or, if bargaining occurs under conditions of zero transaction costs, then there are no costs associated with holding out for a fair deal. Under a zero transaction cost assumption, we may expect either a fair deal or no deal, but no other deal – and so on. In other words, the demands of fairness can be brought in line with the structure of rational choice theory by choosing particular ways of characterizing either the contractors or the environment within which the contractors make their choices.[14]

One final remark: It may be possible to accept everything I've said about the distributive dimension of rational cooperation, including the plausibility of capturing the conditions of cooperation through the vehicle of the rational contract, without believing that the best model of the contracting process is provided by rational bargaining theory. First, the problem of rational cooperation at the level of specifying the framework of political and moral legitimacy is so abstract, knowledge about possible outcomes so incomplete, that although possible solutions to the cooperation problem differ in their distributive dimension, bargaining theory may provide an inappropriate conceptual apparatus for formulating a discussion of the problem.

Second, and perhaps more importantly, there are numerous ways of formulating processes by which individuals might seek agreement, even when there is a distributional dimension to the problem they face. There are compromise, mediation, arbitration, and discussion, in addition to bargaining. Which approach seems suitable may be a function not of the structure of the problem but of its context. In particular, it may depend on how potential cooperators conceive of each other – as friends or strangers, as people engaged in a process with short-term or long-term consequences, whether a small group or a large one, homogenous or deeply divided, and so on. Recognition, even celebration, of the distributive component of rational cooperation is important. But it may not require that the problem be structured as a rational bargain – unless everything that involves compromise or deliberation is viewed as rational bargaining, in which case the concept of bargaining may be so broad as to be vacuous.

Still, none of these alternatives to bargaining eliminates the need to discuss the fairness of holdings obtained prior to commencement of the deliberation process through which the terms of an agreement to cooperate are forged. One cannot hope to eliminate substantive problems by a change of name, for example, from "bargaining" to "deliberation."

2.10 COMPETITION PRESUPPOSES COOPERATION

The market paradigm is committed to the principle of rationality and to the market as its idealized institutional embodiment. The principle of rationality gives cooperative practices their shape and content. The market provides the motivation for engaging in cooperative endeavors. Formally, an agent cooperates if she or he abandons acting on the basis of individually rational strategies in favor of pursuing a joint strategy. To ask when it is rational to cooperate is to ask when is it rational to forgo pursuing individually rational strategies in favor of pursuing jointly maximizing ones. The answer sounds like a tongue twister. Rational agents do not forgo pursuing individual strategies unless there is something to be gained thereby; and there is something to be gained only if acting on the basis of individual strategies leaves room for improvement. There is room for improvement only if individual strategies are not utility maximizing. Thus, the answer to our question is the following tongue twister: It is individually rational to forgo individually rational strategies only when acting upon individually rational strategies is not utility maximizing.

Are individual strategies ever fully utility maximizing? In fact, under conditions of perfect competition, individually rational strategies are utility maximizing. Therefore, forgoing such strategies in favor of joint strategies would not be rational. It follows that pursuing joint or cooperative strategies can be rational only when the conditions of perfect competition are not satisfied, that is, only when markets fail. Rational cooperation is a solution to failed competition. The perfectly competitive market helps us to understand the conditions under which it is rational for agents to cooperate. Cooperation is rational *only* when markets fail.

There is a problem with this aspect of the market paradigm, and it is an important one. But it is not the problem that the conditions of perfect competition are in fact never realized. That is a problem to the extent that the concept of market failure is supposed to be practically and not merely theoretically helpful. This is a problem we address in some detail in Chapter 4. The problem I want to focus on here is internal to the very concept of competition and therefore to the claim that cooperation cannot be understood other than as a solution to failed competition.

The relationship between competition and cooperation is significantly more complex and interesting than that suggested by the market paradigm. The market paradigm holds that cooperation is a solution to failed competition, but it is equally plausible to view competition as a solution to failed cooperation. This argument has the additional consequence of illustrating one important way in which consumers can be the beneficiary, as well as the victim, of the P.D.[15] Let me explain.

The standard proofs of the Fundamental Theorems of Welfare Economics, which hold under conditions of perfect competition and not otherwise, assume n producers and m consumers. The fact is that n producers are not keen to compete with one another because doing so drives prices to marginal cost. As a group, they would prefer to set prices at a higher level and to secure greater profits accordingly. For similar reasons, they would prefer to keep the costs of entry into the relevant markets high. Profits that result because producers can charge in excess of the competitive price constitute a cooperative surplus, a pure rent, attainable by them only if they can agree upon a division of the gains from cooperation and if that agreement is enforceable among them. Thus, they face a bargaining problem embedded within a P.D.: a divisible prisoner's dilemma. That is their collective action problem. *And their failure to resolve that problem of cooperation, of agreeing to and complying with a jointly maximizing strategy, is what gives rise to competition.* Thus, competition is the consequence of failed cooperation and can be explained accordingly.[16] It is as plausible to reconstruct competition as a response to failed collective or cooperative action as it is to view cooperation as a response to market failure.

Not only can we view competition as a response to failed cooperation, the very idea of perfect competition presupposes successful cooperation or collective action. Competition can be viewed as conceptually dependent on cooperation rather than the other way around. Competition presupposes a stable, enforceable scheme of property rights. Any such scheme is a collective or public good. So we must assume that in order for competition to exist, at least some problems of cooperation – for example, the establishment and maintenance of an enforceable property rights scheme – have been successfully resolved. Similarly, markets presuppose the absence of force and fraud. These constraints provide collective goods for individuals who participate in markets. Thus, establishing and enforcing them as norms has a collective goods dimension, and once again, the very possibility of competition is seen to rest in part on solving problems of cooperation. It is just not possible to disentangle competition from cooperation in a way that enables us to conceive of competition as logically or normatively prior to cooperation. Competition can be reconstructed as a solution to failed cooperation, and successful competition presupposes the successful resolution of various problems of collective (cooperative) action.

There is no basis for the proposition that rational cooperation is a response to market failure. This feature of the market paradigm – in many ways, the essence of it, has to be abandoned. Once we abandon that premise in the argument, it cannot be the case that the best interpretation of our legal and moral practices sees them in terms of the role they play in solving problems of market failure, nor can it be the case that the only justification available for such institutions is the role they play in rectifying market inefficiencies.

In abandoning the principle of perfect competition, we have given up neither the principle of rationality nor the centrality of the market to political and moral liberalism. We have given up only the account of the market in political liberalism that the market paradigm sets forth. That is an influential account, however, one that permeates law and economics, and political and moral contractarianism, from Hobbes to Gauthier. If we accept the principles of rationality and the centrality of the market, then we need an account of the role of the market in political and moral liberalism different from the one we have so far explored. On the other hand, this is an account of the market that has to be compatible with the principles of rational choice.

2.11 MARKETS AND CONFLICT

There is no shortage of defenses of the market within the liberal tradition. The market paradigm expresses one role for the market and one defense of it. The market is the primary social institution in which the demands of individual and collective rationality converge, in which individual interest and collective good coincide. Its failure creates not only the opportunity for, but the necessity of cooperation. Although it is true that the failure of competition creates the opportunity for cooperation, competition itself presupposes it. Thus, cooperative schemes may well be prior to competitive ones, not the other way around. This is a thought to which we shall return.

One extremely attractive feature of markets is the fact that they allow interaction among individuals without first requiring or presuming the existence of broad agreement about fundamental values, goods, or ends among exchange partners. That is, individuals can successfully engage in market transactions whether or not they have a common conception of what is important to an individual or to a life. I may disapprove of your interests, find your tastes perverse; you may well find me uncouth, my tastes bovine. We may not make for good friends, but we can transact. Our capacity to interact in the market does not depend on our sharing a common conception of the good. In some ways, this may be a shortcoming of markets, but it is an important virtue as well.

Imagine a large, heterogenous community whose population is geographically dispersed and, in which the benefits and burdens of interaction are spread over time and the bulk of interpersonal relationships are one-dimensional and broad consensus on fundamental values unlikely. If all forms of interaction required shared commitments, little, if any, mutually advantageous and otherwise socially desirable interaction would occur. Were allocation decisions left to the political process, for example, conflict would abound. In contrast, the market has the special virtue of allowing, even encouraging, socially desirable and mutually advantageous interaction in the absence of broad consensus on matters of fundamental importance to the lives of its citizens.

I am not claiming that no questions of fundamental value are involved in markets. Of course they are, including whether to have markets at all, what to allocate through markets, and, because markets reflect existing distributions of wealth, what the appropriate distribution of wealth should be. These are not questions within the market itself, however. Markets will do what markets do, whatever decision on these matters we make.

The success of markets is also connected to other aspects of human relationships, including shared values and interests. Trust, friendship, and convergence of interests reduce the costs of monitoring and increase the probability of compliance with the agreements one makes.[17] Shared values of a certain sort may make market interaction more effective and less costly. Shared understandings of a very general sort are absolutely necessary for existence of even minimally effective markets. Still, the scope of agreement about values is quite minimal when compared with the extent of fundamental disagreement compatible with market exchange. And it is this feature of markets, their capacity to permit widespread social intercourse without agreement about what is valuable in a life or in a community, that I want to emphasize.

This feature of markets takes preeminence in large, heterogenous communities in which the long-term stability of social institution rests in part on the bulk of social interaction not requiring a deep, broad, or enduring underlying consensus. Widespread consensus is difficult to secure and fragile once attained. There may in fact be no basic consensus other than an "agreement to disagree." On the other hand, we might expect to find that in small, homogenous communities defined by shared values and interests, characterized by norms of equality and reciprocity, and where relations are multidimensional and deep, fewer allocation decisions are left to the impersonal market or formal legal mechanisms.[18]

Relations forged primarily through market exchanges may not be deep or significant, but they can be both civil and stable in part because they are compatible with broadly divergent underlying commitments. On the other hand, if market exchange were impossible without more fundamental agreements of value, and required instead a common conception of the good, we should find exchange crippled and ineffective. It is this feature of markets, then, their ability to maximize interaction over a domain of activities without requiring solutions to questions of fundamental value and of the good that in a liberal society so attracts us to them.

From the rational choice point of view, we can capture this property of markets in terms of the contribution they make to social stability. The decision to organize allocation decisions by markets is a political one that has more to do with a desire to finesse or to avoid articulating the nature and scope of fundamental disagreements that may lead to instability than it has to do with the efficiency properties of such arrangements. Even under those unusual conditions in which efficient outcomes could be secured either through deliberative or market arrangements, there would be reasons for preferring market to political alternatives, reasons of social stability. By the same token, the political order reserves for itself the right to withdraw decisions from markets and to place them before public debate precisely when the issues raised are those the resolution of which helps to clarify the polity's identity as a community.

According to the market paradigm, rational cooperation is a solution to failed competition. Political and moral norms constitute schemes of rational cooperation, justifiable only to the extent that they can achieve what the market fails to, namely, efficient social interaction. Cooperative arrangements should mimic, in the appropriate way, competitive ones. In the view I am advancing, the political legal, and moral realms exist at least in part to resolve disputes for which markets are inappropriate and to articulate commitments markets are poorly suited to express.

Unlike market exchange, political and moral institutions are deliberative practices. By conceiving of nonmarket institutions as rational responses to market failure, the market paradigm not only mistakenly implies that cooperation is parasitic upon failed competition, but is also deeply distorts the role of the political, legal, and moral domains within a liberal social-political culture. Rather than being designed primarily to capture gains unattainable by competition under conditions that normally obtain, they are deliberative practices through which values are articulated and communal identity sharpened.[19]

2.12 THE MARKET AND RATIONAL SOCIAL ORGANIZATION

If what I have said about the analytic relationship between competition and cooperation is correct, then we have no a priori grounds for treating one as anymore basic than the other. My view is that the concepts we employ should depend on the question we are trying to answer. Rather than trying to determine whether all forms of social organization are comprehensible by imagining that there must be some problem of market failure, (e.g., high transaction costs or the P.D.) that disables us from organizing in competitive or non-cooperative ways, we will find ourselves asking what sorts of empirical circumstances render one or another form of social organization rational. What factors are relevant to the various forms that social organization takes?

In other words, we begin by imagining ourselves or those whose institutions we seek to understand and evaluate as trying to organize social institutions. With respect to this question, they regard themselves as rational cooperators. As rational cooperators, it is open to them to express their commitment to cooperate in a variety of different institutional forms: in markets, in political processes, and the like. The forms of social organization that are rational for them will depend on a variety of empirical factors, from the size of the geographic area they occupy to the personal histories and cultures they share. No substantive conclusions about the reasonableness or the rationality of the ways in which individuals organize their collective lives together can be derived from an abstraction, from, in particular, the ideal of rationality alone.

Viewed in the way I am suggesting, the fundamental question in all of the social sciences is this: How do, and ought, people live together? Thus I favor a unified, but not a reductionist, social science: unified by the common quest to shed light on this question from a variety of perspectives, not by a reduction to an economic conception of human psychology.[20]

Rational cooperation may be pragmatically more basic than rational competition; competition itself presupposes it. Then we might view subordinate forms of social organization, for example the market, morality, and law, as particular ways of expressing the commitment to cooperate under various empirical conditions. Sometimes the cooperative impulse is expressed through competitive social arrangements like the market and other times not. In order to be understandable or defensible within the rational choice framework, these subordinate forms of cooperation must be rational means of expressing the needs and interests of rational cooperators. Rational choice political and moral theory is part of the general rational choice theory of organizations. In saying this, I

mean explicitly to maintain the normative connection between the theory of political justification and rational choice
theory. Though, as I have said before, such an account, when
properly understood, will reduce the role of the market from
an analytic point of departure, as the idealized expression of
individual rationality, to a particular expression of rational
cooperation, to a form of social organization particularly attractive to rational cooperators under a broad range of empirical circumstances: heterogeneity of values, disparities in
wealth, geographic dispersion, diverse cultural and religious
backgrounds, and the like.

My point is simply this: Even if the fundamental questions
of political and moral theory are part of the more general
theory of rational social organization, answering them in
anything like a useful way requires detailed understanding
of a community's history and its culture. It is of no help to
argue that the institutions that emerge or would emerge
among rational agents at different places and times in different circumstances are a function of "transaction costs" of one
sort or another. For everything that is interesting about a
people and relevant to the determination of rational organization among them falls in the category of transaction costs.

2.13 STABILITY AND RATIONALITY

It would be foolish to claim that the only value of markets is
the one that I have set out: to maximize social intercourse
without raising the questions about the scope and extent of
any underlying consensus, thus contributing to social stability. Markets have other values, values that are, broadly
speaking, both rational and liberal. Free markets embody the
liberal value of autonomy, and markets that work well serve
coordination functions as a result of their ability to provide
and distribute information. My point is the more modest one
that even if markets only inadequately accomplished the feats
economists rightly laud them for, they would still possess
the property I am drawing attention to, a property few have
taken adequate notice of.[21]

Is a preference for stability, however, rational? And if so, under what conditions? It is perfectly possible that a preference for stability as such is not rational. The preference for stability is rational only for social and political arrangements that are defensible *on other grounds*. Then one could argue that only institutions that are mutually advantageous warrant allegiance; only those institutions should create a preference for stability. Commitment to mutual advantage as a condition of rational stability will lead us back to rational cooperation, which will lead us back to failed competition, which will lead us back to the market paradigm – or so the argument might go.

It may well be that a preference for stability as such is irrational. Moreover, it may be that only defensible social practices deserve our allegiance and should generate in us a preference for their stability. It may also be true that within the rational choice framework all such institutions will be mutually advantageous. Still, a mutually advantageous arrangement need not be a response to market failure. Market failure creates the opportunity for mutually advantageous interaction, but mutual advantage does not require market failure. That is precisely the point I have been pressing all along. Markets create opportunities for mutual advantage, but so too do other forms of rational cooperation. And, as I have argued at length, such schemes of rational cooperation cannot themselves be reducible to efforts to solve problems of market failure. Market failure may *suffice* to stimulate rational cooperation but it is not *necessary* for it.

If I am right, then markets are particularly attractive forms of social organization in communities whose values and population are dispersed. The irony is that although markets are especially desirable in such circumstances, the conditions that make them attractive also make them difficult to create and sustain. Markets require contracting or exchange. Exchange is threatened by uncertainty. Uncertainty can be reduced by factors that are endogenous to the relationship between the parties. For example, if potential contractors are involved in repeat play or are members of closely knit communities, then their incentives to defect from transactions will be reduced by reputation effects. But in these sorts of circumstances, pure markets are not as important to social stability as they otherwise would be. For example, we would not think that a family needs to organize itself as a "market" in order to make allocation decisions. And here is the problem: Under precisely those circumstances where markets are most desirable from the point of view of social stability, they are most difficult to create and sustain, whereas in those circumstances most conducive to low-cost market interaction, because of their impersonality, markets may well be less desirable forms of social organization. The solution is to develop bodies of law that provide resources capable of reducing uncertainty and fostering market cooperation. These institutions, for example, the law of property and contract, provide resources when those endogenous to the environment of contracting are in short supply or are otherwise exhausted.[22]

We do not have to accept the market paradigm, or anything like it, to come to understand the ways in which some bodies of the law can arise to respond to market failure problems. Under conditions that typically arise in large, heterogenous communities like our own, rational cooperators will have ample reason to have a variety of allocation decisions made through markets. The conditions under which they may prefer market to collective or political decision rules include those cases in which there are fundamental disagreements about what counts as a good life or makes a life worth living, where the members of a community are diverse in their backgrounds and histories and where they are dispersed geographically. In such cases allocation decisions through public debate may create too much strain on the network of abstract bonds that connect members of the community with one another. Markets do not pressure those bonds unduly. The problem is that for reasons I will develop in detail in Chapters 5 and 6, creating and sustaining markets within such communities is difficult, its difficulty the result of uncertainty. The same virtues that make markets attractive make them difficult to sustain where they are needed most in much the same way that the principles of rationality that make co-operation attractive make it difficult to forge. Indeed, I will invite the reader to treat market interactions as local cooperation problems. Faced with these problems, a community of the sort we described will need to create institutions that make market interaction possible and fruitful where they are needed most. This may well mean the creation of a body of law whose purpose is to create and sustain impersonal exchange relations. This law, a law of contracting, is then best understood in terms of the role it plays in making competition possible. Competition, in turn, is best understood, in terms of the role it plays in sustaining cooperation among people of a certain sort. That is the connection between the argument of this chapter and Part II of this book.

2.14 RATIONAL CHOICE LIBERALISM

Part I of this book was originally motivated by my desire to provide a normative framework for economic analysis of law. That motivation led to a more general theory that could ground not only law and economics, but certain well known forms of liberal political and moral theories. I call that more general theory, the market paradigm. Chapter 1 presents the market paradigm, a foundational theory, liberal in its spirit and minimalist in its normative precommitments, that might provide the bridge to moral and political theory that I and others have argued economic analysis needs. The argument of Chapter 2 is that the theory developed in Chapter 1 cannot be sustained. The idea of competition is not analytically prior to the concept of cooperation in the way the theory requires. The important part of Chapter 2 is not its rejection of the market paradigm, however. Instead, it is the outlined alternative to it, what I call, rational choice liberalism.

The view presented in the last sections of this chapter is that the market is central both to liberal political theory and to rational choice theory.[23] The market paradigm, however, misunderstands the way in which the market is important to the rational choice liberal. The mistake is exemplified, for example, in the moral philosophy of *Morals by Agreement*. The market is not a point of departure for analyzing rational cooperation; it is itself a *form* of cooperation. And it is especially attractive to liberals because of the way in which it can, under a range of conditions, contribute to social stability. Under those conditions, therefore, the market can be defended as a rational means of social organization.

If the market can itself be understood as a rational means of social organization, then there may well be parts of the law that can be understood and appreciated for the role they play in creating and sustaining markets. The form of law and economics, or economic analysis, supported by rational choice liberalism is that which emphasizes markets, not the sort that idolizes efficiency.

The argument of this chapter rejects the market as providing us with the framework within which we can come to understand "constrained" behavior or interaction. The view that the market provides a vehicle for understanding constrained interaction (including cooperation) presumes that the market is itself a form of "unconstrained" interaction, and precisely that is what I have denied.

I have argued that the market is not a form of unconstrained interaction, that it is a form of constrained interaction instead. I have not argued that constrained interaction as such is prior to unconstrained interaction, either conceptually, or normatively. For all I have said against the market paradigm, someone might yet hold the Hobbesian line that unconstrained behavior is normatively prior to constrained behavior, or put another way, that all justification must be in terms of the individual rationality. David Gauthier, for example, might accept my arguments completely, and give up the market as a morally free zone, as the foundation from which moral constraints are to be determined. He need not give up his rational choice contractarianism. For nothing I have said would make someone give up the singular significance of individual rational choice.

Neither rational choice contractarianism nor rational choice liberalism is *entailed* by the arguments in this chapter. For a range of reasons having to do with doubts about contractarianism as a political theory, I have chosen the path of rational choice liberalism, a political theory that is more Humean than either Hobbesian or Kantian.

Given these arguments, the question that remains concerns the extent to which this argument for the market justifies an economic approach to law. Chapter 3 takes up this question schematically. The scope of the argument, moreover, depends on the concept of market failure as well as on those of efficiency and the market. These notions are explored in Chapter 4. Chapters 5–8 develop the suggestion made here and taken up again in Chapter 3 regarding the possibility of understanding contract law along the lines set forth here. Chapter 9 concludes Part II by arguing that the line of argument here may not have the scope of application Chapter 3 claims for it.

Chapter 3

Law and markets

It is ludicrous to suppose that all of the law in liberal democracies is designed either to make markets possible or to rectify for their shortcomings. The Constitution of the United States is not void of economic import or impact, yet it is probably more useful to view it as articulating the basic framework of a political community. It express the fundamental norms and political values that define the American political culture. On the other hand, it is not implausible to suppose that contract law is designed primarily to facilitate market exchange by providing ex ante safeguards against contract or market failure.[1] In this way, contract law may be said to provide a framework of individual *permissions:* norms governing the conditions under which individuals are free to do with their holdings as they see fit. Compare this understanding of contract law with a common conception of the criminal law. In this view, the criminal law can be understood as setting out *prohibitions.* It articulates what we must do, or, more often, what we are not at liberty to do. Some bodies of the law, like contracts, enable. Other aspects of law, like criminal law, disable or constrain. Some bodies of the law do both.

It is plausible not only to view contracts as enabling and the criminal law as disabling, but to view contracts as enabling individuals to move resources to their more highly valued uses and to view the criminal law as disabling individuals from doing things that it would be wrong morally for them to do. Thus, contract law is naturally viewed as an in-

73

strument of market processes, while the criminal law is viewed as the institutional embodiment of a community's morality. If contract law is liberty enhancing and criminal law liberty limiting, how ought we conceive of tort law? Is tort law best understood as an instrument of efficient resource use, or is it instead the expression or embodiment of a category of moral imperatives?

3.1 TORTS, CRIMES, AND CONTRACTS

Arguably, the criminal law prohibits morally wrongful conduct, whereas contracts, provide safeguards against market failure. How does this help us think about tort law, a body of the law that seems to fit comfortably in neither category? If Jones drives his car negligently into Smith's house, Smith will have a claim in torts against Jones for recompense equal to the loss Jones's mischievous motoring occasions. Similarly, if, in order to escape damage at sea from an impending storm, a ship's captain moors his ship to a dock, he will be liable to the dock owner for whatever damages the ship causes the dock should the storm's high winds drive the ship into it. Again, if in the course of dynamite blasting to construct a tunnel or bridge, neighboring property is damaged, the construction company must make the losses good. In none of these examples is the injurer *prohibited* by law from motoring, docking, or blasting, respectively. On the other hand, neither is the injurer *free* to act without responsibility for the harm his conduct occasions. Instead, we might say that in each case, the injurer is free to act provided she pays a certain fee for doing so.[2] We might capture this feature of tort law by saying that the law of torts articulates a framework of *permissions* and *prices*, judgments of what individuals can do and the prices they have to pay in order to do them.

Guido Calabresi has emphasized this feature of tort law, and in doing so has suggested that tort law occupies the conceptual and normative ground between contracts and the criminal law.[3] If we suppose that property law sets out the domain of our legally rightful possessions or entitlements, then we can conceive of contracts as specifying the conditions under which we can do as we wish with those possessions. Contracts specify, in other words, the formulas we must follow in order validly or legitimately to do with our property as we see fit. In contrast, the criminal law specifies prohibitions: actions that are not permissible for us to perform, whether or not we are willing to pay a price for doing them. According to Calabresi, we can view tort law as specifying acts we are permitted to do provided we pay a certain price for doing them.

Contract law sets out the conditions under which I can sell my car. The criminal law says I can't drive the car without either a license or insurance. And tort law says that I can drive the car, thereby imposing risks on other drivers and pedestrians, but that the price I must pay for the freedom to do so is that if I injure someone through my negligent operation of the automobile, I have to render compensation, make good the losses my conduct occasions. I am not prohibited from driving, but my freedom to do so depends on my being in a position to render compensation ex post should my driving somehow go awry. Thus, the rules of tort occupy a middle ground between contract and crimes. I am not free to drive whether or not I injure others. Nor is the fact that I may injure others sufficient to prohibit me from driving. I am free to drive provided I pay the price, which is the cost of compensating those I might injure through my negligence.

Because it occupies a middle ground between permission and prohibition, tort law both expresses a market ideal of efficient resource allocation and articulates public values and commitments. Thus, if we are to understand fully the role of tort law in a liberal, legal order we cannot rely exclusively on either the market model or on derivation from abstract moral principle. As I shall argue in Part III, tort law is in fact a mixture of markets and morals.

Still it would be premature to reach that conclusion on the basis of the argument presented to this point. For one thing, the argument rests on characterizations of both contract law and the criminal law that are controversial. More importantly, it is impossible to draw normative conclusions about the foundation of a body of law by pointing to the logical or conceptual space it occupies between other bodies of law. Analytic premises do not entail normative conclusions.

Calabresi contends that torts occupy the middle ground between contract and criminal law. In fact, I think he is wrong. For it is one implication of this claim that tort law sets out permissions at various prices, and I reject this view as incompatible with the corrective justice account of tort law developed in Part III. For the sake of this argument, however, we can accept Calabresi's view. In that case, contract would be understood as setting out permissions, the criminal law prohibitions, and tort law permissions at prices. Still it would not follow that tort law is a mixture of markets and morals. Whether it is will depend on the correct understanding of contracts and the criminal law. And that is a substantive, not a conceptual, matter. Until that substantive matter is resolved, no valid conclusions about the normative foundations of tort law can be drawn, regardless of the logical space it is thought to occupy between the criminal law and contracts.

3.2 ECONOMICS AND CONTRACT

Nothing about the substantive demands of tort law follows from its alleged analytic connections to contract law on the one hand and the criminal law on the other. Let's try a different approach. Suppose we accept an economic or market conception of contract law. This is in fact the position I defend in Part II. Now we might ask whether someone who is committed to an economic conception of contract law will be led inevitably to defend a similar account of tort law? Is the relationship between contracts and torts such that an economic analysis of contracting entails or otherwise requires an economic analysis of torts? If it does, then we might ask whether similar considerations will force an economic conception of the criminal law on us.[4]

If contract law is designed to facilitate efficient exchange among agents who are in a position to negotiate with one another, then tort law is designed to facilitate efficient "forced transfers" among individuals who are disabled by high transaction costs from negotiating with one another. Tort law imposes ex post as near as is possible the terms parties who cannot negotiate with one another ex ante would have come to had they been in a position to negotiate. Compensation, which is rendered ex post, plays the same normative role in torts that actual ex ante agreement plays in contract. Both legitimate transfer: voluntary but efficient transfer in contracts, involuntary but efficient transfer in torts. This is a conclusion in need of an argument.

In fact, there are at least two arguments for this economic conception of tort law, both of which are based on accepting first an economic interpretation of contract law. One argument rests on considerations brought to the attention of legal theorists by Guido Calabresi and Douglas Melamed in their classic article, "Property Rules, Liability Rules, and Inalienability."[5] In that essay the authors distinguish first between assigning and protecting entitlements and then among three ways of protecting entitlements. *Property rules* protect entitlements by prohibiting nonentitled individuals from reducing the value of an entitlement without first securing the entitled party's consent. Thus, property rules confer powers to exclude and to alienate on terms agreeable to the entitled party. *Liability rules* protect rights by giving rights holders a claim to compensation for whatever diminution in the value of their rights nonentitled parties may impose. Thus, a right protected by a liability rule does not confer a power to exclude or to alienate on terms agreeable ex ante. Instead, under a liability rule, nonentitled parties may take without securing the consent of the entitled party, provided they compensate the entitled party the full value of the loss ex post. *Inalienability rules* protect entitlements by preventing entitled individuals from transferring that to which they are entitled. Inalienability rules, in this sense, protect individuals against themselves.

It is straightforward how property rules protect rights, but

77

it is less clear how liability rules do. Whether or not liability rules protect rights depends on one's theory of what it means to have a right.[6] In the classical liberal view in which having a right entails having autonomy or control over a resource or a domain of actions, the very idea of a liability rule protecting a right seems incoherent. For a liability rule gives *others*, that is, individuals other than the entitled party, the power to transfer by taking; all the entitled party receives is compensation for lost value. Compensation ex post is not equivalent to control ex ante, and it is a fair question to ask how it is that one's autonomy is protected by conferring discretionary authority over one's entitlements on others?

Setting this problem aside for the moment – we discuss it further in Chapter 17 – let's return to the distinction between property and liability rules. Property rules are essential to free exchange and, therefore, central to the idea of a market. For to have one's resources secured by property rules is at once to be able to prohibit others from forced (or fraudulent) transfer and to permit exchange on mutually agreed upon terms. From an economic point of view, voluntary exchange is desirable because it is a relatively low-cost means of encouraging the movement of resources to more highly valued uses. Markets promote efficiency through a series of Pareto improvements, mutually advantageous voluntary exchanges made possible by property rules, and markets promote efficiency in a less costly fashion that might otherwise be required.[7]

Whatever their virtues, under a variety of circumstances, markets fail. The usual explanation is that transaction costs create market failures by blocking the efficient movement of resources. But even a cursory glance at the list of defects that count as insurmountable transaction costs reveals that the category and the explanation it is supposed to provide are too broad to be illuminating. Lumping together the many sources of market failure without regard for the differences among them is analytically unsatisfying for two reasons. First, treating them generically as problems of transaction costs may blind us to important analytic differences among them, differences that might bear on what should count as an appropriate response to the problem each presents. Second, a reliance upon transaction costs as the explanation of market failure suggests a false dichotomy. In the picture that emerges, market exchange is feasible and efficient whenever transaction costs are low, but impossible whenever transaction costs rise above a certain threshold. This is an artificial dichotomy. Even high transaction costs can be overcome under conditions in which the parties have plentiful *endogenous* resources for overcoming them, whereas minor transaction costs may prove debilitating when partners have an impoverished pool of endogenous resources upon which to draw. Even if much of the transaction cost/market failure literature is analytically misleading, it is very easy to illustrate the simple ways in which transaction costs thwart efficient exchange. Motoring imposes risks and thereby reduces every pedestrian's (and other motorist's) security. Suppose each individual is entitled to security from risk, and that this right is protected by a scheme of property rules. That would mean that whenever someone contemplated taking her car out for a spin, she would first have to secure the consent of each person she might put at risk. The search costs alone would prove prohibitive, and no one would drive. Actually people would drive, but their doing so would be wrongful and unjustified: wrongful and unjustified because they had not first secured the consent of those their driving puts at risk.

Instead of requiring each motorist to secure the consent of each person her driving endangers, we permit individuals to drive provided they compensate ex post the victims of their motoring miscues. One way of characterizing this is to say that instead of protecting each person's entitlement to be free from risk by a property rule, which would lead to too little driving – that is, inefficiency – we should protect those entitlements by liability rules.

If property rules enable resources to move to their most highly valued uses when the conditions for contracting are ripe, then liability rules enable resources to move to more highly valued uses when these conditions do *not* obtain. Liability rules accomplish this in two ways. First, they do not require consent as a condition of legitimate transfer. Thus, they are not subject to high ex ante transaction costs, which can thwart ordinary exchange. Second, because they impose a burden of compensation on those who take without first securing the consent of the entitled party, they encourage only efficient forced transfers. If a nonentitled party takes what in fact he values less than the entitled party, then he will have to compensate the "victim" more than the right is worth to him. That will discourage inefficient takings, that is, trades that would not have occurred had transaction costs been trivial or nonexistent.

In short: Liability rules are responses to market failure occasioned by high transaction costs. Applying liability rules mimics the outcome of markets by encouraging efficient takings and discouraging inefficient ones. If contract law is an institution designed around property rules and the markets they make possible, then tort law, too, is designed around the institution of the market. The difference is this: Contract law helps make market exchange possible and efficient by providing ex ante safeguards against contract failure. Tort law promotes efficient outcomes when markets are not available. The economist would have made her point. Tort law may occupy the formal middle ground between contracts and crimes, but the best understanding of liability rules, that is, rules that permit taking ex ante on the condition of compensation ex post, is an economic one.

3.3 DEFAULT RULES AND CONTRACTING

Contracts allocate risks; they specify who bears what costs in the event such-and-such occurs. A fully specified contract is one in which the contracting parties imagine and respond to all potential contingencies. When a contract is fully specified, no term can be rewritten to one party's advantage except at another's expense; and nothing can happen that is not explicitly accounted for by the terms of the contract. A fully specified contract is both complete and efficient.

Fully specifying a contract is not ordinarily possible, relying as it does on a kind of foreknowledge few, if any, of us possess. Were it possible, fully specifying a contract might nevertheless be irrational. Many contingencies are possible but highly unlikely. The benefits of nailing down a particular allocation of risk to cover most extremely unlikely events will often not be worth the costs. Rational individuals will optimize and, therefore, leave at least some things unsaid.

From time to time, unlikely events that contracting parties have not provided for do occur, and the question of who should bear the relevant costs will then arise. When the parties have not spoken to the particular risk ex ante, they will be required to allocate costs ex post. Sometimes they will be able to resolve the matter privately; other times they may not be. In that case, a court may be asked to impose ex post a scheme of rights and responsibilities on the parties in a way that is consistent both with the underlying principles of contract and with the legitimate use of judicial authority. Let's refer to any rule that a judge must apply in such circumstances as a *default or gap-filling* rule: a rule applied in default of the parties not having explicitly resolved the risk allocation problems themselves.

Several theorists, myself included, have suggested that in such circumstances judges ought to apply the following rule: When the parties have not explicitly agreed ex ante to an allocation of rights and responsibilities, the court should impose on them ex post those rights and responsibilities to which they would have agreed ex ante.[8] Whenever it would have made sense for contracting parties explicitly to specify an allocation of risk with respect to some contingency, they would have done so. Therefore, their silence can be interpreted as resulting from high transaction costs. When we say that the silence of the contractors indicates that they have been barred by high transaction costs from nailing down an allocation of risk, we mean that the expected benefits of securing an agreement are outweighed by the costs of transacting. High transaction costs are high not in an absolute, but in a relative sense.

It is also natural to wonder how the phrase, "what the parties would have agreed to," is to be understood. If a contract is a rational bargain, then what the parties would have agreed to ought to be analyzed as a *hypothetical* rational bargain. In order to spell out the default rule, we need a theory of rational bargaining. As noted in Chapter 1, rational bargaining involves three principles of rational choice: collective rationality (Pareto optimality); individual rationality; concession or bargaining rationality.

There is no consensus among bargaining theorists as to the solution of the bargaining problem, which just means that bargaining theorists disagree about the proper principle of "concession rationality." Even if it is impossible in every case to specify the unique solution to the bargaining problem, in the absence of transaction costs rational bargains will be collectively and individually rational.

It is not surprising that legal economists have appealed to the ex ante rational bargain as a way of giving content to default rules. Fully specified contracts among rational agents are efficient, so when the parties are forced by high transaction costs to forgo fully specifying their contracts it is reasonable to assume that had it not been for transaction costs, they would have specified their arrangement in an efficient manner. To impose on rational parties ex post the terms to which they would have agreed in the absence of transaction costs is, in effect, to impose efficient terms upon them. So if the point of the default rule is to replicate the outcome of a rational bargain among the parties, it will assign an efficient or Pareto optimal allocation of rights and responsibilities. Fully specified contracts are efficient, and default provisions which are to apply when unanticipated risks materialize ought to be efficient as well.

3.4 TORT LIABILITY AND DEFAULT RULES

Recall the Calabresi–Melamed framework. Liability rules protect entitlements when transaction costs are high. If transaction costs were low enough, individual entitlements could be secured by property rules. When the conditions are right, property rules are efficient. In the motorist example, motorists cannot transact with all those individuals who might be put at risk by their driving. If they could have, they would have struck a bargain – a rational bargain. Such a bargain would have been collectively rational, that is, efficient. What prevents contracting among motorists? High transaction costs. Liability rules replace property rules in the same way and for the same reasons default or gap-filling rules appear in contract. Both emerge when transaction costs are too high to permit efficient transfers under property rules, when contracting is, in other words, too costly.

Sometimes high ex ante transaction costs make *completing* a contract irrational and infeasible. Therefore, courts apply gap-filling rules that impose costs ex post as an alternative to allocating risk ex ante by contract. Other times, high ex ante transaction costs make entering into a contract irrational and infeasible. Therefore, courts apply liability rules that impose costs ex post. The difference between default rules and liability rules is quantitative. Sometimes transaction costs are sufficiently great as to make completing contracts impossible; other times they are so great as to make contracting itself impossible. Default or gap-filling rules are the solution in the first case; liability rules are the solution in the second case.

In both case default and liability rules are solutions to contract or market failure that results from high ex ante transaction costs. When transaction costs make contracting either incomplete or impossible, the role of the law is to "complete" or "create" the rational contract. If contract law is designed to facilitate markets and the efficient outcomes that markets help make possible, then default provisions and liability rules are designed to rectify market failings that result from high ex ante transaction costs. Indeed, liability rules in torts are simply default provisions in contract writ large. If the point of default provisions is to impose upon the parties allocation decisions that they would have bargained to ex ante, then the point of tort law is to impose upon parties who are barred from contracting with one another by even higher ex ante transaction costs, the terms to which they would have bargained had they been able to. If default rules are hypothetical bargains among contracting parties, then tort liability rules are hypothetical contracts among *strangers*. In either case, the point of the law is an economic one.

3.5 TORTS, CONTRACTS, AND CRIMES

Suppose we accept the economist's analysis of contract law as designed to facilitate market exchange. The difference between contract and torts is the difference between moving resources to their most highly valued uses voluntarily, by ex ante agreement, and moving resources to more highly valued uses involuntarily, by forced transfer. In the contracts case we have consent; in the torts case we have compensation. The move from property to liability rules, from voluntary to forced exchange, from contracts to torts, is precipitated by high transaction costs.

The move from contracts to torts is mediated by default or gap-filling rules in contract. Sometimes high transaction costs require individuals incompletely to specify their contracts; other times, these costs block contracting altogether. The cause in both cases is the same, the solution is designed to serve the same purpose: to impose ex post the terms to which the parties would have agreed ex ante. Because they are rational, the terms to which they would have agreed, would have been efficient.

The point of both agreements is the same. If one accepts an economic conception of contract, then one must accept a similar view of tort law. If contracts make markets possible by providing safeguards against contract failure, then tort law rectifies market failures when contracts are impossible or otherwise irrational. The argument need not stop here. We begin this chapter by working through Calabresi's insight that tort law occupies a middle ground between contract and crimes. Now we can turn the argument around and see if what we have said about contracts and torts suggests a particular account of the criminal law. In fact, it does. Indeed, it is one that Calabresi himself was among the first to note.

In the economic account we have been outlining, property rules secure rights when transaction costs are low and liability rules secure rights when transaction costs are too high. Individuals will almost always prefer to confront another's entitlements as if they were liability rules rather than property rules. But a more important reason is that with damages under a liability rule, the plaintiff only receives market value, whereas with an injunction under a property rule, the plaintiff and defendant bargain over the surplus, which, by definition, exceeds the market value of the rights-violation. One reason for this is that the expected costs of injuring another by taking what he is entitled to will often be less than the expected costs of negotiating for its transfer. Often this will be because a person who takes without consent needs to be found, sued and judged liable, whereas a person who negotiates ex ante is known to the entitled party, and typically cannot secure what he wants without paying for it up front.

Since the probability of being discovered as a taker is less than one, as is the probability of being sued, as is the probability of having a judgment rendered against the taker, the expected costs of treating another's right as a liability rule will typically be lower than the costs of treating the right as a property rule. This means, of course, that nonentitled parties will often have the incentive to treat property rules as if they were liability rules. They need some incentive to abide by the collective decision to protect some rights with property rules and others with liability rules. They need, in other words, an incentive for respecting the property-liability rule distinction. The criminal law, and the punishment it threatens, provide that incentive. The criminal law enforces the property-liability rule distinction. If the distinction itself is drawn in economic terms, as we have just argued, then the best interpretation of the criminal law is also an economic one.

We might refer to this argument style as the *incremental market paradigm*. Instead of arguing, as does the market paradigm, that all law is a solution to market failure because all law is a scheme of cooperation rational only under conditions of market failure, the incremental market paradigm begins with a mild concession – that contract law is plausibly understood in economic terms – and then it converts this concession into a similar view, first about tort law and then about the criminal law. It remains to be seen how much farther the argument can be extended.

Chapter 4

Efficiency and market failure

The argument of Chapter 3 suggests that contract law guards against market failure by reducing uncertainty, and that tort law corrects market failures by inducing forced, but efficient, transfers. Both claims require an analysis of the term *market failure*. Unfortunately, no good account of market failure exists. In fact, our understanding of market failure is about as precise as is our understanding of externality, or, of transaction cost – in other words, not very. Because the usual analyses of market failure depend on the concepts of externality and transaction costs, our understanding of market failure is less than fully satisfying.

4.1 MARKET FAILURE AND PERFECT COMPETITION

Under conditions of perfect competition, agents pursuing individually rational (utility maximizing) strategies induce a Pareto optimal outcome in the core. By now, the concept of Pareto optimality should be familiar. The concept of a *core* probably requires some further clarification. Imagine that the exchange of commodities between two persons is modeled as a game, the exchange game, and that the rules of the game do not prohibit theft. Each player has three options: trade, no trade, theft. There are four possible solutions to the exchange game. In one both players keep what they have. This occurs when both players take the no trade option. In another exchange of commodities takes place. This occurs when both players adopt the trade option. In another one player has all the goodies; in the other solution, the other player has all the goodies. These outcomes occur when one of the players takes the trade option, which amounts to turning over his commodity, whereas the other player pursues the no trade option, which amounts to taking the other's offer without reciprocating, that is, theft.

The outcome in which no trade or transfer occurs is not Pareto optimal because there exists at least one outcome Pareto superior to it: the one in which exchange occurs. The other solutions are Pareto optimal.[1] Only one of these involves exchange. In the exchange game as we have characterized it, the mutual exchange option is not a core solution. The reason is that as long as theft is permitted, each of the players does better acting on his own. In this case, acting on one's own means stealing. Theft is the equivalent of the free rider or defection payoff of the P.D. This is just another way of making the point that the cooperative solution in the P.D. is not a core solution. The defection payoff dominates for both players. As long as each individual can cheat, steal, or lie, each can do better acting on her own than by exchange, the cooperative solution. Formally, a solution is in the core only if no individual actor (or coalition of actors, including the coalition of the whole) can do better by acting on, her (or their) own; and that is why the absence of force and fraud in the competitive situation is necessary to induce a core solution.

The idea of the core helps to illustrate another important feature of competitive markets. In a competitive market, exchange partners are assumed to have a set of initial endowments. An outcome of the competitive game in which any of the parties is worse off at the end of the process than he or she was at its beginning would not fall within the core. The reason is simple. Those individuals who are worse off as a result of competition could have done better on their own by not joining in the process in the first place. This means that in addition to being Pareto optimal, any solution to competition must be Pareto superior to the point at which competition commences. That is, it must render each agent no worse

88

off than he or she was when the game began. The effect of the theorem that perfect competition has a core solution is that from an initial set of endowments, the competitive process induces an optimal outcome that is Pareto superior to the initial starting point. In those circumstances, no one could have done better by sticking with her initial endowments and forgoing competition altogether.

The concepts central to the competitive ideal are the Pareto criteria, autonomy, rationality, competition, and the core. Prohibitions against force and fraud express the idea that exchange in competitive markets is fully voluntary or autonomous. They are necessary, moreover, if competition is to lead to a core solution. Rational utility maximization provides the motivation for individual action. Competition is the framework within which autonomous action by utility maximizing agents occurs. Pareto optimality, or economic efficiency, is the outcome of action motivated by individual utility maximization of autonomous agents within the competitive framework. And Pareto superiority reflects the mutually advantageous nature of the process through which this outcome emerges.

In one analysis, market failure is just the failure to realize the conditions of perfect competition. Within the market paradigm, this conception of market failure is the foundation of legitimate political or moral authority. The same conception of market failure, however, may have virtually no practical use. For if the point of law or politics is to rectify market failure, then law seeks the practically impossible; namely, to recreate the conditions of perfect competition. The problem is that if political authority is not justified unless it succeeds where markets have failed, then there is little reason to believe that a political solution is justified either. There is, after all, no reason to believe that political norms can recreate the conditions of perfect competition, or adequately substitute for them.

If the political is as unlikely as the market to provide public goods at optimal levels, then what makes the political solution more defensible or justifiable than the market solution?

One answer is that the level at which public goods are provided through public institutions more closely approximates the level at which they should optimally be provided. This, of course, is an empirical claim. More importantly, even if markets produce fewer public goods, they may do so in a less coercive way than would be necessary in order to provide more goods publicly. Once we leave the realm of the first-best, we have to evaluate second-best political and market alternatives in both their efficiency and autonomy dimensions. And it is not obvious that even if the political solution is more efficient that it should be preferable on balance. That will depend in part on the relative scope of coercion necessary to provide the relevant goods publicly and privately.

There is no reason to believe that these issues can be resolved a priori. I raise them for an entirely different reason, however, and that is to illustrate how useless the standard of perfect competition is as a criterion of market success. For if markets are successful if and only if they are perfectly competitive, markets are never successful. On the other hand, if political alternatives to markets are successful if and only if they succeed where markets fail, they, too, are never successful. We need an account of market failure that is not just conceptually helpful, but pragmatically and politically helpful as well. If the same account of market failure that proves theoretically useful in political, legal, and moral philosophy is practically useless, we may need an alternative account of more use to us. What might such an account look like?

We can distinguish two questions: Against what standard of market success is market failure to be measured? What fails when markets fail? What is the failure to which "market failure" refers? We have said before that in the perfectly competitive setting a Pareto optimal outcome will be secured by the voluntary, individually rational action of all agents. Is market failure the failure of voluntariness, of individual rationality, of Pareto optimality, or does it merely signify the absence of a core solution? Only if we know what fails when markets fail, will we know what needs to be rectified by our cooperative practices.

4.2 EFFICIENCY IS RELATIVE

If market failure is measured against the criterion of perfect competition, all markets fail, always. Strangely, economists have provided very little help in clarifying the notion of market failure, lending credence to the suspicion that economists are really interested in the concept of inefficiency, not the concept of market failure. The exception is James Buchanan. Buchanan rejects the orthodox analysis of efficiency. In its place, he has offered an account that emphasizes *voluntary choice* and *frameworks of exchange*. In Buchanan's account, a state of affairs is efficient if and only if it is the outcome of voluntary exchange within a given framework of trade (or within an institutional setting). For Buchanan, there is no such thing as efficiency in the abstract. Moreover, social states are efficient relative to particular frameworks within which actual exchange occurs. We might capture these features of Buchanan's analysis by saying that it is *subjective*, that is, dependent on individual choice, and *relative* to particular institutional frameworks.[2]

In the orthodox theory, positive transaction costs often block efficient transfers. The point of law is to overcome or to minimize transaction costs: to create those efficient outcomes that would naturally have occurred but for transaction costs. But what are transaction costs? Some of the classic examples include bargaining or negotiating costs, search costs, distance, time, group size, and the like. In Buchanan's view, these transaction costs are simply facts of the world that shape or define the framework within which exchange occurs.[3] Where the conventional economist sees transaction costs interfering with exchange, Buchanan sees transaction costs as helping to define the framework within which trade occurs.

In orthodox theory, in order to determine what needs to be done to overcome inefficiency, the policymaker must determine what the outcome of exchange would have been in the absence of transaction costs. Buchanan denies that any such question can be relevant or meaningful. The interaction that conventional theory treats as inefficient takes place within a framework of exchange, that framework includes positive transaction costs. Of what possible value would it be to those parties to determine what would have been efficient in the absence of transaction costs. In Buchanan's view, the correct question is, What would have been efficient *in the framework in which the agents are in fact located*, that is, the framework of positive, not negligible or zero, transaction costs?

In Buchanan's view, conventional theory bars itself from responding to market failure problems in the following way. "Yes, I realize that there are externalities, high transaction costs, and the like in our current environment of choice and interaction. Still, I want to know what would be the efficient solution in *this* context." The traditional economist is barred from consistently saying any such thing because as soon as she tries to determine what would have been efficient under current circumstances, the first thing she does is to ask what the outcome of exchange would have been in the absence of transaction costs and externalities.

But that was not the question being asked in the first place. The question being asked was, What is efficient given transaction costs and externalities? Thus, Buchanan believes that, whether they know it or not, conventional economists simply cannot talk meaningfully about efficiency under conditions other than the absence of transaction costs, externalities, and the like. The very notion of efficiency presupposes, in their view, the absence of transaction costs, and that fact alone makes the orthodox approach virtually useless.

In contrast, Buchanan's view is that what traditional economists refer to as transaction costs are really part of an institutional structure or a framework of exchange. Efficiency is defined relative to such frameworks. Therefore, there is no conceptual or analytic difficulty (in theory) in defining efficiency under conditions of high transaction costs and externalities. If Buchanan is right, we should be able to define and talk about efficiency under precisely those conditions under which standard theory believes we can experience only inefficiency, that is, under conditions of externalities and positive transaction costs.

If we can talk meaningfully about efficient outcomes within frameworks of exchange riddled by high transaction costs, then we can have no interest in efficient outcomes attainable under conditions of zero transaction costs and no externalities. The outcome of exchange under ideal conditions is an efficient allocation within *that* institutional framework. That can hardly matter to agents contemplating courses of conduct under very different conditions. Thus, the major implication of Buchanan's view is the utter irrelevance of perfect competition as a definition of market success and, therefore, as a reliable barometer of market failure.

4.3 COMPARING SOCIAL STATES

From these conclusions Buchanan argues that efficiency is relative to institutional frameworks and that efficient outcomes within different frameworks cannot be compared. Moreover, because efficiency is relative to institutional frameworks, the efficiency of an outcome in one framework is irrelevant to determining what steps ought to be taken to enhance efficiency in another framework.

All this seems quite sound. There remains a problem, however, and that is to distinguish among those conditions that are transaction costs *within* a framework of exchange and those that *define* the framework of exchange. If everything that conventional economic analysis treats as a transaction cost turns out to constitute part of the institutional setting, then Buchanan's insights will be gained only at the expense of trivializing the concept of an institutional setting. We need a way of distinguishing among features of the world, those that fall within the institutional framework and those that could conceivably constitute transaction costs within that framework. Setting aside this problem, let's say that Buchanan's insight is that efficiency is always defined within a framework for trade. Frameworks differ, and what will count as a market failure will always be relative to a particular framework.

4.4 EFFICIENCY AND VOLUNTARY CHOICE

Buchanan's analysis of efficiency is not only relative to particular frameworks of trade; it is defined as the outcome of *free exchange* within a framework. Again, this differs from the traditional view, which defines efficiency as a property of social states that can be secured by voluntary exchange, but need not be. We can capture the difference by saying that traditional economic analysis has an *objective* criterion of efficiency, whereas Buchanan adopts a *subjective* theory of it. Buchanan rejects the view that efficiency can be defined as a property of social states independent of the process of voluntary exchange. As a consequence, if we assume some framework of trade, then efficiency is a property of any allocation that emerges from the full and complete process of voluntary trading within that framework. An efficient allocation of resources is that which emerges as the outcome of voluntary exchange within a particular framework or context of exchange.

It appears to follow that within any particular institutional setting governed by prohibitions against force and fraud, there can be no such thing as inefficient equilibria. By definition, where voluntary exchange stops, efficiency exists. It simply makes no sense to talk about voluntary interaction falling short of an optimal result. Efficient outcomes are constituted by the scope of voluntary interactions.

One problem with defining efficiency in this way is that it implies that any given state of the world at any time (ruling out force and fraud[4]) is efficient. Buchanan appears, therefore, to trivialize his alternative to conventional economics. Recall, that he chides the conventional economist for never being able to ask what would have been the efficient outcome of exchange in the circumstances in which the parties actually find themselves as opposed to those efficient out-

94

comes attainable only in the absence of transaction costs. Unlike the orthodox economist, Buchanan can ask this question, but he is disabled from giving anything like an interesting answer to it. The reason is that he is committed to the view that, provided force and fraud are absent, whatever the parties agree to *is* the efficient outcome within a given framework. Thus, the answer to the counterfactual question, What would have been the outcome?, coincides in every case with the answer to the factual question, What is the outcome? Understood in less than a completely generous way, then, Buchanan can be viewed as trivializing both the concept of efficiency and the concept of an institutional setting or framework.

In short, Buchanan is right to criticize orthodox theory, which, whenever faced with an inefficient outcome owing to transaction costs, asks what would have occurred in the absence of transaction costs. Buchanan's objection is that it simply cannot matter what would have happened in the absence of transaction costs. That, after all, marks a different framework of exchange. We want to know, instead, what would have occurred in *this* framework with its positive transaction costs and the like. The problem for Buchanan is that he too cannot give us an interesting answer to the question. The parties find themselves at the end of a process of voluntary choice. So they are precisely where they would have been given transaction costs. Every actual outcome is efficient, given transaction costs.

Given the priviso – the absence of force and fraud – whatever is, is efficient. It looks like Buchanan's view may be even less helpful than the orthodox view he criticizes. A fortiori the equilibrium outcome of the P.D. is efficient because it is the outcome of an autonomous exchange process within the framework defined by the logic or structure of the game. All this would seem to trivialize the notion of optimality or efficiency in a way that greatly reduces its normative significance. In moving from orthodox economics to Buchanan's "constitutional economics," we have done little more than replace one useless construct, perfect competition, for an-

95

other, institutional relativity. That conclusion is a bit premature, however.[5]

4.5 COMPARING FRAMEWORKS OF EXCHANGE

Although it is, strictly speaking, true that assuming the absence of force and fraud every equilibrium is efficient, recall
that, for Buchanan, efficiency is relative to institutional
frameworks. Although efficient states in one framework cannot be compared with efficient outcomes of exchange within
other frameworks, the frameworks themselves can be compared in terms of their efficiency. What would have been
efficient in framework P ("perfect competition") is irrelevant
to determining what would be efficient in framework R ("the
real world"). In other words it is both unhelpful and *impossible* to compare the efficient outcomes, p (in P) and r (in R)
with one another. State p is efficient in P, state r is efficient
in R; p and r are not comparable. They lack a common metric
against which they can be compared. However, P and R can
be compared in terms of their efficiency. The common metric
is voluntary choice. If people choose P to R, P is efficient. If
they choose R, R is efficient. Thus, even if the outcomes of
exchange in two different frameworks are both efficient (relative to the respective framework) and noncomparable (in
efficiency terms), the frameworks themselves are comparable in efficiency terms. The criterion of efficiency at the level
of institutional frameworks remains voluntary choice.

The net effect of Buchanan's definition of efficiency is, in
part, to move attention from particular outcomes to institutional frameworks. It is intentionally designed, I believe, to
emphasize that the important questions in economics are about
rules, not about particular outcomes or social states that
emerge or arise within rule governed structures. For institutions are sets of rules, and what matters are the rules of the
game, not events within the game. What we might view –
and certainly traditional economists would view – as an effort to trivialize the concept of efficiency is, I believe, a con-

scious ploy designed to shift attention away from decisions within the rules to a discussion of rules, as well as a conscious effort to emphasize the role of voluntary choice within economic analysis.

Make no mistake, for Buchanan the normative punch of economic analysis is borne by the voluntariness of exchange, not its efficiency. Although other economists are reductionists of one sort, always trying to reduce deontic categories like autonomy to arguments in utility functions and, ultimately to considerations of efficiency, Buchanan is a reductionist of the opposite sort, trying always to capture the essence of efficiency within the moral category of voluntary choice. For when institutional frameworks are to be compared with one another, the test of their relative efficiency is voluntary agreement.

Because the choice among rules or institutional frameworks is more of a social choice than an exchange, the form of voluntary exchange that is relevant to their assessment is *consent*. (It is in this important sense that Buchanan believes politics must be understood in the model of market exchange, and it is for this reason that he is drawn to unanimity as a collective decision rule.[6]) Notice, moreover, that in determining whether a set of rules is more or less efficient than an alternative, it is consent that does the work. If the relevant decision group consents to framework *R* rather than *P* then *R* is efficient and *P* is not. It would do no good to point out that from some more traditional economic perspective, say, welfare or utility maximization, *P* is more efficient than *R*. If that is so, then normally we might expect people to choose *P* over *R*. If, for whatever reason, they chose *R* over *P*, then that's the end of it: *R*, not *P*, is efficient.

4.6 BUCHANAN IS TULLOCK

It is this conjunction of the emphasis on rules of the game and consent as the basis of justification and as providing the ultimate criterion of efficiency that warrants characterizing

Buchanan as an economic contractarian. But, unlike other economists who have emphasized either the efficiency or rationality of rules, Buchanan is concerned exclusively with whether or not people consent to them. Thus, unlike the theorists described in Chapter 1 who I have elsewhere called market contractarians,[7] Buchanan is what I would call a *libertarian contractarian.* Thus, in my view, the Buchanan of *The Calculus of Consent,* the seminal work in twentieth-century contractarian theory, is really his coauthor, Gordon Tullock.[8] The economic contractarianism of that book is simply not representative of the views Buchanan ultimately defends.

Buchanan and conventional economic analysts develop the relationship between autonomy and efficiency in exactly contrary ways. Orthodox economists believe that efficiency can be defined as a property of social states; and given their definition of it (especially Pareto superiority), it follows logically that people would consent to efficient rules. Consent follows from efficiency. Buchanan puts the matter in exactly the opposite way. What people consent to is efficient. Efficiency follows from consent.

There are many problems with Buchanan's view, most of which result from the identification of efficiency with voluntary exchange and others of which result from an inadequately fine-grained analysis of institutions. The impulse to move the discussion from particular outcomes to the level of rules is a sound one, however. The idea that efficiency is relative to frameworks for trade is an even more important insight.

Following Buchanan part of the way, then, we can define market failure as relative to particular institutional settings, though it will remain to distinguish those features of circumstances that are properly characterized as institutional from those that are not. Now that we have a potentially more useful starting point for characterizing market failure, we can ask ourselves what market failure consists of? That is, what fails when markets fail?

4.7 WHEN MARKETS FAIL

When most economists and lawyers refer to market failure, they mean to draw attention to one and only one missing property: efficiency or Pareto optimality. Market failure is just inefficiency. The focus on inefficiency as such as the criterion of market failure may be more misleading than illuminating. It may blind us to important distinctions among the sources of inefficiency, only some of which could conceivably count as instances of market failure. Instability in property rights or inadequately enforced prohibitions against force and fraud may induce inefficiency. Individuals who are both fully informed and rational in the appropriate sense may nevertheless be imperfect processors of information, and interactions among them may be less than optimal. In these cases, it is hard to see what is gained by referring to the absence of efficiency as constituting a market failure, as opposed, say, to a political failure (in the case of instability in property rights or inadequate enforcement of prohibitions against force and fraud) or a cognitive failure (as in the case of inadequate processing skills).

We want to be able to distinguish the cases in which inefficiency results from political defects from those in which it results from cognitive or other informational defects and both from cases in which it is the result of the logic of human interaction (as in the P.D.) or from gross disparities in wealth. All are inefficiencies, but not all of them are shortcomings *in the market*. More importantly, whether or not they are inefficiencies in the market, they may require different solutions. If we focus only on inefficiency as the signature of market failure, we will see markets as failing when, often, the failure is not in the market but in the normative framework in which it is embedded or in the capacities of agents who interact within it. Because we will lump together causes of inefficiency, we will likely lump together the solutions to them, when, in fact, very different responses to different sorts of inefficiencies are required. Insufficient attention to the sources of market failure – if, indeed, the failure is in the market – lead to blunt, and often, inappropriate solutions.[9]

Market failure implies inefficiency, but inefficiency does not imply market failure. There can be inefficient outcomes of games as well as social choices, neither of which are plausibly characterized as markets. Indeed, in the case of social choice rules, the failing is more aptly characterized as political failure. Therefore, if the motivation for political or collective action is inefficiency, then the notion of *market failure* may be unnecessary, and, in any event, it does very little work. If market failure is the failure of the conditions of perfect competition to obtain, and if the only point of referring to market failure is to introduce the concept of inefficiency as a basis for political action, then it is pretty straightforward, but not necessarily illuminating, that from an economic point of view there will always be a plausible case to be made for political action.

The conceptual difference between inefficiency and market failure has normative consequences, however, and this is the important point. It is one thing to say the law ought to rectify market failure and quite another to claim that the law ought to promote efficiency (i.e., eliminate inefficiency). To see this, consider the claim that the law ought to promote efficiency. Put this way, the claim rests on the premise that efficiency is necessarily preferable to inefficiency. One can object to this premise on a variety of grounds. An inefficient but *fair* distribution may be preferable to an efficient but *unfair* one. This line of objection, however, introduces criteria of evaluation beyond the economic framework, which an economist might be unwilling to accept. The lawyer-economist's claim simply may be that within a purely economic framework – like the market paradigm – efficiency is always preferable to inefficiency. Introducing a criteria of justice or fairness outside the scope of criteria the economist is willing to accept in order to criticize the economist may be unfair.

One need not go beyond economic analysis, however, to find a devastating objection to the claim that the law ought to promote efficiency. Even within a purely economic framework, this claim cannot be sustained. If efficiency is always preferable to inefficiency, then any point on the Pareto frontier – each of which represents an efficient allocation of resources – would be preferable to any point within the frontier – each of which represents an inefficient allocation of resources. But the consequent of the above conditional is false. From a purely economic point of view, only points (including those on the frontier) in utility space to their northeast are Pareto preferable to points within the frontier. All other points – those that do not bear the northeast/southwest relationship to one another – *are Pareto noncomparable.* That is, from an economic point of view, there are no grounds whatsoever for asserting that efficiency is always preferable to inefficiency.[10]

Although it is not true that every Pareto optimal allocation is preferable to every non-Pareto optimal one, for every non-Pareto optimal allocation, there exists a set of Pareto optimal allocations preferable to it. This is an important distinction. The second claim is true, the first is not. Not every efficient allocation is preferable to any inefficient one. On the other hand, if an allocation is inefficient, there are exists at least one efficient allocation that is preferable to it. In utility space, efficient allocations that are preferable to inefficient ones are all those to their northeast. Efficient allocations to the northeast of inefficient ones are not only Pareto optimal, they are mutually beneficial as well. They enhance everyone's well-being.

Therefore, it is one thing to say that the law should promote efficiency, which if it means no more than it says, would be wrong even from a purely economic point of view. It is quite another thing to say that the law ought to promote efficiency in ways that are beneficial to all those affected by it. These are very different claims. Note that the second proposition reintroduces features of the competitive market other than the efficiency of the outcome, and in doing so recalls the discussion in Chapter 1. The law should be designed not simply to compensate for the inefficiencies of the market, but to do so in a way that replicates other features of the ex-

101

change model. By imposing the mutual advantage requirement, we require of the law either that it respect the individual rationality condition of exchange or the Pareto superiority
feature of transactions among rational agents. This recalls
Buchanan's characterization of politics as modeled on simple
exchange. Political solutions to economic problems must, like
simple exchange, be beneficial for all parties, that is they must
constitute Pareto improvements. It recalls as well our claim
that political and legal practices are schemes of rational cooperation.

Economic theories of the law have traditionally focused on
concepts like "market failure," "efficiency" and "inefficiency." In their normative guise, they have suggested that
law be formulated to promote efficiency, reduce inefficiency
or rectify market failures. This chapter has argued that the
relevant notion of market failure is not well understood or
analyzed. It has also argued that there are important conceptual and normative differences between the practice of rectifying market failures and promoting efficient outcomes.
Strictly defined, promoting efficiency as such cannot be defended within any rational choice framework, including the
ones developed earlier in this part of the book. Individual
rational choice theory sanctions only moves to the northeast
in utility space, whereas not every efficient point will be to
the northeast of the point of no agreement for all agents.
Understanding legal rules as facilitating markets rather than
producing efficient outcomes helps avoid this problem.
Moreover, markets are defensible in liberal political theory in
a way in which efficiency strictly construed may not be.

This completes the argument of Part I. One political theory
has been rejected, the beginnings of an alternative sketched.
That alternative, provides a role for the market whose possible scope has been explored in Chapter 3. The next part of
this book takes up the invitation of Chapters 2 and 3 and
considers whether contract law can be usefully illuminated
from the point of view of rational choice liberalism.

Part II

Safeguards and risks

Chapter 5

The rational agreement

Markets are most difficult to create and sustain where they are needed most. A law of contract provides part of the solution to this problem. In this part of the book I argue that the main threat to markets is uncertainty, that in general the real threats to cooperation are epistemic. In Chapter 6, I support this claim and demonstrate some of the ways in which a law of contract can alleviate uncertainty by providing exogenous transaction resources. Part of the claim is that, in liberal legal cultures, the best interpretation of contract law sees contractual norms in terms of the role they play in guarding against contract failure and, thereby, in creating and sustaining markets. Markets in turn are attractive to the liberal because of the contribution they can make to social stability. This theme ties together the arguments in Part I and II.

This part of the book pursues a top-down approach to contract law. Markets involve large numbers of discrete transactions. Some of these occur among individuals who come together only for the purpose of exchange. Others transactions are embedded in long term relationships, both contractual and other. My suggestion is that we think of a discrete transaction, an attempt to forge a contract, as a scheme of "local cooperation for mutual advantage."[1]

To begin, imagine two rational people trying to cooperate or contract with one another in the absence of law. Anthony Kronman refers to this process as "contracting in the state of nature."[2] In characterizing the process this way, we hope to discover the interests the parties have in contracting, the difficulties they might confront in reaching and securing an agreement, the devices they might construct to guard against contract failure, and the conditions under which they might turn to third parties for help and to legal norms in particular.

5.1 THE RATIONAL CONTRACT

Let's begin, then, with an abstract characterization of contracting. The terms of an agreement to cooperate among two or more people, their *contract*, stipulates (1) specific actions by each to be carried out at some time in the future and (2) rewards and penalties to be meted out following compliance or defection. These terms constitute safeguards crafted to minimize and allocate risk. In doing so they create risks of their own. What are the conditions under which rational actors will agree to cooperate if charged explicitly with designing a policy to cope with risk and uncertainty in their environment?

The decision-making calculus that rational actors use in crafting a contract is relatively complex because it requires resolving three distinct but intertwined problems: cooperation, division, and defection. As suggested in Chapter 1, these problems are captured in a type of game termed the divisible prisoner's dilemma. Where other types of games, for example, pure division games, prisoner's dilemmas, and coordination games typically isolate one feature of rational decision that can come into play in contracting,[3] the divisible prisoner's dilemma describes three, the interaction between them, and their informational requirements. The three principles of rationality expressed in the divisible P.D. are rational cooperation, rational division, and rational compliance. Failure to satisfy any one of the three leads to contract failure; satisfying all three is necessary and sufficient for agreement and performance on a contract.

An example of the divisible prisoner's dilemma is depicted in matrix (normal) form in Figure 5.1.

For the moment, assume that each player knows both pay-

106

Player B

| | | Performance | | Nonperformance |
		Contract 1	Contract 2	Nonperformance
	Contract 1	Contract$_1$ 19, 7 C$_1$	Status quo 9, 2 D	B free rides 3, 11 NP$_b$
Player A	Contract 2	Status quo 9, 2 D	Contract$_2$ 16, 10 C$_2$	B free rides 3, 11 NP$_b$
	Nonperformance	A free rides 22, 1 NP$_a$	A free rides 22, 1 NP$_a$	Status quo 9, 2 D

Figure 5.1

offs in all of the cells. Player A (row) and player B (column) each make a three-dimensional choice. Each must decide whether or not to contract; and if the choice is to contract, whether to seek contract 1 or contract 2. In making this decision each of three problems of rational contracting emerges.

The *cooperation* problem may be resolved depending on whether the parties share a common interest in contracting over acting individually. If both prefer to contract, then they solve their cooperation problem; if either or both prefer to act individually, no contract between them is possible. This particular failure to contract results from an inability to solve the cooperation problem. In our example the two contracts represented by cells 1 and 5 represent higher payoffs for both parties than do the noncontract alternatives. Thus, we would expect the players to solve their cooperation problem. Doing so is not sufficient for contracting, however. Two problems

Safeguards and risks

remain. A *division* problem arises if player A prefers contract 1 to contract 2 and player B prefers the opposite. Consequently, opposed preferences on how to contract complicate the common preference for a contract over no contract. And a *defection* problem arises if a player gains from unilaterally defecting from a contract, once agreement is secured. The defection problem is powerfully illustrated by the nondivisible or standard prisoner's dilemma in which the dominant strategy for each player is to defect from whatever agreements he or she has made. In the example, A gains by defecting to cell 7 or 8, and B gains by defecting to cell 3 or 6.

5.2 THREE PHASES OF CONTRACTING

Each problem in the contractual relationship corresponds to a distinct phase of the contracting process and involves a distinct principle of rationality.[4] First, in the *prephase* the decision whether to cooperate, that is, whether to seek a contract, is made. If the parties are rational, each predicates an affirmative decision on expectations that joint gains will be attainable under the contract. Second, in the *negotiation phase* the decision of how to contract is made. That is, the parties agree upon the terms of the contract, specifying the manner in which the gains resulting from the contract and the burdens of enforcing it are to be allocated. Finally, in the *postphase* each party makes the decision to fulfill or to violate the contract and monitors the compliance of the other.

Each phase contains a potential pitfall. That is, individuals may fail to contract because (1) one or more of the essential parties prefers to act independently rather than to seek a contract; (2) the parties fail to agree upon the terms of the contract; or (3) the contract collapses owing to a violation of its terms. Each phase is distinct not only in the sense of carrying its own pitfalls to contracting; to succeed at each phase a contract must also meet the demands of distinct but ultimately related rationality conditions. The phase of contracting and the respective rationality conditions are developed in the following sections.

108

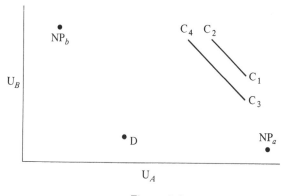

Figure 5.2

5.3 COORDINATION AND JOINT RATIONALITY

No one can expect another rational person to engage in contracting unless each perceives an opportunity for mutual gain.
That surely is the operating assumption when a buyer responds to a seller's "for sale" notice and when labor negotiates with management. Indeed, it is such a common place
that we tend to take it for granted, overlooking its analytic
importance.

We can put this obvious fact about contracting in an analytically precise way. A necessary condition for agreeing to a
contract is that its expected outcome satisfies what may be
termed the *joint rationality* condition. Where U_i is the utility
individual i expects to secure in contracting D_i is i's utility
from disagreement (i.e., the status quo), $U = (U_a, U_b)$ is a given
agreement's utility vector, and $U' = (U'_a, U'_b)$ is any other feasible agreement's utility vector, U is jointly rational if for each
feasible outcome U'

$$U_a \geq U'_a \text{ or } U_b \geq U'_b. \qquad (1)$$

The joint rationality condition can be clarified by analyzing
Figure 5.2. C_1, C_2 represents the contract curve, that is, the
set of Pareto optimal outcomes to the northeast of D. D, in
turn, represents the disagreement point, the outcome of con-

109

tracting that results if the parties fail to reach agreement. NP_a and NP_b are the nonperformance outcomes. NP_a results when A and B reach agreement with which B complies and from which A defects. NP_b represents the outcome that results when A complies and B defects. These are the free-rider outcomes. Both are Pareto optimal in the sense that no points lie to their northeast in the utility–space representation of the game. Though Pareto optimal, they are not Pareto superior to D, and thus they do not lie on the contract curve C_1, C_2. NP_a, NP_b, and all the points on the contract curve C_1, C_2 are jointly rational or Pareto optimal. Only points on the contract curve, however, are Pareto optimal *and* Pareto superior to D.

If information is imperfect or incomplete, each party has an incentive to expend resources to inquire whether a bargain with someone else promises to be advantageous. These resources are *transaction resources*, resources devoted to determining if transacting is rational. At the cooperation or pre-phrase, parties may expend transaction resources to identify and secure D at the outset. Everyone wants a referent from which he or she can evaluate feasible outcomes. Contracting will break down and may not even begin without it (as is the case in labor–management negotiations with newly certified unions whose legitimacy is uncertain). Similarly, individuals cannot take for granted the existence of the contract curve, even though opportunities for more efficient cooperation tend to exist in every relationship. If people must expend resources to determine the location of the disagreement point or the contract curve, some or all of the gains from contracting are consumed – that is, in terms of Figure 5.2, C_1, C_2 moves toward C_3, C_4.

The magnitude of the cooperation problem, roughly the distance between the contract curve and the disagreement point, reflects the social gains forgone by failing to cooperate. It is a measure of the players' joint stake in the game. The greater the attainable gains from contracting, the more resources people are willing to expend to achieve them. However, as they do that, the contract curve lengthens, exacerbating, as we shall see, potential defection and division problems.

Contracting to secure mutual gains consumes transaction resources that are scarce and costly to obtain. In the conventional law and economics tradition, transaction costs are assumed to be low in contracting situations, so that parties are able to gather all pertinent information and to assign all relevant risks.[5] Because it assumes individuals have perfect information, are completely rational, and face no impediments to entering transactions, "it would be surprising if such superhumans were *not able* to manage their own affairs without the intervention of government."[6] As it happens, however, sometimes they are not. The newer law-and-economics tradition emphasizes transaction costs even in contracting situations. Because it assumes that individuals have imperfect information, limited rationality, and encounter substantial impediments in contracting, it would be surprising if such patently imperfect individuals were able to manage their affairs without the intervention of government. As it happens, in some cases, they do.

This discontinuity between "prohibitive" and "nonprohibitive" transaction costs, as I have noted earlier, is an analytic artifice begging for elaboration. The private and governmental controls that people craft depend on the relative size of the transaction costs involved. Because each of the three decision-making problems in any relationship involves unique hazards from imperfect information, the undifferentiated, generic treatment of transaction costs is analytically untenable as well.

5.4 NEGOTIATION AND CONCESSION

Recognizing that contracting would generate benefits in excess of costs is not a sufficient condition for contracting to occur.[7] Contracting requires that parties to the negotiations resolve the division problem, either directly by agreeing upon allocations of benefits and costs or indirectly by agreeing upon a set of procedures by which these allocations are to be determined. The problem is not just the cost of establishing a set of feasible and acceptable outcomes. Even if that cost is nil, the *strategic* nature of the choice may induce a noncooperative outcome.[8] Strategy may require players to disguise their true intentions in pursuit of an agreement, moderating or exaggerating their demands based on their view of how each will respond to the other. Thus, failure to resolve the division problem can complicate the process of contracting even to the point of defeating it.

Returning to Figure 5.2, the division problem arises because the players have opposite preferences regarding where along the contract curve agreement should occur.[9] Expressed in bargaining theoretic terms, C_1, contract 1, is player A's *best hope outcome* because it is the outcome that is: (i) most preferred by A, (ii) no worse than disagreement for B; (iii) feasible; and (iv) enforceable. Similarly, C_2, contract 2, represents B's best hope. The players' best hopes correspond to opposite endpoints of the contract curve. When a *concession* is defined as agreeing to an outcome less preferred than one's own best hope, it follows that agreement requires concessions. Either one player makes all the concessions required for agreement by assenting to the other's best hope outcome, or both players make concessions resulting in agreement at an intermediate point on the contract curve. If bargaining over the allocation of concessions fails, so too does contracting.

Intuitively, we recognize the problem of settling on a division of cooperative gains as endemic in human behavior and know that people resolve it when the conditions are right. Empirical studies confirm that standards of "fair division" sometimes guide rational agreement even in the absence of third party enforcement. In particular, Kahneman, Knetsch, and Thaler have shown that when unanticipated events induce unanticipated divisions, they do not necessarily threaten the economic viability of an arrangement.[10] In other words, individuals sometimes appeal to a sense of fairness to solve division problems when failure to reach agreement on a division may jeopardize an opportunity for mutual gain. Laboratory experiments testing the Coase theorem demonstrate as well that parties are able to secure jointly maximizing outcomes, though different methods of assigning property entitlements influence the division of the gains.[11] Other studies confirm the importance of the status quo in choices over division rules and the heavier weight ascribed to losses than equivalent gains in evaluating outcomes.[12] In short, empirical studies suggest that players are often able to solve their division problem and point to some of the relevant factors in settling on particular divisions: the allocation of initial entitlements, a sense of fairness, the relative disparity in weighing equivalent gains and losses, and so on.

Under a broad range of conditions, then, contracting parties settle on distributions of the gains from trade, which simply means that they allocate concessions. They also have in mind which among the available points on the contract curve they intend to safeguard by the terms of any contract. Put analytically, a necessary condition for agreeing to a contract is that its expected outcomes satisfy what may be termed the principle of *concession rationality*.[13]

Each of the formal models in the literature provides a distinct meaning to the concept of concession rationality. No single point-specific solution to the bargaining problem has gained universal acceptance. But in an abstract or general characterization of the process of rational contracting, it is less important to defend a particular solution to the bargaining problem than it is to identify the parameters that influence the choice of rules for solving division problems. We want a model that applies to a broad range of contractual settings and incorporates fundamental principles universally accepted as affecting the relative bargaining power of parties.

The problem with many bargaining theories is that although they take account of the parties' relative bargaining strength, they assume away many of the other problems that lead to bargaining failure, for example, uncertainty. Thus, they typically yield the result that bargainers will secure a cooperative division of the gains that reflects their initial relative bargaining strengths. This outcome is not surprising, but because of all the evidence of noncooperation (wars, strikes, etc.), these models are neither predictive nor descriptive.[14] Again, though all bargaining models view the relative costliness of conflict as affecting relative bargaining power, many do not take into account the parties best hopes, or aspiration levels, which influence their willingness to incur costs in reaching agreement. That is inconsistent with a sizable body of experimental evidence indicating that aspiration level is positively related to bargaining power.[15]

In contrast, what we call *resistance theory* renders an explicit account of the conditions under which negotiations break down, treats aspirations as part of the decision-making calculus, and describes the information rational contractors require to reach agreement. The attraction of resistance theory, then, is that it illuminates the conditions under which people will expend resources to contract.[16] As conceived in resistance theory, bargainers assess the relative strengths of their strategic positions based on the utility structure of the game – that is, the location of the disagreement point, the location and shape of the contract curve, and their risk and time preferences. The strength with which a bargainer strives to avoid concessions, his or her resistance, depends on the costliness to the individual of the concessions required by the agreement (the greater the concession cost, the greater will be the resistance to the agreement), the costliness of conflict (an increase in conflict's cost increases the willingness to make concessions and diminishes resistance), and the aspiration level (higher aspirations enhance resistance). The very existence of opposing proposals reveals conflicting aspirations. They establish concession limits and distributional expectations based on those assessments. Only outcomes where those limits and expectations overlap satisfy concession rationality.

Formally, where D_i is any bargainer i's utility from disagreement (conflict); B_i is i's aspiration level or best hope – the enforceable outcome on the contract curve that the bar-

114

gainer prefers or, equivalently, the outcome he or she most prefers that is enforceable, feasible, and no worse than conflict for any other bargainer; and U_i is i's utility from a given outcome U, i's resistance to outcome, U, $R_i(U)$ is defined as

$$R_i = (B_i - U_i)/(B_i - D_i). \qquad (2)$$

During negotiations, each bargainer assesses his or her own resistance against that of others. Under conditions of complete information, each will agree to an outcome only if the concessions it requires are at least matched by the relative concessions of others. On the assumption of equal rationality, each party will make equal relative concessions.[17] It is not rational to be exploited. Expressed in terms of resistance, this means that the bargainer will agree to an outcome if his own resistance to it would equal or fall below the resistance of others. Formally, where $R_i(U)$ is any bargainer i's resistance to outcome U and $R_j(U)$ is another bargainer's resistance to outcome U, that outcome lies in the agreement set of i, A_i, if

$$R_i(U) \le R_j(U). \qquad (3)$$

Concession rationality requires that an actor's concession behavior fulfills this requirement. Resistance theory posits that with complete information, people exhibit concession rationality. Under conditions of complete information, rational individuals make equal relative concessions. When information is incomplete, a bargainer will agree to an outcome if his own resistance is matched or exceeded by the expected resistance of everyone else. That is, where i's resistance to U is $R_i(U)$ and i's expectation concerning j's resistance to U is $E_i(R_j(U))$, the set of outcomes to which i would agree, his agreement set A_i, includes outcomes fulfilling the requirement

$$R_i(U) \le E_i(R_j(U)). \qquad (4)$$

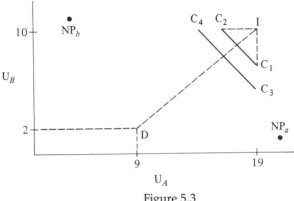

Figure 5.3

Of course, for an outcome to be agreed upon, it must lie in the agreement sets of each individual with the ability to block an agreement. For example, in a system of bargainers A and B, it must lie in the intersection of sets A_a and A_b.

The implications of concession rationality for the outcome of bargaining can be illustrated graphically. Consider Figure 5.3. The outcomes where players' resistances are equal lie on the line connecting the disagreement point D (9, 2), where each resistance equals one, to the *ideal point* I (19, 10), a non-feasible outcome where players simultaneously attain their best hope payoffs and resistances are consequently equal to zero. If person A exhibits concession rationality as defined in Equation 3, his agreement set lies on or to the right of the line ID; and if person B is similarly rational, his agreement lies on or above the line ID. Hence, if both exhibit concession rationality and possess complete information, their point of agreement must lie on line ID.

Resistance theory is one way of specifying the content of concession rationality. Concession rationality in turn expresses a condition of rational cooperation or rational contracting. It specifies a requirement of rational bargaining. Its domain is the division of the gains from cooperation or the parties' joint stakes in contracting.

The division problem can be more or less troublesome. The

116

magnitude of the division problem in a particular case is a function of the discrepancy between the players' best hopes or, equivalently, of the length of the contract curve. If the individuals' best hopes exactly coincide, as in the *nondivisible* prisoner's dilemma game, the contract curve shrinks to a point and agreement requires no concessions. As the contract curve lengthens, the concessions required increase. That in turn makes divisional bargaining an enterprise with higher stakes. Consequently, expending resources to enhance the strength of one's bargaining position becomes more rational, as do any measures to minimize one's own concessions and to maximize those secured from others.

This discussion gives analytic precision to points made less precisely in Chapter 1. Understanding rational cooperation as motivated by the suboptimality of interaction that has the payoff structure of a P.D. emphasizes the compliance problem but ignores the division problem. In doing so it has led theorists from Hobbes on to view the role of the state to be an enforcer of agreements, and has thereby overlooked the role of the state in facilitating negotiations. Also it has led anarchist theorists, like Michael Taylor, who want to resist the inference that the state is necessary because the state of nature is a P.D. to reconceive the state of nature as a re-peated-play P.D. in which cooperation would emerge with-out state intervention. Repeat play is not necessarily a cure to defection incentives in a P.D. More importantly, focusing on the defection problem may lead us from emphasizing the magnitude and significance of the division problem as a bar-rier to cooperation.

5.5 RATIONALITY AND COMPLIANCE

In the nondivisible P.D., the parties' best hopes coincide and no concessions are required. That is why the P.D. is best thought of as illustrating the problem of rational defection, not the problem of rational agreement. The payoffs from co-operation are set, no concessions are required. The defection problem reflects the problematic nature of mutual trust, owing to the presence in most contracts of burdensome provisions and potential loopholes. Frequently, an individual can gain by defaulting on a contract, often at the expense of those who perform according to its terms. A prerequisite for contracting, then, is a system of enforcement with which to preclude or to deter noncompliance or to compensate parties injured by others' noncompliance. Not surprisingly, debate about whether negotiations are undertaken in good faith and careful scrutiny of contracts for hidden loopholes are prominent in virtually all contracting.

The compliance or defection problem can be expressed in terms of a third condition of rationality: A necessary condition for rational agreement to a contract is that its expected outcome satisfies *individual rationality*. Neither player will permit himself to be left worse off than the status quo, or disagreement point. That is, where U_i is individual i's expected utility from participating in a contract, and D_i is i's utility from disagreement, i is *individually rational* if

$$U_i \geq D_i. \tag{5}$$

With reference to Figure 5.3, player A prefers defection if point NP_a is to the right of the point on the contract curve at which agreement occurs, and player B prefers defection if NP_b is above the contract point. Player A would not agree to an outcome lying to the left of point D, such as point NP_b in which B free rides, even though NP_b is jointly rational. Such an agreement would make A worse off than A would be were no agreement made, thus violating the individual rationality condition. Nor would player B accept any outcome below point D, such as NP_a, for similar reasons. Hence, if both players are individually rational, neither will tolerate the other's free riding. The outcomes of Figure 5.3's game that satisfy each player's requirement of individual rationality include the status quo point D, and all of the points on the contract curve C_1, C_2. Rational parties will not agree to contracts they expect to make them worse off; thus, they must find a way to eliminate or minimize the risk of defection. This is no easy task.

A defection problem arises if either player can gain from free riding. The magnitude of the problem depends on the relationship between each player's unilateral defection payoff and the payoff from his or her least preferred point on the contract curve, the other party's best hope outcome $U_i(B_j)$. In other words, a contractor's greatest incentive to free ride arises when the agreement represents the other party's most preferred contract. Notice, however, that a contractor has some incentive for defection even if the agreement represents his best hope or most preferred contract. Every unilateral defection outcome gives him a payoff in excess of *any* cooperative outcome.

To guard against unilateral noncompliance, each party must reduce the other party's incentive to defect. The power of the incentive to defect can be mitigated in several analytically distinguishable ways. Compliance can be made more rewarding, defection less rewarding, or opportunities to defect reduced or blocked. Of these, the second is the most common because the first tends to be more costly and the third tends to be impractical given the near impossibility of removing all opportunities for nonperformance. In short, no party will rationally agree to comply and to let the other party free ride. But because both parties have at least some incentive to free ride, each has an incentive to deploy resources to ensure the compliance of the other.

Individual rationality, then, requires that an agreement be *enforceable*, not just that an individual be protected against an outcome worse than the status quo.[18] To be an enforceable agreement, the parties must expect that each estimates a cost of violation exceeding the gain from unilaterally defecting. That is, no agreement on C_1, C_2 is enforceable without penalties sufficient to deter defection, termed the *force of agreement*.[19]

Viewed graphically, an enforcement system that penalizes defection displaces the defection points NP_a and NP_b toward the origin, making compliance more rewarding relative to defection. In Figure 5.3, for example, if each player faces a violation cost that makes him indifferent between defecting and his best hope outcome, then no points on the contract curve will be enforceable. But if each faces a violation cost that makes him or her indifferent between defecting and the other party's best hope outcome, then the entire contract curve constitutes a domain of enforceable agreements.

In general, the greater an individual's defection incentive, the stronger must be the penalties that would succeed in making compliance rational. Further, the greater the incentive to defect, the stronger are the incentives for the individual to seek to evade or undermine an enforcement system. Put simply, the more a person wants to defect, the harder and more costly it will be to prevent her from doing so. Although it is not rational to accept a contract that is unenforceable – that gives others the opportunity to defect, making a contract enforceable requires expenditure of considerable resources. The greater the incentive to defect, the greater the resources required to prevent it.

5.6 CONTRACT AS BARGAIN

The resistance solution to a bargaining game of complete information can be described in terms of the rationality conditions. Individual and joint rationality, which jointly comprise the classical notion of economic rationality,[20] together suffice to motivate contracting but not agreement on any unique contract. With reference to Figure 5.3, they restrict the outcomes of agreement to a portion of the contract curve C_1, C_2. This contains, of course, many feasible outcomes. In classic economic theory, no choice among them can be said to be more or less rational than any other. The choice among them cannot be a matter of rationality! Thus, in the usual forms of economic analysis, the choice among Pareto optimal (collectively or jointly rational) outcomes is said to be a matter of distributive fairness or equity, not a matter of economics (or rationality).

120

The additional requirement of concession rationality, the signature of the bargaining theory approach adopted here, restricts that outcome to a point on the equal resistance line *ID* in Figure 5.3, so the cumulative effect of these requirements is to specify the intersection of the contract curve and the equal resistance line. For bargainers *A* and *B* with complete information, the outcome of the bargaining *U* satisfies the expression

$$\min[R_a(U) = R_b(U)] \qquad (6)$$

Agreement and performance on a contract occur, then, if and only if the contract satisfies all three requirements for each party to the transaction. Taken together, then, these conditions are necessary and sufficient; they define a party's interests in a contractual relationship.[21]

Bargaining theory differs from the more common forms of economic analysis precisely by its commitment to a principle of concession rationality. This principle is aimed at explaining and defending some outcomes along the frontier as more rational than others. Concession or bargaining theory thus makes the division of the gains from contracting, that is, the distribution of the game's stakes, a matter of rationality. Unlike forms of economic analysis that set aside questions of distribution, rational bargaining theory takes the division problem to be a part of the problem of rational choice. As a consequence, concession theory not only can explain and defend outcomes of contracting as more or less rational depending on the way in which the gains are distributed but it can also explain safeguards in contracting aimed at securing certain divisions and failures in contracting as often resulting from failures to solve the bargaining or concession problem or as owing to the high costs of safeguarding agreed upon divisions.

Chapter 6

Safeguarding

In the model we explicated, bargaining takes place sequentially (at least in logical space–time). First individuals search for potentially advantageous cooperative opportunities; then they seek agreement on distributing the gains; and finally they monitor compliance with the contract's terms. Each phase leaves plenty of room for contract failure. Thus, guarding against failure is rational – up to a point. That is, one does not want to spend more on preventing failure than failure may cost in terms of forgone benefit. The important analytic point is that at least some expenditure of resources to guard against contract failure is rational for all actors. This process of expending resources to prevent contract failure is "rational safeguarding."

The order in which actors safeguard their interests in contracting reverses the order in which they contract (again in logical space–time). In the divisible prisoner's dilemma, both parties have incentives to defect from unprotected agreements. If it is rational for player A to defect from an agreement, then it cannot be rational for player B to bargain with player A over the gains from trade, and vice versa. Bargaining without compliance is simply a waste of resources and is, therefore, irrational. If bargaining over the gains from trade is to be rational, the parties must be reasonably confident of one another's subsequent compliance. Thus, the defection problem must be resolved prior to pursuing a division of the contract's gains.[1] Similar considerations apply regarding the other phases of bargaining. Crafting safeguards to satisfy joint

122

rationality is pointless unless the parties expect both the division and defection problems to be solved. Early phase decisions are dependent upon expectations regarding decisions at a later stage; anticipating breakdown at a later phase may block affirmative decisions at an earlier one. Each party would prefer that the other bear the full costs of safeguarding. In general this preference cannot be successfully insisted on. Concessions are rational and an agreement about distributing the costs of safeguarding can be secured. This "contract," that is, the contract over safeguards, has all the same conditions and pitfalls as bargaining over the gains from trade. So, in the complete rational contract, the parties bargain over both the costs of safeguarding and the gains from trade.

The two games are then analyzed as follows. The first game involves negotiating over enforcement costs. In this game we once again assume that the players command resources adequate to enforce an agreement, so that they need not call upon third-party enforcement mechanisms. (This assumption is crucial; otherwise, the account cannot proceed, for we will generate an infinite regress of nonenforceable contracts.) The only question at this stage – in this game – is, "Who shall bear which costs in solving the defection problem?" If this bargaining problem is solved, then the second cooperative game is played. The players' mutual interest is to bargain over points on the contract curve only. The enforceable solutions to the second game, therefore, lie on the contract curve. Thus, the second bargaining game is over points on the curve.

The first, or enforcement, game is connected to the second, or division of the gains, game in three ways. First, solving the enforcement game is a necessary condition for playing the division game; second, any particular solution to the enforcement game will affect solutions to the division game. How much one is willing to concede in bargaining over the gains from trade may well depend on how much one has had to expend in creating safeguards against defection. Third, because they both are bargaining games, the theory of rational bargaining applies to both. In principle there should be equilibria solutions to the conjunction of these two games that satisfy the rationality conditions.

In general, party A will create a safeguard so long as the potential burden imposed on B to overcome it exceeds the cost to A of creating it; party A expects B to have a comparable incentive.[2] Following these strategies gives rise to an optimizing effect. When parties contract with one another, they bargain so as to minimize the sum of the costs they impose on each other and the costs they must bear to safeguard themselves. Under conditions of complete information both cooperative games are solved so that the following is true: A rational contract minimizes the sum of the costs the players impose on one another and the costs they bear to protect themselves.

6.1 THE CULPRIT IS UNCERTAINTY

Problems in contract arise when information is not complete, when, instead, actors are required to behave under conditions of uncertainty. Almost every contract dispute that winds up in litigation turns on a point about an incomplete contract; the traditional reasons for incomplete contracts are matters of information cost: (1) Some contingencies may be unforeseeable; (2) planning for every foreseeable contingency can be expensive; and (3) some contingencies may involve private information. Indeed, because a complete contract must specify a suitable mechanism for transmitting information to deal with contingencies, it can be particularly costly to devise and, therefore, incomplete and subject to renegotiation.[3]

When bargainers possess less than complete information, failure to identify opportunities for gain or fear of outcomes worse than the status quo can prevent contracting from ever getting off the ground. Once it does, agreement can still be blocked or the point of agreement may diverge from the contract curve's equal resistance outcome. For example, if bargainers underestimate one another's resistance, they demand more concessions than the other will grant and the result is conflict. Unresolved conflict does not entail that the rationality conditions are violated. Rather, divergences from the outcome predictable under complete information can be examined as the expected consequences of rational actors facing imperfect information. Bargaining with incomplete information can be both rational and unsuccessful.

If uncertainty exists, each party may benefit by manipulating information to create the appearance that conflict has become less costly to him or more costly to others. That makes the party's threats credible and signals an unwillingness to give in. Similarly, every bargainer possesses incentives to oversell his or her own preferred contract while denigrating the other's preferred contract. And each possesses incentives to invest in safeguards against precisely this sort of behavior because it threatens the divisions to which he or she would otherwise agree.

One consequence of this analysis is that the main reason for expending resources in contracting is to overcome some sort of uncertainty, uncertainty that threatens the equilibrium solution to which rational actors would otherwise agree. Because the possible sources of uncertainty differ in each phase of contracting, the logical character of the costs that rational bargainers are willing to incur to reduce uncertainty differs as well.

6.2 TRANSACTION COSTS AND INFORMATION

People incur *search costs* because they are uncertain about the feasibility of alternative outcomes. Each bargainer wants information about the group's prospects. In that sense, information about group gains, or the opportunity to secure a Pareto improvement, helps to motivate contracting that satisfies the *joint rationality* condition.

People incur *bargaining and decision costs* because they are uncertain about the acceptability of alternative divisions. Each bargainer wants information about the agreement set. Securing adequate information about one another's resistances is necessary to create an agreement that satisfies the *concession rationality* condition.

People incur *monitoring costs* because they are uncertain about the enforceability of alternative outcomes. Each bargainer wants information about the consequences of the other party's defecting. In that sense, information about the force of the agreement is relevant to creating an enforceable contract that satisfies the *individual rationality* condition.

If an individual need only estimate *his* expected utility for the outcomes possible under a proposed contract against that of the status quo to ensure that its terms are no worse than not contracting, then the information required to judge outcomes by this test is the least stringent of all. But because each party needs to estimate the defection incentive and the force of agreement, then, in addition to the information needed to estimate joint and concession rationality, each must estimate NP_a and NP_b.

Significantly, each phase of contracting entails greater risks than the preceding one because, as an inspection of Equations (1)–(6) in Chapter 5 reveals, more terms come into play at each step, so more information is required by succeeding calculations. This means that more potential sources of uncertainty exist and more estimates must be made, each with a risk of error. In other words, the mathematics suggests that gathering information sufficient to fashion safeguards against defection is more difficult than securing information sufficient to safeguard against exploitive divisions and so on. The more general point is that by incurring search, bargaining, and decision costs, individual contractors are able to mitigate ex ante risks; by incurring monitoring costs they hope to mitigate ex post risks. Thus, one can understand the object of contracting as a joint attempt to minimize the sum of the costs of uncertainty and of its avoidance, where uncertainty afflicts all three dimensions of rationality.[4]

6.3 CONTEXTS AND SAFEGUARDS

Just how much information is necessary to craft safeguards to optimal contracting depends on the degree of uncertainty that exists in particular contract environments. Several different but often related contextual features influence the ability of decision makers to estimate the terms composing the calculus of contracting; that is, they affect the amount and accuracy of the information that must be acquired, verified, communicated, or processed during the course of contracting.

As the *number of principal parties* to the potential contract increases, the number of lines of communication and the amount of information that must be processed during negotiation increase. Opportunities for joint gain can be obscured simply by the noise. Group size affects the defection problem because in larger groups an individual's defection tends to be less noticeable, weakening incentives for individuals to participate in sanctioning defectors.[5] Monitoring compliance in a large group is generally more difficult and more demanding of given resources than in a smaller group. Hence, contracting is riskier.

As *heterogeneity among the principal parties* increases, the bargaining range, if one exists, and defection incentives increase. To be sure, differences of preference are required to provide a basis for exchange and contract, but the less interchangeable the actors, the more difficult the transaction. For example, the commonality among workers at particular job sites facilitates collective bargaining with management. Only minor adjustments are required to adjust for individual differences in seniority, skill level, and work classification. By contrast, when each party to a contract possesses a wholly unique set of attributes and relations to each other participant, bargaining may prove impossible even in a very small group. Any bargain ultimately struck will inevitably leave more people disgruntled and, therefore, will create higher, more disparate defection incentives than would an agreement among a more homogeneous assembly.

As the *spatial dispersion* of the group increases, communication costs increase. Both bargaining and enforcement systems required communication. In geographically concentrated groups, oral communication and incidental observations of behavior may suffice, but linking a dispersed group with equally adequate communication between each pair of individuals is technically more difficult. Conversely, because improvements in the technology of communication, holding dispersion constant, reduce communication costs, transaction resources go further.

As the *temporal distribution* of the costs and benefits at issue in the transaction increases, costs and benefits become more difficult to detect and control. For example, delayed defection costs impede monitoring because the adverse consequences become apparent only long after the fact. Similarly, delayed benefits hamper divisional bargaining because bargaining to allocate anticipated gains may appear to be an exercise in wishful thinking.

Closely related, as the *level of acceptable risk* decreases, monitoring problems increase. In classic economics and game theory, the expected utility of a prospect is the product of its probability and utility. An actor who is rational in that sense is indifferent, for example, between the certainty of losing $10, a 1/10 chance of losing $100, and a 1/100 chance of losing $1,000. Yet such outcomes are not equivalent in their implications for contracting. In contrast to defection that imposes a certain cost, defection that merely creates a risk of damage can remain undetected unless actual harm occurs. Monitoring is especially difficult when defection results in a very small risk of grave damage (analogous to the 1/100 chance of losing $1000), as only a tiny portion of defections actually imposes damage. Just as the absence of damage does not imply that no defection occurred, the presence of a damage does not necessarily prove defection. Risk is simply endemic.

As the *nontransferability of costs and benefits* increases, negotiating becomes more intractable. Bargaining determines how benefits and costs will be allocated, so it requires that at least some benefits or costs be transferable. The problems of

128

quantifying and intersubjectively verifying nontransferable benefits and costs underlie the distinction between fungible and unique goods that has been used, for example, to justify the choice between damages and specific performance in contract disputes.

As *instability* increases within a relationship, more transaction resources are required to secure rational outcomes. The best way to understand how instability increases costs is to understand how stability reduces them. Because decisions themselves convey information about the risks of interacting, frequent and consistent decisions reduce the incentives to expend transaction resources on searching and bargaining over acceptable divisions. Moreover, stability facilitates developing internal systems of enforcement with which to deter defection. For egoists in repeated plays of the same P.D. game, cooperation rather than defection can become optimal because defection would disrupt a mutually rewarding pattern of cooperation.[6] If the short-term gains from defection are consistently offset by larger long term losses, a stable pattern of cooperation emerges.

6.4 SUMMARY

Let's recap the analysis to this point: (1) Rational contractors seek to create mutually advantageous, enforceable agreements. (2) Doing so requires that they satisfy three independent rationality conditions: joint, concession, and individual rationality. (3) These rationality conditions correspond to three phases in the contract process and enable the parties to solve three problems of rational choice: the prephase cooperation problem (joint rationality); the negotiation phase division problem (concession rationality); and the postphase compliance problem (individual rationality). (4) A process of rational bargaining can satisfy these conditions but still fail to reach fruition because of uncertainty deriving from incomplete or imperfect information or from potential defection. (5) Consequently, it will be rational for the parties to create safeguards against contract failure. (6) Creating safeguards

129

requires parties to incur three distinct kinds of cost corresponding to the phases in contracting: search costs (prephase), decision costs (negotiation phase) and monitoring costs (postphase). (7) The magnitude of these costs will depend on contextual factors shaping the extent of uncertainty under particular circumstances. (8) In general, the magnitude of uncertainty is greatest in guarding against defection, less great in securing a division, and least pressing in safeguarding against cooperation failure. (9) Rationality requires that resources be devoted to crafting safeguards. These resources should reflect the extent of the threat to cooperation uncertainty poses. Safeguarding should proceed so as to guard first against defection, then unfair division, and finally, to protect against the possibility of failed coordination. Because the risk of defection dominates in the nondivisible prisoner's dilemma, uncertainty about compliance is greatest and, consequently, crafting safeguards against defection is most pressing. (10) The process of creating safeguards can itself be modeled as a rational bargain over the costs of safeguards. Safeguarding depletes transaction resources.

Typically, contract failure results because of incomplete information, that is uncertainty. The question then becomes to what extent contract or cooperation problems can be resolved when individuals have less than full information. Standard philosophy answers this question by exploring various external or internal constraints that individuals might adopt to deter defection and increase the likelihood of compliance. We canvassed some of these in Part I. I am suggesting an alternative to the traditional accounts. In this section I have outlined how various features of the social environment *increase* uncertainty, thereby, making cooperation more difficult. In upcoming sections I explore ways in which the social environment can be altered to reduce uncertainty thereby increasing the possibility of rational cooperation, whatever the motives of the relevant actors.

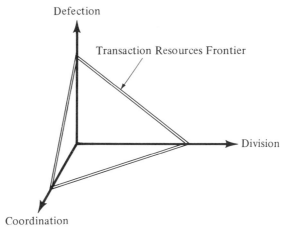

Figure 6.1

6.5 TRANSACTION SPACE

The capacity of the contractors to employ their own resources to reduce uncertainty and create safeguards can be represented graphically.

Figure 6.1 describes the types of interactions to which contractual arrangements may be matched in the form of a *transaction space diagram*. The vertical axis represents the magnitude of the defection problem. The horizontal axis represents the magnitude of the division problem. And the axis perpendicular to both of these represents the magnitude of the cooperation problem.

When a transaction lies near the origin in Figure 6.1, so that the problems are minor, the burden on transaction resources is minimal. At the origin, for example, the parties easily recognize opportunities for gain, and transactions correspond, when described in game theoretic terms, to pure coordination. In transactions at increasing distances from the origin, indicating that the problems of identifying prospects, of bargaining or of defection are more significant, the availability of transaction resources becomes more problematic. The farther any transaction lies from the origin, the greater the transaction costs required for contracting.

131

In contexts where these factors affecting uncertainty are favorable to contracting, only modest resources are required to make contracting possible. For example, small residential groups such as nuclear families possess sufficient endogenous transaction resources with which to develop exceedingly complex systems of mutual understandings. Similarly, conditions in the most hospitable region of transaction space (i.e., the area close to the origin) correspond rather well to those identified in any introductory economics text as conducive to private exchange in perfect or near perfect markets. Even in the (otherwise) most inhospitable regions of transaction space – far upward and to the right of the origin but still within the frontier – ingenious safeguards evolve, such as "exchanging hostages" and giving collateral,[7] where people arrive at and enforce contracts independently.

In contexts where the factors affecting uncertainty are unfavorable to contracting, the parties' transaction resources quickly become exhausted. The worst case arises when members of a large, geographically dispersed group with diverse interests consider negotiating an arrangement where the benefits and costs are delayed, nontransferable, and laden with risk. Locating a national nuclear waste storage facility is an example. Here, the transaction resource frontier will appear to lie relatively close to the origin, indicating that even slight concern over the feasibility of the alternatives or modest division or defection problems exceed the group's ability to contract independently.

6.6 WHAT THIRD PARTIES CAN DO

We need not presume that a forum external to the original setting of a contract – notably, authoritative experts like judges operating under the auspices of the state – will be more efficacious than private ordering in resolving disputes. Third-party intervention must be explained not assumed. And it is more plausibly explained, if we start out presuming that people are never without some endogenous transaction resources with which to contract. That means they do not always rely upon or even want a third party to secure agreements. Endogenous resources, however, are finite. The points in transaction space at which private parties exhaust them define the *transaction resource frontier*. The frontier is simply a way of visualizing the limits to private settlement and the reasons for involving a third party. Attainable gains are lost when contextual features place transactions beyond the frontier and block contracting. That provides an incentive for parties to the transaction to seek third party intervention. When transactions lie outside the transaction resources frontier, principal parties tend to seek third-party support.

A third party can facilitate contracting in any of three analytically distinct ways. First, it can help to resolve the cooperation problem by providing *exogenous transaction resources* to augment the endogenous transaction resources already present in the relationship. If, for example, communication channels are poor, owing to the large number of parties or their geographic dispersion, the centralized channels and information processing services provided by a *mediating* third party may well prove more efficient. Sometimes a mediator recognizes opportunities for mutual gain or audits the status quo more effectively than the principals. Described graphically, this type of intervention expands the transaction resources frontier to encompass a larger area of transaction space. Thus, it increases the region within which contracting among the principal parties becomes possible. It need not entail granting discretion to the mediator to allocate the gains by defining the terms of an agreement or to enforce one by punishing breach.

Second, third parties can help to resolve the division problem by providing *division services*. For example, a *coalition-building* or *arbitrating* third party may be granted discretion to allocate the gains under the contract or merely to narrow the range of divisions possible under the contract. Described graphically, this moves the transaction leftward in transaction space, closer to the origin where conditions for contracting are more favorable. It need not entail granting discretion to the arbiter to enforce an agreement, but arbiters, like mediators, need to be a central agent in processing information.

Third, third parties can help to resolve the defection problem by providing *enforcement services*. For example, a *policing* third party may be granted authority to punish defectors so as to increase the force of contractual agreements. Described graphically, this moves the transaction downward in transaction space, again closer to the origin. It may not entail granting the enforcer discretion to design the terms of an agreement, but to monitor behavior an enforcer needs centralized communication channels like a mediator and in applying the force of agreement across disputants the enforcer's judgments may well involve arbiter-like divisions of responsibility.

6.7 THE PREFERENCE FOR ENDOGENOUS RESOURCES

The existence of finite resources and the need sometimes to expend more than what the parties have available to them provides an incentive for both parties to seek outside help in making and securing contracts. Intervention by a third party, however, may be as problematic as it is promising. First, intervention by a third party complicates the transaction by creating a new contracting problem between it and the principal parties. An *n*-person game becomes an *n* + 1 person game. The more extensive the intervention, the more powerful the third party can become vis-à-vis the principals.

The third party creates a new cooperation problem. The process of searching for a suitable third party and negotiating the terms of performance are costly. Improperly crafted third party services may prove redundant or unnecessarily intrusive. The greater the intervenor's role in processing information and forging communication channels, the greater too becomes the potential asymmetry between it and the principals. That can impede the principals' efforts to monitor it as well as each other. In short, cooperating with a third party may not be worth it, even when it is a prerequisite to contracting.

Intervention is likely to create a new division problem. How are the residual gains from intervention to be allocated among the principal and third parties? Again, the answer depends on their relative bargaining power. The power of the principals depends on how well they can effect divisions to begin with. But the more extensive the intervenor's role in determining how contractual gains will be divided, the greater its potential to either seize a larger than anticipated share or to become embroiled in partisan disputes among principals and empower some at the expense of others.

Intervention also creates a new defection problem. The outside party may fear that the principal parties will default on payments after services have been rendered. Alternatively, the more extensive the intervenor's role in establishing enforcement, the greater its potential to punish exploitatively. Indeed, a third party's special access to and control over information makes more difficult the principal parties' problem of preventing its defection by fraud or misrepresentation.

For these reasons, third-party intervention will always strike the principal parties as potentially more threatening than relying on *equivalent* endogenous resources. The implication is that people will prefer using endogenous resources because they tend to be less costly, more accessible spatially and temporally, and more readily mobilized than functionally equivalent resources that might be provided by a third party. Moreover, having maximum involvement in shaping the contract helps insure that it takes efficient account of their preferences and so strengthens their incentives to honor its terms. Studies of arbitration, for example, show that bargainers who succeed in reaching agreement are more likely to honor it than are those who fail and have one imposed by an arbitrator. Finally, even under the simplest conditions, contracting with a third party is asymmetric because the original parties, being more numerous, must bargain among themselves first.

Many of the problems of third-party intervention can be mitigated by competition among providers of the service. Competition gives principals an alternative and, thereby, a safeguard. Thus, it can reduce their bargaining problem and their fear of exploitive mistreatment. This is an important point, because it gives analytic plausibility to suggestions that under conditions where it is otherwise particularly difficult to constrain a third party, competition among mediators, arbiters, and enforcers may be preferable to a state monopoly on power.[8] Still, establishing and maintaining a mechanism for third-party intervention is no mere technical exercise by which deficiencies in endogenous transaction resources are corrected. Rather, it can be at least as conflictive and politically charged as private contracting. It, too, can fail. Thus, parties have incentives to avoid third-party orderings, such as courts provide, and instead to devise private ordering.[9]

6.8 WHEN ONLY THIRD PARTIES WILL DO

The existence of uncertainty sufficient to threaten contract failure does not provide a sufficient reason for the parties to call upon third-party intervention. As demonstrated, third-party intervention can create costs in excess of gains. Only if the endogenous resources of the parties are inadequate *and* the expected costs of third-party intervention do not exceed expected gains, would it be rational for contractors to require third-party intervention.

Figure 6.1 can be interpreted as depicting the range of cases in which safeguarding against contract failure requires the parties to consume transaction resources.[10] Type I cases fall within the frontier where between them the parties possess adequate resources to resolve whatever problems they face. Moving outward along each axis, endogenous resources prove to be increasingly inadequate. In type II cases the parties possess endogenous resources sufficient to solve division and defection problems but lack those to identify opportunities for cooperation. In type III cases the parties possess internal resources adequate to identify feasible contracts and to solve

136

the division problem but are unable with their own resources to solve the defection problem. In type IV cases the parties possess internal resources sufficient to solve their defection problem but are incapable on their own of identifying or solving the division issues. Off the axes we find a universe of other cases in which the principals in varying degrees lack the resources to resolve combinations of these problems.

This model suggests that we should find that several different types of institutional arrangements emerge in contracting. First, there will exist cases in which private parties are able to solve their problems without recourse to third-party intervention. In fact, we find such institutions, the best example being the competitive market. In the market parties are engaged in bilateral agreements, discrete in time and place. A governmental enforcement mechanism is not necessarily a precondition for exchange; self-enforcing conventions, sometimes called customary business practices, can work just as well. Markets provide ready sources of alternative exchange opportunities that can be sufficient to safeguard against one party's defecting *before* either performs on an agreement. Without resorting to violence or invoking third-party intervention, private parties can depend on reputational effects and devices like hostage giving/taking to safeguard against the risks of defection *after* one party acts in reliance on a promised performance.

Transactions along the search axis beyond the transaction resource frontier pose a risk of joint failure sufficient to exhaust the parties' resources for identifying opportunities for mutual gain; that discourages exchange. The simplest conventions, like drivers slowing down on approaching an intersection and stopping to wave a crossing vehicle through, breakdown. More densely settled areas and a more heterogeneous population of drivers will strain the convention, pushing the risks of motorized travel to the point where people begin to forgo its benefits or endure increasing costs. Someone can reduce the strain simply by setting a rule, almost any rule: When two vehicle approach an intersection simultaneously, the vehicle on the *right* proceeds first; where traffic density makes simultaneity increasingly expensive and variable to judge, a traffic signal is installed.

Contract law has, for example, the mailbox rule: An offeree has power to accept and close a contract by mailing a letter of acceptance, properly stamped and addressed.[11] Little economic justification can be found to support dating the contract from the mailing of the acceptance rather than from its receipt. Its economic justification can be found in the market-expanding properties of having a rule.[12] Like trade associations in various industries that develop consensus standards for product attributes so as to expand the total market for their products, the court expands the resource frontier so that private parties will engage in more transactions.

Beyond the frontier along the division axis, the participants primarily lack resources with which to solve the division problem. The parties would not get to the division problem without having identified an opportunity for productive exchange. Solving the defection problem is less significant, either because of ample endogenous enforcement resources or because incentives to defect are comparatively weak.

Some scholars have noted the significance of the division problem in contract doctrine. But almost all of these scholars have confused the rational division problem as a matter of private law with a social or public theory of "fair distribution." For example, Daniel Farber suggests that contract law has a mandatory risk-sharing system, a social safety net, and it is difficult for parties to bargain around it.[13] Thus, whereas freedom of contract means the power of parties to allocate risks between themselves, some contract rules reveal a countermanding principle of loss spreading – that is, rules against penalty clauses and warranty disclosure for personal injury to prevent catastrophic losses to one party. Similarly, Clare Dalton has claimed that doctrines such as quasicontract, duress, and unconscionability police the limits of acceptable bargains by private parties in the name of social (public) norms of fairness.[14] And Morris Cohen claims that court adjudication supplements an original contract as a means of distributing gains and losses from unanticipated events. In this view, contract law consists of rules by which the courts accomplish this according to the equities of such cases. That follows not from the agreement between individuals but is a way of enforcing some kind of distributive justice within the legal system.[15]

These characterizations of the distributive dimensions of contract law may go too far. The model implies that when courts impose distributive schemes on the parties, their doing so is compatible with the interests of the parties in the contract. No appeal to a global concern for distributive fairness, therefore, is necessary to understand or to justify a court's willingness to impose a distribution of risk among the parties. The legitimate exercise of that authority is restricted to the domain of outcomes the parties would have bargained within, and not to the set of outcomes that would be preferable from the point of view of a principle of social justice or social insurance. However, to the extent that the court, acting as an arbiter, seeks to implement a doctrine likely to resolve a wide range of division disputes efficiently, it may turn to widely accepted principles of social justice for guidance on the grounds that those principles themselves represent an evolved, rational, or efficient solution to a wide range of division problems.

Transactions beyond the frontier along the defection axis indicate that the defection problem is intractable internally but that the cooperation and division problems are soluble. Parties here have relatively abundant endogenous bargaining resources but deficient enforcement resources. Intervention, therefore, takes the form of an externally applied enforcement system that moves the transactions downward, inside the frontier. Within the constraints of that system, individuals retain control over the terms of the contracts they enter.

The features that make a market such an attractive governance system – anonymity, disaggregated decisions adaptive to local circumstances – exacerbate the endemic risks of defection. Classic economists, at least since Adam Smith, have foreseen a productive role for a centralized enforcement agent. If third party intervention diminishes ex post risks, people are freer to expend resources ex ante on searching for and reaching agreements that satisfy joint and concession rationality. Hence, common law, judicially crafted safeguards that penalize contract breach, are widely regarded as promoting economic efficiency. Even third-party safeguards designed primarily to reduce the probability of defection can influence the concession rationality of private decisions. That is because the remedies available under contract cannot escape dividing the residual risks of social intercourse and imposing different burdens of proof on the affected parties when one defaults.[16]

In areas of transaction space away from an axis and outside the frontier, the internal deficit of transaction resources is more profound. Here, assistance is required in solving a combination of problems that afflict contractual relationships. Indeed, even if in absolute terms a relationship is richly endowed with transaction resources, it is virtually assured of falling farthest from the three axes when all of the contextual features we identified impose large obstacles to contracting. Consequently, the degree of third party intervention is greater because regulators must not only enforce contracts but must also specify their terms and bring contractors to the bargaining table.

Chapter 7

Calculus and contexts

To this point we have identified the phases of contracting, three associated conditions of rationality that must be satisfied if contracting is to be rational, three related problems rational actors may face in securing a contract, the safeguards – endogenous and exogenous – available to protect against contract failure, and the factors that affect the nature and scope of the transaction cost problem. Contracting is a form of local, discrete cooperation. We have focused on the ways in which epistemic problems of uncertainty threaten its success and the ways in which endogenous transaction resources can alleviate them.

In many circumstances endogenous resources are inadequate to the task and rational parties will seek transaction resources exogenous to the structure of the environment of their interaction. My suggestion is that we think of the body of contract law in this way, as exogenous resources upon which agents can draw to reduce uncertainty and aid cooperation among them. If I am correct, many cases or doctrines in contract law can be assessed as rational responses to problems of cooperation, division, and defection (breach), corresponding to the three axes that define the transaction resource space.

7.1 CALCULUS AND CONTEXTS

The theory of contracting as rational bargaining exploits two central ideas: the model of rational bargaining and the con-

141

cept of endogenous transaction resources. The former points our attention to developments in formal theory and to empirical work on the psychology of negotiations: the latter to concrete contexts and frameworks of exchange. For it is within those frameworks and contexts in which the resources endogenous to negotiating parties are to be found.

The interplay between abstract theory and concrete context is easy enough to illustrate. The formal theory tells us that whatever the context of their negotiations, rational bargainers are concerned to find common ground for mutual advantage, to secure a desirable division of the gains from trade, and to protect their agreement against one another's potential noncompliance. If, in a given context, the contracting parties know very little about one another, or if their contract represents a one-shot deal, or if the benefits and burdens of the contract are spread over distance and time, it may be difficult for these actors to solve their contract problems without the help of third parties. On the other hand, if in a given context, the parties have ongoing dealings with one another, and their bargain is embedded within a larger competitive market, the incentives to defect are reduced and the range of feasible divisions is diminished. Successful negotiations are more likely.

The theory developed here emphasizes contexts, whereas, because of the need for generality, legal rules are considerably less sensitive to contexts. Nevertheless, certain features of the contexts of contracting are reasonably pervasive. For example, most contracts among businesspeople are embedded within competitive markets. Markets provide low-cost safeguards against defection while simultaneously reducing the bargaining range, thus safeguarding against exploitive divisions. Perhaps the best protection against noncompliance are the availability of alternatives and reputation effects. Competitive markets provide alternatives and are especially good at transmitting information. A potential trading partner's noncompliance is the sort of information everyone has an interest in obtaining.

7.2 CONTEXTS AND DIVISION PROBLEMS

If the framework presented here is plausible, we might expect to find very little of the law of contracts given over to resolving distributive issues: First, the competitiveness of markets reduces division problems by narrowing the bargaining range, and second, the fact that many contracting parties are involved in ongoing relationships reduces the usefulness of contract rules specifying distributive shares. Individuals aware of the legal rules and free to contract around them will treat distributive rules as specifying the point at which negotiations over the gains from trade are to commence rather than as providing a definitive allocation of them.

In contrast, contract rules governing the distribution of gains among strangers or nonrepeat players, or individuals whose negotiations are not embedded in markets, are likely to have a more significant impact.[1] The analysis presented here coincides with the conventional law and economics approach that downgrades the distributional dimensions of contracting. The explanations differ, however.

In conventional law and economics, distributive and efficiency considerations are severed. Courts are particularly well suited to resolve efficiency but not distributive questions. In the case of contracting, moreover, whatever distributive issues arise can be dealt with by side payments. In the rational choice approach, distribution and efficiency are integrated elements of rational contracting. Rational parties are as concerned with the division of the cooperative surplus as they are with finding and protecting it. In competitive contexts in which much contracting occurs, however, the division problem is solvable by transaction resources internal to the framework of exchange. The rational choice approach, therefore, downplays, but does not downgrade, the distributive aspects of contracting.

The calculus of rational contracting suggests that safeguarding against defection is more costly than safeguarding against unfair divisions, which in turn is more costly than guarding against missed opportunities to cooperate. But our earlier discussion demonstrates that features of the context of contracting may make the division problem more tractable than the mathematics suggests it ought to be; and that is why, as I have said, the theory of rational contracting presented here relies on the mix of calculus and contexts. Similar remarks are in order regarding the cooperation and defection problems. The calculus of rational contracting suggests that the cooperation problem should be easiest to resolve and the defection problem most difficult. It is not surprising, therefore, that much contract litigation that comes to the court raises the question of whether a breach has occurred and if it has, what damages are appropriate.

7.3 CONTEXTS AND DEFECTION

It is interesting that even given competition and reputation effects, rational agents risk noncompliance. There are several reasons for this, many of which are suggested by the analysis to this point. It is extremely difficult to estimate accurately the required force of agreement necessary to induce compliance. Because the defection payoff is always greater than any payoff on the contract curve, there will always be an incentive to defect. When the estimated force of agreement is too low, the incentive to defect may be overwhelming.

But should not reputation effects reduce the incentive to defect enough to rectify for inadequate expected penalties? The answer is both yes and no. Reputation effects certainly reduce the incentive to defect. But it is not obvious that a party who is judged at trial to have breached his contract will be unambiguously viewed as a defector. This may be true for at least two reasons. First, defection may be desirable from everyone's perspective, provided appropriate damages are paid. A defector who breaches only when it is rational to do so, and compensates for his breach, may not be a defector in the pejorative sense. He may suffer no loss in reputation as a result. Because he defects only when it is rational to do so, his defection provides evidence of his reliability. Under these

144

conditions, his defection shows him to be a good transacting partner. Second, there is enough uncertainty in most situations that result in breach to make it difficult to view the breach unambiguously as a defection or as involving unfair advantage taking. Finally, even when internal resources are available to contracting parties to reduce the scope of non-performance, "the mathematics can be more powerful than the context," and defection incentives may dominate, resulting in litigation. And, as we have just seen, it is not always possible to interpret the outcome of litigation in a way that reflects unfavorably upon the breaching party.

7.4 COOPERATION REQUIRES CONVENTIONS

If we think of the compliance problem as expressed by the P.D. game, and the division problem as expressed by the rational bargaining game, then we might view the cooperation problem as a *coordination game*. This is a point we first mentioned in Chapter 1. Let's suppose you and I are trying to figure out how we should spend our evening. I want us to go to a Was (Not Was) concert and you want us to go to a lecture on Deconstructionism in Art, Architecture, Athletics, and Carpentry given by the semirenowned Professor Fad. Both of us want to spend the evening together. What that means is that you and I have preferences about the possible evening scene as follows:

	MY PREFERENCES	*YOUR PREFERENCES*
	Me, You	*Me, You*
First Choice	Was, Was	Fad, Fad
Second Choice	Fad, Fad	Was, Was
Third Choice	Was, Fad	Fad, Was
Fourth Choice	Fad, Was	Was, Fad

I prefer most our both going to the concert and least prefer your enjoying the silky sounds of the Motown-on-Acid-Rockers, Was (Not Was), while I am left tortured by the nonsense of the latest Fad. You, of course, would prefer us to

145

Fad-out together; and are duly horrified at the idea of me slumped in my chair half asleep at the lecture while you are forced to press the flesh with your fingers in your ears trying to escape the seductive sounds of the Was Brothers.

The important feature of this coordination game is that if both of us should appear at the Was (Not Was) concert, you will not leave, whereas if both of us are (God forbid!) at the lecture by Professor Fad, I will not leave; neither one of us will change our strategy unilaterally. Either outcome is therefore an equilibrium. But upon which equilibrium will we settle? How will we solve our coordination problem? (Of course the more interesting question is, Why would two people with such contrasting tastes want to spend the evening together in the first place?)

Coordination games are solved by features beyond the logical structure of the game. So if some third person flips a coin – heads to Was, tails to Fad – and if we agree to abide by the result, then we can solve our coordination problem. The simplest example of a coordination game of this sort is the need for motorists to decide whether to drive on the left or the right side of the road. Some may prefer the left, others the right, but all but the perverse prefer that, whichever side of the road is chosen, everyone drive on *that* side. That co-ordination problem is resolved by the state authoritatively setting a standard that creates a convention or social practice. Once the practice exists, it is virtually self-enforcing, as, under normal conditions, no rational motorist has an incentive to defect.

If what economists claim about markets and contracting is true – that much contracting takes place in competitive markets among repeat players – then markets provide the cheapest safeguards against exploitive divisions and defection. It is a fair question to ask whether these same market safeguards work as well to provide salience, or whether, instead, one central but underappreciated role of the court in contracts is to provide salience and in doing so help to solve coordination problems. It is possible that a good deal of contractual litigation is best seen in the light of its role in facilitating coordination.

To put the matter another way: If individuals contract with one another in competitive markets or within relatively homogenous or otherwise closely knit communities, then the market or the community can go a long way toward guarding against contract failures owing to exploitation and defection. Legal rules and other forms of exogenous transaction resources play less of a role in safeguarding against these risks than one might otherwise think. Though markets, which reduce the risk of defection and exploitive divisions, require conventions, they may not themselves create conventions. The most obvious example is property rights. Contracting requires property rights. You and I will have a hard time negotiating the sale of some piece of property if we both believe we own it. In some cases, the conventions necessary for contracting are provided by the "communities" within which the market is itself embedded. In other cases, uncertainty remains and authoritative bodies are called upon to solve the relevant coordination problem.

The calculus of rational bargaining implies that the least difficult problem to solve from an information standpoint, is the cooperation problem. The discussion to this point suggests that the coordination problem, however informationally easy to resolve in theory, may be more troubling in practice. If this is so, then we may find that one of the central roles courts are being asked to play in contract disputes is to solve coordination or cooperation problems, not to rectify breach or guard against exploitive division.

Of course, the court is involved in a relationship ex post, after one or the other party has breached. Often the case will come before a court, therefore, as one involving breach. However, the source of breach is often an unresolved uncertainty at a previous stage in contracting. There is unresolved doubt about the ownership or scope of the relevant property right or the like. As events unfold, this uncertainty proves troublesome and results in breach. The issue before the court

147

is framed in terms of breach or defection, but the role the court actually plays is one of reducing uncertainty about the relevant property right. In doing so its chief function is to aid coordination. By aiding coordination, it facilitates the exchange process, which in turn safeguards against defection and exploitive divisions. In other words, the best interpretation of judicial practice may be that courts play mediating roles even when it looks like they are being asked to play arbitration or enforcement roles.

The hardest part of defending a theory is to show how it might apply to the practice it purports to explain. I said that the account I am offering might help us rethink conventional interpretations of our contract practice. To this end, I want to take a stab at making good on this claim by considering two ways of looking at the famous case of *Laidlaw* v. *Organ*.[2] One approach is represented by conventional economic analysis, another by the theory developed in the preceding two chapters.

7.5 INFORMATION AND PROPERTY RIGHTS

From the perspective of traditional law and economics, *Laidlaw* is hailed as creating a property right in information, which has the beneficial effect of providing incentives to gather information. This view was advanced first, and most eloquently, by Anthony Kronman. According to Kronman, the courts in general have not required the disclosure of private information.[3] This nondisclosure doctrine encourages socially efficient contracting by creating a property right in information. People may retain the benefits of their efforts to secure information relevant to productive exchange opportunities, except in circumstances where they would have come by the information without effort. Where they can come by the information without effort, a disclosure requirement would not reduce the incentive to produce it and so might not be inefficient. In cases of mistake and disclosurue, this argument holds, the court has been called upon as a third-party

148

enforcement agent and it has done so in a way that is consistent with the principle of economic efficiency.

The more secure the right to information, the more an individual will be inclined to invest in producing it. The *social* as opposed to the individual benefits of such a property right, however, are not always obvious, nor is the distinction between information that results from deliberate search and that which has been casually acquired necessarily decisive in establishing the economic efficiency of the appropriate legal doctrine.

7.6 TWO EFFECTS OF INFORMATION

Ultimately, I want to argue for two separate theses: First, the orthodox view of the efficiency of a property right in information is mistaken for a variety of reasons some of which we have already touched upon in Chapter 6. Second, the orthodox interpretation of *Laidlaw* focuses entirely on the dictum of the case, not its holding, whereas the theory presented here gives a more plausible account of both the dictum and the holding.

Kronman's recitation of the pertinent facts of the case is illuminating. Organ, a New Orleans commission merchant, had been bargaining with Francis Girault of Laidlaw & Co., also commission merchants, to purchase 111 hogsheads of tobacco. Early in the morning of February 19, 1815, Organ received news that the Treaty of Ghent had been signed, formally ending the War of 1812. Organ obtained the news from a Mr. Shepard, who had a financial interest in the transaction with Laidlaw and whose brother was one of three gentlemen who brought the news from the British fleet. Before 8 A.M., when the news would be made public in a handbill, Organ called on Girault to consummate the purchase. Girault asked "if there was any news which was calculated to enhance the price or value of the article about to be purchased"; the record is not clear on Organ's response other than Laidlaw's attorney alleging that "the vendee was silent." Nevertheless Girault and Organ entered into a contract.

The price of tobacco quickly rose by 30 to 50 percent as news of the treaty circulated, signaling an end to the naval blockade of New Orleans and the resumption of exporting. Kronman reports that Laidlaw retained possession of the tobacco, but the court record indicates that he first transferred it to Organ, then recaptured it by force. In any case, Organ then brought suit for damages and to block Laidlaw from otherwise disposing of the tobacco. The trial judge evidently directed a verdict in Organ's favor, deciding from the testimony that no fraud occurred. On appeal before the U.S. Supreme Court, Laidlaw's attorney argued, among other points, that this was a matter for the jury to decide.

The Court agreed, reversed the judgment, and remanded with directions for a new trial. Noting that Organ's silence may have been fraudulent, Kronman puts aside questions of fraud. He focuses on the dictum rather than the holding in the Court's opinion delivered by Chief Justice John Marshall. Generally regarded as an accurate statement of the law, it reads:

> The question in this case is, whether the intelligence of extrinsic circumstances, which might influence the price of the commodity, and which was exclusively within the knowledge of the vendee, ought to have been communicated by him to the vendor? The court is of opinion that he was not bound to communicate it. It would be difficult to circumscribe the contrary doctrine within proper limits, where the means of intelligence are equally accessible to both parties. But at the same time, each party must take care not to say or do anything tending to impose upon the other.

The attractiveness, and subsequent longevity of Marshall's opinion derives in Kronman's view, from its consistency with the principles of economic efficiency. It gives contracting parties incentives to get valuable information to the market as quickly as efficient investment in producing knowledge permits. Indeed, "The greater the likelihood that . . . information will be deliberately produced [that is, acquired at a cost that would not have been incurred but for the likelihood that the information in question would actually be produced] rather than casually discovered [by chance], the more plausible the assumption becomes that a blanket rule permitting nondisclosure will have benefits that outweigh its costs."[4] In addition, the administrative costs facing the courts in crafting exceptions are lower compared to imposing limits on a blanket rule creating a duty to disclose. In sum, a rule of nondisclosure is productively efficient.

It is not obvious, however, that a property right in information is always productively efficient. Moreover, what is relevant in determining the efficiency of the rule is not the manner in which the information is obtained (casually or deliberately), but its incentive effects (productive or redistributive). Consider, in this regard, a distinction between technological and distributive dimensions of information first developed by Jack Hirshleifer.[5] Information is valuable because it can affect action. From an individual's perspective, the value of new information, and hence of investing in generating it, derives from *technology*, gains from allocating resources more efficiently, and *distribution*, wealth transfers that follow from price changes. In the case of technology, information makes the pie larger and thus increases ex ante each person's potential share. In the case of distribution, information does not increase the pie's size, only the share of those who have the relevant information.

From society's perspective, the consequences of technological information are largely salutary, those of redistributive information are not. As Hirshleifer puts it, "The distributive advantage of private information provides an incentive for information – generating activity that may quite possibly be in excess of the social value of the information."[6] The argument is this: All information has a technological as well as a redistributive dimension. In many cases, investment in information will be socially efficient because the technological gains will outweigh the costs of investment. However, in some

151

cases, the technological effects will be less significant than the redistributive ones. In these cases, private investment can exceed social return.

Consider two cases. In one case, Jones and Smith each invest $1 to gather information, the technological effect of which is $10, and the redistributive effect is $1.50. Two dollars are spent to secure $10, $1.50 of which goes to the discoverer, say, Jones, with the net gain of $8 shared among the group (including Jones). In the other case, Jones and Smith again invest $1 to uncover information whose social value is only .25, but whose redistributive value is $1.50. Jones and Smith each act rationally, spending $1 to seek at least $1.50, but the net effect is inefficient. Two dollars are spent to create .25. Thus, giving individuals the full benefit of the information they obtain may lead them to act in socially inefficient ways whenever the redistributive aspect of information dominates its technological dimension.

Kronman recognizes that a rule in favor of nondisclosure can create perverse incentives and, therefore, that the decision to permit nondisclosure of certain information forces a practical choice between over- and underinvestment. "Because it is 'certain' that eliminating property rights will result in underproduction and 'merely a danger' that recognizing them will result in overproduction, the economic case for recognizing them is strong ('but not conclusive'), especially where information is deliberately acquired."[7] Neither alternative is optimal, he notes, but assuming legal rules cannot be more finely tuned the latter one is better.

Though Kronman relies upon considerations of the sort Hirshleifer summons, his conclusion – that a property right to information that does not require disclosure is, on balance, efficient – is, if Hirshleifer is right, unwarranted. As Hirshleifer sees it, the incentives to secure a distributive advantage "eliminate any a priori anticipation of underinvestment in the generation of new technological knowledge."[8] That is, investment in information that is likely to be primarily redistributive with little apparent gain in efficiency may be so great under a rule of nondisclosure that the costs of

152

such a rule in terms of inefficient rent-seeking behavior may outweigh its benefits in terms of the production of net social gains. Thus, Kronman ought not confidently claim, as he does, that "allocative efficiency is best served by permitting one who possesses deliberately acquired information to enter and enforce favorable bargains without disclosing what he knows."[9] Whether the social gains created by a property right in information unencumbered by a requirement of disclosure will outweigh the social costs of investment depends on the relative effect – technological or redistributive – of the information.

Kronman nicely summarizes what has become the conventional view: "One effective way of insuring that an individual will benefit from the possession of information (or anything else for that matter) is to assign him a property right in the information itself – a right or entitlement to invoke the coercive machinery of the state in order to exclude others from its use and enjoyment. The benefits of possession become secure only when the state transforms the possessor of information into an owner by investing him with a legally enforceable property right of some sort or other."[10]

The foregoing argument rests on three assumptions: first, that a legal property right in information unencumbered by a disclosure rule is *necessary* to provide the benefits of information; second, that such an approach produces benefits in excess of costs; and third, that the property rule in information cannot cost-effectively be more finely tuned.

The truth of none of these assumptions is obvious. First, the analysis of Chapter 6 suggests that creating a legally enforceable right is not the *only* means to safeguard against risk. Indeed, people may be able to make the benefits of possession relatively more secure by resorting first to their endogenous transaction resources rather than depending upon legal rules. *Laidlaw* in particular was a case in which the parties, commission merchants dealing in a competitive commodities market, were well suited to secure the gains from information in the absence of legal safeguards.

Second, again given the analysis of the last chapter, the

risks of third-party intervention may be sufficiently great that action by the state cannot be assumed to secure benefits in excess of costs. Finally, while circumscribing a duty to disclose might be difficult, as Justice Marshall opined, we cannot a priori rule out its feasibility in all circumstances.

Even if we accept the orthodox understanding of *Laidlaw* as creating a property right in information, we should not accept that such a right is invariably efficient. Moreover, whether such a right will prove efficient does not depend on whether the information is obtained through deliberate search or casually. The efficiency of a property right in information depends on whether the technological or the distributive dimensions of the information dominate. If the information is largely distributive in its impact, a property right in information may well be inefficient. So we should be reluctant to accept the conclusion that the best argument for a property right in information as such is that it encourages efficient investment in gathering information.

7.7 DEFECTION AND ERROR COSTS

The standard account of *Laidlaw*, then, focuses entirely on the dictum, and it is not clear that the arguments presented on behalf of the economic interpretation of it are persuasive. The first thing we want to do is see if we can develop an account of the actual holding in the case consistent with the general theory developed in Chapters 5 and 6.

To explain the Supreme Court's holding in the case, we need first to understand how the case came to court and the question of law the Court was asked to resolve. Recall that we distinguish among three sorts of risks parties will seek to safeguard against, first by deploying endogenous transaction resources and then by pursuing third-party intervention in the event their resources are inadequate to the task or otherwise too costly. These are risks of failed cooperation, division, and defection. When courts are sought to safeguard, we say that they play mediation, arbitration, or enforcement roles, respectively.

The case comes to court framed as a defection problem in which the principal parties are requesting the court to play an enforcement or policing role. Organ brought the case to court claiming Laidlaw's breach. Laidlaw's defense to the charge of breach rested on Organ's alleged fraudulent misrepresentation of the facts. For his part, Organ sued for possession of the tobacco and for his damages, in effect seeking to employ the power of the state to enforce the contract and, thereby, to punish Laidlaw's breach. The trial judge refused to submit the question of fraud to the jury. The jury refused to award damages, preferring instead to award possession of the tobacco. To be sure Laidlaw's counsel raised the division problem on appeal. "Though [Laidlaw], after they heard the news of peace, still went on, in ignorance of their legal rights, to complete the contract, equity will protect them."[11]

Because the issue as presented on appeal was that of fraud, the Supreme Court could not avoid addressing the question of defection. It agreed with Laidlaw that the trial judge erred in refusing to submit the question of fraud to the jury and remanded for a new trial accordingly. On the other hand the Court did not allow itself to be dragged into protecting against unfair divisions under precisely the conditions where the parties could safeguard privately at much lower transaction cost. This is a context of competitive markets in which division problems are more cheaply solved in the market than by courts. That accounts in part for Marshall's concern about the administrative costs of judicial intervention: "It would be difficult to circumscribe the contrary doctrine [disclosure] within proper limits, where the means of intelligence are equally accessible to both parties."

According to the calculus of our analysis, safeguarding against defection is the most information intensive aspect of contracting. For in addition to estimating the other party's best hope and reservation price – necessary for a rational division of concessions – each party must estimate the relevant force of agreement. Doing so requires that each party estimate the other's defection incentive. Thus, the calculus of rational safeguarding against breach is the most complex of all dimensions of rational contracting. The probability of mistake is greatest and, accordingly, so are the costs of guarding against it.

Not only is the probability of mistake greatest in safeguarding potential defection, actual mistakes can be very costly indeed. To see this, consider the difference between errors made in safeguarding against divisions and those made in safeguarding against potential defections. If the parties or a court errs in safeguarding against unfair divisions, it simply moves the parties from one point along the contract curve to another. The parties remain on the contract curve and, therefore, are better off than both would have been had no contract been made.[12]

In contrast, a mistake in discerning or correcting for an alleged breach can make either party worse off than he or she would have been in the absence of agreement. If a court mistakenly determines that no breach has occurred, it enforces the breaching party's nonperformance payoff. In doing so, it makes the other party worse off than he or she was at the point of no agreement, that is, the status quo ante. On the other hand, because the force of agreement is aimed at displacing the defection payoff toward the point of no agreement, imposing a penalty when no breach has occurred forces both parties off the contract curve. Further, when a court determines that a breach has occurred, it sends a message of unreliability to other potential cooperators. It thus chills cooperative endeavors. It reminds the parties of the need to expend transaction resources to reduce the probability of nonperformance; and it reminds everyone that sometimes even the optimal expenditure of resources will not foreclose entirely the chance of being victimized by one's partners in cooperative schemes.

Given these external effects of a court's decisions about defection, it is that much more important that courts reduce the probability of error. Court decisions regarding divisions of the gains from trade have no comparable external effects on markets. In sum: In rational contracting, the probability of making a mistake in discerning or protecting against defection are greatest. The social costs of a court making a mistake about whether defection has occurred are also likely to be substantial.

Statistical evidence suggests over the long run that, between a judge and a jury, a jury is better positioned to determine whether a fraudulent "imposition was practised" and thereby to reduce the risk of error. The reason is rather straightforward. Given the probability of making a mistake and the costs of doing so, it makes more sense to put the factual question to a jury of twelve than to have it resolved as a matter of law by a judge. Remanding for a new trial puts the question of fraud, misrepresentation, and defection before a jury, the lower cost mistake avoider – given that the principal parties could no longer resolve the issue privately.[13]

The case comes to the Court framed in terms of breach. Breach is the highest cost risk to guard against, at least as far as the calculus suggests. Mistakes in determining whether breach has occurred by authoritative bodies like courts are extremely costly. That risk needs to be minimized. Once the question of breach comes to an authoritative body, the question is which sort of body, in this case which court, is in the best position to reduce the risk of mistake. The Supreme Court holds, in effect, that putting the question before the jury is the lowest cost-mistake avoiding strategy. In fact, there is some considerable evidence to support this claim. Thus, our theory provides an extremely plausible account of the case's holding.

7.8 COORDINATION AND PRIVATE INFORMATION

The rational bargaining theory of contract presented in Chapters 5 and 6 provides a plausible account of the Court's actual holding in Laidlaw. We can now turn to the dictum. As already argued, the standard economic analysis of the dictum defends it as creating a property right in information required by considerations of efficiency. We have found that account wanting, and now want to pursue an analysis based

157

on the theory presented in the previous chapters. The first step in any such argument requires us to take a closer look at the context in which the case arose.

The case concerned a contract for a commodity. Conditions in commodity markets represent a close real-world approximation to those found in a theoretical model of a pure exchange economy. Goods are exchanged on the spot, so contracts are well defined in time, place, and purpose. Allowing for readily observable differences in grades, tobacco is a relatively homogeneous and divisible good. Although merchants in a given city who specialize in one commodity might be a relatively small fraternity of members who come to know each other over time, they tend to be sufficiently numerous – or potentially so with relatively low entry costs – so no one sets prices. So long as many exchanges occur, the primary safeguard afforded a tobacco merchant lies in the alternative merchants waiting and willing to deal.

If tobacco merchants buy on their own accounts, as did Organ and Laidlaw, they take on an economic function more than that of sales agents. Commission merchants facilitate market exchange in two ways, both characterized by specializing in *search* activities. First, they collect a transaction fee for bringing buyers and sellers together, narrowing the spread between price bid and price asked. Second, they speculate on extrinsic circumstances, as Marshall phrased it, hedging their exposure to risk by adjusting their inventories. Thus, they spread and reduce risk. In these ways, commission merchants help create markets where otherwise none might have existed.[14] Put in terms of the analysis of rational contracting presented here, the locus of the dispute concerned the pre-phase of contracting, where individuals seek to establish whether cooperation of any sort will be rational, that is, whether there are gains to be had. Demonstrating and creating opportunities for gain is a central role of commission merchants.

Moreover, in the context described here, we might expect merchants to have ample resources for private contracting.

Long before *Laidlaw* v. *Organ*, they invested in information, making deals and allowing producers to specialize in production. And they speculated on events that would influence the value of their holdings, thus creating no apparent need for third party *mediation*. The end of the naval blockade, like a drought or a blight, describes a state of nature inevitably to be revealed to the public: *The risk on which the merchants speculate, then, is less technological than distributive.* So this is not the sort of case, on either Kronman's or Hirshleifer's account, that suggests a nondisclosure rule.

Moreover, these merchants regularly negotiate over quantity, quality, and price. The risks of unfair divisions are mitigated by transforming the decisions into a sequence solvable within the constraints of available bargaining resources held by private parties. As a consequence these merchants do not normally need a third party to *arbitrate*. Finally, alternative exchange opportunities and reputation effects typically mitigate defection incentives without unduly straining enforcement resources. Thus, the merchants need not risk creating a third-party *enforcer*, except to deal with those categories of defections that are unusually costly to safeguard.

In short, given the theory presented here, in which the principal parties are viewed as rational actors embedded in particular contexts, it would appear that neither Laidlaw nor Organ had sufficient reason to seek any form of third-party intervention. The context, which is so important to the analysis, is one that suggests the parties in this case had ample endogenous transaction resources.

One question we need to answer, then, is why the parties turned to the courts for exogenous transaction resources when it appears as if the context in which the dispute arose provided them with all the resources they would need to solve the contract problem. Another, preliminary, question is to determine which contract problem they faced: Was it one of breach, division, or cooperation? These are questions that must be addressed and resolved in our theory, but they are not ones that need arise at all in the conventional view, which is concerned about the *effect* of various rules only, and not with the reasons parties would have for seeking legal intervention in the first place.

It is important to note that however extraordinary an event the signing of a treaty is, it is no more extraordinary than is a blight or drought, all of which create ample opportunities for savvy dealers to enhance their position. But one supposes that part of what makes commodities markets valuable is their ability to respond to such events without recourse to legal action – even when some parties use information for their personal benefit not yet available to others.

After having turned over the tobacco, on the day following circulation of the handbill announcing the Treaty of Laidlaw, "by force," Laidlaw retook possession of the tobacco and withheld it for Organ. That action, should it prevail as a practice, would threaten the network of communication channels that makes market exchange, the specialized normative infrastructure that permits commission merchants to extract payment for their services. The decision to seek to sequester only highlights the extent of the risk, for doing so puts at risk whatever gains had been captured by the initial contractual scheme of cooperation.[15]

Think of the problem this way: Laidlaw and Organ are potential cooperators. They disagree about whether individuals who have private information affecting prices should make full disclosure to their contracting partners. That they disagree about disclosure may be unknown to both of them, and in the bulk of the transactions between them, their disagreement has no impact. In the circumstances presented by the facts of the case, however, the difference of opinion obviously makes a difference. The important difference between the parties, however, is *not* that one of them is right from either a moral or an economic point of view about the duty to disclose. Rather, what is important is the existence of a difference, period. The existence of a difference makes coordination difficult. Bargaining is always easier when property rights are well defined, and it is most difficult when genuine disagreement about them exists.

This disagreement about the norm regarding disclosure or its applicability in the circumstances surrounding the sale is played out in Laidlaw's recapture of the tobacco (or his failing to deliver it, depending on one's reading of the record). This action ultimately invites the Supreme Court to provide an authoritative pronouncement regarding disclosure or misrepresentation. In doing so, the Court will play a mediating role, specifying authoritatively the norms governing market transactions and reducing thereby the risks and costs of cooperation.

We can distinguish between coordination and welfare effects of a rule. In circumstances of the sort commission merchants face, any authoritative rule would solve their coordination problem. This was, as we noted, a highly competitive market in which the principal parties were repeat players. What Laidlaw and Organ needed was an authoritative characterization of the rule, whatever its content. In that sense, either ruling on disclosure would have sufficed. Thus, from a coordination point of view, the rule expressed in Marshall's opinion has no special efficacy with respect to people investing efficiently in information. Once the rule is in place, negotiations between the parties are easier because the threat of noncoordination is reduced.

If it happens that all negotiating parties discover that they could do better under the alternative rule, then the rule the court announces will be unstable or the parties will simply ignore it.[16] No party will diverge from it unilaterally, but all may be inclined to do so jointly. In the case under discussion, as already noted, the private information concerned price changes and was fundamentally distributive, not productive in its impact. Thus, there is no reason to think that a norm requiring disclosure would be any less efficient from a welfare point of view than would the rule the Supreme Court actually advanced. So in the instant case either ruling would be efficient in both the coordination and welfare sense.

The point of the Court's opinion, then, is to facilitate communication by providing salience in the form of a nearly arbitrary choice. With respect to all other matters relating to cooperation, the Court put the burden of deciding how much to expend on safeguarding squarely on the shoulders of those in the best position to exercise that judgment – the principal parties. That is just as it should be. As Michael Taylor has argued in other contexts, by serving an authoritative coordination role unnecessarily, the state decreases the incentives for parties to devise creative solutions of their own. By substituting legal pronouncements for endogenously devised ones, the state weakens the bonds of community or, in this case, weakens the market structure. In short: However disinclined they may become to rely on or to exhaust their transaction resources in favor of a third party solution, where the principal parties remain in the best position to contract efficiently, courts should place the burdens of safeguarding on them. That is precisely what this case does. It provides an authoritative ruling on disclosure that solves a coordination problem, and then it imposes all other risks on the commission merchants who are in the best position privately to safeguard against them.

The court's choice of a rule that does not require disclosure is nearly, but not completely, arbitrary, since, on some occasions, principal parties will lack endogenous transaction resources to resolve privately all conflicts on the terms of cooperation. Perhaps the market in which they transact is inadequately competitive, and therefore too few alternatives exist; or the players are contracting on a one-time basis, in which reputation effects are minimized. In these circumstances the parties may rationally call upon the court to mediate. In that event the rule that does not impose a duty to disclose is easier to administer than likely alternatives to it. Moreover, if the court retained discretion to allocate the search and distributive risks involved here, it might incur high direct costs as well as frequently abuse the notions of fair division held by private parties and communities, thereby calling into question the legitimacy of its value as a third party intervenor.

This is a case about coordination and mediation. As such, either legal rule would have sufficed. Moreover, from the point of view of wealth or welfare maximization, the circumstances of this case provide no argument for the nondisclosure rule. In short, the choice of the nondisclosure rule rests ultimately on considerations of administrative efficiency.

To sum up: Conventional law and economics interprets *Laidlaw* as creating a property right in information, one that can be squared with efficiency. We have argued, first, that a property right in information may not be generally efficient and, second, that a more compelling characterization of Laidlaw, one that follows from the theory developed here, sees it primarily as a case in which the court resolves a coordination problem by providing salience via authoritative ruling. It thus mediates rather than arbitrates or policies and, in that way, protects against a shrinking of the transaction resource frontier.

Though this analysis of *Laidlaw* is at odds with traditional economic analysis, there are bound to be many areas of overlap. After all, nothing we have said diminishes the incentives associated with protecting the right of one party to realize the gains associated from specialized investments in information. However, it may not be necessary or appropriate to reach the distinction emphasized by Kronman between casual and deliberately acquired information in order to explain the case law. A more plausible explanation, we believe, has the court distinguishing among the relative efficacies of alternative safeguards, including judicial intervention, given the risks of contract failure involved, and placing responsibility and discretion with the party or parties who are in the best position to safeguard.

Chapter 8

Filling in the gaps

We have focused so far on the ways in which legal rules can facilitate contracting understood as a form of local rational cooperation. But efforts at cooperation are not always successful, contracting fails. Failed contracting does not necessarily imply the absence of a contract altogether. Sometimes failed contracting leads to incomplete or partial contracts. Then the question becomes, how are incomplete contracts to be interpreted? By what principle are incomplete contracts to be completed.

8.1 GAPS IN CONTRACTS

On the assumption that contracting parties are narrowly rational and fully informed, a contract between them that foresees and responds to all possible contingencies – a fully specified contract – would be efficient, or Pareto optimal. Because a fully specified contract is efficient, it puts the parties to it in a position where neither can improve his or her lot except at the other's expense. Although imagining problems in contract design and execution and devising adequate safeguards against all possible sources of contrast failure is a logical possibility, it remains (for everyone but the gods) a practical impossibility. Were it practically possible, fully specifying a contract might be irrational in that the expected costs of a more complete specification may exceed the expected gains from nailing down a particular solution to an imaginable, but unlikely, possibility.

Unlikely events are not impossible, however. Contingencies arise with which the contractors have not explicitly dealt. Such is the stuff of casebooks. When contingencies arise for which no adequate provisions have been made ex ante, the parties may disagree about their respective rights and duties ex post. Sometimes they are able to resolve the conflict privately, but if not, the parties may find themselves in litigation. What rights and responsibilities can a judge, legitimately exercising his or her authority, impose on them in default of explicit agreement.

We can imagine a range of possible default or gap-filling provisions. A court may be guided by a sense of fairness and use the fact that the parties have not spoken as an opportunity to achieve some measure of fairness the parties themselves may have been unable or unwilling to provide. Or a court may look at the opportunity the parties have provided as an occasion to create efficient incentives of one sort or another. Or courts may use default rules to encourage cooperation at earlier stages of the contractual process, and so on. Or the court could impose ex post terms to which the parties would have agreed ex ante. In effect, the suggestion is that the court complete the contract as the parties would have. If the contract is a scheme of rational cooperation for mutual advantage, then it should be completed by imagining the terms of a hypothetical rational agreement between them. Let's refer to this sort of default or gap-filling rule as the ex ante contract.[1]

Thus, when transaction costs make an explicit agreement too costly ex ante, the court should apply a default or gap-filling rule that "mimics" the outcome of a hypothetical contract between them.[2] The hypothetical contract is the one the parties would have made had transaction costs not made their doing so irrational.[3]

As a default rule, the ex ante contract raises two distinct issues. The first concerns the content of the rule: How are we to model or to understand the ex ante contract. The other concerns the justification a court might have for imposing on litigating parties the rights and responsibilities implied by the ex ante contract. The problem of justification is complicated by the fact that the parties are being held in contract to terms to which they did not explicitly agree. Given the ex post nature of the obligations and rights it distributes, is there any reason to think that one default rule is any more justifiable than another? Is there, in particular, a case to be made for the ex ante contract as the default rule?

The theory presented here invites characterizing the ex ante contract in rational bargaining terms: If the actual contract expresses what the parties take to be a rational agreement between them, then when their agreement is incomplete and needs to be interpreted or filled in by a court it should express what it would have been rational for the parties to agree to. The move from the actual to the hypothetical should not change the content of the principle.

One interesting feature of this version of the default rule is that it or one very similar to it appears to play a part in two radically different theories of contract: consent and economic based accounts of contractual obligation.[4] The problem is this: while it is reasonably easy to understand why the theory of contracting developed here would spell out its default and gap-filling rules in this way – such a rule helps to conserve endogenous transaction resources – it is harder to explain the attraction of either economic analysis or consent theories to the idea of the ex ante rational contract as a default rule. The remainder of this chapter takes up these questions.

8.2 DEFAULT RULES AND CONSENT

One approach to justifying a default rule is to connect it to a general theory of contractual obligation. What kind of argument might the consent or autonomy theory of contractual obligation offer? What, in other words, is the relevant connection between consent and hypothetical ex ante contracting?

In fact, we can distinguish between at least two kinds of arguments a consent theorist might advance to support the claim that the ex ante hypothetical contract is a uniquely appropriate way of establishing ex post the terms of contracts incompletely specified ex ante. The first argument relies on the justificatory force of hypothetical consent. Roughly the argument is as follows: The duties the parties have explicitly imposed on one another are legitimately enforced against them because they are the terms to which the parties have actually consented. The default rule imposes rights and responsibilities to which the parties would have consented. When securing the actual consent of negotiating parties is impossible, determining what they would have agreed to is the best alternative. Hypothetical consent is a proxy for actual consent. Therefore, to the same extent and in the same way that consent justifies a court imposing the rights and responsibilities made explicit in a contract, hypothetical consent justifies imposing the rights and responsibilities that are implied by the application of the default rule. Is the argument persuasive?

In the case of explicit consent, we recognize a difference between *unfree* acts and *irrational* ones. A person may consent to conduct detrimental to his interests (irrational, but free), or he may be compelled against his will to promote his interests (rational, but unfree, as in some forms of paternalism). The distinction between consent and rational self-interest becomes murkier in arguments attempting to establish what a particular person conceived of a particular way would have consented to. This problem in arguments from hypothetical consent and the additional, more fundamental problem of justifying the imposition of duties ex post on the grounds that they would have been agreed to ex ante are illustrated by an example drawn from normative economic analysis of law.

Recall that economists distinguish among three criteria of economic efficiency: Pareto superiority, Pareto optimality, and Kaldor–Hicks efficiency. S^1 is *Pareto superior* to S^0 if and only if no one prefers S^0 to S^1 and at least one person prefers S^1 to S^0. S is *Pareto optimal* if and only if there exists no S_n Pareto superior to it. S^1 is *Kaldor–Hicks efficient* to S^0 if and only if S^1 is potentially-Pareto superior to S^0. S^1 is potentially-Pareto superior to S^0 if in going from S^0 to S^1 resources could be arranged so that no one prefers S^0 to S^1 and at least on person prefers S^1 to S^0. Because the other efficiency concepts are defined in terms of Pareto superiority, we might ask what the relationship between Pareto superiority and consent might be.

The consensual defense of Pareto superiority is very simple, and although it has been employed primarily by Richard Posner in his defense of efficiency, the argument has its roots in Nicholas Kaldor's work some fifty years earlier.[5] The argument is this:

1. S^1 is Pareto superior to S^0 if and only if no one prefers S^0 to S^1 and at least one prefers S^1 over S^0.
2. Therefore, each person would consent to S^1, that is, would choose S^1 over S^0.

Some Pareto improvements, like rational, voluntary market transactions, are in fact consented to, though it remains a further question whether typical market transactions are morally defensible because they are Pareto improving or because they have been voluntarily consummated. In any case, many Pareto improvements are not consented to. Take the famous case of *Vincent* v. *Lake Erie Transportation Co.*[6] A dock owner refused to allow a ship to remain docked beyond the period of time set forth by the terms of a contract between the parties, and ordered it to leave. The captain refused to set his ship free when had he done so it would very likely have been lost at sea, a victim of an impending storm. The ship remained docked, the storm came, and the ship repeatedly smashed the dock, resulting in $500 damages to it.

The court held that even though the ship's captain acted correctly in firmly tying the boat to the dock, he was required to compensate the dock owner. If the ship's captain acted rationally, he was better off taking the risk and compensating the dock owner ex post than he would have been had he set the ship to sea. Provided the dock owner was fully compensated for whatever damages resulted from the ship captain's decision, he should be indifferent between what actually occurred and what would have occurred had the captain set his ship afloat. Thus, the outcome of the case constitutes a Pareto improvement, not one, however, to which the relevant parties had consented. In fact, the dock owner made every effort to express his unwillingness to consent voluntarily to the captain's decision. Here we have a Pareto improvement that could not be justified on the grounds that it had been consented to.[7]

So the consent argument for the legal rule must be that ex ante the parties *would have consented* to it. The premise in that argument is simply the one stated earlier: All the relevant parties are made better off by the Pareto improving state (or at least are made no worse off by it). Thus, they prefer the Pareto improving state to the Pareto inferior one (premise 1). To say that they prefer one state to the other is to say that under normal conditions they *would choose* the former to the latter (conclusion) – thus, the connection of Pareto superiority to hypothetical consent. The premise in the argument expresses the individual rationality of the proposed change; the conclusion expresses the parties' hypothetical consent to it. From the fact that a social state makes someone no worse off (i.e., it is not irrational for him), we are to infer that the agent would have consented to it. Consent follows as a matter of logic from considerations of rational self-interest.

Consequently, in arguments of this sort, there appears to be nothing expressed by the concept of hypothetical consent that is not already captured in the idea of rational self-interest. The distinction between consent and rational self-interest central to moral theory apparently evaporates. The claim that imposing obligations ex post is justified because the parties would have consented to them ex ante adds nothing to a defense of such a proposal that is not already expressed by the argument that imposing obligations ex post is justified whenever such obligations would have been rational for the parties ex ante. Thus, one might say that the reliance on ex ante rational bargaining provides a rationality or welfarist defense of the default rule, not a consensualist one.

A consent theorist needs another way of connecting hypothetical rational bargaining to consent, a way that main-tains both the analytic distinction between the two and the significance of both to a full consensual defense of contrac-tual obligation. One approach could rely on the claims that the relationship between hypothetical rational bargaining and hypothetical consent is *epistemic*, not analytic. What it would have been rational for the parties to bargain to ex ante is not equivalent to, nor does it entail, anything about what they would have agreed to, but it is, nevertheless, *evidence*, per-haps the best evidence, of it. Rather than trying to derive hypothetical consent from rationality, the suggestion is that the former provides presumptive evidence of the latter. In the absence of contradictory evidence, that is, evidence con-trary to that derived from the hypothetical rational bargain, it is legitimate to infer that the parties would have consented to that which would have been the outcome of a rational bargain between them.

Ultimately, the consent theorist's first strategy for defend-ing the ex ante contract as a default rule rests on the claim that what would have been rational for the parties ex ante is extremely strong evidence of what they would have agreed to. What the parties would have agreed to ex ante in turn provides some justification for holding them to those terms ex post. This line of defense, of course, is incomplete pend-ing an account of why it is that something to which individ-uals would have agreed (though they did not in fact) pro-vides a civil authority with grounds for imposing those conditions on them now (when they quite explicitly do not agree to them).

The second line of defense open to the consent theorist is designed to obviate this last problem. In this view, by the very act of contracting, the parties consent not only to a framework of explicitly created rights and duties, but to a jurisdiction for resolving conflicts that might arise in constru-ing those rights and duties. Should the occasion arise, the jurisdiction to which the parties consent is authorized to im-pose rights and duties ex post that were not made explicit ex ante. To contract is, among other things, to consent to the relevant default provisions of a particular jurisdiction. Thus, the rights and responsibilities allocated by a default rule ex post are, in a suitable sense, consented to ex ante. This line of argument eliminates the need to demonstrate either that the terms imposed by the default rule would have been consented to by the parties, or that what the parties would have consented to ex ante provides a reason for imposing those terms on them now. The importance of hypothetical consent simply disappears, and with it the need to establish an evidentiary or analytic connection between it and the ex ante rational bargain.

This approach appears to obviate two problems: specifying the relationship (analytic or epistemic) between rational bargaining and hypothetical consent and explaining the source of the normative punch of the latter. However, new problems are created. If this solution to the problem of connecting consent to the ex ante contract default rule is a good one, it constitutes an equivalently good defense of all possible default rules. For if by consenting to a contract, one consents to a jurisdiction's default rule, then one consents to whatever rule the court applies: from those aimed at reconstructing a hypothetical bargain to those imposing fair terms, to others imposing efficient terms, to those imposing obnoxious terms, and so on. This reconstruction of the consent theory of contractual obligation, in other words, provides no sense in which the ex ante rational contract is special. If the ex ante rational bargain as a default rule has a special attraction for this sort of consent theorist, this line of argument does not do a very good job of expressing or developing it.

If this form of the consent argument for the default rule works at all, it works too well. The next question is whether it works at all. It may make sense to say that two contracting parties consent to the obligations and rights their contract specifies to the extent each has alternative opportunities, or at least provided that none of the contractual terms is imposed unwillingly on either of them. Similarly, the parties could be said to consent to a relevant authority's default rule only if they willingly, that is, noncoercively, choose it. This

171

is not typically the case, however. The default rules of any jurisdiction are generally a nonnegotiable part of their bargain. Though the parties can often contract around them, they cannot substitute the default provisions of other jurisdictions. For that reason, it is questionable whether by consenting to a framework of contractual rights and responsibilities the parties consent to the application of the operative default provisions.

It is no counterargument, moreover, that the parties could reduce the extent to which they rely on the relevant jurisdiction's default rule. Although it is true that the parties could more fully specify their contract and thereby reduce the scope of the default rule's application, this shows only that the parties can reduce or minimize the rule's impact, not that in doing so they consent to the rule's use in those areas around which they do not contract. To hold otherwise is to adopt the "book of the month club theory of consent."

In order for the claim that merely by entering into a contract, parties consent to the relevant default rule to be minimally plausible, we would have to assume something like a competitive market in authoritative jurisdictions. Then the parties would choose jurisdictions based, among other things, on the default rules in effect. If this claim is that a default rule is justified to the extent that it *would be freely chosen* in a competitive market for authoritative jurisdictions, then the defense of default rule itself relies upon arguments from hypothetical, not explicit, consent.

Moreover, the argument likely to be employed to defend the ex ante contract as a default rule would be that among all the possible rules, it is the one that is rational for the parties ex ante. The rationality of the default rule follows from the fact that it reduces the costs of contracting. It enables each party to avoid the costs under other rules of contracting out, of ever more fully specifying their contract, and so on; in other words, it is a rational safeguard against contract failure. Once again, the argument for the ex ante contract ultimately relies on hypothetical consent and a relationship, analytic or epistemic, between what is rational for someone ex ante and what that person would have consented to needs to be specified. In the end, the effort to replace hypothetical with explicit consent does not avoid these problems.

Consent theorists believe that in general the justification for imposing contractual rights and responsibilities is that, through the expression of their rational, autonomous will, the parties have imposed those obligations on themselves; they have agreed so to bind themselves. This is a very different theory of contractual obligation than the one that emphasizes the rationality of such obligations and rights as safeguards against contract failure. Still, in default of explicit agreement, the consent theorist stands prepared to rely in normatively significant ways on the rationality of a bargain as a ground for imposing rights and responsibilities ex post. I have suggested that the best argument available to the consent theorist is that the terms that are rational for the agents provide the best evidence of the terms to which they would have agreed.

8.3 EFFICIENCY AND DEFAULT RULES

The relationship between economic analysis and rational bargaining is illustrated in the work of Alan Schwartz on products liability.[8] Schwartz begins his analysis of products liability by accepting what he calls the principle of consumer sovereignty. This is a principle of contract, not tort. Though he does not explicitly analyze the full range of claims and constraints on contractual relationships that the principle imposes, he claims that it implies minimally that courts ought to enforce the bargains that rational, informed parties voluntarily strike with one another. Such agreements, he notes, are efficient.

The consent theorist is also committed to the principle of consumer sovereignty. In fact, that may be the core principle of contract to which the consent theorist is committed. Efficiency theorists emphasize the Pareto optimality of consensual agreements under the conditions of full information, rationality, and insignificant transaction costs; consent theorists

173

emphasize the ways in which such arrangements express the autonomy of contracting parties. So, under conditions of full information and rationality, there is a convergence between the dictates of efficiency and autonomy, a convergence that is both captured and endorsed by the principle of consumer sovereignty. This turns out to be a particular instance of the more general claim that under conditions of perfect competition laissez-faire markets are rational, autonomous, and efficient. Convergence, then, depends on the background conditions: full information, rationality, and zero transaction costs.

In fact, the information consumers possess about the risks associated with various products is incomplete, and even if they are made fully aware of them, their capacity to assess those risks, is imperfect. Consequently, allocating safety related risks through normal contracts for sale will likely be inefficient. According to the economic analyst, the principle of consumer sovereignty will have to be amended or abandoned completely. An alternative to contracting as a device for allocating risk must be developed. In the standard view, this alternative is products liability law, a branch of tort law.[9] The question, then, becomes: What content should be given to the rules of products liability? How, in other words, ought we to think about who should bear the safety risks associated with product manufacturing when the contractual solution expressed by the principle of consumer sovereignty is unavailable?

The answer we might expect from an economist would be: Impose the risks efficiently. But how are we to determine what constitutes an efficient allocation of risk? Schwartz argues that the rules of products liability should impose on consumers and producers the terms to which they would have agreed under conditions of full information and rationality. These rules would be spelled out in terms of a hypothetical rational bargain or contract among the parties, and the conditions or terms of the contract would, by definition, be efficient. The tort solution – products liability law – should mimic the hypothetical contract solution among rational agents.

When the parties cannot or do not contract to allocate risk, Schwartz claims that at least with respect to products liability the risks should be allocated as rational, fully informed agents would have. Thus, in default of actual agreement, allocate risks according to the dictates of the theory of rational bargaining. Like the consent theorist, the efficiency theorist is also committed to the principle of rational bargaining as a way of giving expression to the content of obligations in the absence of explicit agreement, a way that is consistent with the relevant underlying theory of obligation: consent in the first case, efficiency in the second.

In section 8.2 we argued that the best defense of the ex ante contract as a default or gap-filling rule within a consent theory of contractual obligation is epistemic: The rational bargain between the parties is the best available evidence of the terms to which the parties would have agreed. The question now is whether the economist is justified in relying on the rational bargain as a way of giving expression to the underlying efficiency theory of contractual obligation.

8.4 ARE ALL RATIONAL BARGAINS EFFICIENT?

Default or gap-filling provisions typically apply among parties with *asymmetric information*. It is well known that there are numerous potential solutions or equilibria to bargaining games with asymmetric and imperfect information. Not all of these equilibria are efficient. Because rational bargaining under asymmetric or imperfect information need not be efficient, actually to replicate a hypothetical rational bargain among the negotiating parties may require imposing conditions upon them ex post that are *not* efficient. It is not obvious, therefore, that the desired relationship between efficiency and rational bargaining exists; and further, it is not clear, how the theory of rational bargaining as a way of understanding default rules can be defended on efficiency grounds.

Surely, the economist will not give up so quickly, nor should she. Recall that when faced with a similar problem, the consent theorist defends the rational bargain on epistemic grounds. What the parties would have rationally bargained to ex ante is very good evidence of what they would have agreed to, and so on. Can the efficiency theorist adopt a similar tack? Instead of saying that the outcome of a hypothetical rational bargain is efficient, could the economist claim that the outcome of a hypothetical rational bargain is *evidence* of efficiency?

There are two problems with this approach. First, because of the possibility of multiple equilibria that are not efficient, the outcome of rational bargaining under conditions of asymmetric information may not be reliable evidence of efficiency. Second, the analogy with consent theory is otherwise inapt. When the parties to a contract have not made their preferences clear ex ante, and we are unable to secure their actual consent, the best we may be able to do is develop evidence and make reasonable inferences about what they would have agreed to. In contrast, when the parties to a contract have not made their preferences clear ex ante, we can still determine what would be efficient ex post. We do not have to settle for evidence and inference.

Even if the hypothetical rational bargain could provide *evidence* of what would have been efficient, why settle for it? If, as the legal economist believes, the point of legal rules is to allocate risk efficiently, no need arises for reliance on a theory of rational bargaining.

Consider the following possibility. Under the normal view of the default rules we are considering, whenever transaction costs make it irrational for contracting parties to nail down a specific allocation of risk, courts should stand prepared to impose on them those rights and responsibilities to which they would have agreed or bargained. Because it is relativized to particular agents and their flaws, this particular default rule risks the problem of inefficient equilibria that we have emphasized. To avoid this problem, the economic analyst could suggest an alternative reading of the default or gap-filling rule: whenever transaction costs make it irrational for contracting parties to nail down a specific allocation of risk ex ante, courts should stand prepared to impose on them ex post those rights and responsibilities to which fully informed, rational parties would have agreed or bargained. In other words, simply idealize, rather than relativize, the rational bargain.

This is Schwartz's solution. Moreover, it is a solution that makes it more likely that the outcome of applying the default or gap-filling rule will be efficient. The rational bargain, so understood, is the vehicle through which the principle of efficiency is expressed and given content. I do not want to suggest that this strategy is not available to a defender of the economic analysis of contract. In Schwartz's case, for example, the strategy seems fair enough in that he is attempting to develop a theory of products liability, that is, a set of default rules designed to apply to all consumers and producers. Of course, it hardly seems accurate to claim that such a procedure follows from the principle of consumer sovereignty which applies to particular contractual arrangements between specific contracting parties.

Still, the appeal to an idealized rule for filling in the gaps in particular contracts between particular agents may well be problematic, even disingenuous. What the legal economist is really offering as a default rule, one might object, is not the requirement that a court replicate a bargain between the parties, but that, in the absence of an explicit bargain between the parties, courts should promote efficiency, plain and simple, and the effort to mask this prescription behind the principle of rational bargaining or hypothetical contracting is insincere. Indeed, one would have thought that part of the attraction of the ordinary gap-filling rule is that it makes an effort to complete the parties' contract in terms of which they (on reflection) might have agreed. How can the outcome of an idealized bargain be understood as completing the contract of individuals who are not themselves placed in ideal circumstances?

Isn't this virtually the same point James Buchanan makes about the definition of efficiency under idealized conditions, the same point we discussed in connection with the concept of market failure in Chapter 4? In a way, isn't this the problem critics of ideal political contractarianism point to: Why should someone here and now be motivated to comply with the terms hypothetical, ideal agents would have agreed on? What has the agreement among ideal agents under ideal circumstances have to do with the circumstances in which the parties find themselves?

The appeal to the theory of rational bargaining under idealized circumstances is irrelevant to the interests of the parties to a contract; real agents do not find themselves in anything like ideal circumstances. Their actual bargain reflects the reality of their situation; so should any hypothetical bargain struck between them. Moreover, the appeal to the principle of rational bargaining under idealized circumstances is insincere. It is a mask. Instead of completing, even in an attenuated sense, the contract between the parties, the principle of ideal rational bargaining is just a mask for the real principle: the principle of efficiency.

8.5 NONIDEAL AGENTS AND IDEAL CONTRACTS

Economic analysts like Schwartz accept the principle that incomplete contracts should be completed by the use of the ex ante rational contract. I argued that such an approach may lead courts to impose inefficient terms.[10] That may be inconsistent with economic analysis's commitment to efficiency. To meet this challenge, the economist might try the following strategy. Assume that all contracting parties are rational. Each will seek to maximize his or her utility. Because they have incomplete information, contracting partners may be thwarted in their efforts jointly to maximize wealth. The terms to which they agree may well be less than fully efficient no matter their motivation. Oddly, the fact that the parties have incomplete information that requires courts to fill in the gaps in their contracts may be viewed by contracting partners as an opportunity, rather than as a problem. Here's the trick.

The terms to which rational agents explicitly agree may or may not be efficient. As utility maximizers they are doing

178

their best to create jointly wealth-maximizing contracts. Incomplete information may render their efforts only partially successful. They know this. They also know that ex ante transaction costs in excess of available endogenous transaction resources will require them to leave some terms unspecified. There will be gaps that may need to be filled in by a court. But they look upon that as an opportunity. For they can instruct the court to impose efficient terms on them. The court can do for them ex post what they would prefer, but may not always be able to achieve ex ante, which is a jointly wealth-maximizing or efficient allocation of costs and benefits.

For any given term, *T*, left unspecified in a contract, contacting partners have two options. They can (1) instruct a court to specify *T*, or (2) agree to a procedure by which courts ex post would specify *T* in a way that rational parties with complete information would have. If procedure (2) is always efficient while procedure (1) may or may not be, then *rational* agents would choose procedure (2). In other words, rational parties would have filled the gap in their contract ex ante by leaving it up to a court to impose efficient terms on them. As long as we assume that the parties are rational, whatever their other shortcomings may be, they would have chosen to have the court fill in all the gaps in their contract by imposing efficient terms on them ex post.

The efficient terms to which rational agents would have agreed can be represented by the theory of rational bargaining among fully informed agents under ideal circumstances. To impose those terms on the imperfectly informed agents ex post is to impose on them the terms to which they would have bargained ex ante. Thus, the theory of rational bargaining under ideal conditions is neither irrelevant nor insincerely deployed.

8.6 WHY CONTRACT?

If the parties know that a court will impose efficient terms ex post and that they may fail to secure efficient terms ex ante, won't rational parties have a perverse incentive to maximize the extent to which they rely on courts to allocate risk efficiently? The answer is both yes and no. Individuals will be inclined to rely upon courts to promote their joint wealth, but only to the extent to which they believe that courts are better suited to determine what's in their interest than they are.

In many ways, courts will be no better placed, and often considerably less well placed, than individuals to determine which allocation of risk would be wealth maximizing. After all, even though the court in applying the relevant default rule aims to promote efficiency, there is no reason to think that it will do a better job than will the particular contracting parties. The parties, themselves, also act to maximize their wealth. Whether they are successful often turns on the same considerations that determine whether courts will succeed, for example, the adequacy of information. Moreover, a judicious court will encourage the litigants to solve the problems they face privately whenever they are in the best position to safeguard against contract failure. That, after all, is the central lesson of this entire part of the book.

If the court provides an exogenous transaction resource that safeguards against contract failure owing to uncertainty or incomplete information, then the existence of gap-filling rules can encourage the efficient level of explicit contracting. Parties appeal to the gap filling rules when it is rational to do so and that depends on the resources available. Given their resources, if contracting partners can do a better job of contracting than courts can, they will set the terms of their contract explicitly. If they cannot, they will not. That is the essence of rational contracting.

8.7 RATIONALITY, CONSENT, AND EFFICIENCY – AGAIN

There are technical and substantive objections to imposing on parties ex post what they would have bargained to ex ante. The technical problem arises when a court is asked to determine ex post what parties would have bargained to ex ante. This problem is complicated by the fact that the litigants are likely to offer very different accounts *ex post* of their *ex ante* preferences. The incentive to behave strategically may well be overwhelming. Determining what is fair or efficient may turn out to be considerably easier than determining what the parties would have agreed to.

The normative problem is more troublesome. What parties to an agreement would have agreed to is a function of their relative bargaining strengths. A person's bargaining strength depends on endowments, information available, alternative opportunities, and the like. Even if a court could determine how the parties would have allocated risks ex ante, in doing so it may be doing no more than reinforcing bargaining inequalities. In short, courts may not be particularly well suited to determine ex post what parties would have bargained for ex ante, and even if they could, courts might well exacerbate, rather than alleviate, relative bargaining inequalities.

It is one thing for a court to recognize and enforce bargains that are the result of inequalities in relative bargaining positions when the parties have explicitly agreed to them; it is another for a court to impose unfair allocations of rights and responsibilities in the absence of an explicit agreement among the parties to do so. Rather than using the opportunities created by incomplete contracts to reallocate wealth fairly or in ways that are desirable from some other point of view, the rational bargaining approach instructs courts to replicate a relationship that may be fraught with inequality and injustice.

The default or gap-filling rule is an external transaction resource. It is a legal norm parties can appeal to and rely upon to safeguard against contract failure. The central way in which a default rule contributes to rational contracting is by conserving resources. Imagine the full range of potential default provisions. At one extreme, we can imagine default provisions that are so unattractive to individuals that they would be inclined whenever possible to avoid their application. At the limit, default rules can be so unattractive as to discourage contracting altogether. On the other hand, if the parties know in advance that the terms imposed in default would be precisely those they would have negotiated (as best as a court could determine), then the parties are freed of the need to ever more finely tune their contract. In the limiting case, they may do no more than signal to the court their willingness to have the court impose duties on them. The more closely the default rule approximates what the parties would have done themselves, the more endogenous resources are conserved. Conserved resources can be put to use elsewhere in the contracting process.

If we view the default rule as a rational safeguard, then a case can be made for the default rule that replicates the particular structure of the contracting parties' relationship – even if doing so may lead to outcomes that are neither fair nor efficient as judged by some external criterion of fairness or efficiency. In the rational choice perspective, we are analyzing the default rule from the point of view of negotiating parties and not from the point of view of some conception of justice beyond the transactional framework or from a principle of efficiency desirable from a global or social point of view. A fully developed rational choice default rule may not be fair,[11] but it does provide a rational safeguard and in doing so maximally conserves internal resources among rational contractors.

Chapter 9

From contracts to torts

Default or gap-filling rules provide a safeguard against contract failure. Rational safeguards need be neither fair nor efficient. They conserve transaction resources and in doing so facilitate the exchange process. Contractual norms help to sustain markets. Markets facilitate political and social stability under a broad range of circumstances. In Chapter 3, I suggested that someone committed to a market facilitating view of contract of the sort developed in Chapters 5 through 8 must also be committed to a market failure or *market rectifying* view of tort law. Before leaving the discussion of contracts, we need to revisit and evaluate those arguments for their soundness. We begin with a compressed restatement of them.

9.1 PROPERTY AND LIABILITY RULES

Recall the distinction that Guido Calabresi and Douglas Melamed draw between property and liability rules. Property rules protect rights by conferring on right holders the power to exclude and to exchange on terms agreeable to them ex ante. An individual whose entitlements are secured by liability rules only is not empowered to exclude others, but in the event others act to reduce the value of her entitlement, she is entitled to recover damages ex post. In the case of property rules we speak of free exchange; in the case of liability rules we speak of *forced transfers*.

When the ex ante costs of transacting exceed available endogenous transaction resources, property rules may prove inefficient, as individuals will be disabled from making at least some mutually advantageous exchanges. Under these conditions, rules legitimating forced, but efficient, transfers are required. Liability rules permit individuals who value entitlements more highly to "take" provided they compensate ex post. Liability rules have two essential elements: *taking* and *compensation*. Together these elements yield the idea of a forced exchange. The forced taking dimension of liability rules enables higher value users to overcome high ex ante transaction costs; compensation ex post reduces, if it does not entirely eliminate, inefficient takings.[1] In this way, liability rules rectify market failures. Because tort law is a set of liability rules, the best interpretation of it emphasizes its role in overcoming high ex ante transaction costs.

9.2 FROM CONTRACTS TO DEFAULT TO TORTS

Were it costless to nail down an assignment of risk regarding any and all contingencies, negotiating parties would fully specify their contracts. Transaction costs render full specification infeasible and default rules desirable. Default rules impose rights and responsibilities or allocate costs ex post. They are, in effect, liability rules. Like liability rules in torts, reliance upon them is triggered by the existence of transaction costs in excess of endogenous transaction resources.

Transaction costs sometimes prevent negotiating parties from completely specifying the terms of their contract, other times they prevent parties from entering into contractual relations altogether. Default provisions are solutions to problems of the first sort; tort liability rules are solutions to problems of the second sort. The important point is that both default and tort liability rules overcome inefficiencies that would otherwise occur when transaction costs exceed available endogenous resources. Indeed, tort law is simply contract law by default provision writ large, and is analytically indistinguishable from it. Thus, the same general theory of liability, namely, an economic one, applies to both.

9.3 FROM CONTRACTS TO TORTS TO CRIMES

Contracting ex ante and compensating ex post both can contribute to the efficient allocation of resources. The former is represented by property rules, the latter by liability rules. Each rule is appropriate to different empirical circumstances. The choice between the two depends on the relative costs of compensating ex post and transacting ex ante. Whenever a potential taker expects to pay more to an entitled person ex ante than he expects to compensate that person ex post, he will prefer to take then compensate (if he has to) to pursuing voluntary transactions ex ante.

The individual decision between property and liability rules may depart from the collective decision, however. Individuals may prefer risking tort liability to contracting, when collectively we would prefer individuals to pursue market, not forced exchanges. This problem is exacerbated significantly whenever there is some positive probability that a person who takes first will not be identified, or if identified, will escape liability for other reasons. On the other hand, we may not want individuals to contract around tort liability when they may otherwise be inclined to do so. In other words, we may have sound collective reasons for not wanting individuals to treat liability rules as property rules or property rules as liability rules.

In order to bring private incentives in line with public judgment, an additional inducement may be required. The criminal law provides the additional incentive necessary to induce rational actors to respect the property-liability rule distinction. The criminal law is necessary to bring private incentive in line with public judgment in the same way that enforcement mechanisms may be necessary to bring individual rationality in line with collective rationality in the standard P.D. dilemma.

These considerations suggest a purely "economic" role for the criminal law. In the absence of a criminal law, individuals may be inclined to treat rights secured by property rules as if they were rights secured by liability rules, and vice versa.

The decision to divide transactions into those governed by property rules and those governed by liability rules has already been made on economic grounds. It is, therefore, necessary that individuals be given incentives adequate to induce their compliance with that decision. The payoffs of various decision options must be altered, and that is what the criminal law does.

These arguments present a problem for my general thesis. They appear to show that if someone accepts an economic or market theory of contracting, one will be driven to a similar account of tort. Contract law creates efficient allocations of risk by mutual agreement when ex ante transaction costs permit. Tort law imposes an efficient allocation of risk when ex ante transaction costs are prohibitive. The criminal law encourages agents to pursue market alternatives when they are efficient and to impose force exchanges otherwise (through tort liability). In Chapters 5 through 8 I have articulated and defended a market-based account of contract law. In Part III of this book I present an account of tort law that emphasizes the role of tort law in rectifying wrongs, in implementing the demands of corrective justice, rather than in moving resources to more highly valued uses when ex ante transaction costs exceed available endogenous resources. Either I have to give up the market theory of contract, the nonmarket failure theory of torts, or I have to reject the arguments presented first in Chapter III, then reviewed here that an economic theory of contracts entails an economic theory of torts. Because I am not prepared to make either of the first two concessions, that leaves me no choice but to reject what, on their face, look like very strong arguments linking contracts and torts. And that is precisely what I intend to do.

9.4 COMPLETING AND CREATING CONTRACTS

Default rules provide an analytic bridge between contracts and torts; tort law is simply the default rule of contract writ large. If a rational choice approach to default provisions in contract is appropriate, it is equally appropriate in specifying the place of liability rules in torts.

This is a seductive argument, but not a sound one. When a default provision is employed in contract to specify an allocation of risk, it allocates rights and responsibilities among parties who are already in a contractual relationship with one another. In contrast, tort rules specify relationships among individuals who are not in a contracting situation with one another at all. Default or gap-filling rules *fill-out* contracts; tort rules are *alternatives* to contracts. It does not follow that principles appropriate for filling out contracts between parties who are already contracting partners should govern the relationships of individuals who are not contracting partners at all.

One might respond that in the case of both incompletely specified and nonexistent contracts the source of the problem is the same: transaction costs in excess of available transaction resources. The difference between incompletely specified contracts and no contract is a difference in the quantity of transaction costs only. Sometimes transaction costs are substantial enough to force parties to leave gaps in their contracts; other times the costs are so great as to render contracting impracticable. Reduce the costs in either case, and the result is increased contracting: more finely honed contracting in the first case; contracting of some sort in the latter. In both cases the problem is fundamentally of the same type; so, therefore, should be the solution.

The mistake in this argument is that it draws in inference about what the point of a practice (torts) should be (encouraging efficiency or markets) from the conditions that give rise to it (high transaction costs). There may be no need for tort law in the absence of transaction costs. That does not mean that once there is a need for tort law, its purpose should be to replicate the process of contracting. Moreover, there may well be a role for tort law even under conditions in which transaction costs are trivial.

Let's explore both of these points in a slightly different way. Under conditions of perfect competition, no need would exist for tort liability rules. Therefore, tort liability can only arise because markets fail. If tort liability can arise only if markets fail, tort liability must be a potential solution to market failure. This is the basic structure of the argument we are considering. In the first place, the claim that no tort law would exist under conditions of perfect competition is an analytic truth that follows from the conditions of perfect competition, that is, zero transaction costs and no externalities. No externalities, no social costs. No social costs, no harms to others. No harms to others, no torts. This analytic truth about the conditions of perfect competition tells us absolutely nothing about what we ought to do, what our rules of liability ought to be, when the conduct of some imposes social costs on others.

Even if tort law would not exist under perfect competition, it does not follow that once markets fail and a need for tort law arises, that its point or purpose should be to rectify market failure. That claim is a *normative* one requiring substantive argument. In other words, it may be analytic that perfect competition precludes tort liability, but it is not analytic that imperfect competition requires that tort law be designed to mimic the outcome of perfect competition or its nearest substitute. To derive the conclusion that default rules and tort liability must serve economic ends, we have to add the premise that the point of default provisions and tort liability is to promote efficiency. Unlike the arguments we have been considering so far, such an argument would rely on a controversial normative claim about the purposes of law, and does not depend on the analytic connection between default rules in contract and tort liability.

9.5 FROM PROPERTY TO LIABILITY RULES

In the standard view, liability rules replace property rules whenever the costs of transacting ex ante are too high. It is easy to see the role liability rules play in moving resources to their more highly valued uses when transaction costs are high.

By specifying the terms of legitimate forced transfers, liability rules enable resources to move to more efficient uses, thus rectifying market failures. Because tort law consists in liability rules, tort law is best interpreted as an institution designed to overcome high ex ante transaction costs.

Nevertheless, transaction costs are not a *necessary* condition for the existence of liability rules. Suppose that transaction costs were always sufficiently low so that liability rules would never be needed for the purposes of moving resources to more highly valued uses. In our example, property rules are sufficient to move resources to more highly valued uses; at least transaction costs are never (we are assuming) sufficiently great to present a barrier to the voluntary movement of resources to their efficient uses. Even under a scheme of property rules, however, some actors might be inclined to take without first seeking the consent of others. Transaction costs are not the problem. Defective incentives are. How were we to respond to takings or rights violations that do not conform to the constraints imposed by property rules? One answer is that we can punish rights violators. If the punishments are correctly set, all rational agents will be deterred from takings. Of course, it will probably not be efficient to impose the penalty that is absolutely necessary to deter all wrongdoing. Some takings will occur. If they do, punishment may be appropriately imposed on the injurer. But what of the victim? Normally, we would feel that the victim has a right to have his loss repaired. But if his right is not protected by a liability rule, there will exist no basis for a claim to repair. Remember, it is liability rules, not property rules, that give rise to claims to compensation for damage. In these cases compensation under a liability rule is not designed to legitimate forced transfer. Ex hypothesi, property rules are sufficient for that purpose. Compensation under liability rules is designed to repair a wrong or its untoward consequences. Therefore, even in a situation in which, if followed, property rules would suffice to promote efficiency, or whatever other ends we had in mind, there might yet exist a need for liability rules. Liability rules would exist to ground a claim to repair for wrong done, not to specify the compensation condition of legitimate transfer.

Surely, compensation sometimes plays the role of legitimating forced transfers. The existence of high transaction costs may make this role both necessary and desirable. Still it is a serious mistake to miss the role compensation under liability rules plays in rectifying wrongs. This role may have nothing at all to do with high transaction costs. By focusing primarily on the role of liability rules in moving resources to more highly valued uses when transaction costs are too high to permit voluntary exchange, we will miss entirely the role liability rules play in rectifying wrongful losses. For that reason alone it is perfectly possible to defend a market facilitating theory of contract and a different theory of torts, one that emphasizes the role of compensation in rectifying wrongful losses, not in correcting market failures.

When transaction costs are low, injurers can secure entitlements they value by voluntary agreements. They may, nevertheless refuse to comply with the constraints that property rules impose on them. In doing so, they take without permission. One approach to this mischievous conduct would impose a criminal sanction on those who refuse to comply with the constraints imposed by property rules. That may suffice to discourage wrongful takings, but what of the victim? In the absence of liability rules, the victim has no claim to repair or compensation. By definition, rights to repair are conferred by liability rules. If a right has no liability rule component, its invasion grounds no claim to repair. Liability rules can arise even when ex ante transaction costs are low as a way of rectifying wrongful losses, not simply as a way of legitimating efficient but forced transfers.

9.6 THE GROUNDS OF TORT LAW

According to the argument of Chapter 3, although contracts specify the terms individuals must follow if they are to do with their entitlements as they see fit, and the criminal law sets forth prohibitions – what someone has no right to do with his possessions, regardless of price – tort law sets out what individuals are free to do provided they are prepared to pay the price. In this view, the price is compensation for harm done; and paying the price is sufficient to render the conduct in question permissible.

Nothing I have said so far should be read as denying that *sometimes* compensation under a liability rule is the price one has to pay to be free to act in a certain way. Sometimes compensation is necessary to justify forced transfers. My point is the more modest one that compensation or liability is often for harm done. It rectifies a wrong done, and does not right it. Compensation at least sometimes – often I will argue – does not serve to legitimate what in its absence would be wrong, that is, an unconsented-to taking. Compensation does not change the moral character of the action from wrong to right. Rather, because the conduct is wrong, compensation is the victim's due; it is not the price the injurer pays to secure his victim's "permission." This is the central claim of the next part of this book.

If we are seduced by the arguments with which we began – that tort law is a default provision in contract writ large in which contract law exists to create and sustain markets – we will see tort law largely in, broadly speaking, economic terms. We will have gained significant insight into our practices, but we will miss as much as we have seen. In particular, we will miss or misunderstand the role of wrongfulness and wrongdoing in tort liability. It is time now to develop a theory of tort law that gives prominence to wrongfulness as a basis of both liability and recovery.[2] This is the theory of corrective justice.

9.7 REVIEW

Before moving on to the argument that accident law is largely a matter of corrective justice, I want to repeat what I take myself to have been arguing for so far. I reject the market paradigm, and in its place offer rational choice liberalism.

191

Like the market paradigm, rational choice liberalism begins with two primitives: the principle of rational choice and the centrality of the market. In rational choice liberalism the market is important because of its contribution to social stability. In the market paradigm the market is important because it creates efficient outcomes under highly restrictive conditions. The kind of economic analysis that falls out of the two competing theories may overlap, but their differences are important. In the view I defend efficiency matters primarily as an instrument in the pursuit of other goals or as a dimension or aspect of those goals. It is not an independent moral ideal. I want to shift the focus of economic analysis away from efficiency back toward markets.

In Part II, I take a first step at working out this program. I look at contract law from the point of view of someone who accepts rational choice liberalism, someone unconcerned with efficiency as such. Instead the focus is on market transactions as micro or local cooperation problems. Solving those problems is important for a variety of reasons. First, it enables individuals to get on with their lives with one another in ways that satisfy their interests and needs, and, second, it creates conditions of stability. Nowhere do I mean to suggest that economists are wrong to look at contract law from the point of view of efficiency. There are a variety of good reasons for doing so, some of which I touched upon in the Introduction. Still, I am interested in the normative dimension of the practice, not the predictive dimensions of it. I think markets, stability and autonomy are important in this regard in ways in which efficiency simply is not.

I fear that some readers will misunderstand another aspect of the argument in Part II and I want to take this opportunity to try to make clear what I was not doing in this Part of the book. I was not defending rational bargaining theory as a better normative theory than conventional law and economics. At the normative level I am defending markets as against efficiency. That is the only normative bone I have to pick with conventional law and economics. The preference for bargaining theory as against conventional economic analysis

192

is not normative; it comes in at an entirely different level of the argument.

Accept for the moment the argument in Part I on behalf of rational choice liberalism. I claim that we should take that argument as an invitation to reconsider certain legal practices from the point of view of the role they play in creating and sustaining markets. That leads me to apply the theory to contract, arguably a part of the law that sustains market relations. Now I need a way of getting at the ways in which contract law sustains markets. My suggestion is that we look at the typical discrete market transaction as a local cooperation problem. Then I suggest that the best way of modelling the problem of local cooperation is as a divisible prisoner's dilemma. And then I claim that we can conceptualize the divisible P.D. as a bargaining game of a certain kind. Therein lies the preference for bargaining theory. My claim is not that bargaining theory is a better normative theory than conventional economic analysis. Rather, it is that bargaining theory might more fruitfully capture the elements of rational contracting, something we will need to do if we are to see the ways in which the norms of contract law can contribute to sustaining markets.

Part III

Rectifiable wrongs

Chapter 10

The goals of tort law

If contract norms are safeguards to contract failure, then contract law can be interpreted as having the point of helping to sustain markets. That is the argument of Part II. Markets, in turn, contribute to social stability by allowing a broad range of interaction to take place among individuals with significantly different conceptions of the good. This is their attraction to liberalism, or so I have argued in Part I. Markets are most needed where they are most difficult to create and sustain, that is, under conditions of significant uncertainty. A law of contracts alleviates many of these problems. That is the connection between Parts I and II.

When ex ante transaction costs are high, resources may not move to their most highly valued uses. Therefore, it is natural to view tort law as created for the purposes of moving resources to move efficient uses when the contract option is unavailable. Such a view sees liability and compensation under liability rules as ways of legitimating forced transfers. The argument of Chapter 9 is that sometimes liability and compensation under liability rules is for wrong done. We have at least two ways of understanding tort law; one that emphasizes its role in substituting for efficient contractual exchange; the other emphasizes its role in rectifying for wrong done. Which is the better interpretation of our current tort practice? That question occupies the remainder of this book.

10.1 MIDDLE LEVEL THEORY AND TORT

Part III of this book approaches tort law from the perspective I referred to in the Introduction as middle-level theory. At the core of tort law is a certain practice of holding people liable for the wrongful losses their conduct has occasioned. This is not the entirety of tort; it may not even reflect the majority of cases litigated in tort. Often individuals are compensated for losses that are not wrongful; individuals are sometimes required to repair losses when they did no wrong; and other times individuals are held liable for losses, wrongful and otherwise, for which they are not in any obvious sense responsible.[1] Along the way, I hope to have something interesting to say about these and other dimensions of tort law, departures, justifiable and otherwise, from its core. Still, my real focus will be on tort law's core, the practice of holding individuals liable for the wrongful losses they impose.

My claim that this is tort law's core will of course be controversial. My defense of that claim is simply that when one thinks about or teaches tort law, no matter what else one feels compelled to explain or to understand, one is required to understand two features, one structural, one substantive. The structural feature is that in the typical case decisions about who should bear a loss are rendered within a framework restricted to victims and those individuals they identify as their injurers. The question is not; who in the world should bear this loss? Instead, it is: should the injurer or the victim bear it? The substantive feature is that if a victim can show that her loss is wrongful in the appropriate sense, the burden of making good her loss falls to the individual responsible for it. An account of tort law that fails to provide a persuasive understanding of these elements, whatever it may illuminate, simply does not understand tort law.

On the other hand, I am not claiming that the core of tort law is in any sense immutable or unchanging. Scholars reading this book twenty five years from now – surely that is an optimistic prediction – might find my discussion entirely unhelpful as what I am calling the core of tort law shrinks to a

198

point or disappears into a normative black hole. Though tort law has undergone significant changes, some of which I will discuss, and not all of which can be reconstructed as natural extensions of its core, part of what I am assuming is that the core remains – at least for now.

It might surprise some readers of what follows that I do not advance the view that those areas outside the core of tort ought to be rethought to better reflect tort law's core commitment. It will surely surprise many readers that I do not argue that the core of tort law must be maintained if the practice is to warrant our allegiance and reflective acceptance. I do not argue that all departures from corrective justice constitute moral mistakes in part because I accept what many readers may find both a controversial and unsettling thesis about the scope of corrective justice that I set forth in Chapter 19. Briefly, my view is that whether corrective justice imposes moral reasons or duties within a community will depend on other practices, including legal ones. For that reason, corrective justice may not provide an independent standard against which all such practices are to be measured.

Chapter 11 sets out the substantive rules of liability that all tort theorists seek to provide a convincing account of. Chapters 12–14 consider various attempts to defend those rules of liability as expressing various norms, some economic (Chapter 12), some moral (Chapters 13 and 14). Chapter 15 begins the development of my conception of corrective justice. The analytic structure of the principle is set out in Chapter 16. Its subsidiary components are developed in Chapter 17. Chapter 18 asks whether the principle so conceived is at the heart of accident law, defined by the substantive rules identified in Chapter 11 and a structural component first introduced in this chapter. Chapters 19 and 20 explore departures from the corrective justice core and defend those departures in part in the light of the claim that social practices can sometimes constrain legitimately the scope of corrective justice. Chapter 21 tries to tie the entirety of the arguments in Parts I, II, and III together.

At the heart of middle-level theory is the conviction that

199

one has to immerse oneself into a practice in order to understand the norms that inhere in it. This chapter, in particular,
argues that we can only go so far in understanding accident
law if we begin by trying to understand it as having certain
goals and policies external to it that can be identified without
regard to the practice itself.

10.2 TORT LAW AS A FORM OF ORDERING

Let's call any account that holds that the justification of the
practice depends on its capacity to achieve or implement certain goals or purposes instrumentalist. In any *instrumentalist*
account of the law, the substantive ambitions or purposes of
the law shape the structure of the legal institution and determine its content. We can contrast a formalist conception of
tort law with the instrumentalist one. According to *formalism*, tort law is a body of law defined by the fact that it has a
structure of a certain kind. Whereas the instrumentalist believes that the substantive aims of tort law determine its
structure, the formalist believes that the structure of tort law
determines the extent to which various goals can be pursued
through it. In its most extreme version, formalism denies that
tort law has any goals or purposes external to the practice.
The only goal of tort law is to be tort law, and that is to
capture in law the way in which injurers and victims are related to one another in the world in the relationship of injuring and suffering.

Ernest Weinrib, the leading formalist of modern private
law, puts the difference between the instrumentalist and the
formalist in terms of two different forms of orderings:

> There are two ways to conceive of an ordering of several as-
> pects. In the first way, the aspects are intelligible only through
> the integrated whole that they form as an ensemble. Every
> aspect contributes to the meaning of the whole, and the whole
> gives meaning to its constituent aspects. . . . The aspects be-
> long together and are unintelligible in isolation. Such an or-
> dering can be termed "intrinsic."

In the second way, the aspects are independent of one another. . . . The aspects of a legal ordering in this second sense come together because positive law happens to bring them together, or because a single designation ("tort law") happens to apply to them in combination. Because the linking of the constituent aspects reflects the contingencies of social practice and linguistic usage, we can call such an ordering "conventional."[2]

Conventional orderings are instrumental. According to Weinrib, there are aspects of tort law, however, that are so general and pervasive that they are indispensible to our conception of what tort law is. They characterize tort law in the literal sense of providing indicia of its distinctive character. Were they completely removed, we would no longer be able to recognize what remained as tort law. These features together constitute the basic structure of tort law. Because it is impossible for us to conceive of tort law without them, a theory of tort is necessarily a theory of these features.[3]

Tort law has a certain essential character, form, or structure. In order for something to count as tort law, it must have certain properties or attributes. And its justification as an institution depends on the way in which it orders the relationships among these central properties. For Weinrib in particular, that means that the relationships among the concepts in tort law – injurer, victim, causation, and wrongdoing – mirror the ways in which these concepts are connected in the world, in the experience of injuring and suffering.[4] Thus, essential to tort law is the fact that respective victims bring suit against their particular injurers and, in the event the victim is entitled to repair for her loss, she recoups her damages from the wrongdoer. These features of tort law – that victims sue injurers, and, when they are entitled to repair, recover from their injurers – "define" the practice of tort law. Understanding tort law requires a comprehension of the ways in which these features of the law map onto the relational experience of injuring and suffering in the world.

It may well be that an institution of tort law conceived as

an ordering relationship of a certain kind is nevertheless poorly suited to reduce or spread risks or to achieve other "goals" of a desirable social policy toward accidents. The formalist does not deny that optimal risk reduction or spreading are important, or even that some institution should be created in order to facilitate those ends. Instead, his view is that institutions designed specifically to reduce or spread risk need not be tort law, and that it would be a mistake to treat tort law as inadequate or otherwise unjustified if it fails adequately to reduce or spread risk. For his view is that tort law may well be inadequate to the instrumental ambitions some have had for it, but that as long as it coherently connects its essential properties that themselves express a conception of justice or moral agency, tort law is both justifiable and comprehensible.

The difference between the formalist and the instrumentalist is now clear. For the instrumentalist, the criteria of justification are *extrinsic* to the practice. Tort law is justifiable provided it turns out to be a good way of pursuing those human ends and ambitions it is designed to achieve. Features of tort law that are essential to it within the formalist account are, within the instrumentalist account, merely contingent. Thus, it makes sense for victims to sue wrongdoers only if doing so has desirable social consequences, including, perhaps, minimizing search costs and maximizing the availability of reliable evidence relevant to determining the validity of the victim's claim. Similarly, it makes sense for injurers to pay victims only if doing so has desirable consequences, including optimal deterrence and insurance. According to the instrumentalist, the ordering of injurer and victim in tort law depends on the relationship of each to the goals of tort law, not on the relationship of each to one another. Thus, the ordering of injurer to victim is conventional rather than intrinsic – depending on the relationship of injurer and victim to the "external" goals of tort law rather than the relationship of injurer and victim.

If we accept an instrumentalist approach to tort law, then we can evaluate its success or failure. We can compare it with

202

alternative means of achieving certain goals and principles, for example, accident cost avoidance and justice. If the formalist is right, however, we will not be assessing tort law if we judge the institution by its success in achieving certain goals. To understand tort law is to understand why injurers and victims are brought together in litigation in the way in which they are – as reflecting their relationship in the world – and, indeed, in the way in which they must be if tort law is to be intelligible to us.

10.3 TWO FORMS OF INSTRUMENTALISM

Only instrumentalists believe that tort law has goals. We can distinguish among instrumentalists in terms of the goals each believes are appropriate to tort law. The important dichotomy is between moral and economic instrumentalists. Both contract and tort are legal instruments for allocating risk. In contracts risks are allocated among individuals according to the terms they voluntarily settle on. They are able to allocate risk contractually only when ex ante transaction costs are low enough. In contrast, tort law allocates risks among individuals when the ex ante transaction costs exceed available endogenous transaction resources. Tort law allocates risk by enforcing standards to which private individuals could have agreed had they been in a position to bargain with one another. The norms of tort law replicate efficient private arrangements – thus, the reliance on the hypothetical contract as the model of tort liability. This is the core of the economic instrumentalist approach to torts.

Moral theorists typically view tort law as embodying public standards of behavior. The rules of tort liability allocate risk, but they do not do so on the model of the private contract. Tort law is not simply a necessary response to the impossibility of contract, but a genuine alternative to contract as a device for allocating risk. Public standards are not simply responses to the failure of private arrangements, justifiable only to the extent they mimic or emulate private arrangements that might have been; public norms are genuine

203

alternatives to private arrangements, desirable on their own terms, in particular, as expressions of the demands of justice in the allocation of risk.[5] This is the starting point of moral instrumentalism as an account of tort law.

10.4 THE GOALS OF TORT LAW

Instrumentalists believe that tort law has goals and that its defensibility depends on the extent to which it satisfies them. Once we identify the goals of tort law, our next project will be to characterize the basic substantive rules of liability. Then we can ask whether the rules of liability, or which rules of liability, satisfy the relevant goals. Finally, we will characterize the structure of tort law, the way in which it orders the relationships of victims and injurers. Once we do that, we can determine whether this structure is best interpreted in the light of tort law's substantive goals or as a way of expressing the relationship between injurer and victim.

The first task is to identify the goals of tort law. We can distinguish between two kinds of goals: economic and moral. It may be more useful to think of the moral demands of tort law not as goals but as principles that are either expressed through tort law or that serve as constraints on the extent to which the law may legitimately pursue its policy objectives.[6] The economic goals of tort law have been succinctly captured by Guido Calabresi, who distinguishes among primary, secondary, and tertiary costs.[7] Primary costs are the dollar equivalent of the damages caused by accidents. Secondary costs are the costs of bearing the costs of accidents. These are the costs associated with various schemes for distributing the primary (and tertiary) costs of accidents. Secondary costs are reduced when they are spread maximally over persons and time, or when they are borne by those individuals in the best position to bear them. Tertiary costs are the administrative costs of any system, including the tort system, for determining who should bear the costs of accidents.

Deterrence reduces primary costs; insurance reduces secondary costs; and who knows what can reduce administrative costs. We might say that the economic goals of tort law are risk reduction (primary), risk spreading (secondary), and administrative cost avoidance (tertiary). Tort law should be designed to minimize these costs. Not quite. The costs of minimizing these costs also figure in the formula. We would not want to minimize accident costs by spending more in prevention and avoidance than what accidents actually cost. Thus, instead of minimizing, we want to *optimally* reduce costs. We want, in other words, to use Calabresi's useful phrase, to minimize the sum of the costs of accidents and the costs of avoiding them.

10.5 TWO ASPECTS OF PRIMARY ACCIDENT COSTS

The total primary costs of accidents are a function of two variables: the *level* at which individuals engage in an activity, and the *degree* of care they take. For any harmful activity, the more of it, the greater the likelihood of harm. The greater the number of harms, the greater the total cost (other things being equal). Similarly, for any level of a risky activity, the less careful one is, the greater the probability of harm. The greater the number of harms, the greater the total cost (other things being equal). Optimal risk reduction is aimed at both degree of care and activity levels.

10.6 INSURANCE

Insurance does not reduce risk; it spreads it. There is a distinction between first- and third-party insurance. In first-party insurance the victim purchases coverage against losses that she might suffer, those occasioned by the actions of others as well as other kinds of misfortunes. One can purchase first-party insurance against the consequences of both injustice and misfortune. In third-party insurance, someone purchases insurance to protect herself against liability or other judgments made against her. As long as individuals can purchase either first- or third-party insurance, liability decisions are really decisions about which party has the responsibility of purchasing which sort of insurance. The question of which party should be liable is often the question of which party should have the burden of insuring. Who should have the burden of initiating risk spreading?

Because decisions about who should be responsible for accident costs are basically decisions about who should buy which kind of insurance, we could argue that liability judgments in torts should take into account their insurance consequences. If it turns out that with respect to certain accidents, first-party insurance is preferable to third-party insurance, that should affect whether liability should be imposed on the injurer (third-party insurance) or remain the responsibility of the victim (first-party insurance), and so on. Because liability decisions have insurance implications, why not take those implications into account in rendering liability judgments in precisely the same way that we take into account the effects of liability rules on accident rates in determining the relevant liability rules?

There is another way of looking at the relationship between insurance and tort law, however. According to this account, it is important to distinguish between insurance as an institution that arises in order to enable individuals to discharge their substantive duties under the law and insurance itself as a goal of the law, as capable of providing independent grounds for imposing substantive duties under the law. In the first case one's substantive obligations under the law of torts are presumably determined on other grounds, then they are discharged by insurance contracts. In the second case one's substantive obligations under the law of torts are determined in part by one's capacity to insure optimally. Advocates of the first view argue in effect that even if liability judgments that enforce substantive duties under the law have insurance implications, it does not follow that those consequences should feed back into liability judgments. Insurance is not, in their view, a goal of tort law.

We might strengthen the intuition that insurance is not a goal of tort law in two ways. First, insurance depends on the existence of liability rules. Without liability rules, we do not know who is responsible for losses. If we do not know who is responsible for a loss, then we do not know who should buy insurance to cover it. Because insurance depends on the existence of liability rules, it cannot provide a ground or reason for imposing liability in one way rather than another. Second, consider the possibility of insuring against criminal liability. Few, if any, thoughtful observers would feel that when a defendant is found criminally responsible, his being required to shoulder his full criminal sentence creates a missed opportunity to spread the losses maximally over persons and time. The costs the state imposes on the wrongdoer are his and his alone. By imposing them on him, the criminal law does not spread the costs, but, then, virtually no one believes that spreading the costs is something the criminal law ought to do. This example illustrates that spreading costs in general is alien to institutions that impose liability in ways that reflect judgment of individual responsibility.

There are important differences between criminal and tort law, some of which we will develop later in this chapter. One difference is that in torts, accidents create losses that must be borne by someone or other. A loss exists and will not go away. It is, as economists say, sunk. The fundamental issue in torts is deciding upon its incidence. In contrast, criminal liability is the imposition of a *new* cost, not the allocation of an existing, sunk cost. One reason for imposing that loss on the wrongdoer is that he *deserves* it. If he deserves it, then the loss should be his to bear. It makes no sense, to spread the cost over persons and time, among individuals who are not otherwise deserving of criminal sanction. It makes no sense, in other words, to create a new loss specifically for the defendant, then try to spread it to reduce its impact. If we had in mind reducing its impact, we could have done that by imposing a lesser cost in the first place, or no cost at all. The whole point of the punishment is to impose such a cost, one suitable to the defendant's just deserts.

One could argue that tort law is different in this respect. Instead of imposing additional costs, it seeks to allocate existing costs only. In this context it makes very good sense to allow individuals to arrange to have the loss spread among members of an insurance pool. If this is a good argument, however, it shows only the risk spreading is something tort law enables us to do, not that risk spreading is something tort law should aspire to do. We need to be careful not to confuse the fact that liability decisions have insurance implications with the very different claim that insurance implications should dictate liability decisions. On the other hand, one could argue that the reason risk spreading or insurance is not a goal of the criminal law is that the relevant conceptions of justice and personal responsibility simply prohibit it. The principles of justice and responsibility expressed in tort law, however, permit risk spreading. Once it is permitted, as it is in torts, then why not count it as a goal of tort law, even if it may well be relegated to a subsidiary role?

The argument against tort law's having an insurance function is too broad to be compelling. For the very same argument should count against the claim that tort law has, or should have, a risk reducing function. Why should risk reduction be a plausible goal of tort law, if risk spreading cannot be? When we say that risk reduction is a potential, permissible goal of tort law we mean to say really is that pursuing it is not prohibited by the relevant principles of responsibility and justice. Moreover, because different liability rules will have different effects on overall risk, it makes perfect sense to consider these effects in making liability decisions. In other words, if it makes sense to wonder whether strict or fault liability is better at reducing accident costs, then it makes perfectly good sense to wonder whether third of first party insurance has more desirable risk-spreading consequences. If it is permissible to fashion liability rules based on their effects on reducing risks, it makes as much sense to fashion liability rules based on their effects on spreading risks. The only question is whether the relevant principles of justice and responsibility preclude our doing so.

The relevant principles of responsibility and justice in the criminal law may preclude risk spreading as a goal. Of course, in some views of those principles, criminal justice precludes risk reduction or deterrence as a goal of the criminal law as well.[8] The fact is that the relevant principles of justice in tort law appear to rule out neither risk reduction or spreading. As for the argument that insurance presupposes liability rules, therefore insurance can never be a ground of liability rule, the antecedent is false. Whether or not there are liability rules, there are accidents. Accidents create costs. It is the existence of accident costs, not liability rules that create the incentive for insurance. Without liability rules, losses will fall to victims who will purchase insurance to guard against disaster. Once this response to loss becomes apparent, it is natural to ask whether victims or someone else should have the responsibility of guarding against risk by purchasing insurance. In answering that question, it makes perfectly good sense to wonder whether injurers or victims are better insurers. And so on.

10.7 THE MORAL GOALS OF TORT LAW

Tort law does not compensate all victims of accidents. And it is a very costly way of compensating the victims it does. No one seriously believes that all victims deserve to be compensated for their losses. At least some victims deserve the losses that have befallen them. Even victims who do not deserve to suffer may have no right to repair. Compensation simpliciter is not a goal of tort law. O. W. Holmes recognized this fact and concluded that compensation could not be a goal of tort law.[9]

Even if compensation as such is not a goal of tort law, it does not follow that identifying rightful claims by imposing liability is not one of tort law's central concerns. Indeed, I want to argue not only that identifying and vindicating rightful claims to repair are legitimate aspirations of a law of tort, but that the best explanation of current Anglo–American tort law sees the practice primarily in terms of its efforts to meet these demands of justice – what I call corrective justice.

It is a further question whether tort law can or ought to pursue other norms of justice or morality generally. Should tort law be concerned to *redistribute* wealth among the parties to particular private litigations? Surely, holding the injurer liable to the victim has the effect of shifting wealth from the activity in which the injurer is engaged to the activity in which the victim is. Liability decisions have wealth redistributive consequences. Why should we not take these into account in forming liability judgements in particular cases or in categories of cases? Should tort law aspire to *cultivate character?* Liability judgements affect individual incentives to take care. The care one shows to others reflects one's character. Why not take these potential consequences into account when choosing liability rules? Liability judgments allocate costs ex post, but in doing so they provide guidelines to managing risk ex ante. Tort law is a piece of the larger puzzle of risk management. Should the rules of liability in tort be shaped as part of a general theory of *risk management?* These are all worthwhile goals, principles, and policies, and they are all capable of being affected by tort law. Should tort law aim to do whatever of each it can?

My general view is that once we accept some form of instrumentalism or institutional consequentialism we simply cannot decide in the abstract what the goals of practice should be. To determine tort law's legitimate goals, we need a theory of *institutional competence.* By that I mean an account of what particular institutions are competent to do consistent with the demands of institutional integrity. That requires a more general political theory, an account of legitimate institutional forms. Why do we believe that it is permissible to redistribute wealth through taxation (if it is permissible to do so at all), but not through the private law of contract?[10] Why do we think that the criminal law should reflect a deep theory of personal responsibility or moral agency, but that environmental law should not? Why do we believe, generally, that some goals and principles of justice are suitable to some institutions, and others are not?

We can only say that some goals and principles are suitable to a body of law once we have a theory of institutional competence, a political theory of institutions. Such a theory will have two components corresponding to two senses of competence: epistemic and normative. Some institutions are poorly placed to gather and develop the information relevant to making certain judgments and deciding on policy. Judges in contracts suits and in private litigation generally are not in a good position to gather the sort of information necessary to determine what the appropriate distribution of wealth should be. In contrast, legislators who take evidence from experts on such matters are epistemically better suited than are judges to render the appropriate judgments.

Some institutions are poorly placed normatively to enforce certain standards or principles or to pursue certain policies. Thus, some might argue that in a political democracy courts are better suited to protect individual rights than are legislatures, whereas because of their representative nature legislatures are better suited to make decisions about the provision of public goods. These arguments reflect considerations of political morality, not epistemology.

There is little more to be gained by trying to identify the legitimate goals of tort law. Instead, I suggest that we focus on the practice itself. We need to take a look at the substantive rules of liability and the structure within which those rules operate; then we can ask ourselves what provides the best normative interpretation or understanding of the mix. That will enable us to see what goals and principles the law itself seeks to accommodate or implement, what principles and understandings of justice (or economics) it expresses.

Chapter 11

Fault and strict liability

Holmes takes the view that losses should lie on victims unless some compelling reason exists for shifting them to someone else. Let's refer to the principle that losses should lie on victims as an *initial liability rule*. The responsibility for presenting a case for shifting the loss falls to the victim. If the evidence fails to convince, the burden of shouldering the costs is the victim's. The initial liability rule, therefore, has both epistemic and normative implications.

Liability rules specify the conditions the victim must establish in order that her loss be made the responsibility of someone else, usually, but not always, the injurer. The law of torts distinguishes generally between two sorts of liability rules: fault and strict liability. If a case is governed by a principle of *strict liability*, the victim must show that

1. She has suffered a compensable loss.
2. The injurer acted.
3. The injurer's conduct caused the loss she seeks to have repaired.

If the case is governed by a principal of fault liability, the victim must show that:

1. She has suffered a compensable loss.
2. The injurer acted.
3. The injurer was at fault in acting.
4. The injurer's fault caused the loss she seeks to have repaired.[1]

Fault and strict liability

11.1 LIABILITY RULES AND EPISTEMIC BURDENS

In each case the burden of establishing that the relevant conditions for shifting losses have been met typically falls to the victim. Thus, liability rules apply in response to the initial liability rule that victims are responsible for the costs of accidents. There are procedural devices, however, that reduce the extent of the burden to victims. In some cases, the nature of the accident strongly suggests that it would not have occurred but for the injurer's fault. In such cases courts sometimes apply the doctrine of res ipsa loquitur.[2] When the doctrine is applied, the victim is presumed to have met her burden of establishing a prima facie case that the injurer was at fault, and responsibility shifts to the alleged injurer to show that he was not. Although the doctrine is applied to reduce the difficulty of establishing fault, the victim is still required to establish that an injury occurred and that it was caused by the defendant.

Sometimes an analogous procedural device is applied with respect to the victim's responsibility to establish a causal connection between her injury and her alleged injurer's conduct. The case of *Summers* v. *Tice* illustrates this point.[3] Two individuals negligently fire at a third, but only one of the bullets strikes the victim. It is impossible for the victim to determine which bullet did the damage. Had the case proceeded along the usual lines, the victim would have been required to establish a causal connection between his injury and the conduct of the alleged injurers. His failure to meet that burden would have left him responsible for his losses, and the two wrongdoers, one of whom is not only a wrongdoer but responsible for the plaintiff's injury, free from liability. This case differs from those involving res ipsa loquitur in that in *Summers* the plaintiff establishes fault, but cannot establish the relevant causal connection, whereas in the typical res ipsa loquitur case the plaintiff can establish causation, but not fault. Both causation and fault are necessary to establishing the prima facie case for liability under the fault rule.

213

The fact that a plaintiff might be able to establish fault is inadequate to shift his loss to someone else. After all, it may be reasonably easy for any victim of a traffic mishap to establish the negligence of some driver, somewhere. Usually, we expect more than that. The plaintiff in *Summers* can establish more. He can establish with virtual (perhaps actual) certainty that his injury was caused by the *disjunction* of the faulty acts of the shooters. He can show, in other words, that either one or the other person negligently shot him. Under these conditions the court finds it appropriate to treat the plaintiff as having met his burden, thus shifting the burden to each of the individual defendants to show, if he can, that his bullet did not do the damage.

One argument for shifting epistemic burdens from victims to injurers is that in some cases injurers have more reliable or better information than do victims. So courts might allow the burden to shift from plaintiff to defendant when it has grounds for believing that the defendant, but not the injurer, has better information material to determining what happened.[4] Interestingly, in *Summers* the defendants are in no better position to illuminate what really happened than is the plaintiff. Requiring the defendants to show the absence of a causal connection is tantamount to imposing liability upon them, and, cannot be justified as a way of developing reliable evidence about what happened. In the conventional view, the best rationale for shifting the burden in *Summers* simply is that as between an innocent victim and two negligent defendants, it is better to let the loss fall on a negligent person whose conduct was in fact harmless than to have the loss fall on a party who was in every sense free from fault or blame.[5]

Rules that impose epistemic burdens have liability implications. If the burden is shifted to defendants to show that a loss is not their doing on the grounds that defendants have more reliable information about what has occurred than do victims, then whenever a defendant is unable to convince a jury that he was not at fault or otherwise responsible for the harm, he would be liable. On the other hand, if the burden of presenting evidence to a jury adequate to establish that the harm was the defendant's fault falls to the victim, failure to meet the epistemic burden would leave the victim liable for her losses.

The same liability rule – for example, the rule that injurers are liable only for the losses their fault occasions – can have very different substantive outcomes depending on the procedural rules in effect. The most important of these rules are the ones imposing epistemic burdens. The choice of these rules is driven in part by epistemic considerations. Which party is in the best position to know what happened? On the other hand, the rules governing epistemic burdens are not designed simply to develop the best available information. At bottom they appear to reflect the view that the burden of presenting evidence and of convincing a jury should, other things being equal, fall to that party who seeks to apply the public power to enforce the imposition of her loss on another. Thus, epistemic and other rules of administrative justice are constrained by considerations of political morality.

11.2 POSITIVE DEFENSES

If and when a victim is able to meet the burden of presenting evidence adequate to shift her loss to the injurer, the injurer is normally given the opportunity to present countervailing evidence aimed at defeating her responsibility. For example, suppose the victim can show that the injurer's fault substantially contributed to her injury with a degree of warrant so compelling that were the defendant to offer no resistance, any jury would find the injurer liable to her. Rarely can we expect a defendant to offer no evidence on her behalf. The question at this juncture is what is a good reason for shifting the loss back to the victim.

When defendants attempt to defeat responsibility after the prima facie case against them has been made, they offer *positive defenses*. These defenses can take many forms, ranging from establishing one's immunity from liability[6] to demonstrating the plaintiff's contributory negligence. The relationship between the procedural rules and the substantive ambitions of tort law has been insufficiently addressed by theorists, and I am as much at fault in this regard as anyone. Moreover, with the exception primarily of Richard Epstein, few theorists have analyzed the role of positive defenses in the theory of liability.[7]

To this point, I have distinguished between two kinds of substantive liability rules: fault and strict liability. I have also suggested that the same rules can produce different outcomes depending upon the organization of the epistemic burdens of the parties. And I have pointed out the familiar fact that the liability rules themselves are not conclusory, that in a typical case, meeting the demands imposed by the liability rule shifts the relevant burdens. The ultimate effects of tort law on the goals of accident law are a function of the interplay among substantive rules, positive defenses and epistemic burdens. Any fully adequate theory of tort law should explore all dimensions of the problem.

11.3 INCOMPATIBLE STANDARDS OF LIABILITY

A defendant performing the same action under the same conditions can be liable for whatever losses her conduct occasions if the act in question is covered by a principle of strict liability, but free from the burdens of repair if the issue is to be resolved by applying a fault standard. And what of victims who can recover under one rule but not under the other? Surely one can argue with some force that either the fault of the injurer is relevant to determining whether one has a right to repair or it is not. How can it be that fault matters if the injury is the result of a car accident caused by another motorist, but is irrelevant if the auto accident is the result of a defect in the way the car is manufactured? And what of the uncertainty at the margins of any scheme of liability that distinguishes cases that are covered by one liability rule from those covered by another liability rule? Uncertainty diminishes the welfare of all; unprincipled uncertainty, that is, uncertainty without justification, wrongly and unjustifiably reduces everyone's welfare. At first blush, it would seem odd

216

at least, and unjust at worst that some cases are governed by a principle of strict liability while others are covered by a standard of fault liability.

Is there a principled way of drawing the distinction between fault and strict liability? Are both forms of liability defensible? Are they defensible on different grounds? Is the best explanation of fault liability that is required by justice, whereas strict liability is defensible as a departure from justice necessary to reduce accident costs? Or can only that body of cases governed by fault liability be defended? Or is strict liability defensible and fault liability not?

11.4 THE FAULT IN FAULT LIABILITY

The fault principle holds that an injurer will not be required to make good his victim's losses, even if he has caused them, unless he is at fault in having done so. When an individual acts, we can distinguish two aspects of the situation that might be at fault. On the one hand, the *action* may be at fault; on the other, the *actor* may be at fault for having done it. We distinguish between fault in the doing and fault in the doer. An action is at fault when it fails to measure up to the relevant standard of conduct. An actor is at fault in his doings whenever his conduct exemplifies some shortcoming in him, usually a defect in character or motivation. Faulty doings need not evidence defective motivation, and defective motivation need not result in faulty doings.

These two aspects of fault are illustrated by the distinction we draw between two ways of defeating them: excuses and justifications. When an actor offers an *excuse* for what she has done, she might accept that what she has done falls below the relevant standard of conduct. Instead, she denies that her conduct, if wrong, is attributable to any shortcoming in her character or motivation. She ought not be blamed for what she did, even if what she did is the sort of thing people in general get blamed for doing. In contrast, when an actor *justifies* what she has done, she denies that the action is, all things considered, wrong. By this she might mean that the

217

action in fact does not fall below the appropriate standard, or that her conduct satisfies the more basic or important norm that grounds the particular norm from which her conduct appears to deviate, or even that her action is an exception to the principle that action contrary to the relevant norm is wrong.

In offering an excuse, an actor typically seeks to deny responsibility or blame for action she may be otherwise prepared to acknowledge is wrong. In contrast, in offering a justification, an actor often embraces responsibility for conduct she contends is, at the least, permissible and, on occasion, obligatory. In the conventional view, conduct that is excusable is not generally conduct that ought to be encouraged – even if the agent ought not be blamed for having performed it – whereas conduct that is justifiable ought to be encouraged. Or, somewhat more weakly, even if we do not mean always to encourage conduct for which individuals have a justification, we mean never to discourage it.

Tort law distinguishes among three ways in which conduct can be at fault: A person can act negligently, recklessly, or with wrongful intent. In the first case, the actor imposes risks a reasonable person would not have, and it does not matter whether he is alert to the fact that the risks are unreasonable. In contrast, a reckless person acts in conscious disregard of risks he knows to be unreasonable. It is not a condition of intentional torts that the person intended to do harm or to act wrongfully, that is, to act in violation of some rule or standard. Rather, someone commits an intentional tort if she intends to perform some act, does perform it as a result of her intending to, and the act is wrong under some description of it. If the act turns out to be harmful, the tort is an intentional one, even if the agent does not intend to do it under the description that makes it wrongful.[8]

The bulk of fault liability involves negligence. In torts, an actor is negligent if she fails to exercise the care of a reasonable person of ordinary prudence. The failure to exercise the care of a reasonable person is a failure to exercise due care, and a failure to exercise due care is negligence. Negligence, then, "is conduct, not a state of mind."[9] In order for a person to be negligent in torts, it does not matter whether he knows that the risks are unreasonable, nor does it matter whether he could have done other than what he did. Failure to measure up to the standard of reasonable care, whether or not one is capable of doing so, suffices to render one's conduct negligent. In this sense, ascriptions of fault (negligence) are not normally defeasible by excuses.[10]

An individual can be at fault in torts even if he has an excuse for the shortcomings in his behavior. If a person has a good excuse for what he has done, he is not to blame for his conduct. Liability that is not defeasible by excuses, is liability without blame. In torts, liability for negligence is liability that is not defeasible by excuse.[11] Fault liability in torts, especially liability for negligence, therefore, does not require culpability or moral blameworthiness. Blameless agents can be held liable in torts; and fault can be the basis of their liability. Fault liability may be liability without blame.[12]

This suggests the rather odd conclusion that fault liability in torts is really a form of liability without "fault." This apparent contradiction can be resolved by recalling the distinction between fault in the doing and fault in the doer. Fault liability in torts refers to fault in the doing, not in the doer. An agent is at fault in torts whether or not the fault in his conduct marks a shortcoming in him.

11.5 THE STRICT IN STRICT LIABILITY

In torts, fault liability may be liability without blame. In the *criminal law*, liability without blame, that is, liability that is not defeasible by an excuse, is strict liability. Does that make fault liability in torts strict liability? If fault liability in torts is a form of strict liability, then what is strict liability in torts?

An individual who is charged with negligence in torts is still capable of defeating liability by showing that what she did was, all things considered, reasonable. Reasonableness is a defense against fault liability. To show that what one did was in the circumstances reasonable is to show that what one did was justified or permissible. Thus, ascriptions of fault liability are defeasible by justifications, if not by excuses. We can then define strict liability in torts as liability that is defeasible *by neither excuses nor justifications.*

There is an element of strict liability in fault liability in the sense that it is not ordinarily defeasible by excuses, and so a person can be liable for her fault without being to blame for anything. On the other hand, if the conduct is negligent, then it is wrongful in the sense of being unreasonable. Strict liability in torts is imposed not only if the agent is blameless *for* her conduct, but also if her conduct *is* blameless, even if, in other words, it is the right thing to do in the circumstances. Fault liability may be strict, but strict liability really is.

We can put the difference between fault and strict liability in terms of the distinction between fault in the doing and fault in the doer. Fault, especially negligence, liability requires fault in the doing, but not in the doer. Strict liability requires neither.

11.6 TORT LIABILITY AND MORALITY

Most philosophers who have come to study tort law – and, unfortunately, few have – do so after they have learned something about the criminal law. Their understanding of the role of excuses in law is developed within the theories of criminal and moral responsibility with which they are familiar. The reason that alleged wrongdoers are given the opportunity to offer excuses to fend off criminal liability or moral responsibility is that we believe it is wrong or inappropriate to sanction, punish, or blame someone for conduct that reveals no defect of character or motivation. H. L. A. Hart, for one, treats the restriction on punishment that only the guilty be punished to be a demand of justice.[13] How is it that both fault and strict liability in torts have missed or chosen to ignore this obvious truth about the way in which justice constrains liability?

The common understanding of the role of justification in

the theory of liability is similarly nurtured by the philosopher's familiarity with the conditions of criminal and moral responsibility. Conduct that is justified is conduct that is, on balance, correct, or at least permissible. Conventional wisdom is that it is wrong to discourage the desirable. Strict tort liability in torts does precisely that, however. Strict liability in torts, after all, is liability imposed upon individuals whose conduct, all things considered, may be reasonable or desirable. How is it that tort law has failed to appreciate this fact about conduct that is justified?[14]

All liability in torts is fundamentally strict liability in the sense that it is imposed whether or not the agent is to blame for her conduct. And sometimes it is worse even than that, as at least some of the time, liability in torts is imposed for the consequences of perfectly desirable or defensible activities. We said at the outset that a defensible tort law would reduce accident and administrative costs and meet the demands of justice. Chapter 12 details some of the ways in which fault and strict liability, separately or jointly, can serve the economic ends of tort law. But it appears obvious, at least at first blush, that everything in tort law flies in the face of justice.

Losses almost always fall at least initially on victims apparently for no reason other than it would be costly to shift them to someone else. Victims rarely cause their own injuries, nor are they typically at fault in having done so. This appears to be an injustice to victims. Occasionally, losses do get shifted from victims to others – usually, but not always, injurers. But the losses are shifted either on the basis of fault or strict liability principles. Both impose liability without regard to the blameworthiness of the injurer; they "punish" someone who may have done nothing wrong. Strict liability imposes losses on some people who have not only not done something morally wrong; they may well have done something morally desirable. This appears to constitute an injustice to injurers.

Tort law is unjust either to victims or injurers, probably to both. How can anyone hope to find expressed in tort law any

221

of the demands of justice? Perhaps we would be better served simply to admit that tort law is a legal aberration; it is not designed in any way to satisfy the demands of justice. Rather, it is an institution whose singular purpose is an economic one: to minimize accident costs, to allocate risks efficiently ex post when contracting to do so ex ante is unavailable.

It is too soon to give up. The obstacles are clear and formidable. Our task is to provide an account of the demands of justice that makes defensible the principles of both fault and strict liability, as well as the need to settle some cases under one principle and others under the other. We must begin by forgetting just about everything we have "learned" from studying the philosophy of the criminal law.

11.7 TORTS AND CRIMES

The differences between torts and the criminal law are so fundamental that the net result of applying one's understanding of the criminal law to torts is bad philosophy and total confusion. Let me illustrate by emphasizing two differences. When an accident occurs, costs are created. Someone has to bear those costs. No matter how hard we may wish them away, they won't disappear. The only question is, Who should bear these costs? If, for example, we restrict the decision of who should bear the costs to the victim and her injurer, then a decision that the injurer should not bear the loss implies that the victim should.

This feature of tort law has no analog in the criminal law. Suppose a defendant is charged with committing a certain crime punishable by ten years imprisonment. Let's suppose further that although the defendant has acted in a way that fits the objective criminal standard – the *actus reus* requirement – he did so under duress or by mistake. These are typically thought of as excusing conditions, and the defendant's failure to exhibit *mens rea* is adequate to free him from criminal responsibility. But if the defendant goes free, there is no other person, for example, the victim – if there is one – who must then serve ten years behind bars. The costs in the sense

of the relevant prison term don't have to be borne by someone or other. They have to be borne by whoever is responsible for the crime, and if no one satisfies the conditions of
responsibility, then they are not to be borne by anyone.[15]

Tort law allocates risk. Every case is an opportunity to affect the nature and level of risk-taking activity. The law of
torts affects risks ex ante by assigning liability ex post. Tort
law affects risks by shifting or redistributing losses. We need
not deny that the criminal law also allocates risk or that it
aims to reduce risk. Even if the criminal law does reduce
risk, it does so by imposing costs in addition to those that
arise as the result of criminal misconduct. Tort law reduces
risk by allocating the costs of accidents, not by adding costs
to those that it imposes on injurers while letting the other
costs fall on victims.[16]

The demands of justice in tort law have to be sensitive to
its central feature, namely, that any decision is a liability decision: losses always must fall on someone. Similarly, the demands of justice in the criminal law must be sensitive to its
central feature, namely, that punishment is the imposition of
an additional cost which need not be imposed on anyone,
which no one other than the deserving need bear – costs, in
fact, that no one other than the deserving should bear.

Another fundamental difference between tort and criminal
law warrants our attention. Insurance contracts may be perfectly appropriate for discharging one's obligations under the
law of tort. Insurance contracts spread risk. As noted in
Chapter 10, it would be hard to imagine that insurance contracts would be permissible vehicles for discharging one's
criminal responsibilities. To see this, suppose we put together a group of twelve of us in an insurance pool to share
the risk of criminal sanction for fraud. Imagine that the penalty for fraud is twelve years. One of us commits insurance
fraud and each of us serves a year in prison. Now there are
all sorts of good reasons – from moral hazard to adverse selection – for doubting whether such insurance would be offered in the market. That's not the point. Even if such insurance were available, most of us would find the practice of

223

allowing individuals to insure against criminal liability deplorable.

11.8 FAULT, JUSTICE, AND EXCUSES

Whether imposed strictly or based on the fault principle, tort liability is not generally defeasible by excuses. The standard of liability is objective in this sense. Now suppose an accident occurs. If we frame the question of who is to bear the costs of a particular injury to exclude everyone other than the victim and the injurer, then to hold that the injurer should be free of the burden of rendering compensation because, although she injured the victim, she did so through no culpable fault of her own, is to impose those costs upon the victim, who may be both free of fault of any sort and in no way causally responsible for bringing the loss upon herself. There may be, in other words, even less justification for letting the loss remain the victim's responsibility than for shifting it to the injurer. The injurer may be without moral fault, but if she is legally at fault, that may mark a morally relevant difference between her and her victim in deciding which of the two ought to bear the costs of the accident.

Now suppose that the accident occurs, but that neither the victim nor the injurer is even legally at fault. Legal fault cannot mark the relevant moral difference. Nevertheless, the loss must fall either on the victim or the injurer. If we decide that we ought not impose the loss on an injurer who acted reasonably though injuriously, then we leave the loss on the victim who may also have acted reasonably and *not* injuriously. Here the fact that neither injurer nor victim is at fault in any sense does not distinguish injurer from victim. The difference between them may be that the injurer, but not the victim, caused the loss, and that may be difference enough to impose the costs on him. This conclusion may be controversial. Even if it is, recognizing the way in which the problem of who pays is structured leads us away from total condemnation of strict liability. Though strict liability imposes the costs on an injurer who may have acted reasonably, it

224

still imposes the costs on the injurer, rather than on a "passive" victim.

We began this discussion by condemning strict liability. Then we showed that fault liability has an element of strict liability. That made us dubious about fault liability. We are now in the process of trying to salvage them both. The first argument we have advanced is based on emphasizing the distinction between criminal and tort liability. Tort law allocates risk. It allocates risk ex ante among agents by imposing costs ex post. Its domain is losses. When an accident occurs, there are losses that must be borne by someone; they will not evaporate. Liability without blame may be inappropriate in the criminal law, but legal or tortious fault may be a morally relevant reason for deciding on the incidence of a loss when the loss must be borne by one party or the other. And in cases in which no legal fault is present, the fact that one person caused the loss may also count as a morally relevant difference between them for the same purposes. Thus, within this framework, there can be a limited defense of both strict and fault liability.

But what about the charge that strict liability in particular is counterproductive? Strict liability in torts imposes costs on permissible or justifiable conduct. The point of allowing individuals to free themselves of the burden of liability by offering a justification in morality and in the criminal law is that we do not want to discourage conduct that is in fact justifiable. Liability discourages conduct. It should not be imposed on justifiable conduct, that is, conduct that we do not want to discourage. Therefore, strict liability in torts is wrongheaded at best, indefensible at worst.

At some level, this objection is both valid and unhelpful. Strict liability is necessarily imposed on one party or the other whenever an injury results for which no one is at fault. Not to impose liability on the injurer is to impose it on the victim, and vice versa. Both, ex hypothesi, are faultless. Liability on either is strict liability. Consequently, the costs of engaging in either the victim's or the injurer's activity will go up, however reasonable engaging in either may be. One or the other reasonable activity will be "discouraged."[17] It is hard to condemn a practice as morally wrongheaded when it is logically inescapable.

11.9 FAULT AND STRICT LIABILITY — AGAIN

In defense of strict liability, we have argued that sometimes the fact that one person's conduct injures another may suffice to impose the loss on the injurer when one or the other must bear the cost. But if the injuriousness of a person's conduct is sufficient to impose liability, does not that make the fault condition otiose? Whenever there is fault liability, the causal condition is also satisfied; and if the causal condition is satisfied and marks a morally relevant difference between injurer and victim, the fault condition cannot be necessary. If causation suffices from a moral point of view to distinguish defendants from plaintiffs, then our defense of strict liability has undermined our hopes of finding a defense of fault liability.

If the fault principle is unnecessary from the moral point of view as a condition for justly settling on the incidence of a loss, there is much else that can be said against it. The costs of administering a fault system are extraordinarily high.[18] For most torts in the modern world, the amount of information which has to be developed and correctly interpreted is staggering. Just consider how difficult it is to determine whether a manufacturer has created a product according to the best available design. Determining the best available design will require that the jury determine the appropriate expenditures in research and development, and so on.[19] Administrative costs are reduced, sometimes significantly, if claims to repair can be assessed without regard to the fault of the parties. If fault is unnecessary to decide justly on the incidence of a loss, then get rid of it.

We have to avoid reaching strong conclusions too quickly. In truth, we never eliminate fault from the liability formula; even strict liability typically has a fault dimension. Let me explain. We can distinguish liability rules from one another in at least two dimensions. The first dimension concerns the conditions that must be satisfied in order for the presumption of the initial liability rule to be overcome. So the fault liability rule holds that the initial presumption in favor of victim liability is overcome if the victim can show that the injurer is at fault. This differs from the strict liability rule in that under strict liability the same presumption is overcome if the victim can show that the injurer caused the victim's loss.

The second dimension of a liability rule concerns what we referred to earlier as the positive defenses that someone can offer on her behalf once the initial presumption is overcome. In this regard, consider two versions of the rule of strict liability. In the first case an injurer is strictly liable and he is given no opportunity to defeat his liability by pointing to some failing in the victim's conduct. In the second case an injurer is strictly liable but is given the opportunity to defeat his liability by showing that the plaintiff himself is at fault in contributing to the accident's occurrence. Strict liability often allows the defendant the positive defense of victim negligence or fault.

The principle of strict liability with the defence of victim fault has the following logical form:

1. The injurer has to bear the victim's losses unless the loss is the victim's fault.[20]

Now let's put the principle of fault liability in logical form. What is it that the fault principle implies? We usually think of it as a principle of injurer liability, and we state it roughly as follows:

2. An injurer is liable to his victim if and only if he is at fault in causing her harm.[21]

But that's not all the principle implies, is it? No; the fault liability principle implies that if the injurer is not at fault, the loss remains the burden of the victim, *whether or not the victim is at fault.* The rule of fault liability, therefore, has a rule of victim liability contained within it, and it is a rule of strict liability. If we wanted to capture completely the rule of fault liability, it would read something like this:

3. The victim is strictly liable for her losses unless she can establish the fault of her injurer in having occasioned them.

If strict liability is really the principle that an injurer will bear the costs of accidents unless she can establish that the harm is entirely or largely the victim's fault, then fault liability is the principle that the victim will bear the costs of accidents, whether or not she is at fault, unless she can establish that the harm is the injurer's fault. And that means that the principle of fault liability has an element of strict liability, strict victim liability, at its core, and that the principle of strict liability has an element of fault liability at its core.

11.10 WHAT MIGHT WE MAKE OF THIS?

Suppose you did not know much about the actual substantive principles of tort liability, but you had some rough understanding of the conventional distinction in ordinary moral theory between a person's being held strictly liable and his having liability imposed on him only if he is at fault. It is very likely, I would guess, if forced to choose between strict and fault liability for accident costs, that you would choose fault liability. Considerations of fairness or justice would seem to favor such a judgment, quite without regard to economic or cost-avoidance considerations.

If we have shown anything, it is that this initial judgment may not be warranted, or at least that the intuitive grounds on which it likely rests are indefensible. First, we have seen that because fault liability, especially for legal negligence, is objective – conduct, not a state of mind – it is not defeasible by what would ordinarily count as an excuse. That makes negligence or fault liability a kind of strict liability, that is, liability without blame. Second, we have seen that fault liability has another, deeper dimension of strict liability. For under fault liability, victims are strictly liable if their injurer is not at fault. Both aspects of strict liability figure in the rule of fault liability. But it gets worse for the advocate of fault liability. In strict liability the injurer is held accountable only if her conduct causes another harm, whereas the sort of strict liability imposed on victims under the guise of the fault rule does not require that the victim cause her own loss. She may be liable even if the harm she suffers is *caused* by her faultless injurer. And this is not a result that would have obtained had her case been litigated under a rule of strict (injurer) liability.

If anything, the argument to this point suggests that strict liability may be preferable to fault liability. As long as we understand that both are really forms of strict liability defeasible by a positive defense of the other party's fault or negligence, the choice between them is a choice about who should bear the costs of accidents when neither party is at fault. And if the fact that one person's conduct causes the harm is a morally relevant feature of the situation, then, other things being equal, the loss should fall on injurers when it must fall strictly on someone. Strict injurer liability expresses this conception of fairness (if it is one); strict victim liability does not. Thus, from the moral point of view alone, strict liability is preferable to fault liability. That, I take it, is a surprising conclusion.

11.11 TWO CONTROVERSIAL PREMISES

This conclusion, like others we have been drawn to, may also be a bit premature. The argument to this point makes two claims. The first is that strict and fault liability are mirror images of one another; both are forms of strict liability at their core. Strict liability is strict *injurer* liability; fault liability is strict *victim* liability. The plausibility of this claim depends on treating the situation under the fault rule in which a court refuses to shift a loss from the victim to her faultless injurer as a form of victim *liability*. The second claim is that insofar as both strict and fault liability rules are both strict liability rules, strict injurer liability is preferable to strict victim liability. The difference is that under strict injurer liability, faultless injurers are liable only if they *cause* harm, whereas under fault liability, faultless victims can be held liable whether or not they cause harm. Therefore, strict injurer liability is preferable to fault, that is, strict victim, liability.

The plausibility of both these claims depends on the plausibility of controversial premises. Strict injurer and fault liability are mirror images of one another only if the failure to shift losses from victims to injurers is a form of victim liability. As liability rules, strict injurer liability rules are preferable to fault liability rules only if the fact of causation makes a relevant moral difference. I explore the claim that causation matters from the moral point of view in Chapter 14. I do not think that causation matters in the way in which this argument requires it to. I want to close this chapter, however, with a brief discussion of the claim that we can treat a court's refusal to shift losses from the faultless victim to his faultless injurer as a form of strict (victim) liability.

11.12 IS STRICT VICTIM LIABILITY, LIABILITY?

There is no doubt that we can refer to the victim as having to *bear* a loss that she is not at fault for having brought about or for which she is not otherwise responsible. The issue is whether we can refer to her having to bear that loss as a kind of *liability* being imposed on her. The answer will depend on what we mean by "liability." In one sense, liability requires that a judgment be made that the party having to bear the cost is judged appropriate or deserving of it. The rule of strict victim liability neither requires nor makes any such judgment about the victim. It does not claim, for example, that the victim must bear his own loss because he acted in such-and-such way, or because he has defective character or the like. Instead, we can understand the court to be saying something like this: The victim must bear his loss, not because of anything about him but because of something about his injurer, namely, that there is nothing the injurer has done that warrants imposing the loss on him.

There is a significant difference between a court shifting a loss from someone else to you and calling you liable for those costs, and its refusing to allow you to shift those losses to someone else, refusing in other words to find anyone else liable for them. When the court refuses to shift the loss to the injurer, it does not say that the reason it *leaves* the burden on the victim is that the victim is, or ought to be, liable for the costs.

This objection rests on the proper use of the term liable, and the role such judgments play in conveying information about the underlying reasons for imposing liability. But this objection can be overcome once we remind ourselves of the information that is in fact conveyed by liability judgments in torts, as opposed, for example to those made in a criminal law. After one reads this chapter, for example, one would be hard pressed to claim that a liability judgment in torts conveys anything other than the following: For a complex set of reasons having to do with cost avoidance, insurance, and as yet unspecified demands of justice, the "liable" party has been determined to be in the best position to shoulder these costs. There is no explicit or implicit judgment of moral fault or character defect. Liability in torts is, on the face of it, a risk allocation judgment, not a moral one.[22]

Alternatively, one can object to the characterization of fault liability as a form of strict liability by drawing on a supposed difference between the public power being called upon to shift a loss from one person to another and its simply letting the loss lie where it has fallen. The latter does not involve liability, whereas the former does. The former involves *legal* events the latter, *natural* ones.

The doctrine that the loss should fall on the victim does, however, presuppose a kind of liability rule. It is not a statement about the natural course of events. Analytically, losses fall initially on victims. But the fact that the legal system proceeds in its determination of who should ultimately bear the loss by putting the burden of shifting losses on the victim itself involves a *judgment*. It is not analytic within tort law that losses *should* lie initially on victims. That they should lie on victims is a normative judgment, a judgment that for whatever reason – usually administrative cost avoidance – the burden should fall to victims. The claim that letting the loss lie on a faultless victim imposes no liability judgment is true only because the loss begins as the victim's "legal responsibility." It imposes no *additional* liability judgment, because it already presupposes one. The victim's legal responsibility is itself a function of an initial liability rule.

That losses lie on victims is either an analytic truth or a normative judgment. When we develop a legal institution for determining if and when losses that naturally (analytically really) fall on victims should be reallocated, we are working within a normative framework. When we say that the responsibility for making the case for shifting a loss should fall to victims, we are making a normative judgment. We are not describing natural facts. As a consequence of these reasons in favor of the initial victim liability rule, when we feel that a particular injurer has not acted in a way that warrants shifting the loss from the victim to him, we are *affirming the initial liability judgment*. We are not simply refusing to interfere with the natural course of events.

To sum up: (1) Fault liability based on the injurer's negligence is not ordinarily defeasible by an excuse. In that sense, both fault and strict liability in torts are forms of strict liability. (2) Strict liability in torts differs from fault liability in that an injurer can defeat liability neither by excuse nor justification. (3) Fault liability is really the rule that victims are strictly liable for their losses unless the injurer is at fault. (4) Strict (injurer) liability is really the rule that injurers are strictly liable for the losses their conduct occasions unless the victim is at fault. (5) Thus, fault and strict liability are mirror-images of one another. (6) Therefore, there are two dimensions of strict liability in fault liability. A *victim* can be liable whether or not she has done wrong, provided her injurer is not at fault. An injurer who is at fault can be liable even if his fault is not culpable, even, in other words, if he has an excuse for his doings. (7) One difference between strict and fault liability is that in fault liability, innocent victims who have not caused their losses can be liable for them, whereas under strict liability, innocent injurers can be liable only if they have caused another's loss. (8) If causing a loss is a morally relevant fact about someone, then strict liability may be preferable to fault liability. And that would be a surprising conclusion for anyone who begins by assuming that, if anything, fault liability would be preferable to strict liability.

This chapter sets the stage for the argument that follows. If fault and strict liability stand or fall together, then a defense of one must also be a defense of the other. Chapters 12–14 each consider accounts of tort law designed to defend both strict and fault liability. If strict liability is preferable to fault liability, it is because causing harm is a morally relevant aspect of an injurer's conduct. The moral relevance of causation is taken up in Chapter 14.

I deny that fault and strict liability stand and fall together. I deny as well that strict liability is morally preferable to fault liability. I do, however, accept one conclusion of this chapter, namely that letting a loss fall on the victim involves a kind of liability decision. I deny, however, that the only grounds for this liability decision are economic ones. Rather, as I will argue in Chapters 16–18, it may be permissible to impose liability on the victim when there is no one else who has a duty in justice to bear her costs. The duty to bear her costs, in turn, often derives from corrective justice. Corrective justice, moreover, provides the moral defense of fault liability we seek. It also has implications for strict liability. Before developing these arguments, we consider first those theories that seek to unify tort law under a single coherent principle. We begin with the principle of efficiency.

Chapter 12

The economic analysis of torts

Chapter 11 argues that all liability rules have an element of strict liability at their core. If this argument is correct, there may be no defense of the fault principle that is not also a defense of strict liability. If strict liability is not a matter of morality, then neither is fault liability. If the only defense of strict liability is an economic one, then the only defense of fault liability is an economic one as well. Only an account of tort liability rooted in considerations of economic efficiency can ground both fault and strict liability.

12.1 FAULT AND RETRIBUTIVISM

This argument moves too quickly. Perhaps there is a defense of the fault principle that we have not yet considered that renders fault liability a matter of justice, not just economics. One such argument rests on the principle of *retributive* justice. There are any number of ways of capturing the requirements of retributive justice. For the sake of this argument, suppose that retributivism is the view that wrongdoing deserves its comeuppance, or that a wrongdoer ought to be punished or sanctioned for his wrongdoing. By imposing liability on faulty injurers equal to the costs of the harm their wrongdoing occasions, we impose a penalty on them, and in doing so give them their just deserts. No such argument is available for the principle of strict liability. If sound, the retributive argument would render only part of tort law morally defensible. Strict liability would have to be defended, if it could be defended at all, on other grounds, perhaps economic ones. In that sense, tort law would be a mixture of markets and morals.

There are several problems with the retributive defense of the fault principle, however. First, doing retributive justice requires only that the faulty injurer suffer some penalty. It does not require that the penalty take the form of liability for the consequences of the wrong. Second, the wrong can be very slight and the damage enormous; or the wrong can be grave and the damage minuscule. In either case, making the victim whole will be unconnected to the extent of the wrongdoing. Third, even if liability for the costs of the harms one's faulty conduct occasions is the suitable penalty for wrongdoing, retributive justice fails to explain why the injurer compensates the victim. The aim of retributive justice is equally well served when the faulty injurer is made to forfeit a sum of money to the general tax coffers that reflects the degree of his culpability. Yet injurers paying compensation to victims is at the very heart of tort law, and the retributive principle gives us no account of that key feature of the practice.

Fourth, all individuals who are at fault are wrongdoers in the appropriate sense, though only some of the conduct that is at fault causes harm to others. Whereas the retributive principle holds that all equally faulty behavior should be subject to the same penalty, in torts, only faulty conduct that occasions loss is subject to liability. Tort practice cannot be explained as a matter of retributive justice; otherwise everyone who is at fault in the appropriate sense would be subject to tort liability, and they are not. Only those whose fault occasions harms of a particular sort are candidates for liability.[1] Finally, an individual can be at fault in torts without the defect in his conduct expressing a moral shortcoming in him. It is unlikely, therefore, that individuals who are at fault in torts are necessarily deserving of punishment, sanction, or any other expression of disapprobation. All this is implicit in the practice of allowing individuals to discharge their obligations in tort through insurance contracts. The retributive argument is unable to provide us with the explanation of the morality of fault liability that those who defend the existing practice as moral seek.[2]

12.2 OTHER OPTIONS

Efforts to ground tort law in a retributive interpretation of the fault principle must be abandoned. What options remain? One strategy is to deemphasize fault. This can be accomplished in a number of ways. Consider two alternatives. First, one can argue that both fault and strict liability are instances of a deeper criterion of liability. This is the approach taken by George Fletcher, who has argued that the deep principle of liability in torts is *nonreciprocity of risk*.[3] Individual injurers are liable if they impose nonreciprocal risks on their victims, and victims are entitled to recover whenever they are injured by nonreciprocal risk taking. Fault and strict liability simply articulate ways in which individuals under different circumstances impose nonreciprocal risks on one another. The second alternative does not so much deemphasize fault as much as it simply abandons it. It relies instead on the causal condition that is common to both strict and fault liability. The moral dimension of liability is captured by the fact that one person's conduct causes another harm, not the fact that in doing so one person, and not the other, is at fault. This approach is generally associated with Richard Epstein's work.[4] We touched on it in Chapter 11, and it is more fully discussed in Chapter 14.

These views either embed the fault principle in a deeper principle of liability and recovery, a principle in which strict liability can also comfortably rest, or else they simply deny the relevance of fault altogether. In contrast, one can try to reestablish the centrality of fault liability, and in doing so locate fault in some principle other than that of retributive justice, for example, the principle of corrective justice. This is the view I develop and defend in Chapters 15 through 18.

Each of these alternatives to the retributive argument has limitations. Non-reciprocity of risk denies that either fault or strict liability is fundamental, yet our tort practice suggests the primacy of both fault and strict liability. The theory of strict causal liability ignores fault altogether, when fully one half of every torts case book is devoted to explicating and evaluating fault liability. The principle of corrective justice encourages us to emphasize the justice of fault liability, but may have less to say about the justice of strict liability.[5]

It is against this background of failed and fragmented moral accounts of tort law that we ought to evaluate the economic alternative. Only economic analysis takes both fault and strict liability on their own terms. Only economic analysis offers a defense of both. Only economic analysis can explain why some cases are decided under the fault rule, and others are adjudicated under the standard of strict liability. Only economic analysis is comprehensive and coherent. If the goal of rational interpretation is to understand our practices as coherent and unified, only economic analysis can provide the sort of explanation we seek.

12.3 BASIC ECONOMIC ANALYSIS

Liability in torts can be either strict or based on fault. Consider fault liability first. If fault in torts is not coextensive with the conditions of moral fault or moral responsibility, that is unsurprising, because all the court ever means in ascribing fault to someone is to identify that person's conduct as economically inefficient. To be at fault is to act inefficiently. Negligence marks an economic failing in an action, not a moral shortcoming in the agent.

Suppose that you were both the injurer and the victim, so that whatever accidents we might imagine you causing someone else were ones you really caused yourself. Which of the accidents that you cause yourself would it be rational for you to prevent? How, in other words, should you determine your investment in prevention? Imagine that if you undertake a particular course of conduct, you would injure yourself, and that your injury would cost you $100 to repair. If you did not undertake that course of conduct, you could have prevented the injury, but you would have lost the opportunity to gain $25. You could prevent a $100 injury by incurring a $25 opportunity cost. Assuming that you are rational, that is precisely what you would do; you would prevent the greater injury at the lesser cost. On the other hand, if you would have to forgo $250 in benefits in order to prevent $100 in damages, you would not, as a rational agent, forgo the benefit. Instead, you would pursue the course of conduct, secure the gain, absorb the loss.

Generally, when the costs of prevention are less than the costs of the harm, you take precautions; when the costs of prevention exceed the costs of the harm, you incur the harm and save the costs of prevention. If there is uncertainty about the likelihood of the harm's occurrence, you will prevent all and only those injuries whose costs of prevention are less than the expected value of the harm.

This is the basic economic strategy.[6] Treat the injurer and victim as one person, then determine what investments in safety rationality requires. Because the individually rational strategy is always to maximize expected utility, the rational agent invests only in those precautions whose cost is less than the expected value of harm. That is the definition of rational prevention; rational agents take all and only cost-justified precautions. Once we know what the rational individual would do, we can determine the investments in safety that we want injurers and victims to make. If the law is to be rational, then we want liability rules that encourage them to act rationally in the same way that you do when you are both the injurer and the victim. In other words, we would want both injurers and victims to take all and only cost-justified precautions.

An agent who takes all and only cost-justified precautions acts reasonably.[7] The risks his conduct imposes are, therefore, reasonable risks. By the same token, the agent who fails to take cost-justified precautions acts unreasonably, and the risks he imposes are unreasonable. To be at fault in torts is to take unreasonable risks, and to take unreasonable risks is to fail to take cost-justified precautions. Thus, to be at fault in torts is to act in an economically inefficient manner; negligence is the failure to make optimal investments in safety.

It should come as no surprise, then, that we have had such difficulty in constructing a moral theory of fault. To be at fault is not to act in a morally culpable way or to fall below a standard of care with which one is morally compelled to comply. To be at fault is to act inefficiently; no more, no less.

12.4 THE MEANING AND GROUNDS OF FAULT

We can distinguish between analytic and normative dimensions of fault: What do we mean by fault? Why do we *impose liability* on the basis of fault? The economic argument we have just outlined provides an economic answer to both of these questions. To be at fault is to act in an economically inefficient manner. Liability is imposed on the basis of fault in order to discourage inefficiency. The distinction between the analytic and the normative questions is important because one can defend an economic theory of the meaning of fault, but a noneconomic or moral theory of the reason for imposing liability on the basis of it. For example, suppose that to act wrongly is to act inefficiently. Individuals who are injured by faulty conduct, so conceived, are wronged; their losses are wrongful ones. Still we might say that liability is imposed on the basis of fault, not to discourage inefficiency but to rectify wrongful losses.[8]

Thus, we can have an economic theory of the meaning of wrongdoing or fault and a moral theory for imposing liability on the basis of fault so conceived, the moral theory in this example being the principle that wrongful losses ought to be annulled. Even if the economist is correct in his analysis of fault, it will not follow that he is correct in his account of why liability is imposed on the basis of it.[9] An economic theory of fault, then, does not entail an economic theory of the point or purpose of imposing liability on the basis of it. So even if economic analysis provides the best interpretation of fault it

239

may not provide the best interpretation of the practice of imposing liability on the basis of it.

For similar reasons, it is possible to advance an economic analysis of liability based on fault without holding an economic analysis of the meaning of fault. For example, such a view might hold that liability is based on fault to discourage faulty behavior, but by faulty behavior we might mean conduct that violates norms of fairness or reciprocity. Typically, however in an economic analysis of tort law, the principle of efficiency provides both the understanding of negligence and the justification for imposing liability based on it.

12.5 EFFICIENCY AND STRICT LIABILITY

Strict liability is liability that is not normally defeasible either by excuses or justifications. A person is strictly liable in torts even if she could not have done otherwise, or even if she did what she ought to have done, that is, even if she acted with all due care. Strict liability is like fault liability in that a person may be held liable for the causal upshots of his doing even when he has what would ordinarily count as a good excuse for his conduct. Unlike fault liability, however, an injurer can be strictly liable for conduct that is reasonable or otherwise justifiable.

Again, we can distinguish between analytic and normative questions pertaining to strict liability. In what sense is strict liability a matter of efficiency? Why impose liability strictly? From the economic point of view, strict liability is an embodiment of the practice of internalizing externalities (or social costs). To hold someone strictly liable is to force him to shoulder the full costs of the activities in which he is engaged, whether or not he has an excuse or a justification for imposing some of the costs he does. Strict liability just means requiring someone to bear the full costs of his conduct. To return to the example in which the injurer and the victim are one person, strict liability is the practice of always making the victim's loss part of the injurer's cost calculations. In that way victim and the injurer are "one" – at least with respect

240

to the costs of accidents. Strict liability forces the injurer always to take into account the costs his conduct imposes on
others – thus, the phrase, "internalize externalities."

Like the rational person who is both injurer and victim, a
person held strictly liable will be driven to take all cost-justified precautions. Strict liability makes the injurer and the victim one person in this sense. Doing so forces agents who
pursue individually rational investments in safety to secure
collectively rational or Pareto efficient outcomes. Thus, one
good economic reason for imposing liability strictly is that it
encourages injurers to make optimal investments in safety.

The practice of internalizing externalities also enables us to
resolve a puzzle we first confronted in Chapter 11. Strict liability imposes costs on individuals who may have acted reasonably. In doing so it increases the costs of engaging in the
activity. In increasing the costs of the activity, it discourages
the activity. How can discouraging reasonable or otherwise
justifiable conduct be a good or desirable thing? That's the
puzzle. In response, we noted that in the case of faultless
accidents, strict liability will necessarily be imposed on either
reasonable injurers or reasonable victims, depending on
whether the underlying liability rule is strict or fault, respectively. In effect, we said that even if it is always wrong to
discourage reasonable or justifiable conduct, doing so is
sometimes unavoidable.

The practice of internalizing externalities enables us to understand the ways in which imposing costs on justifiable
conduct can be defended as permissible, not simply toler-
ated as unavoidable. Strict liability increases the costs of engaging in various activities, and thereby discourages them,
but it does not discourage individuals from engaging in desirable activities at appropriate or optimal levels. Provided
the marginal benefit of engaging in the activity at a given
level exceeds the total marginal cost, the agent will engage
in the activity even if he is held fully liable for its social costs.
Because the benefits exceed the costs, the activity is desirable. Imposing the social costs on the agent is more costly to
him than not doing so, but it does not prevent him from

engaging in desirable activities at the levels at which it is *socially* desirable for him to do so. When the total marginal cost exceeds the marginal benefit of an activity, it is no longer desirable that the agent engage in the activity at that level, and his having to shoulder the social costs of the activity will discourage him from doing so. Strict liability just means internalize externalities. Internalizing externalities is desirable because it promotes efficient resource allocation. And it does this by placing the burden of deciding whether the benefits exceed the costs on the relevant agent, that is, the injurer. In short, strict liability does not discourage desirable or justified activities. Instead, it encourages agents to engage in all activities at their optimal (desirable) levels. That is precisely what efficiency requires and strict liability produces.[10]

Again, there may be noneconomic justifications for a practice that encourages individuals to internalize externalities. In one such view, if individuals are not compelled to internalize externalities, they are permitted to treat those individuals who are the victims of their conduct as means to their own ends, and not as ends in themselves. Externalizing costs would be a violation of the Kantian requirement of treating others as ends in themselves. Thus, it may be possible to defend the principle of strict liability and its requirement that injurers internalize externalities on Kantian grounds. I am not defending this view any more than I am defending economic analysis. Instead, I am trying to illustrate the point that the same analysis of the practice is often compatible with different normative theories of it, as well as the distinction between the meaning of strict liability (or fault), on the one hand, and the reasons for imposing liability on the basis of it, on the other.

There is an economic analysis of both fault and strict liability in both of the senses we have discussed above, an analysis, in other words, of both the meaning of the relevant standard and the reason for imposing liability on the basis of it. In both strict and fault liability the key idea is inducing individuals to take cost-justified precautions. Failure to take such precautions constitutes fault. In fault liability, *courts* determine whether someone is at fault in this sense and impose liability if he is, not otherwise. In strict liability, the *liable party* determines whether accidents are worth their costs (to him). If he is rational, he will take all and only cost-justified precautions. The difference between the two, then, is who determines which actions are worth their costs: courts under the fault rule, and potential injurers under strict liability.[11]

If both strict and fault liability can be defended on grounds of economic efficiency, the only question that remains is why in some cases liability is imposed on the basis of fault whereas in others cases it is imposed strictly. How, moreover, should we decide which cases are to be resolved under which standard?

12.6 WEALTH EFFECTS

Strict liability shifts wealth from injurers to victims, and fault liability shifts wealth from victims to injurers. One reason for imposing strict liability in some cases and fault liability in others would rest on the existence of a social preference for shifting wealth to victims at the expense of injurers under some conditions, a preference that is presumably reversed in other categories of cases. Thus, we may have strict manufacturer or products liability, not because fault liability is any less efficient but because there is a social preference for shifting wealth from manufacturers to consumers. In ordinary automobile accident cases we have a rule of fault liability, which some might take as evidence of the existence of the opposite social preference for the distribution of wealth.

This argument relies on the distinction between the efficiency and distributive dimensions of liability rules. Two equally efficient liability rules can have different distributive consequences. Distributive concerns are important in torts in a way in which they may not be in contracts. Thus, the difference between strict and fault liability, that is, the fact that some cases are decided on the basis of strict liability, and others are based on the fault principle, is to be understood on distributive grounds.

This argument is not persuasive, however. First, it would be surprising were there a social preference for victims in some cases but for injurers in others. I am hard pressed to imagine that the victims of defective products are to be favored in this regard and the victims of automobile accidents are not. Second, what could count as evidence of such a preference other than the fact that some cases are decided under the rule of fault liability whereas others are adjudicated under strict liability? Third, and most importantly, it is simply not true that the only dimension on which fault and strict liability differ is the distributive one. In fact, fault and strict liability differ from one another along efficiency and insurance dimensions as well as along the distributive dimension.

12.7 ONE- AND TWO-PARTY ACCIDENTS

The discussion so far has assumed that all accidents that should be prevented can be prevented, or their risks optimally reduced, by a rule that imposes one or another kind of liability on the *injurer*. This is the assumption that only the injurer's conduct is relevant to preventing those accidents worth preventing or to reducing optimally the probability of their occurrence. In fact, we can distinguish this case from two different kinds of cases. In one, although the injurer can take cost-justified precautions adequate optimally to reduce the probability of harm, so too can the victim. Imposing liability, either strict or fault, on either the victim or the injurer would suffice to secure optimal deterrence. Imposing liability, either strict or fault, on either of them is not necessary, however. What I mean by this is that if we want to reduce optimally the risk of harm, it's not necessary that we impose liability on the injurer, nor would it be necessary that we impose it on the victim. It is necessary, however, that we impose it on someone, but that's not something we have to worry about, because the problem is structured in such a way that we cannot avoid doing so. Imposing liability on the injurer would do the trick, as would imposing it on the victim, which is equivalent simply to refusing to impose it on the injurer.

How should we decide? Here, Guido Calabresi's famous dictum, that we should impose the loss on the cheapest cost avoider, provides the answer. Either strict or fault liability will do. When both parties can optimally reduce risk, the loss should be imposed on that party that can reduce the risk at the lowest cost: the cheapest cost avoider.

We can contrast the case in which either party's taking precautions is sufficient optimally to reduce the costs of accidents with the case in which the conduct of both parties is separately necessary and jointly sufficient optimally to reduce the costs of accidents. In this case, both injurers and victims must take all cost-justified precautions. In such cases a rule of strict (injurer or victim) liability cannot be efficient. The reason is obvious. Consider the case of strict injurer liability. Under such a scheme the victim is always fully compensated for her loss. Thus, she is indifferent between not being harmed, on the one hand, and being harmed and fully compensated for the harm, on the other; she is indifferent between her positions ex ante and ex post. In these circumstances she has no incentive to take precautions. *Ex hypothesi*, if the probability of the accident's occurrence is to be optimally reduced, she must take all cost-justified precautions. Therefore, a rule of strict liability cannot be efficient in this case – what economists call the two-party accident case.

In order for any rule of liability to be efficient, it must encourage all relevant parties to take all cost justified safety measures. The rule of strict liability imposes the full costs on only one of the parties, and therefore fails to coordinate the behavior of victims and injurers in the two party case. We need to augment the strict liability rule in a way that encourages victims to take precautions. We can do this by allowing injurers to defeat liability by showing that the victim is at fault. This would be the rule of strict liability with the defense of (plaintiff) contributory negligence (or fault), that is the rule of strict liability as we characterized it in Chapter 11.

On the usual assumptions of rationality and agent competence, such a rule will be efficient in the two party case. Victims know that they will have to bear *all* of their costs whenever they fail to take rational, that is, cost-justified precautions. In taking such precautions they insure that they will never bear the full costs of any accident that might befall them. Whenever the costs of precautions are less than the expected costs of the harm, taking such precautions is rational. Injurers know that this is the way rational victims will operate, and know therefore that they will be liable for the full costs of any accident that they cause. Therefore, they cause only those accidents that are rational for them, that is, those accidents whose marginal benefits exceed their marginal costs. *Strict liability with the defense of plaintiff fault is efficient.* In the two party case, we first divide the problem into two parts. We determine which liability rules would induce efficient investment for victims and which would induce efficient investment for injurers. Then we conjoin the two. Like the mathematician, we take a complex problem, then reduce it to simple problems we have already solved.

Interestingly, the rule of simple negligence is also efficient in the two party case. In fact, two different arguments we have already discussed entail this conclusion. If the rule of strict liability with the defense of plaintiff negligence is efficient, then it follows logically that the rule of simple negligence or fault is efficient also. Why? The answer is that the rule of fault liability is really the rule of strict victim liability with the defense of injurer negligence, which is the mirror image of the rule whose efficiency has been demonstrated. If one is efficient because it coordinates the behavior of both parties, so must the other, and for the very same reason.

Victims will take all rational efforts to reduce the costs they must bear. But that would be true whether they would be held strictly liable or liable only when they are at fault. The contributory fault aspect of the fault liability rule is simply superfluous in this regard, that is, as an incentive imposed on victims to take cost-justified precautions. Once they know that their injurers, if rational, will never be at fault, they have all the incentive they need to take optimal precautions. They don't need a rule telling them they will be liable otherwise. They will be liable in any case, and what they want to do is minimize their costs.

Although both strict and fault liability are efficient in the one-party accident case, strict liability is not efficient, though fault liability is, in the two-party case. Strict liability with the defense of plaintiff negligence is also efficient in the two-party case, as is the rule of fault liability with the defense of contributory negligence.

12.8 ACTIVITY LEVELS

At any given level at which individuals engage in risky activities, various liability rules, alone and in combination with one another, can be efficient. Liability rules, however, may differ from one another with respect to the ways in which the benefits of optimal risk reduction are distributed. This is not surprising. If we imagine a world in which there are only two activities, one in which the victim engages and one in which the injurer does, equally efficient rules will make one of the activities more costly relative to the other. So if the victim's activity is watching television in his basement and the injurer's activity is driving cars into peoples' basements, then a rule of strict liability will make basement wrecking more expensive relative to television watching, whereas a rule of fault liability (provided we can imagine nonnegligent basement wrecking) will make the costs of watching television rise in relation to the costs of driving into basements. This in turn may cause some people to move away from television watching and take up basement wrecking, and that will increase the amount of basements being wrecked at the hands of former television addicts.

The general point is that the distributive dimension of the liability rule affects the efficiency of the rule because it can affect activity levels. In a one-party accident at a given level of activity, both strict and fault liability will be efficient. Because fault liability will shift wealth to injurers, it may increase the extent to which individuals engage in the activity

247

relative to the extent to which they would do so under a rule of strict liability. These efficiency and distributive dimensions of liability judgments are inextricably linked to one another.

The usual distinction in the formulation of strict fault liability rules is that a plaintiff trying to make a case under the latter has to prove everything that someone trying to make a case under the former does and she has to prove fault as well. It follows, therefore, that the costs of litigating fault cases must be higher than the costs of litigating strict liability cases. This differential would be particularly striking in products liability cases, where establishing the existence of a design defect would call for extremely expensive (and often baffling) expert testimony. So the conventional view is that litigating fault is much more expensive than litigating strict liability.[12]

The conventional view is probably correct, but one should not misinterpret its implications. In those cases covered by strict liability, the costs of litigation can be quite high because so much may ride on establishing the causal connection between injurer action and victim harm. Issues of causation, which may not be fully and expensively delved into in the fault context, may be extensively and expensively pursued under strict liability. So the differential between the two liability rules need not be as great as one might otherwise think. Sure, fault is expensive to determine, but causation can be expensive as well, especially when demonstrating fault is not at issue. Resources spent in litigating fault under the fault rule may be shifted to litigating causation under strict liability.

Once at trial, litigating under fault is more costly than litigating under strict liability, but how about the incentives these rules create to litigate in the first place? If we assume that a case that requires a plaintiff to demonstrate the truth of fewer claims is an easier case to make than one that requires her to

248

show more, then strict liability is easier for victims to litigate than fault liability is, other things being equal. If it's easier to win, victims are more likely to sue, other things being equal. So strict liability encourages litigation as compared to fault liability, provided the rewards for successful litigation are similar. If the awards are the same, then the only difference is the probability of obtaining them. Higher probability means higher expected value. The higher the expected value of an activity, the more of it we are likely to see. Strict liability is administratively cheaper, but it encourages more litigation.

The conventional view is that fault liability increases un-certainty relative to strict liability. That is because even if it is hard enough to determine who caused what, it is harder still to know what a court or jury will say about whether there was fault on either the plaintiff's or the defendant's part. It is also part of the conventional view that the more both parties to litigation agree about what is likely to occur at trial, the more likely they are to settle.[13] As between the two, then, strict liability is more likely to encourage settle-ment than is fault liability. Strict liability may encourage liti-gation, but may also encourage pretrial settlements of in-completely litigated disputes.

It is a further question whether settlements are, from the point of view of optimal risk reduction, a good thing. When injurers settle, do they pay too little to be adequately in-duced to take all the necessary precautions, and so on? Even if settlements adversely affect deterrence, they have a salu-tary effect on cases that do get litigated. If individuals were prohibited from settling disputes once litigation had begun, all disputes would be litigated to conclusion. If we assume a finite budget for litigating at the public's expense, this means that all sorts of resources would be used that could have been saved by allowing parties to settle. Those resources could have gone to litigating the more difficult cases in which the disagreement about the expected outcome may be greatest. So there is a way in which we can think of settlements as allowing us to spend our resources where they are most needed.

12.10 INSURANCE

One important way in which strict and faulty liability differ is with respect to the system of insurance contracts that grows up around them. A system of strict liability encourages individuals to buy insurance against the losses their conduct may cause others; this is third-party insurance. Victims have no incentive to buy insurance against injury if they will be compensated by their injurers. On the other hand, under a fault system, injurers will buy insurance against liability for their fault and victims will seek coverage to protect themselves against faultlessly occasioned losses. The nature of the liability rule determines the distribution of first and third-party liability insurance.

All forms of insurance spread risks. Nevertheless there are important ways in which first and third-party insurance schemes differ from one another. In an important series of articles, George Priest has argued that relative to first-party insurance, third-party insurance increases the costs of moral hazard and adverse selection.[14] Moral hazard has both ex ante and an ex post components. Ex ante, the mere fact that someone is insured against loss increases the probability that he will engage in risky activity. Ex post, moral hazard affects victims more than injurers. If a victim knows that her costs are fully covered by insurance, her incentive to keep those costs down to their efficient level is reduced.[15]

The problem of adverse selection arises in trying to put together an insurance pool. In its worst form it leads to what can be called *pool unraveling*. An insurance company charges each member of an actuarial group the cost of insuring the average person in that group. To make a profit, members of the insurance group must be optimally diverse with respect to the risks they pose. The spread can be neither too small nor too large. When the spread is too large, the least risky members of the pool have an incentive to leave because they are being charged far too much. If they are able to leave – a function in part of the competitiveness of the industry and the capacity of other insurers to segregate risk – then the average level of risk rises, as does the average cost of guarding against it. What was true first of the least risky individuals in the pool is now true of the next least risky in the set. They are now being charged far too much. They leave, the process continues, and the pool unravels.

The capacity of an insurer adequately to segregate risks into suitable risk pools depends on the information available to the insurer about the relative riskiness of insureds. The conventional view is that such information is more easily obtained under a first-party regime. Just compare the amount of information your life insurance company is able to get about you that would be relevant to its assessment of your chances for a life of a certain duration with the information a company insuring blenders against defects has about the people who use blenders. Wouldn't the insurance company be better able to devise optimal insurance if each blender user sought out insurance to protect him – or herself from loss owing to defective blenders? The success of insurance depends on information available to the insurer and that in turn depends on the liability rule in effect.[16]

Chapter 13

Reciprocity of risk

We can identify at least three different moral solutions to the failure of the retributive argument. In one, the morality of tort law depends on downplaying the significance of the fault principle. Alternatively, the morality of tort law may depend on eliminating the fault principle altogether. Finally, one can accept the fault principle, but think it is grounded in some other principle of justice.

One can *downplay* the significance of fault by showing that fault is not itself fundamental but is, instead, one way of exemplifying a deeper, more fundamental standard of responsibility or justice in liability and recovery. One can *rid* the moral theory of tort law of its reliance on fault by arguing that some other aspect of the formula for liability and recovery, for example, the causal requirement, expresses the morally relevant component of both liability and recovery in torts. The fact that an injurer has caused another a loss, not the fact that she is at fault (she may not be) for having done so, morally grounds recovery and liability. Finally, one might argue that a moral principle other than the principle of retributive justice can explain and justify the relevance of fault to both liability and recovery in torts. Perhaps tort law expresses the ideal of corrective, not retributive, justice.

In Chapter 12, I summarized aspects of the economic analysis of tort liability. In Chapters 15 through 18, I develop the theory of corrective justice in tort law. In Chapter 14, I discuss the theory of strict liability as a way of eliminating tort law's reliance on the fault principle. In this chapter,

Reciprocity of risk

I want to consider ways in which the fault requirement can be downplayed by exploring the sense in which it expresses a more fundamental, general principle of liability and recovery: the principle of liability for nonreciprocal risk taking. This is the view generally associated with George Fletcher.[1]

13.1 LIABILITY AND RECOVERY

The principle of nonreciprocity of risk begins with the important distinction between the grounds of recovery and liability. This is the distinction between the reasons that justify a victim's right to recover and those reasons that warrant imposing liability upon someone. Though Fletcher distinguishes between the grounds of recovery and liability, he argues that nonreciprocity of risk grounds both. An individual is entitled to compensation if she is harmed by another's nonreciprocal risk taking. An injurer is liable if she harms someone through her nonreciprocal risk taking *and she has no excuse* for doing so.[2] "[A] victim has a right to recover for injuries caused by a risk greater in degree and different in order from those created by the victim and imposed on the defendant – in short, for injuries resulting from unexcused nonreciprocal risks."[3]

The formula for liability has two elements: injury through nonreciprocal risk-taking and the absence of an excuse. The fact that a defendant can defeat liability by having an excuse implies that there are cases in which victims are entitled to repair – because they have absorbed losses that result from someone's nonreciprocal risk taking – but for which no one, including the injurer, has a responsibility grounded in considerations of justice to make good her losses – because the injurer has an excuse adequate to free her from the burden of liability.

We need to ask three questions about Fletcher's proposal. What makes risks reciprocal (or nonreciprocal)? What principle of justice or morality makes liability and recovery based on the principle of nonreciprocity of risk a matter or morality

253

or justice? Can the law of torts be plausibly construed as exemplifying the principle of nonreciprocity of risk?

Risks are reciprocal when they offset one another. When the
risks A and B impose on one another are of the exact same
type and magnitude, they are reciprocal. That's the easy –
and the least likely – case. Nonreciprocal risks are different
in degree or kind from one another.[4] When the risks individuals impose on one another fail to cancel one another out in
this neat way, can they still be reciprocal or offsetting? If the
only risks that are reciprocal are ones that are equivalent in
both degree and kind, then almost all risks individuals impose on one another will be nonreciprocal. Fletcher himself
is not especially helpful in this regard. I want to suggest that
we can do better. My suggestion is that we define nonreciprocity of risk in terms of expected value or disvalue.

A imposes risks of type a^* on B. B imposes risks of type b*
on B. The risks A and B impose upon one another are offsetting if and only if the expected value of the harm created by
A's conduct $p(a^*)$ is equal to the expected value of the harm
with which B's conduct threatens A, $p(b^*)$; the risks A and B
impose on one another are reciprocal if and only if $p(a^*)$ equal
$p(b^*)$; otherwise, they are nonreciprocal.

It is natural to wonder whether this quantitative account
of offsetting or reciprocal risks reduces reciprocity of risk to
a form of economic analysis. If it does, the standard of nonreciprocity of risk might then fail to be a genuine alternative
to economic analysis. Let $p(a^*) = A^*$, and $p(b^*) = B^*$; then either
$A^* > B^*$ or $A^* < B^*$ or $A^* = B^*$. However great in absolute terms
A^* and B^* may be, A and B impose reciprocal risks on one
another whenever $A^* = B^*$; otherwise, the risks A and B impose on one another are nonreciprocal.

Under reciprocity of risk, if $A^* = B^*$ then recovery would be
unavailable for either A or B, whether or not A and B are
negligent. If $A^* > B^*$, A would be imposing non-reciprocal risks
with respect to B, whereas if $B^* > A^*$, B would be doing the

same with respect to A. In the first case, B could recovery in justice for whatever harms A's conduct causes him, whereas in the latter case, A could recover in justice for whatever harms B's conduct imposes on him. Liability is a function only of the relevant inequalities in expected value.

In economic analysis, the expected value of a harm plays a different role in determining whether liability or recovery is appropriate. In economic analysis, liability based on the negligence of the injurer is a function of the relationship between the expected value of the harm and the costs of preventing it, not on the relationship between the relative expected disvalues of the *injurer's* and the *victim's* conduct. This means that even if $A^* = B^*$, A may be at fault and B not, or B may be at fault and A not. The costs to A of preventing the harm, PA^*, may be considerably less than A^*, whereas the costs to B of preventing the accident, PB^*, may be greater than B^*. in other words, it is possible that $PA^* < A^*$ and $PB^* > B^*$, even when $A^* = B^*$. Therefore, even if $A^* = B^*$, A would be at fault from the economic point of view, but B would not be. From a purely economic point of view, A can be liable to B, even though neither could recover against the other under the principle of reciprocity of risk.

A simple arithmetic example might help. Suppose the expected value of the harm A imposes on B is 100, and that the expected value of the harm B imposes on A is also 100. Then the risks A and B impose on one another are reciprocal. In the event of an accident between them, neither A nor B could recover against the other under the theory of reciprocity of risk. On the other hand, suppose it would have cost A 50 to prevent the harm to B, whereas it would have cost B 200 to prevent the harm to A. Thus, in economic terms, A would have been negligent, but B would not have been. Thus, in economic analysis even though A and B impose reciprocal risks on one another, A can be negligent with respect to B, but not vice versa. In the event of an accident, B might be able to recover against A, whereas A would not be able to recover against B.

Reciprocity focuses on the risks individuals impose on one

255

another, whereas efficiency focuses on the risks individuals impose relative to the costs of prevention each would have to incur. Reciprocity of risk moves beyond cost-benefit standards of recovery and liability toward a standard of liability and recovery that emphasizes the *relationship between injurers and victims* or among the members of a community of risk takers.

13.3 FAULT AND STRICT LIABILITY

We can illustrate how the principle of reciprocity works by considering some examples. In one case you are mindlessly watching MTV in the basement recreation room. All of a sudden a car slams through the foundation into the room, runs you over, destroys the television, and generally disrupts your good time. Your first instinct is that the culprit must be Tip Gore, but, alas, it is the rhythm section of the Dead Milkmen. (Apparently, they are a particularly hard-driving, hard-core band.) The risks you impose on the band by sitting mindlessly in front of your television set are different from those – both when you watch and listen to the Dead Milkmen on MTV, and when they bombard your basement – the band imposes on you.

In another case you and I are motorists. As long as we drive nonnegligently, we impose roughly the same type and magnitude of risk on one another. In order for one of us to impose nonreciprocal risks on the other, either you or I would have to drive in a fundamentally different way, for example, negligently. There are some activities that by their very nature impose nonreciprocal risks. One example is provided by the case of the Dead Milkmen. In contrast, other activities involve communities of reciprocal risk takers. Motoring is one such activity; playing risky sports, like hockey and football, is another. Reciprocity of risk calls for a standard of strict (injurer) liability in cases of the first sort, whereas it suggests a fault standard in the cases of the latter sort. That is, in cases involving a community of reciprocal risk takers, imposing nonreciprocal risks amounts to imposing risks beyond the level of normal risk. Risks beyond the norm within a community are negligent or faulty ones.

Nonreciprocal risks are always characterized relative to a background of risk imposition. In the Dead Milkmen example, that background implies that any risks the band imposes on you will be nonreciprocal in the relevant sense. The expected loss the band imposes on you exceeds the expected loss you impose on it. In the motoring example, the community of nonnegligent driving defines the relevant background of risk taking. Nonreciprocal risks must stand out against that background. In order for that to occur, the risks must be beyond the norm, that is, they must be what we otherwise refer to as negligent.

If everyone in our neighborhood keeps pet dogs, then provided we take reasonable precautions with respect to their care and maintenance, all of us impose reciprocal risks on one another. If, however, a new neighbor decides to bring a pet mountain lion onto his property, then it does not matter one bit how much care he exercises in maintaining it safely on his property. The presence of the animal imposes nonreciprocal risks on everyone else. Should the lion escape and cause damage to persons or property, it will be no defense that the owner took every reasonable precaution to maintain the animal safely. The standard of liability is strict. Understood in this way, it follows that a community of individuals all of whom keep pet mountain lions on their property would, other things being equal, be imposing reciprocal risks on one another. That would make the case of the mountain lion more like the motoring example. In order for liability to be imposed for an escaped mountain lion, one would have to show negligence in the way in which the owner maintained his "pet."

The community of risk takers defines the background of risk. Thus, in *Rylands* v. *Fletcher* the court held that storing water on one's property could, in some circumstances, be the sort of thing that subjects one to strict liability.[5] Two theories were advanced to support the holding, both of which could be recast in terms of the reciprocity of risk formula: (1) Building reservoirs in rural England is not the sort of activity in which people generally engage; and (2) water is the sort of material like a mountain lion that is harmless when it is safely tucked away on one's property but is likely to cause significant damage should it escape. A person who keeps water in a reservoir is imposing the sort of risk that is uncommon to the community of risk takers; it does not constitute part of the background of risk. Not only is the risk of escaping water unusual, it is dangerous. Thus, it is different both in kind and degree from the sort of risks members of agrarian England typically impose on one another.

In sum, fault and strict liability are not fundamentally different standards of liability. Rather, they are distinct ways of giving expression to the same basic principle of liability and recovery suitable to differing circumstances, namely, the principle of nonreciprocity of risk. This is the sense in which the principle of reciprocity of risk downplays fault.

The reciprocity of risk theory of liability and recovery is ambitious. It promises, if sound, to provide an account of liability and recovery that spans the entirety of tort law, both strict and fault liability alike. In this respect, it is like economic analysis. Whereas the economic analysis understands strict and fault liability as different expressions of the general principle of efficiency, reciprocity of risk conceives of fault and strict liability as different embodiments of the general principle of reciprocity of risk. Thus, reciprocity of risk shares with economic analysis the ambition of providing a unified account of the entirety of tort law, as well as the analytic strategy of interpreting the difference between fault and strict liability as different ways of expressing a commitment to a more fundamental principle under different circumstances. Unlike economic analysis, however, reciprocity of risk seeks to provide a moral foundation for tort practices, not an economic one.

13.4 RECIPROCITY AND EXCUSES

One feature of the retributive argument is that it makes a person's liability depend on the relationship of his conduct to a criterion of blameworthiness. It does not impose liability on the basis of any relative features of the victim's and injurer's conduct. That distinguishes it from the principle of reciprocity, which appears to focus entirely on the relationship between injurers and victims.[6] So the standard of justice that the principle of reciprocity of risk exemplifies should reflect the standing of individuals relative to one another in some appropriate dimension.

As Fletcher conceives it, the principle of reciprocity of risk permits the imposition of liability on injurers only if they lack an excuse for their conduct. The possibility of an injurer's defeating liability by presenting an excuse seems oddly out of place within a theory that focuses primarily on the relationship between injurers and victims. In contrast to both retributive and economic theories, reciprocity is designed to draw our attention to the relationship between victims and injurers, and away from evaluations of the conduct of either against independent standards of efficiency or blameworthiness. The emphasis on excusing conditions appears to express a concern for the relationship between the injurer's conduct and some standard of responsibility independent of the injurer's relationship to the victim. To that extent, the emphasis on excusing conditions appears inconsistent with the thrust of the overall thesis. If the flaw in a person's conduct is the imposition of nonreciprocal risks, why should it matter whether a particular agent is morally to blame for this shortcoming in his conduct? Is there a sense in which allowing excuses to defeat liability can be made compatible with the overall theory?

Let's begin by drawing a distinction between two ways in which excuses can defeat ascriptions of liability.[7] We discussed one of these at some length earlier when we contrasted excuses with justifications. In this sense, an excuse defeats liability by showing that the actor's conduct exemplifies no defect in his character or motivation. Excuses of this sort defeat liability by defeating the ascription of blame upon which liability can sometimes be grounded. Liability in torts, especially for negligence, does not require blame as a condition of liability, however, and for that reason, it is not generally defeasible by excuses of this sort. Were these the sort of excuses Fletcher had in mind, his account would fail to provide anything like a plausible interpretation of our current practices for the same reasons the retributive argument fails to do so.

On the other hand, liability appears to require human agency. Therefore, one way of defeating liability of any sort is to show in a particular case that the conditions of human agency are not satisfied. Actions are a subset of events; they are things done by individuals volitionally or intentionally. Moving one's body under a hypnotic trance is something that happens to one, not something one does. Liability is for the consequences of actions performed; actions require agency. Excuses that defeat agency are essential to any theory of liability, including the theory of liability for nonreciprocal risks.[8]

Even if we accept the distinction between those excuses that are designed to defeat liability by defeating ascriptions of culpability and those designed to defeat liability by defeating ascriptions of agency, we need an account of why agency matters to a theory of liability, whereas culpability does not. One answer is that even if an individual can be held liable for what she has done, whether or not her doing it is culpable in any way, she cannot be held liable in justice for things that, although they involve her, happen to her, not by her.

Suppose Jane mistakenly shoots Joe, thinking he's a bear. She may not be to blame for her honest mistake. Nevertheless, we can imagine a theory of liability according to which she must make good Joe's losses. Mistakenly or not, she did shoot him. On the other hand, if Sarah places a device in Jane's brain that, unbeknownst to Jane, triggers Jane's shooting Joe, then Joe gets shot but through no action of Jane's. In a sense, Jane discharges the rifle, but her doing so does not constitute an action of hers, and for that reason she does nothing for which she can be held liable. Liability requires agency whether or not it requires blame. Or so the argument goes.[9]

This explanation of the role of excuses in the theory of liability has some obvious appeal, but it is not without its share of problems. I have argued that a decision by a court to let a loss fall on the victim under the negligence rule when the defendant is not at fault should be understood as a form of victim liability. Indeed, following Guido Calabresi, I would want to refer to the fault rule as a form of strict victim liability.[10] If that is correct, then *tort law is always holding people liable for losses in which their autonomous agency is not implicated.* Victims are often held liable in the absence of agency under the fault rule. Thus, in tort law at least, liability does not require agency. If liability does not require agency, excuses that defeat agency should be as irrelevant to the general theory of liability in the same way that excuses that defeat blame or culpability are.

In short, there are no grounds for holding Joe, the victim of Jane's shooting, responsible for his own losses or for holding Jane responsible for them when she was the unwitting instrument of Sarah's diabolical device. Neither Joe nor Jane acted. The shooting is something that involves both of them, to worse effect in Joe's case, but the agency of neither. Suppose that for whatever reason Sarah could not be liable to Joe. Then the choice would be to let the loss fall on Joe or to shift it to Jane. If we claim that Jane cannot be held liable on the grounds that she performed no action, why shouldn't the same argument be available to Joe? If the absence of autonomous agency is adequate to defeat Jane's liability, it should be adequate to defeat Joe's as well. However we decide this question, we cannot rest our decision on the principle that it is never fair to hold people liable for things that happen to them rather than for things that they do.[11]

There is an important distinction between excuses that defeat agency and those that defeat culpability, but it is not obvious that the distinction is adequate to justify the role of excuses in the theory of nonreciprocal risk taking. Victims as well as injurers can fail in a particular case to act, and to impose a loss on the victim because what the injurer does fails to exemplify human agency is to impose the loss on the victim who may also have failed to act in any way that makes the loss her doing. However relevant the distinction between these two kinds of excuses may be, it will not do the needed work in the theory of liability.

Let me suggest an alternative. To uncover why excuses matter, rather than looking to the legitimacy of holding the injurer liable, we should look to the *victim's claim to repair*. The reason it matters whether Jane acted when she discharged the shot that hit Joe has more to do with Joe's potential right to recover than it does with the grounds of Jane's liability. To see this, forget about Sarah's role in all this, and suppose that Jane shot Joe as the result of an unexpected, uncontrollable twitch. Twitches are not actions, and harms that result as a consequence of twitches do not involve human agency. If we put the matter before us in terms of the relationship of excuses to liability, we would have no reason for imposing liability on either Jane or Joe. If human agency were a condition of liability, neither's conduct exhibits the sort of human agency that could count as a ground for liability.

Rather than asking whether Jane or Joe should be liable, we might ask instead whether Joe has a *right* to compensation in justice. It might turn out that someone can have a claim in justice to compensation only if the loss he suffers is the result of another's agency. This, I believe, is true of corrective justice.[12] If tort law seeks to implement corrective justice, which I believe in large part it does, then Joe has no claim in justice to recover. That is not to say that he has no claim in utility or charity or benevolence to repair. He may well, but so, too, do the victims of natural disasters like hurricanes and earthquakes. Those losses, however real, do not typically trigger claims to recovery in torts, nor are the claims they trigger matters of corrective justice. When someone like Joe suffers damage from another's bodily movements, but not the actions of others, his losses are like those that result from natural disasters or acts of God. My view, then, is that excuses that defeat agency are relevant, not because an individual who has not acted cannot be held liable but because a person who is injured as the result of events that do not implicate human agency has no right in justice to repair.

If Joe has no right to repair, then Joe might end up bearing his own costs. He is liable for his costs not because he deserves them; certainly not because he acted in some way that makes them his doing. He is liable because he has no right in justice to their repair, and (we might suppose for this argument) there are no other grounds for imposing his costs on someone else. In my admittedly unconventional view, excuses that defeat agency are essential in tort law, not because they defeat liability but because they are relevant to the legitimacy of the victim's claim to recovery.

We have considered three different accounts of the role of excuses in the theory of liability for nonreciprocal risk taking. The first is that excuses are relevant to a just theory of liability because a theory of liability can be just only if it imposes liability on the basis of *culpability.* Excuses defeat culpability and, therefore, liability. I reject this account of the role of excuses in tort liability if for no other reason than tort liability is typically unconcerned with culpability. The second theory argues that excuses are relevant if and when they defeat *agency,* because liability can be imposed justly only if it is imposed for conduct that implicates the injurer's autonomous agency. I reject this thesis as well, largely because liability in torts does not require autonomous agency. Strict victim liability under the fault principle is liability without agency. The third theory argues that excuses are relevant because only individuals who are injured as the result of human action have a claim in corrective justice to repair, and part of the inquiry in any torts case is whether in fact the victim has such a right.

Which of these views of excuses is compatible with Fletcher's account? Which account, if any, does he advocate? Fletcher recognizes as well as anyone that liability in torts does not require culpability. Thus, he would not defend excuses on the grounds that they demonstrate the absence of blame or fault. Only excuses that establish the absence of autonomous agency are relevant to tort law. These accounts fall into two categories: those in which the absence of agency defeats liability and those in which the absence of agency defeats the claim in corrective justice to repair.

There is some reason to think that Fletcher himself adopts the view that excuses matter because the absence of human agency undermines justice in liability. Recall that his general thesis is that whereas an individual who is injured by a non-reciprocal risk taking of another is entitled to repair, only those whose nonreciprocal risk taking is unexcused (in the relevant sense) are candidates for liability. He explicitly claims that being injured by nonreciprocal risk taking suffices to ground a claim to repair whether or not the "event" that creates the risk is the result of an autonomous human action. On the other hand, only autonomous human actions are candidates for liability.

This view is wrong on both sides of the liability–recovery equation. First, liability does not require agency, as is true of strict victim liability. Second, individuals can have nonreciprocal risks imposed on them by sources other than autonomous human agency. Lightning imposes nonreciprocal risks, yet the victims of lightning are not generally thought to have claims to repair in corrective justice or in torts.

Only the third account of the role of excuses in a just theory of liability is defensible. Though there are grounds for thinking that this is not Fletcher's view, the most sympathetic reading of his overall thesis would require substituting it for the thesis he appears to hold. From here on, we shall say that in any theory of justice in torts, excuses are relevant because they bear on a defendant's agency, not his culpability. Agency, in turn, matters because the victim's claim to repair in justice depends on his being the victim of another's conduct. Agency matters to recovery even if it does not bear directly on liability. There is an important difference between issues of liability and recovery on the one hand and those of moral right and duty to repair, on the other. I have argued that because an individual can be held liable in torts even if the loss for which he is liable is not his doing, not, in other words, the result of his doing, torts does not require human agency as a condition of liability for loss. Therefore, to the extent excuses that defeat agency are allowed to excuse an individual from liability, it cannot be because liability cannot be imposed on individuals who have not acted. There must be another explanation.

My suggestion is that often in deciding on the incidence of a loss, the court begins by trying to determine whether the person who seeks repair, the plaintiff, has a *right* grounded in morality to compensation. It may be that under the relevant principles of justice (as I will argue), the victim can have a right to repair only if there is someone who has a duty in morality to compensate him, and someone can have a duty to repair only if he is responsible for imposing a wrongful loss upon the victim. Excuses are then relevant to this inquiry about the moral rights and duties of the litigants because they bear on whether the injurer is responsible for the victim's loss in the sense required by the relevant moral principle. If the defendant has an excuse, then the victim has no moral right to repair under the relevant principle of justice. Because the loss remains to be allocated, determining that it cannot be allocated under the relevant principle of justice does not conclude the inquiry. It may be imposed either on the victim or the injurer, though in neither case will it be imposed because in the appropriate sense the loss is the liable party's doing. And that is why excuses are relevant to an agent's duty to repair in justice, but not to liability. An agent can be liable for a loss in tort law though he has an excuse,

Rectifiable wrongs

whereas he cannot have a duty in corrective justice to make amends under the same conditions: a duty in morality that could otherwise provide a ground of his legal liability.

13.6 RECIPROCITY AND JUSTICE

In what sense is liability and recovery under the principle of reciprocity a matter of justice? In defense of the reciprocity thesis, Fletcher cites Aristotle on corrective justice, but the argument he advances on its behalf relies on Rawls.[13] The difference is important. Rawls is concerned to articulate principles of distributive justice; Aristotle is concerned with corrective justice. We will explore corrective justice as a basis of tort liability later. For now, let's focus on the underpinnings of reciprocity of risk in a Rawlsian conception of distributive justice.

Citing Rawls, Fletcher argues for nonreciprocity of risk by constructing a principle of distributive justice that he takes to be an analog of Rawls's first principle of justice. Rawls holds that everyone is entitled to the maximum degree of liberty compatible with a like liberty for all. Fletcher contends that each individual is entitled to the maximum degree of security compatible with a like degree of security for all. Fletcher's security principle is neither a proper analog of Rawls's first principle nor a principle of justice. The security principle can be satisfied by a complete prohibition on human conduct. Security is maximized when free action is minimized. Maximum political coercion is not a requirement of justice, however.

Elsewhere Fletcher defines security as freedom from harm without compensation.[14] So defined, everyone has a right not to be harmed without compensation. This does not mean that individuals have a right not to be harmed; nor does it mean that injurers do wrong when they harm. Harm requires compensation. If an injurer harms another, then he must compensate his victims. Understood in this way, it is the fact that one has suffered harm that triggers the right to repair. Reciprocity of risk has nothing to do with it.

To maintain the centrality of the concept of reciprocity to the general thesis, Fletcher might reformulate the principle that is to confer moral relevance upon it. This can be done in a number of ways, each of which is problematic. First, he might redefine security so that it means freedom from exposure to nonreciprocal risks. The right to security is the right to be free from nonreciprocal risks. If the right one has is to be free from nonreciprocal risks, then recovery and liability do not depend on actual harm being done. Exposure is the wrong; harm is incidental to or evidentiary of it. The effect of this proposal is to eliminate from both liability and recovery what is currently central to both, the requirement of actual, as opposed to threatened, harm. And of course we still need a principle that tells us why individuals who have their security interest harmed are entitled to compensation. That is the heart of the tort remedy, and that part of it goes untouched by principles that seek only to articulate the nature of the underlying entitlement or interest.

It will not do to redefine security more narrowly, as freedom from loss owing to nonreciprocal risks, as that would merely restate the principle in need of justification as the criterion that is supposed to justify it. People are entitled to recover for harms caused by the nonreciprocal risk taking of others because there exists a principle that holds that individuals have a right to recover for harms caused by the nonreciprocal risk taking of others. Nothing Fletcher himself offers comes close to providing a defense of the moral relevance of nonreciprocity of risk.

If compensation in torts is sometimes a matter of justice – as I believe it is – that cannot be because all individuals have a right to the maximum degree of security compatible with a like security for all. The best argument for the principle of nonreciprocity of risk depends on arguments to be presented in the chapters that follow. Nevertheless, it can be sketched here. Suppose that there exists a principle of corrective justice that asserts that wrongful losses ought to be annulled. Then we can treat the principle of nonreciprocity of risk as one way of fleshing out the relevant conception of wrongful-

267

ness. Which losses ought to be annulled? Wrongful ones. Which losses are wrongful? Those that result from nonreciprocal risk taking.

13.7 RECIPROCITY AND THE CASES

The question that remains is whether nonreciprocity of risk can provide a plausible explanation of the cases. Unfortunately, it cannot. To see this consider two different sorts of cases. In one case a *nonnegligent* motorist hits a *negligent* pedestrian crossing the street against the traffic light. There is no account of reciprocity of risk that yields the result that the motorist and the pedestrian impose reciprocal risks on one another. I don't care how slowly an automobile moves or how powerful a pedestrian may be, cars impose nonreciprocal risks on pedestrians. Nevertheless, the motorist imposes no wrongful loss on the pedestrian; if anything, through his negligence, the pedestrian is responsible for his own demise. Tort law does not allow recovery in such cases, and the reason cannot be that the pedestrian and the motorist impose reciprocal risks on one another. This example shows, among other things, that the fault criterion is not just another way of expressing nonreciprocal risk taking. For here is a case of fault in which the faulty conduct is not the one that imposes the greater risks.

The second example involves *two negligent* motorists. Because the risks they impose on one another are roughly of the same degree and kind, we can say that they belong to a community of reciprocal risk takers. Now let's suppose that it is Hank's negligent driving that causes the harm to Charlie. That is, though both parties impose non-reciprocal risks on one another, only the negligence of Hank, not that of Charlie, contributes to the accident. In torts, Charlie can recover against Hank, and for the very good reason that he suffered a wrongful loss in virtue of Hank's mischief. If the theory of reciprocity of risk were correct, we could not explain Charlie's recovery.

It should be obvious that nonreciprocity of risk is an inadequate criterion of wrongfulness within the domain of corrective justice. Moreover, as this last example shows, nonreciprocity of risk is insensitive to the role of causation. Two individuals can impose reciprocal risks on one another, but liability and recovery can nevertheless be warranted provided the risks are negligent and those imposed by one party are causally efficacious. However attractive and ambitious the principle of reciprocity of risk may appear at the outset, it fails to provide the moral foundation for tort law we seek. If the theory of reciprocity fails to account for the cases because it fails to capture adequately the relevance of causation, let's turn our attention to an alternative account that rests almost entirely on the claim that the morality of both liability and recovery is a function of the fact that defendants *cause* injurers harm. This is the theory of strict liability.

Chapter 14

Causation, responsibility, and strict liability

No course in the first year curriculum is more baffling to the average law student than is torts, and for good reason. In the first two weeks, the student learns that causation is necessary for both fault and strict liability. Two weeks later the student learns that causation is meaningless, content-free, a mere buzzword. Whereas every torts instructor preaches to students the centrality of causation, virtually no tort theorist takes causation seriously.[1]

14.1 BUT-FOR AND PROXIMATE CAUSE

Ordinary lawyers and law professors are as confused about causation and the role it plays in liability and recovery as are their students. Lawyers analyze cause-in-nature, or metaphysical cause, what they call cause-in-fact, in terms of the *but-for test*. *A* is a but-for cause of *B* if and only if *B* would not have occurred but for *A*. The damage the cows cause the corn would not have occurred but for rampaging cattle; but it would not have occurred but for the corn being in a position where it could get destroyed by the cattle. Both the ranching and farming activities are but-for causes of the harm; the harm to one could not have occurred but for the other. Because both activities are causes in the but-for sense, the causal relationship that exists between them is too indiscriminate to justify imposing liability on either ranching or farming.

To solve this problem, tort lawyers introduce the concept

270

of *proximate cause*. Proximate cause picks out from the set of necessary conditions, or but-for causes, that event that liability can be legitimately grounded on. Determining which activity is the proximate cause of an event's occurrence will depend on considerations of policy and principle. For example, if the goal of liability is to reduce the probability of harm, then the proximate cause of some injury is that action (or omission) that could have reduced the harm's occurrence at the least cost, and so on. If the but-for test is too weak to ground liability, proximate cause is too strong. It is conclusory, not evidentiary. It is no wonder that tort theorists, who as torts teachers preach causation's centrality, as scholars find it nearly useless. But it is a mistake to give up on causation.[2] What we need, then, is an account of causation that is more restrictive than the but-for test, but which is weaker than the conclusory proximate cause test. In other words, we need an account of causation that can provide reasons of some weight for imposing liability.

14.2 CAUSAL PARADIGMS

This is the task Richard Epstein sets for himself. In a series of articles beginning with the classic "A Theory of Strict Liability,"[3] Epstein develops his theory based primarily on the concept of causation. Any such theory requires an account of causation that neither trivializes nor renders otiose the causal inquiry. As it happens, Epstein offers no general theory of causation.[4] That is, he gives no analysis of the truth conditions for propositions of the form X causes Y. Instead, he offers a series of paradigm cases in which we would normally speak of the conduct of one person as being the cause of another's loss. The strategy is to suggest to the reader that we generally have no difficulty in identifying causal connections, that there is no need, first of all, to hit on a theory of entitlements in order to determine the direction of the causal relationship, and that, when properly developed, the causal inquiry can provide morally relevant grounds for imposing liability.

271

Epstein distinguishes among four paradigm cases, those involving force, fright, compulsion, and the setting of dangerous conditions. Jones hit Smith; Charles scared Norma; Linda compelled Sam to frighten Martha and to hit Jody. These are all examples of sentences expressing causal relationships. Each fits into a more general category of causal relationship: force in the first case, fright in the second, and compulsion, force, and fright in the third. In each case the verb used to express the sort of causal relationship involved is transitive, which suggests that to the extent our language reflects the way in which we experience the world, the relevant causal relationship is directional, not reciprocal. Epstein's more important claim is that in each case in which it is true that *A* forces or frightens or compels *B*, and in which *B* suffers a loss as a result, there is good reason for imposing *B*'s losses on *A*. In each case causation provides a relevant moral reason for imposing liability on the injurer.

Epstein also emphasizes the distinction between the prima facie case and the conclusory case. His view is not that satisfying the causal condition is sufficient to warrant imposing liability on the injurer. Rather, his view is that satisfying the causal condition is sufficient to establish the prima facie case for both liability and recovery. If the victim meets her burden, the onus then shifts to the injurer to establish that he should nevertheless not be held liable. The injurer would have to present a similar argument to shift the loss back to the victim. That is, he would have to show that the victim actually caused the harm or contributed significantly to its occurrence. If he is unable to make his case, the prima facie case becomes conclusory.

There are three kinds of questions we can ask about Epstein's account corresponding to those we asked about George Fletcher's: Is the account of causation he gives adequate? By that I mean has he provided a theory of causation that falls somewhere between the innocuous and the question-begging? Does causation so understood provide morally relevant grounds for imposing liability and awarding recovery? Does the theory genuinely help us understand the practice?

14.3 CAUSATION AND RESPONSIBILITY

Originally, Epstein defended the causal condition as being required by a more general theory of personal responsibility, and he believed as well that the theory of responsibility he advocated could itself be defended on libertarian grounds.[5] During that period his entire work was very much antiutilitarian, antieconomic analysis and expressed the same concerns and cares that animates Fletcher, namely, that to the extent tort law makes recovery depend on the social utility of an individual's behavior, it can never adequately explain the sense in which recovery is a matter of right and compensation a matter of duty. Epstein no longer fears utilitarian or economic analysis, and in his latest work he toils to establish the fundamental compatibility of utilitarianism and libertarianism. He has even recently attempted to formulate a utilitarian theory of natural rights.[6]

Through the changes, Epstein has not given up the relevance of causation to the justice of liability and recovery. What's changed is the alleged principles of justice and morality that render causation relevant. Epstein has defended strict liability on at least four different grounds corresponding to four distinct normative theses: the responsibility thesis, the equilibrium thesis, the rights thesis, and the property thesis. According to the responsibility thesis, justice requires that we impose liability on all and only those individuals who are responsible for a harm's occurrence. Liability requires responsibility. The scope of one's responsibility is, in turn, coextensive with the causal upshots of one's volitional conduct.[7] One is responsible for all and only what one causes. Causation is morally relevant to establishing the prima facie case because responsibility is, and the causal relationship provides, the necessary link between responsibility and liability.

Epstein's account holds that there is a connection, first, between causation and responsibility and, second, between responsibility and justice in tort liability. One can object to Epstein's analysis by denying that either (or both) of these connections obtain. That is, one can deny that justice in tort liability requires that liability be imposed on the basis of responsibility. Or one can accept that tort liability can be justly imposed only if it is imposed on those who are responsible for their doings, but deny that responsibility is coextensive with causation.

The problem is exacerbated somewhat by the fact there are two different notions of responsibility. In one sense, responsibility is a matter of authorship. The author of an act is the person who is responsible in the sense that the act is his, not someone else's. But being the author of the act in this sense is not normally sufficient for imposing liability. Though the fact that it is my act may be a reason for holding me rather than you liable for its consequences, it is not yet a reason for holding me liable. In the normative sense of the term, responsibility is a reason not just for holding me rather than you liable; it is a reason for holding me liable. There is a loss in the world that I am responsible for, that I might be fittingly held liable for. In this sense, however, causation is neither necessary nor sufficient for responsibility.

Suppose it has snowed in your neighborhood for two weeks running, and you've done nothing about shoveling the snow from your walkways. Someone coming to visit you slips on the snow and breaks her leg. It is plausible to maintain that you are responsible for the injury and for the losses she has suffered. However, what caused her injury was her slipping on the snow. There was snow to slip on just because you were negligent in failing to shovel it; and you are responsible just because you were negligent in failing to shovel it; and you are liable just because you are responsible for her injury. You did not cause the harm. You could have *prevented* it, however, and you should have. Because you did not prevent the harm when you should have and could have, you are responsible for it; and you are liable for it because you are responsible for it. Here is a case of responsibility without causation. Liability may require responsibility, but responsibility does not require causation.[8]

In addition there are harms one causes, for which one is

responsible, that do not ground a claim to liability or recovery. In competitive markets producers try to undersell one another and, in doing so, attempt to take business from one another. When they succeed, it makes perfectly good sense to say that they have caused one another to suffer losses. The victims of competition are harmed no less than are the victims of traffic accidents. Still those individuals who, through their business acumen, are able to advance their positions at the expense of others are not normally viewed as having a duty either in morality or law for making good the losses of those who get the short end of the stick.

On the other hand, a businessperson who harms a competitor can sometimes be liable for the losses his conduct occasions. Whether he will be subject to liability depends on whether his business practices abide by the relevant norms. If someone drives out his competition by fraud and misrepresentation, then he may be liable for damages. But, then, it is not causation as such that provides the basis of liability. Rather it is the *wrongfulness* of the behavior, its failure to comply with the norms governing competitive business practices. Wrongfulness in this sense is a kind of fault in one's conduct. If the wrongfulness of a person's conduct is a condition of justly holding that person liable, then we would have failed in our bid to rid the moral theory of tort of its reliance on fault. We would have turned the theory of strict liability into a theory of fault liability.

14.4 CAUSATION AND EQUILIBRIUM

If we think of the world statically, we can, by taking some license with the term's more technical usage, refer to a full description of it at any time, t, what probability theorists call a state description of it, as constituting an equilibrium. The relationships among all the relevant parties are well ordered or balanced. The balance between the parties can be upset by one party imposing a cost or a loss on another. The only way to reestablish that equilibrium is to nullify whatever gains and losses have occurred. By requiring the injurer to make good his victim's losses, tort liability nullifies both the relevant gains and losses, thereby reestablishing the preexisting equilibrium. The principle of tort liability necessary and sufficient to reestablishing the preexisting equilibrium is the principle of strict liability.

This argument is as unsatisfying as it is simple. Nullifying gains and losses may be a good thing, it may even be the right thing to do, but it cannot be the right thing to do because in doing so one re-creates the same equilibrium that existed before, and for two very different kinds of reasons. First, under the best of circumstances, by annulling all gains and losses the most one could do would be to create a different equilibrium that has normatively relevant properties in common with the preexisting equilibrium. One can nullify gains and losses; one simply cannot nullify *events* in the world.

Second, there is no reason to think that to the extent that doing so is possible, recreating the status quo ante is always defensible or desirable, let alone a requirement of justice. For the sake of argument, let's suppose that by rendering compensation to his victim an injurer could re-create the status quo ante. What reason would we have for claiming that justice requires re-creating any and all equilibria by nullifying all departures from it? Can justice impose such a demand independent of the justice of the preexisting state? The claim that it does may be no more than a particularly unenlightened form of status quo-ism.

The underlying idea must be either that the preexisting state is just and, therefore, worthy of constant re-creation, or that certain ways of departing from the status quo are inappropriate or unjust independent of the desirability or justness of the status quo ante.[9] In the first case the preexisting state's justness is supposed to provide an enduring and sufficient reason forever to re-create it. This is a wholly unsatisfactory idea, plausible only if we could imagine no ways of altering even a desirable state of the world justly. As soon as we recognize the possibility of altering the status quo justly – say, by gifts and voluntary exchanges – we cannot seriously advance the view that, even if it is just, the status quo should forever be re-created. This shifts our attention at least momentarily from the justness of the status quo to the kinds of possible departures from it. Voluntary exchange and donations are legitimate ways of departing from the status quo; negligently harming or intentionally defrauding are not.

The equilibrium thesis brings us to roughly the same place that the responsibility thesis does. The status quo may be either just or unjust. If it is unjust, it is not obvious that departures from it that result from the causal agency of someone should create a duty to re-create it. If the status quo is just, we nevertheless permit certain ways of departing from it to be sustained. In both cases what counts is the way in which departures from the status quo come about. Wrongful departures, through force, fraud, negligence, or the like, may trigger a claim to repair or a duty to make good another's loss. But the underlying claim in such cases is not the fact that one person's conduct harms another; rather, it is that one person has *wrongfully* injured another. Reliance on *wrongfulness* as a condition of justice and recovery once again puts the defense of strict liability in doubt.

14.5 STRICT LIABILITY AND HARM

What in addition to loss, action, and causation is necessary for the imposition of liability and the provision of compensation to be required as a matter of justice? The very plausible answer, fault, is not available to a proponent of strict liability like Epstein, whose thesis is that causation, not fault, expresses the moral dimension of tort law. We can distinguish among three candidates, each of which purports to supplement the causal requirement in a way that does not introduce fault but which nevertheless renders liability and recovery matters of justice. The first alternative relies on the concept of harm. To harm is to set back a person's legitimate interests, and in that sense to wrong that person. Conduct that is harmful in this sense creates a duty to repair consequent losses. Because harming is a form of wronging, justice requires righting the wrong.[10] The existence of the duty to right the wrong does not depend on whether the conduct that wrongs is otherwise at fault.

Individuals have interests in things. Not every interest is a legitimate one. The thief has an interest in the television set he has recently acquired illegitimately, an interest that may mean more to him than the interest I have in the television I recently purchased. Normally, my interest would count as legitimate, the thief's not. Our actions affect other people's interests in any number of ways. Sometimes our actions advance the interests of others; other times our actions set back those interests; still other times we miss opportunities to advance the interests of others at little or no cost to us. In the first case we talk of benefiting others; in the third case of wrongly not benefiting others; and in the second, we talk of harming others.

If harming is supposed to provide morally relevant reasons for imposing liability and providing repair, the interest harmed must be one that creates a morally relevant ground for respecting it. The thief's interest in the stolen television, however real, is not ordinarily viewed as legitimate. When the police confiscate the television, it is unlikely that the thief has grounds for repair. In short, if being harmed is supposed to provide the missing ingredient in the formula for liability, then harming has to be more than setting back any interest of an individual; it has to be an interest that is qualified in a morally relevant way. The usual way of qualifying interests is to distinguish legitimate from illegitimate ones. To harm is to set back a legitimate interest.

Is harm, so understood, the missing ingredient? The answer may depend on how we analyze *legitimate interests*. Fortunately, for our purposes, we do not have to present a full account of *legitimate interests* to know that there are all sorts of harmings that do not call either for compensation or for liability. One can quite justifiably, for one's own benefit or for the benefit of others, interfere with or set back another's legitimate interests. After all, the reason the unsuccessful suitor or businessperson has no claim to repair is not that his interests are illegitimate. The businessman's interest in the success of his company may well be legitimate, whether or not he succeeds. If he is driven from business by more successful competitors, he is harmed, his legitimate interests frustrated. Still, it is unlikely that he has a claim to compensation provided the businesswoman who outduels him abides by the relevant conventions and competes fairly. The concept of harm adds something to the formula of strict liability, but it does not add enough to explain the sense in which both liability and recovery are matters of morality and justice.

14.6 STRICT LIABILITY AND LEGITIMATE EXPECTATIONS

Alternatively, one could argue that the reason the unsuccessful businessman is not entitled to repair for his losses is that he has no legitimate *expectation* of success in his venture. A person who goes into business cannot expect that others will not compete against him, and as a result always runs the risk of failing. Roughly the same can be said of competitors for the affections of others. On the other hand, someone who enters business can expect to compete only on fair terms, and if he is the victim of unfair business practices he can recover his losses. Thus, one can recover for losses that result from the frustration of legitimate expectations, but not for losses resulting from the frustration of expectations generally.

A modern businessperson has reason to expect that some competitors will cheat if they can, in the same way that retailers expect certain shoppers to steal. It would be unreasonable to expect otherwise, and no reasonable person could expect otherwise. If it is reasonable for a businessperson to expect a certain degree of unfairness in competition, then her suffering loss as a consequence of such practices cannot be described as involving the frustration of a legitimate expectation. As long as the loss results from unfair competition that falls within the scope of legitimately anticipated unfair-

279

ness, no frustration occurs, and no grounds for liability or recovery exist.

The concept of legitimate expectations is ambiguous. If we claim that a person has a right to recover only for losses resulting from the frustration of legitimate expectations, then we need to distinguish between expectations that are legitimate in the sense that someone has good and sufficient *epistemic* reason to have them and those that are legitimate in the *normative* sense that some rule or principle gives someone the right to have them. It is not reasonable in the epistemic sense for any motorist to expect that all motorists will follow the rules of the road; the empirical evidence available to all motorists suggests that no motorists follow all the rules. On the other hand, the rules of the road give all motorists normative grounds for expecting the compliance of others. I have a right to expect compliance, but no grounds for expecting that my expectations will be realized. In other words, I have legitimate normative expectations and no legitimate epistemic grounds for anticipating that those expectations will be realized.[11]

The unsuccessful businessperson has no right to recover for damages that result from fair business practices, but does have a right to recover for damages that result from unfair practices – even if she has no reason to believe that competitors will comply fully with the relevant legal constraints. If that is correct, then the relevant criterion of expectation is normative, not epistemic. If each individual is entitled (normatively) to expect from others that they not impose unreasonable risks of harm, then the concept of normatively legitimate expectations implicates the concept of fault. People are normatively entitled to expect that others will not be at fault with respect to them. Recovery for frustrated normative expectations is recovery for fault. Fault does the work; normative expectations provide the cover. The concept of normative expectation appears to help explain recovery and liability in a way in which the concept of harm fails to, but it may do so only by reintroducing the concept of fault or wrongdoing.

The problem of course is that the concept of normative

expectations is itself not basic or fundamental. One's normative expectations depend on the relevant norms and conventional practices. If reasonable care provides the relevant norm, recovery and liability are matters ultimately of fault. At best, the concept of legitimate normative expectations is only partly helpful. The degree to which it is helpful depends on the underlying norms that create the relevant expectations. But once we have a set of underlying norms, the concept of normative expectations becomes otiose; losses that result from the violation of those norms are compensable because the conduct is wrongful. At worst, normative expectations play no role in the argument whatsoever.

14.7 STRICT LIABILITY AND RIGHTS

Suppose that harming someone consists neither in setting back a legitimate interests nor in frustrating a normatively legitimate expection of hers, but in acting contrary to her rights. To harm is to violate or infringe a right. Then compensation would be due and liability imposed as a matter of justice whenever one individual harms another just because harming violates or infringes a right. Harming is a kind of wrong because harming is action contrary to an individual's right. Because it is the fact of action contrary to a right that gives rise both to compensation and to liability, it does not matter whether the action is in any way wrongful or otherwise at fault. Thus, we have the makings of an account of liability that is both strict and just.

Either we can say that action contrary to a right is a form of harming, and that the theory being presented is another version of the principle of liability and recovery for harm; or we can say that the rights thesis is a distinct theory, in which case liability and recovery are for rights invaded, not for harms done. For reasons that will become clearer in subsequent chapters, I prefer to distinguish harmful conduct from rights invasions or infringements. To harm is to set back a legitimate interest. Though rights protect legitimate interests, not every legitimate interest is secured by rights. When a legiti-

281

mate interest is secured as a right, then its invasion, or so the argument holds, creates a claim in justice for repair. And because the right can be invaded permissibly as well as wrongfully, the claim in justice for repair does not depend on fault. Thus, the rights thesis can provide the needed defense of the theory of strict liability.

Rights invasions are actions contrary to the demands rights impose. We can distinguish between two ways of invading rights. In one case rights are *violated*. That occurs whenever without justification someone acts contrary to the demands rights impose on him. In the other case, rights are *infringed*. Infringements are justified or permissible invasions of rights. We can illustrate the distinction with the help of an example. Suppose Hal takes something of Carla's that she has a property right in. Let's say that to have a property right in something is to be in a position (normatively) to prohibit others from taking or using one's property without consent. Property rights in this sense entail powers of exclusion and alienation. We can imagine circumstances in which Hal, for no good reason, recklessly and gratuitously destroys Carla's property. It is natural to refer to what he has done, among other things, as being a violation of her rights.

On the other hand, suppose that both Carla and Hal are diabetics. Hal's insulin supply is lost in an accident, and before he lapses into a coma he rushes to Carla's house only to find that her insulin is there, but she is not. He takes the necessary insulin only after he assures himself that there is enough left for her daily dosage. Normally, we would want to be able to say that Carla has a right that Hal not do what he did, because her right means that anyone who would use or take her insulin could do so legitimately only on receiving her permission or consent.[12] Hal did not secure her consent, and so what he did was contrary to the constraints her right imposed on him. On the other hand, Hal has acted permissibly in the circumstances, and only someone who had no understanding of human need and motivation could think otherwise. Therefor, he *rightly* acts *contrary* to the demands

Carla's right imposes on him. If we feel that he owes her compensation, it cannot be because what he had done was in any way at fault. What he has done is right. If Hal has a duty to make good Carla's loss, then the ground for recovery and liability is the fact that his conduct, however permissible, was contrary to Carla's right.

Some actions that are contrary to the demands rights impose on us are at fault or otherwise wrongful. We refer to those as rights violations. Other actions, however, can be both contrary to the demands of rights and not at fault. In those cases, there can be both liability and recovery in the absence of fault. So action contrary to a right does not necessarily entail fault. Therefore, a proponent of strict liability might try to define compensable losses in terms of rights invasions, and in doing so avoid the charge that he has done no more than supplement his theory with the principle of fault.

In those cases of permissible invasions, that is, infringements, compensation derives from the invasion of the right, not from the wrongfulness or fault of the injurer's conduct. There is no wrongful conduct of which to complain. In cases of culpable invasions, that is, violations, the case for compensation is overdetermined. There is both wrongful conduct on the injurer's part and conduct contrary to the victim's right. The infringement cases suggest that conduct contrary to the victim's right is sufficient for liability as well as recovery. Thus, though the wrongfulness of the injurer's conduct may be sufficient, it cannot be necessary. If liability and recovery can be explained as required by justice without having recourse to the wrongfulness of the injurer's conduct, then we have provided a genuine theory of strict liability – a theory that makes liability both strict and just.[13]

This is the strongest version of the theory of strict liability. Though I do not believe that the argument ultimately succeeds, I need to postpone full consideration of it until in Chapter 16. Rights play a role in the correct theory of liability and recovery, but not the one theory of strict liability sets forth. Before we explore an alternative to the theory of strict liability, we should first state the theory and give some idea of the line of objection to be developed later.

The theory of strict liability holds:

1. Liability and recovery are matters of justice for all and only losses that result from the invasion of rights.
2. Compensation can never be a matter of justice in the absence of a right.
3. Compensation in torts is always for action contrary to rights.

There is much in the theory of strict liability that is insightful and defensible; much of it is not, however. The theory of strict liability holds that liability depends on rights in all cases. That is wrong. Rights are secured interests. Sometimes interests are legitimate but not afforded the protection of rights. Legitimate interests can be wrongfully harmed, and when they are, losses that result can be compensable as a matter of justice.

Compensable losses do not require the existence of a right. Moreover, even where compensation requires rights, compensation is not always required to *rectify* losses resulting from conduct contrary to rights. Sometimes compensation is required in order for an injurer's conduct to count as *respectful* of the victim's right. There are three kinds of cases in which compensation is someone's due. In one case it is for wrongful *harmings;* in another, it is for rights *invasions;* and in the third it is required in order to *respect* rights. Rights do play a role in the correct theory of liability, but not the role defenders of the theory of strict liability have in mind. Chapter 15 goes part of the way toward developing this claim.

Chapter 15

Liability and recovery

The theory of strict liability is a response both to the failure of the retributive theory of fault liability and to the success of the economic analysis of it. It expresses the idea that justice in tort law must eliminate entirely the role of fault in recovery and liability. The theory of strict liability rightly notes that liability and recovery in torts do not always depend on fault. It goes astray both as an account of our current practice and as a moral defense of it precisely because it fails adequately to appreciate the relevance of fault to the imposition of liability in practice and to the justice of that practice. Fault is central both to the institution of tort law and, in my view, to its ultimate moral defensibility. The principle of justice that grounds the fault rule is corrective justice.

This chapter begins the account of corrective justice. Several distinctions are important to the account of corrective justice and to the role I claim for it in tort law. This chapter develops four of these distinctions.

15.1 RECOVERY AND LIABILITY

The first distinction is the one for which I have been given undue credit, and that is the distinction between the grounds of recovery and liability. The distinction between the grounds of recovery and liability is analytically unassailable, but the truth is that our current tort practice does not appear to take advantage of it. In torts, the costs of particular accidents are allocated between particular plaintiffs and defendants. Tort

285

litigation is structured so that if a victim has an adequate case for recovery, then liability is almost always imposed on his injurer; a case that is adequate for recovery is almost always deemed adequate for liability. By the same token, if the injurer is not liable, then the victim is treated as if her claim to redress is unworthy in the appropriate sense.

This feature of tort practice is particularly troubling when neither injurer nor victim is at fault or otherwise responsible, for a harm's occurrence. This is a point we have already touched on in Chapter 11. As tort law is currently structured, liability may unavoidably fall to either an innocent victim or an innocent defendant. Were we to implement the analytically sound distinction between the grounds of recovery and liability, then we might develop institutions that would compensate victims without unduly burdening morally innocent injurers. For example, we might repair faultlessly occasioned losses through a general or public insurance scheme, thus protecting the legitimate interests of victims in having their losses rectified. Because the costs of compensating victims would be spread throughout the population as a whole, innocent injurers would not be required to bear any greater costs than anyone else.

Another problem with the current practice is that it imposes liability only on those whose fault causes harm to others. Equally faulty conduct that is "harmless" in this sense goes without sanction or liability. One might object to luck playing such an important role in allocating accident costs. The problem can be solved by paying heed to the distinction between the grounds of recovery and liability. Suppose we accept as our principle of recovery that individuals who suffer harm at the hands of the faulty are entitled to recover, then instead of imposing the costs of particular accidents on respective faulty injurers, we might distribute the total costs of accidents among all agents who are at fault, whether or not their fault occasions harm to anyone.

We need to take note of two points. First, I do not mean to be defending any of these proposals. I am just identifying some pressure points in current practice and showing how attending to the distinction between the grounds of recovery and liability frees us to imagine alternative arrangements that may alleviate the pressure. Second, the distinction between liability and recovery does no justificatory work. It does not allow us to say, without the benefit of moral or political argument, that institutional arrangements separating questions of liability from those of recovery are preferable to current practices, nor does it imply that such schemes of liability are fully compatible with the relevant norms of justice. It does, however, encourage us to reassess current practice in the light of its ability to answer both concerns, recognizing that current practice treats as unified a variety of questions that can be treated as distinct. Thus, among the elements of current practice that need an explanation as well as a justification is this fact, that is, the merger of the grounds of recovery with those of liability, what I will call in subsequent discussions the structure of tort law.[1]

15.2 GROUNDS AND MODES OF RECOVERY

The next distinction is between the grounds and modes of recovery (or liability). The grounds of recovery specify the conditions that must be satisfied if a person's claim to compensation is to be justified. Once we determine that a victim is entitled to repair, we have the further question of how compensation ought to be provided. Should valid claims to repair be made good through funds in the treasury? Should they be the responsibility of the injurer; or should they remain the responsibility of the victim – however legitimate the underlying claim to repair may be? In other words, should valid claims to repair be made good through public or private insurance? If we opt for private insurance, should the claims to repair be made good through third-party (injurer) or first-party (victim) insurance?

In answering this question we are attempting to determine the appropriate *mode* of rectification. Again, we can make similar remarks about the mode of liability. Once we reach the conclusion that an injurer ought to be held liable for conduct that causes harm or damage, should her liability be to the victim or should she be made to pay into a general fund, perhaps the same fund from which victims draw compensation?

In torts, a victim is entitled to repair only if her injurer is a candidate for liability; and if a victim is entitled to repair, her claims are against her injurer. Tort law makes good the legitimate claims of victims by imposing the costs on their respective injurers. Once again, the question we want to answer is whether, and to what extent, this practice can be justified. With all the options available for allocating costs, why impose them on particular injurers? Why not spread them among the class of injurers? Or among those injurers who are at fault? Or among those who are at fault whether or not they are injurers? Or among those best able to reduce the risk of injury at the lowest marginal cost? Or among those who are the best risk spreaders? Why, in other words, allocate liability for loss as the tort system does?

15.3 GROUNDS AND SCOPE OF LIABILITY

I want to introduce now a distinction that I have not emphasized much in my previous work but that is both obvious and important. This is the distinction between the grounds of the right to recover and the scope of the right. There is an analogous distinction between the grounds and scope of liability. Suppose that an injurer should be liable to a victim only if he is at fault in harming her. It is a further question whether the scope of his liability should extend to cover all the damages that result from his negligence, or whether instead it should be limited to those of the victim's damages that were or should have been foreseeable? These are important and interesting questions about the scope of liability and recovery, but they are not the questions of fundamental interest in this study.

Suppose that an injurer is at fault in causing another harm; suppose further that whenever an injurer is at fault in causing another harm, she secures a gain thereby, and that because the gain is the result of wrongdoing, it is a wrongful gain. Setting aside questions of foreseeability, what is it that justice requires of her liability: the annulment of her wrongful gain, or the annulment of the wrongful loss her conduct occasions, or both?

The injurer's wrongful gain can exceed, be equal to, or be less than the loss his conduct imposes upon the victim. In the event that the victim's loss equals the injurer's gain, no special problem emerges; annulling the injurer's gain also annuls the victim's loss. The other cases can create problems. If the injurer's gain is less than the victim's loss, then if justice requires only that her wrongful gain be annulled, doing justice may leave the victim without full relief. On the other hand, in the event the victim's loss is less than the injurer's gain, giving the victim full relief is inadequate to rectify the injurer's wrongful gain. To give the victim more than full compensation as a way of rectifying the injurer's wrongful gain is to give the victim more than she deserves. When the victim's loss exceeds the injurer's gain, imposing the victim's full costs on the injurer may involve imposing a cost in excess of what is permissible as a matter of justice. And so on.[2]

Of course, the extent to which these cases present problems depends on the extent to which liability and recovery are merged in a single legal practice. If we create separate institutions for rectifying wrongful gains and losses, then it may be possible to do both in ways that are compatible with the demands of justice. It is also possible that corrective justice permits imposing liability in excess of wrongful gains. We can imagine two cases. First, it might be that a person cannot be liable *unless* he has secured a wrongful gain. Once he has, the scope of his liability does not depend on the extent of the gain. Securing a wrongful gain makes him a candidate for liability in corrective justice. The scope of liability depends on the loss his wrongdoing occasions, not on the gain he secures.

It is also possible, however, that the grounds of liability have nothing to do with the injurer's having secured a wrongful gain. Perhaps justice requires that an injurer be held liable for the wrongful losses his conduct causes whether or not his wrongdoing otherwise benefits him. Securing a wrongful gain is not a condition of liability. Still, wrongdoers sometimes do secure unjust benefits. When they do, justice requires that those gains as well as the losses they cause be annulled. Justice need not require that tort liability be imposed on the wrongdoer as a way of rectifying those gains. Those gains can be rectified in some other way, perhaps through restitutionary remedy of some sort.

The second set of questions regarding the distinction between liability and the scope of liability has to do with the distinction between pecuniary and non-pecuniary losses, a topic to which we shall return in the discussion of product liability law in Chapter 20. For now it is enough to note that there is a distinction between those losses a rational individual would insure against (pecuniary) and those he would not insure against (non-pecuniary).[3] Suppose an injurer has acted in a way that makes her liable to her victim. Should she be liable for losses, like emotional distress or pain and suffering, that the victim herself would not have insured against? Why would it be rational for the law to impose a duty to insure against a category of losses that victims themselves would not find rational to insure against? Put slightly differently: Liability rules impose insurance burdens.

If a victim would not insure against nonpecuniary losses, why would the law impose the duty on third parties to provide that insurance? If it is irrational to insure against a loss, then it is irrational to insure against it, no matter who has the burden of providing the insurance. On the other hand, if these losses are occasioned by the fault of the injurer, they are, in a suitable sense, wrongful losses; should not wrongful losses be annulled? Failure to hold individuals liable for the full costs of their mischief may lead to inadequate deterrence. Thus, although we may feel that a victim should not recover for a loss that he would not have insured against, freeing the injurer from the burden of making good that loss may well have perverse incentive effects. The wrongfulness of a loss is different from whether it is a loss rational individuals would insure against. Which standard, rationality or wrongfulness, should determine liability and recovery in justice and torts?[4]

15.4 COMPENSATION AND JUSTIFICATION

The theory of tort law I propose depends not only on these three distinctions but on a fourth set of distinctions as well. We need to distinguish among at least three ways in which the justifiability of an agent's conduct can relate to his victim's claim to repair.

1. Sometimes a person owes another compensation only if the loss he causes is the result of unjustifiable or unreasonable conduct. In this sense, acting justifiably is a bar to recovery; fault or unreasonableness on the injurer's part is a necessary condition of the right to compensation.
2. On other occasions, an individual can suffer loss owing to the justifiable conduct of another, but the justifiability of the conduct precludes neither recovery nor the duty to repair.
3. On yet other occasions, an injurer's conduct is justifiable only if the injurer pays compensation for whatever losses his conduct occasions. In such cases the rendering of compensation is a necessary condition of the justifiability or reasonableness of what the agent does. In that sense, it helps to right what in its absence would be a wrong.

In the first kind of case compensation depends on the character of what the injurer does. Because the injurer has done something wrong, the victim has a claim to compensation for the losses that ensue. In the third, compensation *changes* the moral character of what the injurer does. Compensation rights what in its absence would be wrongful conduct. In the second case compensation does not right a wrong, nor is it owed because the injurer has acted wrongfully. What, then, is the basis of compensation in cases of this sort? I want to suggest that compensation is owed because even in acting justifiably an injurer can sometimes *infringe* the rights of oth-

291

ers. Losses that result when rights are infringed are compensable in justice.

These cases represent possibilities in logical space. Though examples may prove controversial, I want to provide illustrations of the kinds of cases that fall into each category, and in doing so, illuminate the importance of the distinctions involved. If I drive reasonably, as would a reasonable person of ordinary prudence, I am justified in imposing the risks I do. If you are injured as a result of my doing so, ordinarily you would have no claim to compensation against me. This example falls into the first category in which the justifiability of what I do defeats any claim to compensation for loss that you might hope to press. On the other hand, the case I considered in Chapter 14 in which Hal justifiably takes a portion of Carla's insulin to prevent himself from lapsing into a coma is a case in which his conduct is justifiable, but the justifiability of his conduct does not preclude the legitimacy of Carla's claim to repair, nor does it preclude the possibility of Hal being obligated to provide it. This example falls into the second category in which the justifiability of what the injurer does is adequate to free him from fault, but is inadequate to defeat the victim's claim to repair for the taking.

Often I lunch at the local Korean produce market. My eating the salad they offer is justified provided I pay them what they (fairly) charge me for it. If I ate the salad but refused to pay, I would have done something wrong. Some might call it theft. In any event, it would constitute a taking of something to which I had no right. So my rendering the market their due by paying the tariff is a condition of my legitimately eating their food. This is an example of the third sort of case in which there is justification in the doing only if compensation is paid, not otherwise.

15.5 NECESSITY

Admittedly, any set of examples is likely to be controversial, and the examples I have offered are no exception. I have suggested that the insulin example falls into the second category of cases. The insulin case is like Feinberg's back-packer.[5] Both are like the famous case of *Vincent* v. *Lake Erie* discussed earlier.[6] All involve claims of necessity. I have ten-tatively placed these cases in the second category, but some might argue that they belong in the first category, and others in the third. Consider how the argument for placing neces-sity cases in the first category might go.

As long as Hal acted reasonably in taking the insulin, he owes Carla nothing. If we accept that the gravity of his cir-cumstances renders his taking justifiable, then we must ac-cept the consequences of that judgment. If his conduct is justifiable or reasonable, then he has not wronged Carla. If he has not wronged Carla, then Carla has suffered no loss that is the point of justice to correct. The justifiability of his conduct defeats her claim to repair, and if that is so, the ex-ample belongs in the first category, not the second. Neces-sity provides a justification and individuals who harm others justifiably owe no compensation in justice for the losses their conduct occasions.

On the other hand, even if Hal justifiably appropriates Carla's insulin, it hardly follows that Carla has no right to recover. After all, the insulin is hers. Hal takes what is right-fully hers, what he has no right to. Even if we do not mean to condemn Hal for what he does, we still have Carla's claim to her insulin to contend with. Why would someone think that the gravity of Hal's situation extinguishes her claims? We need a reason for the view that the appropriateness of what he does operates on her property rights in the way in which this argument says it does. Why does the justifiability of Hal's conduct extinguish what we would otherwise rec-ognize as Carla's legitimate claims? We need reasoned argu-ment, not mere intuitions.

One argument rests on the proposition that necessity forces private property to revert to the *common pool*. In other words, we accept that Carla has a property right in her insulin. That means that typically she has the power to exclude others from using it without her consent. Necessity changes all that, and it changes it in a special way. It extinguishes, if only temporarily, her property right in the insulin (at least against those with claims of necessity), and in doing so renders the insulin part of the common pool of resources on which those in distress can draw. In virtue of the urgency of his need, Hal is free to draw on the common pool. Carla has no right to exclude Hal's use, because, with respect to Hal's claims, her property right has been temporarily extinguished. Hal, in turn, does nothing wrong in calling on resources in the common pool, and so the legitimacy of Hal's conduct defeats Carla's claim to liability. Because "her property" is now part of the common pool of resources, he owes her nothing for having appropriated it.

When Hal's life is imperiled, he justifiably takes the insulin. We can agree to that. But is his conduct justifiable because he is drawing on resources in the common pool? No, and for the simple reason that the property does not revert to the common. The "public" is not responsible for distributing the loss that results from Hal's use of the insulin. The public did not purchase the insulin in the first place, nor will it fall to the public to replace it. The original purchase and the cost of repurchase fall entirely to Carla, and no effort is made to distribute her costs among the population as a whole. Hal is not availing himself of a public commodity; he is availing himself of Carla's. It is Carla, not the public at large, who bears the costs of Hal's conduct.

If necessity causes private property to revert to the common, Carla would have no claim to compensation. But it would not follow that Hal would have no duty in justice to replenish the common. The same problem arises whether the property is Carla's or part of the common pool of resources. The question of whether the justifiability of his appropriating the resource suffices to free him of the burden of repair or compensation remains.

Instead of claiming that necessity compels private property to revert to the common, one could hold that the reason Hal has no duty to repair Carla's loss is that necessity makes each of us our neighbor's insurer. The necessity of Hal's situation makes Carla, and anyone else who might possess insulin necessary to keep him alive Hal's potential insurers. In the same way, Hal may someday be Carla's insurer. The insulin is Carla's, not the public's. The gravity of Hal's situation does not change ownership of the insulin or property rights in it. Instead it alters the claims on Carla's property that Hal can make. Carla, in effect, becomes his insurer. Under conditions of necessity, our neighbors have claims to our aid; we have no claims to repair when we provide it, even when we "provide" it involuntarily. That is why Hal owes Carla nothing, not the fact that the gravity of his situation causes Carla's property to revert to the common. That, after all, is not what happens. The neighbor-as-insurer principle provides a good reason for treating necessity cases as if they fell in the first, not the second, category of cases; necessity justifies conduct that would otherwise be wrong. The justifiability of the conduct then defeats the victim's claim to compensation.

Now let's consider an argument for treating necessity cases as if they fall into the third category of cases, those in which the justifiability of what an agent does depends on his compensating those who are injured as a result of his conduct. Consider the following argument. Suppose Carla had been at home when Hal came knocking at her door seeking aid. Presumably, before he would have been justified in appropriating a portion of her insulin, Hal would have had to secure her consent. It is possible that Carla would have given her consent only if she were adequately compensated. Transaction costs makes it impossible for Hal and Carla actually to contract. Therefore, the best they can do is replicate ex post what a rational contract between them would have been. That amounts to Hal being at liberty to appropriate her insulin provided he compensates her, not otherwise. Understood in this way, the insulin case is like the restaurant example. If you are not prepared to purchase the meal, you are not justified in eating it. The insulin case is an "ex post contract" case in which compensation is a condition of the justifiability of the conduct. Carla's presence or absence is relevant to whether they can contract with one another; it cannot be relevant to the justifiability of his taking without compensation. Compensation ex post is a second best alternative to contracting ex ante, necessary when the contractual solution is unavailable.

We have identified plausible arguments pulling us in different direction, for there are grounds for treating the conflicts created by necessity cases, those like *Vincent* v. *Lake Erie*, Feinberg's backpacker, and the insulin example, in either of three ways:

1. If necessity renders each of us our neighbor's insurer, then as insurers we have no claim against our neighbor when necessity compels her to take our resources without our consent.
2. On the other hand, necessity should not entitle someone to take from another in her absence if one would have had to negotiate a price under normal conditions. Necessity allows one to take without first securing consent, so that one is not prevented from taking, but then one is not justified in doing so unless one stands prepared to compensate after the fact.
3. Or necessity permits one to take whether or not one is prepared to render compensation. Sometimes the gravity of the situation justifies the taking on those grounds alone. The person whose life is imperiled need not stand prepared to compensate in order for what he does to be permissible. On the other hand, it does not follow that the gravity of his situation extinguishes all claims against him that the victim of his conduct has. While the victim's right to exclude the endangered person's appropriation may be overcome, (if not extinguished), the right to compensation may be neither overcome nor extinguished. Thus, the imperiled individual is justified in taking from another, full stop; but those from whom he takes have a right to repair against him, while she has a duty to make amends to them.

Which solution to the conflict of interests is the correct one?

15.6 RIGHTS AND COMPENSATION

Instead of treating the neighbor-as-insurer solution as a principle of justice applicable to determining how the costs that arise in necessity cases ought to be allocated, we might treat it as a *convention* that might plausibly be adopted as a way of determining the distribution of those costs. As a convention it represents a sensible solution to conflicting claims in morality, claims that derive from more basic moral norms. The neighbor-insurer principle, then, is not a principle at all, but is instead a convention for responding to a conflict of principle. In the case of necessity those principles ground both the victim's claim to repair and the justifiability of the injurer's conduct.

As a conventional solution to necessity cases, the neighbor-as-insurer solution has some important advantages. It increases the likelihood that those in jeopardy will be able to extricate themselves from danger, and reduces transaction costs by eliminating the need for negotiations, and so on. On the other hand, because it requires no compensation in individual cases, it may invite inefficient or otherwise unjustifiable appropriations. Further, it will likely create a need for an institution to determine whether the appropriations are justifiable. Therefore, even if the insurance solution reduces ex ante search costs, it may increase ex post litigation costs. The costs of securing consent and paying compensation are reduced; the costs of determining whether the taking is appropriate may well be increased.

Similarly, we might find it helpful to think of the argument for placing necessity cases in the third category as an invitation to adopt a different kind of conventional solution to the problem created by conflicting moral norms. The convention in this case is that when faced with necessity individuals can take without first seeking permission but only if they stand prepared to compensate their victims. They owe their victims a fair market price determined by a hypothetical contract between them. The convention is itself seen as an unavoidable, second best alternative to actual exchange.

If we understand the insurance and hypothetical contract approaches in this way, then we see them as alternative *conventions* we might adopt as ways of accommodating conflicting interests and claims. In this case these are represented by the injurer's interest in fending off disaster and the victim's property interest in her insulin. The underlying moral claims may be that the injurer is justified under certain conditions in appropriating another's property *and* the victim is entitled in justice to repair in the event she suffers a loss as a consequence of the injurer's conduct. These are the moral claims justified under the relevant moral principles, principles that apply separately to the injurer's conduct and to the victim's claims. Sometimes an individual is justified in taking another's property for his use if doing so is necessary to save his life. On the other hand, in doing so, the individual may invade the property rights of others, rights that give the right holder, not others, control over the property's use.

Once we have these two legitimate moral claims grounded in distinct principles, we can determine how best to accommodate them in practice. What conventions or practices provide the best overall way of accommodating these claims? It is at this level that the insurance solution and the hypothetical contract apply – as potential ways of accommodating conflicting legitimate claims – claims whose legitimacy is already established independent of the relevant convention. For those who would place necessity cases in either the first or third category implicitly assume the legitimacy of the conflicting claims that make placing them, at least initially, in the second category plausible.

My claim is not that placing necessity cases in the second category provides the best accommodation of the conflicting interests. Quite the contrary: it is that my view explains the sense in which there is a conflict of claims that needs to be accommodated; and that is because necessity morally justifies the appropriation – thus giving rise to the injurer's claim – and the property right of the victim justifies the claim to repair. Only this account explains why there is a need in justice to find a conventional solution in the first place.

15.7 INFRINGING AND VIOLATING RIGHTS

The argument to this point depends on the claim that an injurer's claim to repair for loss can be independent of the moral character of the injurer's conduct. The idea that conventions may arise to accommodate independently sustainable moral claims to appropriation on the one hand and to compensation on the other presupposes the truth of this more basic premise. At the very least, then, I owe an account of how it is that the victim's right to repair is independent of the moral character of the injurer's conduct. This account relies on a particular analytic theory of rights. That theory is fully developed in Chapter 19, but the gist of it can be spelled out in sufficient detail here to provide an explanation of the sense in which the victim's right to recover can be separated from the moral character of the injurer's conduct.

There is a difference between the content (or semantics) and structure (or syntax) of rights. The syntax of rights identifies what is true of rights analytically. In my view, rights consist in sets of valid claims covering a variety of domains. The content or semantics of rights determines which claims get associated with particular rights. The syntax is a necessary feature of rights as such; the content of a right, that is, the claims it gives rise to, are not analytic features of rights but contingent ones. The claims associated with a particular right are a function of the underlying normative theory of rights. The syntax of a right is a matter of philosophical analysis; the semantics of a right is a matter of normative argument.

If rights protect autonomy in the libertarian sense, then all rights give rise to the claims libertarians associate with property rights, typically, exclusion and alienation; rights are secured liberties. On the other hand, a welfarist theory of rights may give rise to one set of claims under some conditions and different claims under others. For example, when transaction costs are low, rights may give rise to claims based on principles of exclusion or alienation. Voluntary exchange may maximize welfare at the lowest cost. When ex ante transaction costs are high, however, the content of rights may be given by liability rules.

We might say that wrongs are actions contrary to rights. To act contrary to rights is to fail to respect the claims associated with them. There is as well a distinction between two ways of invading (or acting contrary to) a right: violation and infringement. A violation is a wrongful invasion of a right. An infringement is a non-wrongful or justifiable invasion of a right.

When necessity motivates Hal to appropriate Carla's insulin, his conduct is permissible or morally justifiable. It does not follow that he has not wronged her thereby. In other words, though permissible, his conduct may, nevertheless, be contrary to the demands her rights impose on him. It is the fact that her right has been invaded that grounds her claim to repair. That claim, moreover, is independent of the moral character of his conduct. And that is why we can separate the morality of his action from the justice of her claim. That is why we have two legitimate claims, one in morality, the other in justice, that we might seek to accommodate through a variety of conventions and practices.

Unfortunately, the argument is not over. We need to specify the sense in which Hal's conduct is "action contrary to" Carla's right. Here's the problem. Suppose for no good reason, that Hal goes to Carla's house and appropriates all her insulin without her consent. We have no difficulty in holding that he acts unjustifiably (i.e. without good reason) and that in doing so he violates her property right. For no good reason he appropriates it without her consent. Now suppose that Hal takes Carla's insulin for a very good reason. He acts in a morally permissible fashion, but we need to be able to say that in doing so he acts contrary to her right. Otherwise we cannot ground her claim to repair. In what sense is his action contrary to her right?

The justifiability of the injurer's conduct calls for an overall assessment of it. In responding to dire circumstances, we might come to the view that Hal did the right thing; in the circumstances, his conduct, all things considered, is justifiable. It is justifiable, moreover, even though it invades or infringes Carla's right. It is Carla's right and the fact that Hal infringed it that grounds her claim to compensation. That claim, in other words, is independent of whatever overall moral assessment of his conduct we come to. So far, so good. The skeptic will not allow the argument to end here, however. He might accept the idea that Carla's right to compensation depends on her right being infringed, not on an overall assessment of Hal's conduct, but exactly what was it that Hal did that infringed Carla's right? Or put another way, in what sense was Hal's appropriation contrary to Carla's right?

One answer is this. Property rights confer powers to exclude and alienate. The power to exclude entails that someone cannot appropriate the property of another without securing that person's consent. Consent is a condition of legitimate transfer within property rights. Hal does not secure Carla's consent, and, in that sense, his conduct infringes her right; it is contrary to the claims her rights impose on him.

We need to keep in mind the distinction between wrongdoing and wrong. The victim has the relevant property right. That means that he or she can exclude or just say "no." Had she been home when danger happened upon Hal, Carla could have excluded Hal's use. Had the cabin owner in Feinberg's example been at home, he could have excluded the backpacker. In each case, doing so would have been action within the victim's rights. On the other hand, right holders may unreasonably or wrongly insist upon enforcing their rights. They may do so maliciously, without reason, or otherwise unjustifiably. At some point, we might feel that someone's acting within his rights is so unreasonable as to subject the right holder to moral, if not legal liability, for the consequences of exclusion. That is one gloss we might put on the dicta in *Vincent* v. *Lake Erie* and the holding in *Ploof* v. *Putnam*. Rather than saying that the victims have no power to exclude under conditions of necessity, we might say instead that the victims have the power to exclude, but that they may be responsible for the consequences of wrongfully exercising that power. For our limited purposes, however, the key point of this discussion is that because the victim retains the power to exclude, the injurer's failure to secure consent constitutes action contrary to the victim's right.[7]

One way of understanding those who argue for the neighbor-as-insurer or hypothetical contract approaches is to view them as trying to present a tidy moral or political theory: tidy in the following way. Both want to argue that once we have settled on the justifiability of someone's conduct, then no further claims remain or can be sustained. In one case, this is the view that if the conduct is justifiable, no claims to compensation can be sustained. In the other, compensation is a condition of justifiability. In both cases, once the conduct is deemed justifiable, no one is in a position to press additional claims. Settling on the conditions of justifiability may well be difficult and controversial. But once the justification-conditions are specified, there are no residual claims. (This is very much like the approach in tort law that seeks to unite questions of liability and recovery. If the injurer acted justifiably and should not, therefore, be held liable, then the victim has no claim to compensation in justice. Settling on the morality of the injurer's conduct puts an end to all inquiries regarding the claims of victims.)

These approaches are tidy, but they achieve their neatness at a cost. For settling on the justifiability of someone's conduct, no matter how difficult or controversial a matter that may be, does not preclude the existence in justice or morality of residual claims, including those to compensation. And it is providing a foundation for those claims in necessity cases that leads us to consider the principle of corrective justice itself. For recovery in such cases may be a matter not only of welfare maximization, but of justice as well.

Chapter 16

The mixed conception of corrective justice

To this point we have considered accounts of tort law that seek to bring the entirety of the practice under the umbrella of a single principle. In part, this effort has motivated by the argument in Chapter 11 that there is a sense in which fault and strict liability are mirror-images of one another. If a principle is to count as an account of the role of either principle in torts, it should count as a defense of the other as well. Thus, we have been led to consider an account of tort law based on the principle of economic efficiency as well as accounts based on reciprocity of risk and causal responsibility. Though these accounts of accident law share the ambition of providing a unified and coherent interpretation of the practice as a whole, they differ with respect to the cornerstone principles of the interpretation: one grounds the practice within a larger theory of efficient resource allocation, the others within more general moral principles of justice between the parties.

I reject the idea that the practice can be understood as a unified whole. Instead, my view is that accident law implements a variety of different principles and policies. Some of these are economic, others moral. In the next few chapters I want to spell out the sense in which tort law is a matter of morality, leaving it until the end to explain the sense in which it is a matter of markets. In addition to consisting in a set of rules for imposing liability, tort law is a structure, an institution of a certain sort, through which its goals are pursued and in which its principles are embedded. The immediate

303

goal is to explain the sense in which both the underlying claims and the structure of tort law reflect moral principles. The next few chapters develop the claim and that corrective justice is embodied in the structural and substantive core of tort law. I begin by developing the relevant conception of corrective justice.[1]

Let's suppose that you are extremely well off financially. Your wealth exceeds that of the Rockefellers. Assume, moreover, that there is no possible principle of distributive justice with which your current wealth is compatible. You have more, in other words, than you would be entitled to under even the most inegalitarian, but defensible, principle of distributive justice. My situation, let's suppose, is just the opposite. I'm poor, dreadfully so. I have less than I would be entitled to under even the most inegalitarian, but defensible, conception of distributive justice. Neither of our positions can be sustained under any plausible theory of distributive justice. As luck would have it, one day I ram my car into yours, causing you to endure a significant financial setback. You are now less wealthy than before, and, a fortiori, closer to the demands of distributive justice. And, just to complete the story, suppose somehow the wealth you lose is transferred to me. Maybe an auto accident is an implausible way to transfer wealth. In that case, simply suppose that I defraud you of your money.

The question is whether you have a right to repair or to compensation against me? After all, you have no right to your wealth under the relevant principle of distributive justice; and if you have no right to your wealth, how can you have a right to have it restored when I reduce it? That is the problem. We can imagine a range of reasons for compensating you that have nothing to do with compensation being a matter of justice or right. For example, the possibility of securing compensation gives you a reason for suing me. Suing me for my negligence or wrongdoing is a way of privately enforcing the norm of safe driving. Compensating you also increases the cost of my negligence and provides me with an incentive to drive safely. Can compensating you be a matter of justice as well, and, if so, what principle of justice?

It may be good social policy to compensate you and in so doing to re-create or protect an unjust distribution of wealth. That may seem like a price worth paying in order to create the right incentives: yours to sue, mine to drive safely. I want to suggest, however, that compensating you under conditions that generally obtain can also be a matter of justice, and, therefore, that entitling you to repair may be required by justice, even if that means sustaining a less than fully just distribution of holdings. One consequence of this view is that justice may permit sustaining an unjust distribution of wealth. This is what I believe one must be committed to if your claim to repair against me can be a matter of justice. If sustaining or protecting a less than fully just distribution of wealth or resources can sometimes be a matter of justice, it cannot be a matter of distributive justice. Then what sort of justice is it that permits, if it does not explicitly, endorse distributive injustice?

The answer is, corrective justice.[2] Before we say anything more about the demands of corrective justice and the way those demands fit with those of distributive justice, it is important that we distinguish between endorsing injustice and implementing a policy that has the effect of permitting or sustaining injustice. The difference goes to the point or purpose of an institution or the intentions of the agents within it. Meeting the demands of corrective justice may have the effect of re-creating or sustaining a less than fully just distribution of holdings, but endorsing distributive injustice is not part of the point of corrective justice. Of course, if it turns out that meeting the demands of corrective justice has the effect of entrenching distributive injustice, that might well count as a reason against devoting substantial resources to meeting the demands of corrective justice.[3]

Rectifiable wrongs

16.1 THE ANNULMENT CONCEPTION OF CORRECTIVE JUSTICE

In this chapter I want to distinguish among three different conceptions of corrective justice, and defend one of them. I call the first of these, the one I have previously defended in my writings, the annulment thesis.[4] According to the annulment thesis the point of corrective justice is to eliminate, rectify, or annul wrongful (or unjust) losses.[5] Thus, to make use of a distinction introduced in the Chapter 15, corrective justice, so conceived, specifies grounds of recovery and liability; it does not specify a particular mode of rectification. It does, however, constrain the set of possible modes of rectification. Wrongful gains and losses cannot be annulled so as to create other wrongful gains or losses. Any mode of rectification that does not create wrongful gains and losses is compatible with corrective justice; and any mode of rectification that creates wrongful losses violates corrective justice.

Only wrongful losses (and gains) fall within the ambit of corrective justice. Therefore, any conception of corrective justice will require a substantive account of wrongfulness. It is wrongful losses that must be annulled; and the threat of creating new ones that restricts the institutions we might develop for rectifying existing ones. Indeed, different conceptions of wrongfulness will identify different losses as wrongful and different institutional mechanisms as permissible modes of rectification. To illustrate this point, if it is wrongful to impose a loss upon someone who does not agree to have the loss imposed, then whenever someone injures another person who has not assumed the risk or otherwise consented to his injury, the victim has suffered a wrongful loss deserving of repair. The victim's loss can be rectified in any way that does not create a wrongful loss. And that means that imposing the loss on anyone other than those individuals who agree so to bind themselves would be impermissible. Of course, the injurer or wrongdoer may not agree so to bind himself, and if he does not, imposing liability on him would be impermissible, a violation of corrective justice. (This

306

may be one reason for rejecting the view that involuntariness of a loss is a sufficient condition of its being wrongful.)

In contrast, if a loss is wrongful only if it results from inefficient conduct, many victims who have not agreed to run certain risks or to have losses imposed upon them may have no claim in corrective justice to repair. In the event someone does have a legitimate claim in justice to repair, any mode of rectifying it would be permissible provided that liability could be justified on efficiency grounds. Imposing the victim's loss on the cheapest-cost-avoider, for example, would fall within the ambit of permissible liability schemes even if the cheapest-cost-avoider has not agreed so to bind himself; indeed, even if he is in no other way responsible for the loss in question.

As I have characterized it, the annulment thesis strictly prohibits all institutional forms for rectifying wrongful gains and losses that create additional wrongful gains and losses. This constraint may be too strong. Suppose a very substantial loss could be rectified by creating a rather minor one. Can corrective justice really mean to prohibit implementing an arrangement that would reduce the extent of wrongful losses in the world simply because doing so may occasionally require the imposition of another wrongful loss? Should not corrective justice look at both sides of the loss equation?

If corrective justice requires rectifying wrongful losses but prohibits doing so if doing so creates other wrongful losses, then corrective justice may permit considerable wrongful loss. On the other hand, if corrective justice permits the imposition of wrongful losses in order to eliminate even greater losses, then at least it minimizes the total amount of corrective injustice in the world. Which is the proper way of understanding the demands of corrective justice?

One problem with imposing corrective injustices in order to annul greater wrongful losses is that it may turn the principle of corrective justice into a form of the principle of efficiency. Thus, rather than saying that justice requires eliminating wrongful gains and losses, it may be advocating the policy of minimizing the extent of corrective injustices in the world. The underlying principle is the economic one of minimizing the sum of x and the costs of reducing x, where x is replaced by "corrective injustice." Thus, we are led to the claim that someone who has suffered a wrongful loss at the hands of another has no claim in justice to repair as such. Instead, like everyone else, she is entitled to the least corrective injustice in the world. That might mean that she is entitled to repair if compensating her is "corrective-injustice minimizing," but not otherwise.

Within the annulment thesis, there is a way of responding to this problem that allows us both to treat claims in corrective justice adequately and to impose some corrective injustices in order to eliminate significant ones. First, it is always wrong to create a corrective injustice in order to rectify a wrongful loss if it is possible to correct the loss without doing so. Second, we can reject the claim that corrective injustices ought to be minimized. Instead, we might hold that it is sometimes permissible to impose a wrongful loss in order to eliminate another wrongful loss only if there is a significant or substantial difference between the loss eliminated and the loss created, not otherwise. Thus, a proponent of the annulment thesis can reject the "optimizing" conception of corrective justice. While he admits that sometimes it is permissible to impose wrongful losses in order to annul other wrongful losses, he rejects the marginalist form of reasoning about when doing so is permissible.

However plausible or intuitive this solution is, nothing I have said so far represents a defense of it. I have no intention, moreover, of providing the needed defense here, other than by analogy (a style of argument, I should add, that I believe we ought to shy away from generally). The analogy I have in mind concerns the way we normally think about rights and claims based on rights. Claims based on rights can be defeated by considerations of, say, utility. But part of what it means to have a right, part of its syntax, is that claims based on rights cannot be defeated by merely marginal increments in utility. The claim of right establishes a "significance" threshold. The gain in utility must be substantial before claims of rights are overcome or defeated.

Thus, one can accommodate claims of rights and claims of utility in a way that does justice to both. On the other hand, if claims of marginal advantage could defeat claims based on rights, we would not be able to say that people really have rights; rather, we would be optimizers or utility maximizers with no real account of rights. That is one reason, for example, why David Lyons, for one, has denied that there can be a utilitarian theory of rights. Utilitarians are committed to incrementalist reasoning in a way that is incompatible with the significance threshold entailed by rights.[6]

Something like this is what I am suggesting might be true of claims to repair in corrective justice within the annulment thesis. Corrective justice specifies grounds, not modes, of rectification. It constrains modes of rectification to the extent that it does not normally permit the creation of wrongful losses as a way of eliminating other wrongful losses. However, on some occasions, when no other alternatives are available, and the difference between the loss created and the loss eliminated is sufficiently great, it may permit the creation of what would otherwise be a wrongful or unjust loss.

Let's return to the basic structure of corrective justice as it is conceived by the annulment thesis. Corrective justice requires that wrongful losses be annulled, but on whom does the duty to repair fall? The annulment thesis does not appear to impose this responsibility on anyone in particular. In other words, corrective justice, so understood, gives no one in particular any special reason for acting, for annulling wrongful gains or losses.

Suppose we hold the view of justice and morality as action guiding. Principles of justice and morality do not simply provide answers to metaphysical questions about which things in the world are really good or right; they are designed to give agents reasons for acting. Their importance depends on the role they play in practical reasoning. One way in which corrective and distributive justice might differ, then, is with respect to the ways in which they figure in an individual's practical reasoning. Corrective and distributive justice are distinct principles of justice. That just means that typically they give individuals different kinds of reasons for acting. But if we accept the annulment thesis, this is not how corrective and distributive justice differ. For, as I have characterized it, the annulment view appears to hold that justice requires that a certain state of the world be brought about, not that anyone in particular has a special reason in justice for bringing it about. And this is precisely the way we think about distributive justice. Therefore, in terms of their reason-giving properties, corrective justice is indistinguishable from distributive justice.

At the outset, I suggested that one might appeal to considerations of corrective justice in ways that might sustain certain distributive injustices. This was part of the point of the Rockefeller example. If that suggestion is plausible, corrective justice must be logically and morally independent of distributive justice. The argument to this point suggests, however, that if corrective justice is understood in terms of the annulment thesis, it creates reasons for acting in the same way (and of the same type) as does distributive justice. If the difference between the two is to be reflected in the reasons for acting that each creates, the annulment thesis seems disabled from distinguishing corrective from distributive justice. It would fail, then, as an account of corrective justice.

An example might illustrate the basic problem. If Josephine steals Ronald's radio, then corrective justice should be the kind of principle that gives Josephine a reason to act that neither you nor I have. It is not as if each of us has a responsibility, if any of us does, to see to it that Ronald's radio is returned or, if it is damaged, that he is compensated. Rather Josephine has a reason for returning the radio that none of us has. The same might not be true with respect to at least some of our other important duties to Ronald in distributive justice. If distributive justice required that certain of Ronald's needs be met, then each of us might have the same

310

kind of reason in justice to see to it that those needs were met.

If corrective justice provides individual agent-relative reasons for acting in this sense, it cannot be a principle that provides only grounds for claims to recovery and liability. It must be a principle that specifies individual rights and responsibilities. And if it specifies a system of correlative rights and responsibilities, it also specifies a particular mode of rectification. Those who have the duty in corrective justice to make repair must in justice be made liable to do so. Any other scheme of liability is an offense to justice. Josephine's wrong is taking Ronald's radio; corrective justice imposes the duty on her to return it, or, if she has ruined it, to replace it. No one else in justice has the reason for acting Josephine does; no one must do what she must do.

The annulment view has two general problems that are related. First, it seems unable to account for the distinction between distributive and corrective justice. Second, it provides only grounds for recovery, whereas a proper conception of corrective justice will specify a mode of rectification as well as a reason for doing so. Rectification in corrective justice will be the duty of someone in particular. This suggests that the annulment view must be augmented or abandoned. Before considering alternatives to it, let's develop these objections to the annulment conception of corrective justice more fully in the hopes of establishing their ultimate persuasiveness.

16.2 THE RELATIONAL CONCEPTION OF CORRECTIVE JUSTICE

Until recently, I believed that the annulment conception of corrective justice provided the only plausible interpretation of the concept. Joseph Raz, Ernest Weinrib, and especially Stephen Perry[7] have convinced me that the annulment thesis is untenable. Weinrib in particular has pressed an alternative conception of corrective justice. In what follows, I want, first, to summarize the objections of Perry and Raz that have persuaded me to abandon the annulment thesis, and then, second, to characterize an alternative conception of corrective justice with which Weinrib in particular has been associated.

One problem with the annulment thesis is that it provides no one with any special reason for acting. If someone has suffered a wrongful loss then that loss should be eliminated. But how and by whom? The answer implicit in the annulment view appears to be that it depends. So justice itself does not tell us who should do what to repair the damage. It merely warns us against rectifying the loss in any way that creates additional wrongful losses. This feature of corrective justice reduces it to a form of distributive justice, a line of objection suggested earlier. Let's now develop it in considerably greater detail.

In one view of distributive justice, we all have reasons for acting in certain ways, for providing each member of the community with whatever it is that the principle of distributive justice requires of us. This responsibility falls to each and every one of us, but coordination in efficiently discharging this duty is difficult. Therefore, we create a larger institution, the state, that acts as our agent and sees to it that we discharge our obligations under distributive justice. For similar coordination related reasons, we may empower this state to do all sorts of other things as well, like provide public goods. Indeed, this is the sort of public goods argument for the state as an agent of distributive justice that one might defend as consistent with the general theory presented in Part I.[8]

We have other responsibilities to one another that are not matters of distributive justice; they are owed by us to other persons as a result of actions we undertake and relationships we form. Some of these duties are contractual; others derive from commitments of one sort or anther; still others result from unjustified advantages we take of one another, or the harms our conduct occasions. If I take your watch, I have a duty to return it. No one else has that duty. If I have somehow destroyed it, then I owe you compensation. No one else does.

It may turn out that if I take all your possessions, you will fall below the social safety net. And everyone has a responsibility to see to it that people are situated above the safety net. I now have two connected responsibilities: one to return what I have taken; the other to see to it that you rise above the safety net. I can discharge both by returning your possessions to you. Suppose I do not. Then you are below the safety net. In that case the duties of others under distributive justice apply. Each person has a duty to see to it that you rise above the safety net. In this case, that might mean working to get me to return your possessions, or failing that, to see to it that you are compensated for your loss. Usually that duty will be discharged by the state in some way, for example, through welfare or other forms of social insurance. But the state is merely acting as our agent in discharging our duties under distributive justice.

Notice that the duty in distributive justice that each of us has to come to your aid is triggered only when you fall below whatever it is that distributive justice claims is your entitlement. No one has a responsibility to make good your loss as such. Only the injurer, that is, me, is responsible to return your possessions or to make good your losses *independent of considerations of distributive justice.* Only I have a duty to return or repair in corrective justice. That is the essential point of what I am calling the relational conception of corrective justice. It is a point whose difference with the annulment theory is worth emphasizing.

In the annulment thesis, wrongdoing creates no special reason for the wrongdoer to do anything. Rather the focus appears to be entirely on the loss the victim has suffered. That loss should be annulled. In general, we have an interest in the well-being of the victim. We are sensitive to shifts in her wealth. Should she suffer a diminution in welfare because of a flood, a hurricane or other misfortune, then we might feel that her loss is undeserved and should, if pos-

313

sible, be eliminated. The losses she suffers at the hands of others are also of this sort. They are losses that are undeserved, and should, if possible, be eliminated. Or so justice demands. In the same way that losses owing to misfortune create grounds for annulment, so too do losses owing to the wrongful mischief of another. If the argument for eliminating losses in one case is benificence, then so too is the argument for doing so in the other. If it is our responsibility in distributive justice to eliminate losses owing to natural disasters or undeserved handicaps, then the argument that brings wrongfully inflicted losses to our attention is also one in distributive justice. Losses owing to wrongdoing are among the set of losses that generally ought to be eliminated.

The problem for the annulment thesis is that corrective justice provides particular persons with reasons for acting, and it is that fact about it that distinguishes corrective from distributive justice. Without the imposition of a duty or responsibility, corrective justice is, at best, reducible to one or another form of distributive justice. That would seem to be an implication of the annulment thesis: to wit, wrongfully imposed losses are among the kinds of losses that should be compensated for, but so are (arguable) losses that result from handicaps, natural disasters, and misfortunes generally.

In the annulment view, the point of corrective justice is to eliminate or rectify certain gains or losses. It says nothing at all about who has this duty, if anyone does, in justice. The alternative conception of corrective justice, what I call, the relational view, makes exactly the opposite claims. It denies that corrective justice has any point or purpose with respect to gains and losses. The existence of a *loss* is not necessary to trigger claims based on corrective justice, nor is the point or purpose of corrective justice to annul or eliminate a loss. Rather, it specifies a framework of rights and responsibilities between individuals. In the relational view, it is the wrong, not the loss that must be annulled, that specifies the content of the relevant duty. It claims, in effect, that corrective justice operates on the relationship between persons in the following way. If one person has wronged another, then corrective justice imposes a duty on the wrongdoer to rectify his wrong. In the annulment thesis, in contrast, the fact that one person wrongs another can create a state of the world that is the concern of justice, but perhaps not of anyone in particular, including the person responsible for the wrong. In the relational view, the fact that one person wrongs another affects the system of rights and responsibilities *between* them.

We have isolated two important differences between the annulment and relational views. In the annulment view, corrective justice is triggered by wrongful losses (or gains). Its point or purpose is to rectify them. In doing so, it does not appear to impose a responsibility upon anyone in particular to repair the distortion. In contrast, wrongful losses are of no direct consequence in the relational view. Corrective justice has no point or purpose, let alone the specific purpose of annulling gains and losses. In the relational view, justice merely creates a scheme of rights and responsibilities between individuals. Thus, unlike the annulment thesis, it creates specific, agent-relative reasons for acting.

It is important to distinguish the relational view from other conceptions of corrective justice with which it might be easily confused. Richard Epstein, for one, appears to hold the view that justice requires that the individuals responsible (casually) for the losses of others be held liable in order to make those losses good. If I understand his position correctly, Epstein shares with the annulment thesis the view that the point of corrective justice is to eliminate wrongful losses. His view differs from the annulment thesis in holding that such losses ought to be eliminated by imposing liability on particular wrongdoers. The annulment view is agnostic with respect to liability for loss. It shares with Epstein, however, the view that the normatively significant aspect of the relationship between persons (from the point of view of corrective justice) is the existence of wrongful losses.

Though the relational view appears similar to Epstein's position, in fact it denies both of its central tenets. In the relational view, wrongful losses as such are normatively unimportant. Their existence does not trigger the application of

315

the principle, nor is it the point of the principle to eliminate or rectify them. The fact that someone *wrongs* another creates the relevant duty in corrective justice. Losses have nothing to do with it. Moreover, whereas Epstein believes that losses should be annulled by imposing liability upon particular wrongdoers, the relational view does not assert that there is only one institutional form through which the debts under corrective justice can be discharged that is compatible with justice. Thus, while it rejects annulment as the point of corrective justice, it accepts the distinction between the claims of corrective justice and the institutional forms available for satisfying them. In this regard, it is similar to the annulment thesis.

Because the relational view is concerned entirely with the ways in which individual rights and responsibilities are altered as a consequence of wrongdoing, it is also possible to confuse it with the attempt to embed corrective justice in a particular account of what it is to have a right, and in doing so to provide a foundation for that conception of the principle. The problem of providing a foundation for the relational conception of corrective justice is important because it is natural to wonder why corrective justice has no point or goal beyond merely identifying the ways in which wrongdoing alters the normative relationships among agents. The relational view merely imposes a scheme of rights and responsibilities. And one reason it does so, one might argue, follows from our understanding of what it is to have a right. Corrective justice, in this view, is simply part of the meaning of rights.

Suppose we analyze rights in the following general way. To say that you have a right that I not harm you, for instance, is to say, among other things, that I have a duty not to harm you. These are correlative rights and duties that are *primary*, or fundamental, to the content of the right in question. However, part of what it means for you to have such a right is that you have a variety of *secondary* rights as well; these are, or can include, meta rights – rights about your primary rights. One such right is the one you have that I compensate you in the event that I invade or violate your first order right that I not harm you. Similarly, we might say that I have a series of second order duties correlative of your second-order rights, and among these, presumably, is the right that I compensate you in the event that I fail to discharge my first order duty not to wrong you. Thus, when I harm you in a certain way that violates your first order right, you have a second order right against me to repair the resulting damage, and I have a corresponding second order duty to provide it.

This argument, which purports to provide a conception of corrective justice, in fact does not mention corrective justice at all. Instead, it draws its conclusions from a particular account of what it is to have a right. It is plain that the relationship between secondary and primary claims or rights relies on normative, not analytic, considerations. Even if we accept the view, which I do not, that correlative of every right is some specifiable set of duties, and that rights are to be analyzed in terms of the relationships between or among the rights and duties, it hardly follows that the existence of certain primary rights entails, in any sense, the particular list of secondary rights or claims that includes the claim to repair. After all, the right not to be harmed can be protected in any number of ways, each of which may give rise to very different secondary claims, and some of which may give rise to no secondary claims at all. Surely, how we should secure or protect the important interests marked by rights is not a matter of logic but a matter of substantive moral argument. (Similar remarks obtain with respect to the relationship between primary and secondary duties.)

If the duty to compensate and the right to compensation do not follow as a matter of logic from the nature of what it means to have a right, but follow, instead, from a suitable normative principle, the question is, Which principle? The obvious choice is the principle of corrective justice. In other words, the duty to compensate and the right to compensation for the invasion of rights derive from the principle of corrective justice. Or, to put the matter somewhat differ-

317

ently, the second order right to repair and the corresponding duty to compensate are ways in which the principle of corrective justice requires that first order rights be protected and duties enforced. But then the principle of justice does not *derive* from a plausible theory of rights. Instead, it is the moral principle external to rights that gives rights a certain content; it is an element of an underlying foundational theory of rights, not part of the meaning or syntax of rights. In other words, we cannot defend a particular conception of corrective justice by showing that it follows from our understanding of what it is to have a right when it is that conception of corrective justice itself that grounds that understanding of what it is to have a right. So one thing we might say about the relational conception of corrective justice is that it grounds a particular conception of what it is to have rights of a certain kind.

16.3 A MIXED CONCEPTION OF CORRECTIVE JUSTICE

The annulment conception of corrective justice runs into trouble because it seeks to do no more than to articulate *grounds* of repair. As such, it only identifies a category of losses that something ought to be done about. In the limit, the focus on the wrongfulness of the loss as such obliterates the distinction between corrective and distributive justice. This is one objection the relationalists have successfully pressed against my earlier position. The other is that by focusing on the loss in the way in which my previous work has, my account provides no explanation of how it is that corrective justice gives rise to reasons for action in some agents but not in others. The radio example illustrates this point. If Josephine takes Ronald's radio, then corrective justice gives Josephine a reason for acting that no one else has. She has a duty to return it or repair the damage, a duty that no one else has.[9]

These objections have convinced me that the annulment thesis is inadequate. My aim here is to provide a new ac-

318

count of corrective justice that accommodates both the relational and annulment conceptions of corrective justice. I do not want to claim that this conception will satisfy every objection, nor do I believe that the changes in my view will delight, rather than disappoint, those who have followed me in analyzing corrective justice in terms of annulment or rectification only. I claim only to be providing a plausible (and, I hope, interesting) conception of corrective justice that is closer to the truth of the matter than anything I have previously defended.

The central insight of the relational view I want to incorporate is that there is a difference between the reasons for acting we have as a result of the actions we undertake and those we have by virtue of our being members of a particular community. As a citizen of the United States I have reasons for seeing to it that others are adequately housed and clothed. If I promise to meet you for lunch, then I now have a reason for acting that I did not have before I promised to lunch with you, one which I might not have had I not so promised and one that no one else may in fact have. It is a reason for acting that is the result of my act of promising.

In the same way that promising can create reasons for acting, my harmful or wrongful actions can also create reasons for acting. If I negligently injure you, then I may have reasons to act that I very likely would not have had I not injured you, reasons to act that others who have not injured you very likely do not have. In the case of promising, the reasons derive from the accepted conventions governing the practice. In the case of my negligently injuring you, the reasons for action and the content of them derive from the principle of corrective justice. I want to accept this aspect of the relational view: namely, its emphasis on the way in which corrective justice creates agent-relative reasons for acting.

Wrongs are invasions of rights. In the relational view, corrective justice requires that wrongs be annulled by imposing a duty to repair them on the right-invader. Understood in this way the relational view denies the normative relevance of wrongful losses as providing a ground as well as the content of the duty in corrective justice. This feature of the relational view is unacceptable. Instead, I want to defend that aspect of the annulment thesis that emphasizes wrongful losses as both an aspect of corrective justice and part of its point. Thus, I want to articulate and defend what I will call the mixed conception of corrective justice.

Let's begin by stating precisely the relational conception of corrective justice. Corrective justice imposes a duty, but what duty? It imposes the duty, moreover, in virtue of something a person does, but what is that something that creates the duty? In the conventional interpretation of the relational view, it is the fact that one has done something wrong that triggers corrective justice. Corrective justice then operates on the action performed to create and impose a duty that would not otherwise have existed. It is a duty to correct or to annul. Correct or annul what? It is a duty to correct or annul that which one did that triggered corrective justice in the first place, namely, the wrong. Thus, a natural understanding of the principle of corrective justice is the following: *Corrective justice imposes the duty to repair the wrongs one does.*

The relational view emphasized the wrong one does and not the losses that might result as a consequence. The duties one has in corrective justice arise as a result of wrong or wrongdoing, not as a result of wrongful loss. The duty is to repair the wrong. What, then, is the connection between repairing the wrong (or wrongdoing) and repairing the loss? Indeed, the problem with the relational view is that it cannot take us from "repairing the wrong" to "repairing the losses." Moreover, if repairing the loss is not part of the duty in corrective justice, then what can the point of corrective justice be? If repairing the wrong is unconnected with repairing the losses it occasions, doing corrective justice may well leave innocent victims without visible means of claiming compensation in justice. In that case, corrective justice may have nothing to do with the practice of tort liability for loss, a practice, after all, that takes the victim's loss as its point of departure.

We might make the problem facing the relational view

concrete with an example. Suppose Steven negligently rams his car into David, causing him $1,000 in damages. The annulment thesis holds that David has suffered a wrongful loss that needs to be eliminated; it then asks whether the best way of doing justice in this case would impose the loss on Steven or somebody else. What does the relational view say? First, it notes that what Steven has done constitutes a wrong. Second, it holds that as a result Steven has incurred a duty to repair the wrong he has done. The problem is figuring out what the wrong he has done is, for only then can we figure out what needs to be done in order to repair it.

To focus the discussion further, let's suppose that Michelle drives negligently in the same way that Steven does, but that Michelle is lucky. Her negligence causes no damage to anyone. In one view, Steven's wrong is his driving negligently and putting people, David included, at risk. The negligence is the wrongdoing that needs to be repaired. Michelle is a wrongdoer in precisely the same way, and we might suppose for the argument, to the same extent. Each has a duty to repair the wrong each has done. We can imagine some plausible ways in which both can repair the wrong they have done. Steven and Michelle must apologize to those they put at risk. Or they must make a public statement conveying the judgment that they were wrong to treat others as means to their ends. Or perhaps the only way of annulling the wrong is to imprison them or otherwise to subject them to expressions of public indignation and disapprobation.

But what are we to say about the $1,000 loss that David has suffered? One thing we might say is that repairing the wrong does not involve repairing the loss. In that case, David is out of luck. Or we might say that his "wrongful loss" is the concern of distributive, not corrective justice. In that case, we might rectify or eliminate it through funds raised from the treasury. Alternatively, we might say that Steven's wrong includes the loss he imposed on David. Thus, his wrong is different from the wrong Michelle committed. Then repairing his wrong would involve both apology and compensation, whereas repairing hers would require apology only.

The claim that Steven's wrongdoing is different than Michelle's just because David suffers a loss as a consequence of his mischief begs the question. What principle makes David's loss part of Steven's wrongdoing rather than an untoward consequence of it? What did Steven do that Michelle did not? Each drove negligently, that is, wrongfully. What differs is the consequences of wrong, not the wrong itself.

Instead of arguing that Steven's wrong differs from Michelle's just because the consequences of their mischief differ, we might argue that even though the wrongs are the same, the content of the duty to repair differs because the consequences of their mischief differ. Both have done the same wrong; they have driven negligently. Both, therefore, have the same duty under corrective justice; each has the duty to repair the wrong. To annul a wrong is to eliminate its effects in the world, as much as is feasible. It is to return the world to where it would have been had the wrong never been committed. In this sense, fully to repair the wrong is to repair not only the wrong but its consequences as well. That would mean giving up whatever gains one has secured as a result of the wrong as well as compensating for whatever damage one has caused others to suffer. Though Michelle and Steven have committed the same wrong, this account of what it means to annul or repair a wrong explains why Steven and Michelle have different duties in corrective justice as the result of committing the same wrongful act. Steven's having to compensate David is a matter of corrective justice because it is part of what Steven must do to repair his wrong. It is part of what he must do to make the world as if his wrong had never occurred within it. Michelle's negligence harms no one; repairing her wrong does not require that she compensate anyone. The same wrong can yield different concrete duties under the same abstract duty to repair that wrong.

More importantly, this account explains why Steven must compensate David in corrective justice without making the fact that David has suffered a wrongful loss part of the reason – let alone all of the reason (as in the annulment view) –

for having to do so. In this account, the wrongfulness of the loss has nothing to do with the nature of Steven's duty. Repairing the wrong means making it as if the wrong had never occurred; and that means compensating the victims of it. This, I take it, is how the pure relational view would ultimately want to deal with the appropriateness of the damage remedy.

The problem with this account of the relationship between the wrong and the losses that result from it is that it is based on an unacceptable understanding of what is required in order to "repair" or annul a wrong. Here is an example of the sort of case that creates a problem. I am scheduled to take a plane from New Haven to Washington. Five blocks from the airport, the taxi hits another car. My leg is broken; I'm taken to the hospital; I miss my flight. The plane I would have taken crashes. There are no survivors. Had I caught the plane, I would have died. Only the taxi driver's recklessness keeps me alive.

There is no doubt that the taxi driver acted wrongfully, and that as a result of his doing so incurs a debt under corrective justice to repair the wrong he has done. But if we understand repairing the wrong in the way we do in Steven's case, then the cabbie has a duty to make the world as if his wrong never happened in it. In that world, I would have died in a plane crash; my being alive is a consequence of his wrong – one for which I am grateful. But can the taxi driver really have the duty to bring about my death? I do not see how he could. The duty to repair is not the duty to annul all the consequences of one's wrongs. It is, I want to suggest as a first approximation, the duty to repair the wrong – in whatever sense we can ultimately make of that phrase – and all the *wrongful* consequences of it. The gist of my suggestion then is that the wrongfulness of the loss is an independent aspect of corrective justice. Repairing the wrong and repairing the wrongful losses occasioned by it can be distinct duties under the principle of corrective justice. If I was wrong in my earlier work to focus entirely on the wrongfulness of the loss as the point of corrective justice, then I would com-

323

mit a greater error by accepting the pure relational view that treats the loss as only coincidentally connected to the duty to repair.

These considerations suggest the following characterization of what I will call the mixed conception of corrective justice. Corrective justice imposes on wrongdoers the duty to repair their wrongs and the wrongful losses their wrongdoing occasions. The duty to repair the wrong follows from the relational view; the importance of wrongful losses to the demands of corrective justice is the remnant of the annulment view: thus, the "mixed" view. This conception of corrective justice stands in need of further amendment, however. Indeed, I want now to argue that repairing the wrong itself, the cornerstone of the relational view, is no part of corrective justice at all. The view I want to defend is that the duty of wrongdoers in corrective justice is to repair the wrongful losses for which they are responsible.

16.4 A WRONG IS NOT ALWAYS A WRONG

There are two problems with the notion that corrective justice requires annulling wrongs. The first is that the wrongs that typically are the concern of corrective justice are not wrongs in the sense that usually calls for annulment. Second, to the extent individuals commit such wrongs, there already are principles of justice designed to deal with them. In the typical case an injurer is at fault for failing to take the care that a reasonable person of ordinary prudence would have. Fault judgments of this sort are not ordinarily defeasible by what we would think of as an excuse. To use the language I developed earlier and will take up again later, in the typical case the fault or wrong is in the doing, not in the doer. The agent need not have done something for which he is to blame, something that displays a lack of proper motivation or a defect in his character. The wrongdoing is *objective*. Similarly, wrongs that are invasions of rights need not be culpable in the ordinary sense. In the infringement cases, they are the result of conduct that is, on balance, justified and not culpable at all. Excusable conduct can be at fault; justifiable conduct can be rights-invasive, and constitute a wrong in that sense.

The wrongs that fall within the ambit of corrective often do not mark a moral defect in the agent or in her action. It is hard to see why annulling them would be a requirement of justice. On the other hand, there are cases of genuine wrongdoing that mark a fault in the agent and in the action. The reckless imposition of unjustifiable levels of risk; the intentional harming or injuring of another. These can be genuine wrongs. Perhaps a case could be made for the proposition that justice requires annulling them. But there already is a principle of justice that holds that such wrongs should be annulled: the principle of *retributive* justice.

Annulling moral wrongs is a matter of justice: retributive, not corrective, justice. There is a legal institution that, in some accounts anyway, is designed to do retributive justice, namely, punishment. The bulk of cases in which claims in corrective justice are valid do not involve wrongs in this sense. If we abandon the view that corrective justice requires annulling wrongs as such, we are left with the claim that corrective justice imposes the duty on wrongdoers to annul the wrongful losses their conduct occasions.

Does this mean that we have returned to the annulment thesis, that we have given up the relational view altogether? No. *Corrective justice imposes on wrongdoers the duty to repair the wrongful losses their conduct occasions, losses for which they are responsible.* Thus, it provides wrongdoers with reasons for action that are peculiar to them – agent relative reasons in that sense – to annul losses they are responsible for. The insight of the relational view is that wrongdoing changes the nature of the relationship between the parties; it creates duties where none had previously existed. It gives agents reasons for acting that they did not previously have. The problem with the relational view is that it gets the content of the duty wrong. The annulment thesis has the correct interpretation of the content of the duty: thus, the mixed conception of corrective justice.

In the relational view, the fact that he has done something wrong gives the wrongdoer a duty to repair the wrong. In the mixed view, the wrongdoer has no duty to repair the wrong. Instead, he has the duty to repair the wrongful losses that are his responsibility. What grounds that duty? It is not the fact that the injurer has done something morally blameworthy or otherwise culpable, something, in other words, that might in fact ground a duty to right his wrong. He may in fact have done nothing morally reprehensible at all. Still, he has done something wrong. Because it is wrong, the loss that results is wrongful, or so I will argue in Chapter 17. Moreover, because he has done wrong, the loss may be his fault, his responsibility. And if it is his responsibility, corrective justice imposes on him the duty to repair. That is the way in which corrective justice connects agency with wrongful interferences with an individual's well-being. Its core idea is that when individuals are linked to wrongful losses by the relationship of responsibility there arises a duty of repair.

Corrective justice has two dimensions. First, losses are the concern of corrective justice if they are wrongful. They are wrongful if they result from wrongs or wrongdoings. The wrong grounds the claim that the losses are wrongful (and thus within the ambit of corrective justice.) Secondly, the duty to repair those wrongful losses is grounded not in the fact that they are the result of wrongdoing, but in the fact that the losses are the injurer's responsibility, the result of his agency. The duty to repair those losses under corrective justice is grounded in the injurer's connection to them. They are, in a suitable sense, his responsibility, they are his, and, therefore, his to repair.[10]

16.5 GROUNDS AND MODES OF RECOVERY – AGAIN

In Chapter 15, I argued that there is a difference between the grounds and modes of rectification, and that distinction still stands. Nothing I have said about corrective justice in this discussion provides a reason for amending a perfectly defensible analytic distinction. The question is whether the distinction is applicable to corrective justice as I now understand it. In the mixed conception, corrective justice provides both a grounds for liability and recovery *and* a reason for claiming that compensation is someone's moral duty. Thus, one might be tempted to hold that the principle of corrective justice provides both the grounds and the mode of recovery. Wrongful losses ought to be annulled means that victims have a right to repair; and because wrongdoers have a duty to repair in corrective justice, the proper mode of rectification is one that imposes liability for those costs on them. In that case, any mode of rectification other than imposing the victim's costs on the injurer would violate corrective justice. Is this constraint on liability entailed by the mixed conception of corrective justice?

Even if the injurer has the duty to repair in justice, it does not follow that justice requires that the duty be discharged by the injurer. We need to distinguish between the grounds of the duty and the institutional mechanisms that are permissible ways of implementing the duty. One simple example might illustrate the general point. The duty to repair is a debt of repayment. People who take out loans incur debts of repayment. We might even say that these are debts in justice. But it does not follow that an injustice is done whenever someone other than the indebted individual pays back the debt. So if Donald Trump decides to pay back all my debts (for which I would be suitably grateful), and does so (for which I would be even more grateful), all claims against me would thereby be extinguished. If the loans are repaid by someone other than me, no injustice has been done. This is true even if it is me, not Donald Trump, who has the duty in justice to repay the debts. It is true, moreover, even if Trump does this all on his own, without any encouragement from me, or in the absence of a contractual or other understanding between us.

This example illustrates that someone other than the indebted party can discharge the duty without doing so constituting an injustice. Therefore, it does not follow from the fact that one is required to make repair as a matter of corrective justice that any institutional arrangement (or mode of rectification) that discharges that duty in some other way (for example, through the general tax office) would be unjust. So one question we have to consider is this: What modes of rectification are compatible with the mixed conception of corrective justice? This is the issue that will preoccupy us in Chapters 18 and 19.

Whatever conception of corrective justice one adopts – the annulment thesis, the relational view, or the mixed conception – the central concept is "wrongdoing" and its siblings "wrong," and "wrongful." We need to develop an account of the concept of wrongfulness within the principle of corrective justice, the task to which we now turn.

Chapter 17

Wrongfulness

Corrective justice imposes a duty to repair wrongful losses on those agents responsible for them. In this way corrective justice mediates the relationship between agents and a subset of losses that individuals absorb. Its central feature is that it brings agents together with these losses by creating agent-relative reasons for acting. The particular duty it imposes is to repair the loss. There may be other agent-relative reasons for acting that arise as a consequence of wrongfully injuring another, for example, the duty to apologize or to forbear from future harming, but these are not derived from corrective justice.

There are two essential components in the concept of corrective justice. These are wrongfulness and responsibility. Only wrongful losses fall within the ambit of corrective justice. Responsibility for them grounds the agent-relative duty to repair. The principle of corrective justice requires a theory of wrongfulness and a theory of responsibility. This chapter develops the relevant conception of wrongfulness and outlines the relevant theory of responsibility. We begin with the theory of wrongfulness.

A theory of wrongfulness will have both analytic and substantive components. The analytic theory will provide an account of the conditions of wrongfulness. The substantive theory will tell us what sort of losses are wrongful within the meaning of corrective justice. Thus, it may turn out that losses are wrongful if they result from conduct harmful of legitimate interests. The substantive theory will then determine which interests are legitimate. The substantive theory awaits a preliminary analytic inquiry, and it is to that endeavor we now turn.

The thesis is that wrongfulness applies to losses. Conduct can render a loss wrongful, and it can do so in either of two distinct ways: by *wrongdoing* and *wrong*. In order to illustrate the distinction between wrongdoing and wrong, we need first to distinguish among interests, legitimate interests and rights. I can have many interests, not all of which are legitimate. I can steal a television and develop an interest in its possession. In general, arising as it does from theft, my interest will not be legitimate. Were the television destroyed, my interest would have been injured. I would have suffered a loss. Normally, injuries to non-legitimate interests do not call for relief or repair in justice. Nevertheless, there may exist all sorts of good reasons for legally protecting even these interests in a limited way. For example, we may want to discourage individuals from randomly destroying property. In order to create a system of private enforcement, I may be entitled to seek compensation if you destroy my TV, even if I have no claim in justice to it. It is not part of the case for compensating me that I have a right to repair. My interest, however real, cannot morally ground such a claim. Instead compensating me is a way of reaching you, not a way of sustaining or recognizing the "legitimacy" of my interest.

The destruction of my TV injures me and, under circumstances of the sort just described, can give rise to legal protection. Though injured by its loss, I would not be *harmed* by it. I reserve the moral category of harm for cases in which *legitimate* interests are injured. There are many things that a person may have a legitimate interest in, but no right to – including a successful career and a generous reception of one's books. Bad reviews and wily competitors can be harmful. Nevertheless, neither recovery nor liability is warranted when a bad review or effective competition is damaging. Certainly, neither is required by justice, even if liability for unflattering reviews might have the salutary effect of reducing their incidence.

Even if there is no right to a favorable review or to a successful career, an individual who recklessly and without justification sets back those interests wrongfully injures or harms the victim. Though a negative review need not violate anyone's rights, it can harm nonetheless. And if it harms wrongfully, for example, by distortion or gross misrepresentation, the loss that results from the harm may well be a wrongful one. Sometimes legitimate interests are so important that they are rights. Part of what that means is that losses arising from actions contrary to the constraints imposed by rights ought to be repaired in justice. This is one way, I argue, that rights can be distinguished from legitimate interests more generally, that is, by the nature of the protection afforded them.

We might then distinguish loosely among interests, legitimate interests, and rights according to the claims in justice to which interference with them gives rise. Though we can imagine all sorts of very good (policy) reasons for allowing victims to recover against their injurers, losses that result when mere interests are set back do *not* give rise to a claim in justice to repair. (Perhaps, the injurer has acted in an unjustifiable fashion and by allowing the victim to recover against the injurer, we establish a system of private enforcement.) In contrast, legitimate interests *can* give rise to claims in *justice* for their repair, but not always. Fair competition can be harmful of legitimate interests, but it does not give rise to a claim in justice to repair. Only losses that result from unjustifiably injured legitimate interests require compensation in justice. Rights differ from legitimate interests in just this way. Invasions of rights give rise to claims in justice to repair whether or not the injurer's conduct is justifiable.[1]

With these distinctions in mind, I want now to return to two ways of creating wrongful losses, by wrongdoing and wrong. First, wrongful losses can result from *wrongdoing*. Drawing upon the previous distinctions, we might say that wrongdoing consists in the unjustifiable or otherwise impermissible injuring of others' legitimate interests. Wrongdoing is unjustifiable harming. Business losses that result from unfair business practices may be of this sort. The businesswoman has a legitimate interest in the success of her enterprise, but no right to it. If a competitor succeeds in driving her out of business through permissible means, then the businesswoman has no claim in justice to repair. On the other hand, if her competitors violate norms governing fair business practices, they act impermissibly and in doing so wrongfully harm her legitimate business interests. Those losses are wrongful, the result of wrongdoing.

Secondly, wrongful losses can result from *wrongs*. Wrongs are actions contrary to rights. Wrongs can be justifiable or not. Suppose Carla has a property right in her insulin. When Hal takes the insulin in order to prevent his lapsing into a coma, he invades her right permissibly. Should he take the insulin for no other reason than to put her at risk, he invades her right wrongfully. In both cases her losses are wrongful in the appropriate sense.

Corrective justice imposes the duty to repair wrongful losses. Losses are wrongful if they result either from wrongdoings or wrong. Wrongdoing consists in unjustifiable or impermissible harming. Wronging is action contrary to rights. The discussion to this point remains incomplete, for at the very least we need an account of the sort of conduct that is unjustifiable or impermissible within the meaning of corrective justice. Suppose someone does the best she can, but manages nevertheless to set back another's legitimate interest. If she has failed to take reasonable care, then her conduct falls below an *objective* standard of conduct, but one she is incapable (under the circumstances) of meeting. Does her conduct constitute the sort of wrongdoing or unjustifiable conduct contemplated by the principle of corrective justice? We might say of such a person that she did the best she could, that she is not to blame for her failure, that she has an excuse for her shortcoming. Could we say, nevertheless, that though excusable, her conduct is unjustifiable? Corrective justice requires unjustifiable harming. What is the relevant theory of unjustifiability? More precisely, what is the relationship between excuses and wrongdoing in corrective justice?

Wrongfulness

17.1 EXCUSES AND WRONGDOING

Because our larger project is to determine the extent to which the principle of corrective justice applies to it, it will be helpful if we recall the concept of wrongdoing applicable in torts. In torts, conduct is wrongful if it is at fault. Conduct is at fault if it is either negligent, reckless or intentionally mischievous. Intentional misconduct in torts is somewhat of a misnomer in that an injurer is said to have committed an intentional tort if she intends to commit an action that is, under some true description of it, wrongful, whether or not the actor herself believed the act to be wrongful or would have desired to perform it had she had known or believed it to be. Conduct that is at fault because it involves what the law of torts calls "wrongful intent" may be anything but intentionally wrongful in the usual sense.[2]

Most of the damage for which individuals seek redress in torts is the result of accidents, and of the cases involving accidents, the bulk of these are adjudicated under the negligence rule. Negligence in torts is the failure to take reasonable care, and, as we have already noted, the standard of reasonable care is objective or external to the actor. An actor is negligent for failing to take the care of a reasonable person of ordinary prudence, whether or not she is capable of exercising that care.

How can the injurer's conduct be *wrongful* when measured against an external or objective standard of negligence? In what sense can an injurer who does the best he can, but fails nevertheless to act as would have a reasonable person, be said to have acted wrongfully?

The answer lies in the distinction between fault in the doing and fault in the doer. Ascriptions of fault in the doing can be defeated by justifications, whereas allegations of fault in the doer are ordinarily defeasible by excuses. Whether tort liability is strict or imposed on the basis of fault, it is not normally defeasible by excuses designed to establish the absence of moral or other fault in the doer (i.e., culpability defeating excuses). Thus, the standard of fault in torts is that

333

of fault in the doing. The question is whether corrective justice implicates a similar notion of fault or wrongdoing.

It does. To see this, recall that some wrongful losses result from wrongs. Wrongs are invasions of rights. Some wrongs are infringements, that is, permissible or justifiable invasions of rights. The losses that result from infringements are wrongful in the sense required by corrective justice and are thus compensable in justice, though the injurer acts in a permissible or praiseworthy, not culpable, fashion. Losses therefore, can be wrongful in the absence of culpable agency and agents who create such losses can have a duty in corrective justice to repair them. Thus, culpability is a necessary condition neither of the relevant conception of wrongfulness nor of responsibility implicated by corrective justice.

If culpability is not a condition of the duty to repair another's loss in cases in which a right has been invaded, why should it be a requirement of corrective justice in the standard case of wrongdoing? The failure to abide by the relevant norms of conduct is enough to render the action a form of wrongdoing (in the same way that failure to abide by the constraints imposed by rights renders conduct a wrong) and the losses that result wrongful (in both cases) even if it is inadequate to render the agent a culpable wrongdoer, someone who would be worthy of blame, sanction or punishment.

The sort of wrongdoing required by corrective justice is objective. It does not require moral culpability or blame. It requires only that the conduct in question fail to comply with the relevant or appropriate norms of conduct. In the typical case, this failure is the failure to exercise reasonable care; it is a failure to abide by governing *community* norms.[3] Because wrongdoing is objective in this sense, culpability-defeating excuses are normally irrelevant to the demands of corrective justice.

Agency-defeating excuses are important in corrective justice even if those that defeat culpability are not.[4] Agency, not culpable agency, is implicated by the concept of corrective

334

justice. In corrective justice excuses that aim to defeat agency are relevant for two different reasons.[5] First, in order for an agent to have a duty in corrective justice to repair a loss, the loss must be wrongful in the appropriate sense. It must result from either wrongdoing or wrong. Both involve human agency. Therefore, an individual who has an agency-defeating excuse undermines the victim's claim that his is a loss falling within the ambit of corrective justice. Second, corrective justice imposes the loss upon the injurer, not simply because it wrongful, but because the loss is, in some appropriate sense, his responsibility. An individual who has a suitable agency-defeating excuse may be on the way to showing that there is no sense in which the victim's loss is his responsibility. (His having a good excuse does not strictly imply that the loss is not his responsibility because being connected to an event by the agency relationship may be only one of the many morally relevant ways of being responsible for it.) Thus, agency-defeating excuses are relevant in corrective justice because they bear on the "injurer's" responsibility as well as on the moral character of the victim's loss.[6]

17.2 THE CONTENT OF RIGHTS

Conduct that is invasive of a right constitutes a wrong. The same conditions of agency apply to wrongs as to wrongdoing. Culpability is not a condition of a wronging for some of the same reasons that it fails to be a condition of wrongdoing under corrective justice. Indeed, in the case of some wronging, the injurer's conduct is actually morally praiseworthy or, at least, permissible. These are the infringement cases. Wronging can sometimes create wrongful losses even in cases of justifiable conduct. In cases of wronging, neither the absence of blame nor the presence of praiseworthiness is sufficient to defeat a claim that a loss is wrongful. The wrongfulness of the loss derives from the fact that the conduct is a wrong, and the conduct is a wrong just because it is invasive of a right. Because wrongs are defined in terms of rights, we need an account of what it is to have a right, and what it is that makes conduct invasive of a right. This section presents the relevant conception of rights and of rights-invasion, and in doing so revisits the discussion in Chapter 15 regarding the relationship between the content of rights and the underlying normative theory of them.

The place to begin is with the distinctions owed to Calabresi–Melamed among property, liability and inalienability rules as ways of protecting or securing entitlements. These distinctions should be familiar by now, but a brief review will be helpful for the discussion that follows. Property rules protect rights by conferring on right holders the power to exclude and to alienate. Consent ex ante is a condition of legitimate transfer under a property rule. Liability rules protect rights by conferring a right to compensation on right holders in the event that someone takes that to which the right holder is entitled. Under liability rules, compensation ex post legitimates forced transfers. Inalienability rules protect entitlements by prohibiting right holders from transferring that to which they are entitled by either consent ex ante or compensation ex post.

Now let's contrast this account of rights with the classical liberal theory. In classical liberal theory, to have a right is to have a protected sphere of autonomy or control. To say that I have a right to something is to say that I, not you or anybody else, have control over its use. I make those decisions, not you. There is an obvious conflict between the classical liberal conception of rights and the Calabresi–Melamed framework. How can a liability rule in the Calabresi–Melamed sense protect my right when it gives you and others certain important discretions with respect to the uses to which my right can be put (provided that you compensate me for whatever damages, if any, the uses to which you put my holdings impose on me)? A liability rule in this sense gives you options or control with respect to the resources to which I am entitled. Isn't the notion of a liability rule incompatible with the classical liberal conception of a right? How can liability rules protect liberal property rights?

The answer is that liability rules cannot and do not protect classical liberal property rights. Something, apparently, has to give – either the liberal theory of rights or the Calabresi–Melamed framework. Neither alternative is altogether satisfactory. There is a third alternative, however, and it is the one I want to defend. It requires that we give up both the classical liberal conception of rights and the Calabresi–Melamed framework.

The analysis I offer relies on the distinction between the meaning and content of rights, or what I have elsewhere called the syntax and semantics of rights.[7] The syntax of rights specifies what is true of rights analytically: what, in other words, is part of the meaning of rights. Ronald Dworkin, for one, claims that part of the meaning of rights is that they act as trumps in political and moral arguments.[8] For him, their *function* is part of their syntax. Were his claim true, it would be true of all (political or moral) rights as such. In contrast, Joseph Raz claims that rights *ground* duties.[9] For Joel Feinberg, rights are valid claims of one sort or another.[10] The set of valid claims can range over a variety of domains including use, alienation, and transfer more generally. That rights are valid claims is part of their syntax. If true, it is true of them necessarily.

The syntax of rights does not specify the content of any right in particular. When we say that rights are valid claims that range over a variety of domains, we have said nothing about the content of any particular right. The content of the claims associated with rights ownership is given by the semantics of rights. The semantics of rights is not given a priori, and is not true of rights as such. That rights include some set of valid claims is an aspect of the syntax of rights. The specific claims associated with particular rights constitute the right's semantics.

An example might help to illustrate the way in which the semantics of rights are constructed. Suppose it is a norm in our community that in order for someone legitimately to obtain what is owned by another, she must first secure the entitled party's consent. Under this norm consent would be a condition of legitimate transfer. The right holder would then have the (moral) power to require others to seek and secure her consent as a condition of obtaining that to which she is entitled. Alternatively, we might say that someone can take what another is entitled to provided he compensates ex post for what he takes. In that case the right holder has no moral power to demand consent as a condition of legitimate transfer; instead she has only the power to demand compensation ex post. She has rights in both cases, the syntax of which is the same. That is, she has a set of valid claims expressing powers derived from the relevant norms governing transfer. The content of the right changes as a consequence of the relevant norms governing transfer. With the change in content comes the change in claims associated with the right.

The content or semantics of rights is not given a priori; the claims associated with rights ownership are not part of their meaning. Instead, the content of rights derives from the *norms* governing the particular domains constitutive of rights ownership. Those norms themselves derive from the underlying *normative* foundation or theory of rights. The normative or substantive theory of rights specifies the point or purpose of the set of rights, the goals or purposes of the practice or the ideals the practice expresses or aspires to. If I am correct, the content of rights derives from normative argument, not conceptual analysis.

We can now reinterpret the Calabresi–Melamed framework in a way that eliminates any conflict it appears to have with the liberal conception of rights. Instead of saying that the Calabresi–Melamed framework specifies ways of protecting or securing rights, we should say that it constitutes a framework of norms designed to specify the terms or conditions of legitimate transfer. It constitutes a framework for specifying the *content* of particular rights with respect to the terms of their transfer. The Calabresi–Melamed framework tells us what conditions must be satisfied in order for transfers to respect rights. In other words, the mistake in the conventional interpretation of the Calabresi–Melamed thesis is

338

treating liability and property rules as ways of protecting rights, when in fact they are norms that help to specify the content of rights within the transactional domain. *Liability and property rules determine the conditions of legitimate transfer, the conditions that must be satisfied if transactions are to respect the rights of others.*

Here is a sampling of the ways in which property and liability rules work to specify the content or semantics of particular rights: (1) If someone has a property rule right, then she has a valid claim requiring those who seek her resources to secure her consent first. Failure on the part of others constitutes action contrary to her right, and taking under those conditions constitutes a wrong to her. Given the analysis of wrongs, such a taking would be a wrong even if the taker was justified, on balance, in forgoing efforts to secure her consent. (2) If someone has a liability rule right, then she has a valid claim to compensation in the event another individual secures her resources without her consent. Liability rule rights do not confer on right holders the power or authority to exclude or to demand consent as a condition of transfer. One who has such a right cannot exclude others from enjoying that to which one is entitled. If liability rule rights can be rights, then the classical liberal theory must be rejected as an account of the *meaning* of rights. It may be considered as a potential normative theory of the content of rights, however. As a normative theory, it would hold that the content of all rights should be given by rules that express the role of rights in protecting and securing individual autonomy. Thus, it might hold that almost all rights should be property rule rights enabling exclusion and alienation. This is, roughly speaking, the libertarian theory of rights.

We can combine property with liability rules to specify the content of rights, and we can do so in either of two ways. (3) In one case the content of a right is given by the *disjunction* of property and liability rules. Thus, the right holder is entitled either to consent ex ante or to compensation ex post as a condition of legitimate transfer, but not both. Thus, in order to effect a transfer in accordance with rights, someone would have to negotiate with the right holder or, in the event he chooses to forgo negotiations, would have to pay compensation. (4) Alternatively, we can specify the content of a right by the *conjunction* of property and liability rules. In that case, the right holder is entitled to exclude another's use and to alienate on terms agreeable to her ex ante. Failure to respect voluntary exchange as the appropriate condition of transfer constitutes a wrong – action contrary to the right holder's rightful claims. The liability rule gives the right holder a claim to compensation for consequential damages. In the case in which the content of a right is given by the disjunction of property and liability rules, both specify possible conditions of legitimate transfer. In the case in which the content of rights is given by the conjunction of liability with property rules, compensation arises as a valid claim whenever someone fails to comply with the terms of transfer set out in the property rule. Compensation rectifies a wrong done; it does not right what in its absence would constitute a wrong.[11]

17.3 WRONGS AND RIGHTS

This account of the ways in which property and liability rules specify the content of rights provides the foundation of an understanding of the concept of a wrong. Wrongs are actions contrary to rights. The kind of wrong depends on the kind of right. The kind of right depends on the transaction rule applied. The transaction rule applied depends on the underlying normative theory of rights. Property rule rights are invaded whenever the agent fails to secure consent as a condition of transfer[12] Liability rule rights are invaded only when the agent fails to compensate ex post for the taking. In these cases compensation legitimates forced transfers and rights what in its absence would have been a wrong. Rendering compensation is a way of respecting the claims associated with rights ownership in the case of liability rule rights;

it is a way of repairing wrongs in the case of property rule rights.

In the case of rights whose content is given by the disjunction of property and liability rules, there is a wrong only if the agent fails to secure consent and fails to render compensation ex post. Either would have sufficed to render transfer legitimate.[13] In the case of rights whose content is given by the conjunction of property and liability rules, the wrong consists in the failure to secure consent as a condition of transfer. If Carla's right to her insulin is given by the conjunction of property and liability rules, then Hal justifiably wrongs her by taking her insulin in order to prevent lapsing into a coma. Under the analysis presented here, Carla has a right to repair in justice. By rendering compensation, however, Hal does not right the wrong he has done her; he merely compensates her for it. In doing so, he respects her claim to repair against him. Should he fail to compensate her, which is her right, then he would have doubly wronged her. He would have invaded both aspects of her right, to consent as a condition of legitimate transfer and to compensation in the event consent is not secured. It is a further question whether his doubly wronging her could be defended as permissible or justifiable in anything like the way his wronging her to save his life might be. The appropriateness of various institutional arrangements for responding to his doubly wronging her, whether or not he is justified in doing so, create further problems and raise additional issues. Nothing about the justifiability of his conduct nor the appropriateness of various institutional responses, however, follows from the syntax of rights or wrongs. Each requires substantive normative argument.

The underlying normative theory of rights tells us what the appropriate transaction rule should be in various empirical circumstances. The transaction rule in turn specifies the conditions of legitimate transfer and in doing so gives content to particular entitlements. Only then can we determine whether compensation is owed, and, if it is, whether it is owed because a right has been invaded, or because rendering compensation is part of what one has to do in order to respect the constraints that rights impose. The conceptual framework provides the meaning of analysis of rights; it helps us understand what wrongs are. The normative framework determines which of a person's actions wrong the rights of others.[14]

17.4 RIGHTS AND WELFARE

Compensation under liability rules can sometimes respect rights, a fact that suggests a particular conception of rights. If compensation justifies a forced transfer, it does so because compensation gives the entitled party her due. Therefore, rights must be no more than guarantees to a particular stream of welfare or utility, otherwise compensation could never fully respect a right. Because rights are streams of welfare only, providing a "victim" full compensation, that is, rendering her no worse off ex post than she was ex ante, respects her rights; it gives her the full measure of her entitlement.

Voluntary exchange and compensation are two ways, suitable to different circumstances, of seeing to it that one gets what one is entitled to. Under property rules, the right holder is responsible for obtaining the relevant stream of welfare by refusing to accept an unsatisfactory offer. Under liability rules, the right holder obtains the relevant stream of welfare by compensation. Both voluntary consent and compensation can respect the same rights only if the content of that right is given by the disjunction of property and liability rules *and* only if rights themselves are analyzed as a protected level of welfare or utility. This is the underlying conception of rights implied by economic analysis.

17.5 RIGHTS AND AUTONOMY

If we focus only on those cases in which compensation justifies forced transfers we will miss entirely the role compensation plays in rectifying wrongful losses. The core of the theory of strict liability is the idea that compensation is owed

342

because a wrong has been done, a right invaded. And it does not matter from the point of view of justice whether the wrong is the result of wrongdoing (unjustifiable conduct). It is the wrong that grounds the claim to repair. Liability serves not to legitimate forced transfers under the auspices of rights, but serves instead to rectify wrongs done to rights; it is a debt owed because the conditions of legitimate transfer under rights have been violated or disregarded, not respected.[15]

In the theory of strict liability, only property rules specify the conditions of legitimate transfer. Liability rules ground ' claims to repair in the event the terms set out by property rules are disregarded or inadequately respected. Thus, in the theory of strict liability, rights are to be understood as protected spheres of autonomy or control. Property rules empower right holders to exclude and to alienate. These are ways of expressing individual autonomy. Legitimate transfer within rights must respect individual autonomy. At the very least, this emphasis on the conjunction of property and liability rules underscores the classical liberal foundation of Richard Epstein's earliest version of the theory. It enables us to understand why Epstein believes that libertarian political philosophy grounds a theory of strict liability in torts.[16]

We have argued that property and liability rules specify the content of rights over the transactional domain; that is, they specify the conditions that must be satisfied in order for transfers to comply with the constraints imposed by rights. Whether the content of rights is given by property or liability rules or by some combination of the two depends on the underlying normative theory of rights. When both the classical liberal and economic theories are correctly understood as substantive normative theories of rights and not as accounts of the meaning of rights, we can determine both the conception of rights each has as well as the rules governing transfer each favors. In economic analysis, rights are themselves streams of welfare or utility, and the rules of transfer are determined by fitting them to the overall ambition of increasing welfare under different empirical circumstances. In the classical liberal theory, rights secure autonomy, and in order that they succeed in this regard their content is to be given by the conjunction of property and liability rules. It is in this way that the theory of strict liability falls out of a general libertarian or classical liberal political theory.

17.6 CORRECTIVE JUSTICE AND RIGHTS

In Chapter 15, we distinguished among three ways in which the justifiability of someone's conduct figures in the claims of his victims to repair. In the first, compensation is one's due only if the conduct that creates the loss is somehow wrongful or unjustified. In the second, the conduct is justifiable, but the injurer is nevertheless required to make good his victim's loss. In the third, compensation is owed as a condition of making the injurer's conduct justifiable. The arguments of the last two chapters have provided us with the tools for grounding these intuitive categories. In cases of the first sort, there is wrongdoing. Cases of the second sort involve wrongs. Both wrongs and wrongdoings can create wrongful losses that require repair under corrective justice. That is why the victim is entitled to compensation in both cases. Cases of the third sort are not wrongs or wrongdoings. In these cases compensation is a response neither to wrongdoing nor to wrong. Instead, compensation respects rights by respecting the conditions of legitimate transfer set forth in them.

The theory of strict liability makes two fundamental mistakes. Because it downplays the concept of fault, it misses the importance of wrongdoing or fault as a basis of liability and recovery in justice. It countenances wrongdoing only in the case of wrongful invasions of rights, that is, violations. But in the case of violations, rights are invaded, and that is enough for the strict liability theorist to justify both liability and recovery. The wrongfulness of the invasion is, in effect, otiose. The second problem comes from failing to appreciate the variety of ways in which compensation can derive from rights. Compensation can be a way of respecting the demands of rights, and is therefore not only a way of correcting for wrong done.

In contrast, the economist overemphasizes cases of the third sort. In these cases compensation legitimates transfer; it respects the underlying transactional rights. This view of compensation grows out of the more general economic analysis in which rights are analyzed as streams of welfare; where the point of assigning rights is to promote efficiency; and where the need for a law of tort derives from high ex ante transaction costs. Compensation is, in such a view, a normative equivalent, but second best alternative to, voluntary agreement, suitable to circumstances in which transaction costs block efficient voluntary exchanges.

The view I am pressing is that cases of both the first and second varieties involve the principle of corrective justice though only the second involves rights. Cases of the third sort can involve rights, but not corrective justice. If all of the cases of tort liability and recovery were of the third sort, the proper explanation of tort law would be an economic one; tort law would be a matter of markets, not morals. But tort law also involves cases of the first two sorts in which losses result from wrongdoing or wrong; and those cases implicate the principle of corrective justice, or so I argue in Chapter 18. Thus, tort law is a mixture of markets and morals, or so I argue in Chapters 18–20. So much for the analytics of wrong and wrongdoing. Before turning to the substantive theory of wrong and wrongdoing, I want to outline the relevant analytic theory of responsibility implicated in the principle of corrective justice.

17.7 A THEORY OF RESPONSIBILITY

The conception of corrective justice I defend holds that an individual has a duty to repair those wrongful losses that are his responsibility. Corrective justice requires a particular conception of wrongful losses. I have provided the analytic structure of that conception in the preceeding sections of this chapter. It also requires a particular conception of responsibility. This section outlines the relevant theory of responsibility.

There is an important connection between the theories of wrongfulness developed above and the theory of responsibility. There are two ways in which an individual's conduct can create wrongful losses, by wrong and wrongdoing. Wrongdoing presupposes fault, wrong does not. Thus, responsibility for loss can sometimes require fault, other times not. In other words, the conditions of responsibility may change depending on the source of the wrongfulness of the victim's loss.

In the case in which an injurer is responsible for another's loss as a result of his wrongdoing, his responsibility depends on the truth of the following proposition: the victim's loss is his fault. The sentence, "*P*'s loss is *D*'s fault," is true only if the following set of propositions is true.

1. *D* is at fault.
2. That aspect of *D*'s conduct that is at fault is causally connected in the appropriate way to *P*'s loss.
3. *P*'s loss falls within the scope of the risks that make that aspect of *D*'s conduct at fault.

A loss cannot be someone's fault unless his conduct is in some way at fault. And it cannot be his fault unless his fault causes the loss for which he is being held responsible in an appropriate way. Moreover conduct can be at fault and causally efficacious in the appropriate way without the agent being at fault for the losses that result. For example, a motorist can be at fault for driving without his license. If the motorist injures someone while otherwise driving nonnegligently, the loss is not his fault even though his conduct is both at fault and the cause of harm. The relevant connection does not exist between the loss and that aspect of the conduct that is at fault. In order for the loss to be his fault, the loss must be connected in the appropriate way with that aspect of his conduct that is at fault. Even in those cases in which harm results from those aspects of one's conduct that are at fault, the loss may not be of the sort that falls within the scope of the risks that make the conduct at fault in the first place. These last two conditions of responsibility narrow considerably the scope of responsibility for loss. Causation is simply not enough.

This account sets out necessary conditions of responsibility. It does not claim that these conditions are jointly sufficient. For example, it may be that a loss can be someone's fault only if it falls within the scope of risks that make the conduct at fault *and which are foreseeable, or reasonably foreseeable*. In addition to being insufficient for these reasons, the account I outline is incomplete in other ways. Responsibility depends on the agent's conduct being causally connected to the victim's loss in the appropriate way, but I have not offered an account either of causation or of appropriate causal connections. I favor a counterfactual account of causation of the David Lewis variety, but I am not in a position to defend it here. These tasks are left for another occasion. I bring them to the reader's attention only to make clear that I am not offering a full account of the principle of responsibility implicated by corrective justice. My goal is to provide an outline of the kind of theory required.

Not every wrongful loss results from wrongdoing. Some wrongful losses arise from wrongs that are rights infringements. The theory of responsibility outlined above will not apply to these cases if for no other reason that in the rights infringement case there is no fault in the doing; the loss is wrongful, but no one's fault.[17] That does not mean, however, that it is no one's responsibility. In these cases, it is enough that the loss be causally or otherwise connected in the appropriate way with those aspects of the agent's conduct that make it rights invasive. This outline of the theory of responsibility completes the analytic structure of corrective justice and of its component parts, wrongfulness and responsibility.

17.8 CORRECTIVE JUSTICE AND WRONGDOING

However rights or holdings are allocated, there will be a set of norms governing their transfer. These norms will specify the conditions that must be satisfied if that to which individuals are entitled is to be transferred legitimately. These norms are principles of transfer. Corrective justice is layered upon the relevant theory of transfer. The question before us is whether the principle of corrective justice requires a particular substantive theory of legitimate transfer? Does it constrain the set of possible theories of legitimate transfer, or is it compatible with any consistent theory, whether libertarian, egalitarian or utilitarian? Moreover, do the claims in corrective justice reach beyond the rules of transfer and extend to the substance of the underlying entitlements themselves?

The fact that corrective justice is layered upon substantive norms of transfer raises two doubts about the independence of corrective justice as a moral ideal. First, how can corrective justice both depend on a substantive theory of transactional norms and yet remain an independent moral ideal? Second, if corrective justice provides *moral reasons* for repairing a loss, then the underlying claims sustained by corrective justice must themselves express requirements of distributive justice. This connection between distributive and corrective justice is necessary if corrective justice is to be morally compelling, or so one could argue. By the same token, this relationship appears to rob corrective justice of its moral independence, and greatly reduces its potential as a principle underwriting our current legal practices, practices that do not require that underlying entitlements protected by law meet the strictest test of justice. Corrective justice appears both to depend on an underlying substantive theory of norms and to restrict the set of such norms. How can this be?

Corrective justice imposes the duty to repair the losses occasioned by one's wrongdoing. Its content depends on a substantive theory of wrongdoing, *but its point of purpose does not*. Even if we accept the economic theory of wrongdoing, there remains the important difference between the claim that

348

liability in torts is imposed on injurers in order to promote efficiency. If the law of torts adopts the economic conception of wrongdoing, liability may well be imposed on the very same people in both economic analysis and corrective justice, but the grounds or reasons for imposing liability will differ. It may yet be that the best interpretation of tort liability sees the practice as an attempt to meet the demands of justice of righting or redressing wrongful losses. It is just that in meeting the demands of justice to redress wrongful losses, tort law always promotes efficiency. It promotes efficiency, moreover, because the wrongs that give rise to a duty to redress are economic ones.

This discussion recalls similar disputes in the theory of punishment. We might draw a distinction between the justification of penal liability and the substantive theory of criminal law. With this distinction in mind, the question might be whether a retributive theory of punishment is compatible with a utilitarian theory of the underlying criminal prohibitions. Most compatibilists believe that it can be. Utilitarianism provides the criterion by which the conduct that ought to be prohibited is determined. Then, when an individual inexcusable and without justification violates one of these norms, he deserves to be punished. Retributivism provides the justification for punishment; utilitarianism provides the criterion of punishable acts. The same might be said of the relationship between corrective justice and economic efficiency. Efficiency tells us which losses ought to be annulled. Corrective justice arranges for annulment by imposing the duty to repair on the wrongdoer. If this argument is a good one, it does not appear to matter to corrective justice whether the underlying theory of wrongdoing is an economic one. Even if it is, corrective justice can remain a morally independent principle and capable of providing the best interpretation of our current tort practice. Corrective justice depends on a substantive theory of wrong or wrongdoing, but its point or purpose does not. In that sense, it can remain an independent principle, not swallowed up by the norms it sustains or protects.[18]

Rectifiable wrongs

17.9 CORRECTIVE AND DISTRIBUTIVE JUSTICE[19]

The argument of the previous section is that the point or purpose of corrective justice is distinguishable from the underlying theory of wrongdoing upon which it is layered. It is possible that conduct is wrong only if it is inefficient, and therefore that losses are wrongful only if they are the result of inefficient conduct. Nevertheless, that alone would not make corrective justice a matter of efficiency, for, as I have argued, the point of corrective justice, to impose duties to repair wrongful losses, need not itself be understood as expressing an economic ideal.

If I am right, an underlying economic theory of wrongfulness will not threaten the moral independence of corrective justice. The same would obviously hold of distributive justice. Even if the underlying theory of wrongfulness is given by the relevant theory of distributive justice, it would still be possible to distinguish the point of corrective justice from the underlying theory or the norms it sustains. The point would be to impose reasons for acting of a certain kind, whatever the underlying norms and the theory that grounds them.

Ought we conclude that corrective justice is compatible with any underlying theory of wrongdoing, whether rooted in efficiency or distributive justice, or something else altogether? I think not. Its moral independence assured, the question before us is whether corrective justice itself constrains the norms it can sustain. I argue that it does, and in important and interesting ways.

The claim that corrective justice constrains the underlying substantive theory of wrongfulness rests on the insight that the point of corrective justice is to provide agents with *moral* reasons for acting; it imposes *moral* duties on them. The underlying theory of wrongdoing and wrong must be compatible with this feature of corrective justice. Before someone could have a moral duty to rectify those losses, there must be a moral reason for doing so. In other words, the losses ought to be of the sort it makes moral sense to be concerned about.

Thus, corrective justice must impose constraints on both the substantive theories of wrongdoing and wrong. The set of underlying entitlements may be unjust or wrong, or it might conform to the demands of justice. The norms governing their transfer might also be unjust or they might conform to the demands of justice. This is the distinction between the underlying entitlements and the transactional domain with regard to them. We might agree that corrective justice imposes constraints on the kinds of norms it sustains, but it remains for us to determine the scope of those constraints. Does corrective justice constrain only the norms governing transfer? Is it a dimension of transactional justice narrowly conceived? Or does corrective justice reach the underlying entitlements as well as the norms governing their transfer?

The justice of holdings depends on both the underlying distribution and the relevant transaction norms. If the net effect of securing and sustaining a system of norms and rights in transfer is to embed a fundamentally and uncontroversially unjust distribution of holdings, then one would be hard pressed to say that doing so is a requirement of justice. It does not help to say that doing so is required by corrective justice, but that the demands of corrective justice in such cases are very weak when compared to other reasons for acting that an agent might have. There may be no reason in morality for sustaining injustice, not even a weak one – or so one might argue.

We appear to have two alternatives; neither is fully satisfactory nor plausible. I want to take a stab at outlining a more promising line of argument. If we drive a wedge completely between the norms governing transactions and the justice of the underlying entitlements, we will sometimes find it impossible to explain how corrective justice can provide agents with moral reasons for acting. On the other hand, if we require that claims in corrective justice be ultimately supportable by the distributive justice of the underlying entitlements, then the scope of corrective justice will be narrow indeed, so narrow as to give us reason to doubt that it could play any useful role in understanding any legal practices in a patently second-best world like our own.

The rights sustained by corrective justice must be *real* rights; they must be compatible with the fact that corrective justice imposes moral reasons for acting. Nevertheless, these need not be rights that can be shown to be defensible within the best theory of distributive justice. We need to identify the middle ground that is picked out by the fact that the principle of corrective justice provides agents with moral reasons for acting. Here is an abstract characterization of a solution to this problem. In order for the principle of corrective justice to apply to the underlying system of rights sustained by its application the rights must be such that they are worthy of protection against infringement by the actions of others, even if they would not be protected against infringement by state action designed to replace them with the set of entitlements which could be defended as required by the best theory of distributive justice.[20]

Other things being equal, the state would always have the moral authority to impose that allocation of rights required by the best available theory of distributive justice. Doing so would be disruptive. It would involve the infringement of many "rights" that individuals could otherwise claim against others. The idea here is that since the point of state reallocation is to give each person what in fact he has a right to, it cannot be the case that his real rights are infringed by state action. No one's real rights are being infringed; no claims to repair are sustainable. On the other hand, the state may have this authority to reallocate resources in a way in which individuals do not, even if certain individual reallocations might have the effect of making a more distributively just world. In order for a scheme of rights to warrant protection under corrective justice, then, they must be sufficiently defensible in justice to warrant being sustained against individual infringements. Entitlements that fail to have this minimal property are not real rights in the sense that their infringement cannot give rise to a moral reason for acting.

In order that their infringement by other agents matters from the moral point of view, the relevant "rights" must be real rights. We can cash out by saying either that those rights are supported or even required by the principles of distributive justice that apply in the second or third best world, or that there is a general moral principle that requires protecting certain entitlements in the real world even if those entitlements are not the ones that would exist under a system that implemented the best theory of distributive justice. Not every set of putative entitlements will satisfy either of these conditions, and, therefore, not every infringement of them will give rise to claims in corrective justice to repair.

I have stated the condition that must be satisfied in order for the infringement of a right to give rise to a claim in corrective justice. I have also mentioned two possible groundings for this condition, one in moral theory and one in distributive justice itself. I have not yet defended either the condition or the principle that justifies it. Nor have I suggested how we might know whether the condition is satisfied in a particular community, or whether it is satisfied in our own. All this remains to be worked out on another occasion, but on behalf of the general condition, I note that some such condition must be implicitly, if not explicitly, accepted by nearly everyone. No one I know believes that the underlying allocation of holdings in the United States, for example, exactly coincides with what distributive justice requires. On the other hand, it is not implausible to think that infringements of those holdings by the conduct of others normally gives rise to claims in justice to repair. Moreover, each of us can imagine political institutions that so unjustly distribute resources that no one could have a reason in justice for sustaining them by making repair.[21] The important point here is that there is at least some good reason for thinking that nearly everyone is committed to the existence of some such condition by which the "real" entitlements are to be distinguished from the pretenders. Real ones in this sense will be accorded the protection of corrective justice, that is, their invasion by responsible human agency can create moral reasons for acting of a certain kind, even if they will not be protected against action by the state to implement that allocation of rights required by the correct theory of distributive justice.

We set aside questions about whether this condition is itself grounded in distributive justice or morality more generally for another time. Ultimately whether some set of "second best" entitlements warrants protection in justice or morality more generally will depend on the extent to which they contribute to creating and sustaining important social institutions and arrangements. For example, some set of property rights will be important to sustaining markets. Perhaps the existing set of property rights is not what it would be ideally under the best theory of distributive justice. Nevertheless, within limits, the rights in place may help to sustain an institution that generally improves individual well-being and social stability, and that does so in ways that encourage individual fulfillment, initiative and self respect. Those rights would then be worthy of respect even if they did not exactly coincide with the best or most just distribution of resources. Roughly this is the status most of us accord to the scheme of rights protected by private law in liberal political cultures like our own.[22] The kind of wrongfulness required by corrective justice, therefore, must consist in departures from norms and rights that satisfy this condition. Ultimately in this relationship between corrective and distributive justice resides both corrective justice's independence and attraction to us as a moral ideal.[23]

17.10 JUSTICE BETWEEN THE PARTIES

Corrective justice imposes a duty to repair the wrongful losses for which an injurer is responsible. This chapter has developed the relevant theory of wrongfulness and sketched the requisite account of responsibility. It has also argued that because corrective justice imposes moral reasons for acting, it constrains the underlying norms it can sustain. This section explains two senses in which corrective justice is "justice between the parties." In doing so, it reveals the sense in which corrective justice relies on community norms and conventions.

One sense in which corrective justice is between the parties depends on the responsibility relationship on which it is predicated. An actor has a duty in corrective justice to repair a loss only if that loss is his responsibility. Corrective justice applies only between agents who bear this relationship to one another. One is responsible for the other's loss in a way in which others are not. This fact of responsibility is the basis of liability in corrective justice: liability between the parties based on the responsibility of one for the losses of the other. In this sense, corrective justice is between the parties.

The other sense in which corrective justice is between the parties invites us to consider the kinds of norms corrective justice typically sustains. Distributive justice is global in the sense that it applies to all the members of the relevant community. It applies to the entitlements of all members of the relevant community. Resources are distributed justly when each member of the community has what he or she ought to have (under the correct principle). Efficiency is global in an analogous way. It applies to the preferences and welfare of all members of the relevant community. Resources are allocated efficiently when there is at least one person who prefers this allocation to the alternative candidate, for all possible alternatives. I have already argued that one distinctive feature of corrective justice is that it creates agent-relative reasons for acting. In this way it differs from the usual understanding of one's duties under distributive justice. I want to argue now that another way in which corrective justice differs from distributive justice is that the former is local in a way in which the latter is normally not. In doing so, I want to give content to the idea that corrective justice is between the parties. The remarks that follow are sketchy and tentative, but, I believe, point us in interesting directions.

Suppose Joseph harms Ronald, and that all we can say about what Joseph has done, other than harm Ronald, is that he took inefficient risks. If efficiency were the sort of norm that could be sustained by corrective justice, then Ronald's loss would be wrongful and Joseph responsible for it. Joseph would then have a duty in corrective justice to repair Ronald's loss. Now suppose that Herbert harms John, and that all we can say about what Herbert has done, apart from harming John, is that in doing so he has disrupted the correct distributive scheme. If distributive justice is the sort of norm that could be sustained by corrective justice, then John's loss would be wrongful and Herbert responsible for it. Herbert would have a duty in corrective justice to repair John's loss.

I want to suggest, however, that the duties Joseph and Herbert have are not duties in corrective justice. Joseph's is a duty in economic efficiency; Herbert's is a duty in distributive justice. The reason is that efficiency as a norm is inadequately local to function within the ambit of corrective justice; the same is true of distributive justice. If I upset a just distributive scheme, and in doing so you lose out and I benefit, it is not corrective justice – understood as justice between the parties – that provides for me the relevant reason for making repair and restitution. Repair and restitution are required by the principle of distributive justice that entitles you to X and me to Y. If distributive justice says you should have X units of something, and I take one unit away, then you have less than what distributive justice says you are due, and I have more. If I am required to return what I have taken, it is in order that you have what distributive justice says you must. If this were all there was to doing corrective justice, it would surely be an aspect of distributive justice, or so one might argue.

Similar remarks, I believe, apply to the norm or efficiency. If it is inefficient of me to injure you, then it is the demand that I be efficient that requires me to pay you, and so on. Surely if efficiency is desirable, then departures from it will be inefficient and therefore undesirable. In order for my duty to you to be a duty in corrective justice, it must be because I have *wronged you* in an appropriate sense. It is not enough that I did something wrong globally. I had to have invaded a norm regulating the affairs between us, or failed to discharge a duty *I owe you*. Efficiency and distributive justice as concrete norms, rather than as principles that ground or justify norms that regulate the affairs between us, fail to specify concrete responsibilities we owe one another. My claim is not that corrective justice cannot sustain norms that are distributively just or those that are efficient. Rather, my claim is that corrective justice does not sustain distributive justice or efficiency conceived as norms regulating the relationships between injurers and victims. Efficiency and distributive justice may *ground* or *justify* norms sustained by corrective justice, but cannot themselves constitute the norms on which corrective justice is layered. The reason is that they are inadequately local to fall within the idea of justice between the parties. If I have acted inefficiently, I may have done something wrong; if it is wrong to act inefficiently, then surely I have done something wrong. But in doing so, I have not wronged you. I have not violated a norm regulating our affairs, one that imposes responsibilities on each of us to the other.[24]

How "local" must norms be if they are to fall within the ambit of corrective justice? At one extreme, we might hold that the norms sustained by corrective justice must be particular to the injurer and his victim. This suggests that the only wrongs to which corrective justice might apply would be those the parties agree to impose on one another – as they might be in a long-term contractual relationship. This approach is too narrow and misleading. Agreements create local norms only in the context of a broader social practice that recognizes agreement or consent as a way of creating norms.[25]

The principles of efficiency and distributive justice are too global to be the kinds of norms sustained by corrective justice. The norms that arise from private contract-like arrangements are both too local, and, in the end, depend on broader norms for their efficacy. How local is local enough? Let us consider the following strategy. Reasonable people reject the idea that it is permissible to impose unreasonable risks. This much may be analytic or otherwise obvious. But how are we

357

to determine which risks are reasonable? My idea is that informal conventions typically arise within communities of individuals as ways of giving local expression and content to the prohibition against unreasonable risk taking. These conventions govern the behavior of local communities; members of the communities develop expectations about the behavior of others and internalize constraints regarding their own behavior. These conventions are local, not global. It is failure to comply with them that typically grounds duties in corrective justice.

Central to the idea of wrongdoing in corrective justice is this conventionalist notion of local norms. Wrongful losses can result from wrongdoing. Wrongdoing involves a departure from an appropriate norm. If we understand corrective justice as justice between the parties, often these norms will reflect conventions within the relevant community of individuals. Of special interest are those norms and conventions that express what members of a community regard as reasonable risk taking activity and the conventional understandings by which those norms are to be interpreted. Though I am sure that he had nothing like this in mind, conventional practices regulating the risk taking activities of members of various communities expresses the real insight in George Fletcher's concept of nonreciprocal risk taking. It also makes concrete his important distinction between background and other risks.

In many communities, the conventions governing reasonable risk taking will be in the interests of most participants. Such is the nature, if not the logic, of conventions. There will be a sense, therefore, in which the norms will tend to be efficient or mutually advantageous within their domain. It should not be surprising, therefore, if advocates of economic analysis who study the practices that implement corrective justice find so much efficiency in them. Given this argument, it is even less surprising that someone like George Fletcher could look at the same practice and see in it the possibility of both an economic and a corrective justice understanding. When economic analysts of law look at the rule of liability for unreasonable risk, they see economic efficiency at work: Unreasonable risks are inefficient ones. But their vision is inadequately rich. If I am right, what a theorist really sees is different conventions arising in different communities of risk takers as ways of giving expression to the common understanding of reasonable risk taking behavior. And it is because such conventions typically arise in ways that are mutually beneficial to the members of the community who adopt them that they are efficient in that sense. The core idea in the rule of negligence is that of a convention giving expression to a common understanding of reasonable behavior. There need be no ambition to reduce risk optimally expressed by such a convention. Rather, the need is to coordinate behavior. Successful conventions are efficient in the sense that they coordinate behavior, not necessarily in the sense that they optimally reduce or spread risk.

To this point we have suggested how conventional practices and norms arising within communities can be sufficiently local to fall within the ambit of corrective justice. Corrective justice imposes moral reasons for acting. Therefore, we need to say something about the ways in which conventions, so understood, can create moral reasons for acting. Generally, local norms and conventions are created and sustained by behavior. They govern relationships among members of the community and provide agents who accept the norms from an internal point of view with reasons for acting in compliance with them. Though social norms, they may also be able to create *moral* obligations in those governed by them. Because conventional practices enable members of a community to coordinate, they provide benefits for everyone. The moral duty to comply derives from the prohibition against free riding on the compliance of others. Some might view the duty of compliance as grounded in the general duty of fair play. Conventions create expectations, both epistemic and normative. Typically, individuals rely on these expectations in formulating and pursuing their projects and plans. The importance of social norms and conventions to the pursuit of projects and plans can also ground an individual's moral responsibility to sustain the practice, to comply with its demands, and to repair one's failure to do so. The moral rights and duties created by conventional norms to act in accordance with them and to sustain them through other practices fall to all members of the community provided the norms are social norms or conventions in the appropriate sense, that is, provided the norms are accepted by the bulk of the populace from an internal point of view.

Corrective justice sustains practices of this sort by requiring that individuals responsible for losses resulting from failure to comply with these norms have a duty to repair them. The underlying norms are important to major institutions affecting individuals' lives. They govern reasonable risk taking activity among members of a community. In that way they contribute to each agent's capacity to anticipate the behavior of others that might be disruptive to their ability to act on plans they have formulated. Corrective justice contributes to individual well-being in two ways: first by addressing diminutions of welfare or wellbeing; second, by sustaining a system of norms that provide legitimate expectations (both normative and epistemic) about the behavior of others. These expectations enable coordination and contribute to the ability of individuals to promote their own welfare by pursuing projects and plans of their own choosing within a stable framework. Thus, there is a connection between corrective justice and the institutions that implement it on the one hand and the conditions of rational social stability on the other. This is a point to which we shall return in Chapter 21.

Chapter 18

Corrective justice and tort law

A loss falls within the ambit of corrective justice only if it is wrongful. Losses are wrongful if they result from either *wrongdoing*, that is, unjustifiable departures from the relevant standards of permissible behavior or, *wrongs*, that is, invasions of rights. Corrective justice responds to such losses by imposing on individuals a duty to repair them. An actor incurs the duty to repair a loss in corrective justice only if it is in an appropriate sense his responsibility. The theory of wrongfulness determines which losses fall within the domain of corrective justice. The theory of responsibility provides the connection between the particular agent and those losses sufficient to impose the moral duty to repair. Chapter 16 developed this conception of corrective justice. Chapter 17 developed the relevant conceptions of wrongdoing and wrong, outlined the relevant theory of responsibility, and explored some of the ways in which the underlying norms sustained by corrective justice are constrained by the facts that corrective justice imposes moral reasons for acting and constitutes a kind of justice between the parties. This chapter develops the connection between corrective justice so conceived and the core of Anglo–American accident law.

Tort law has substantive, procedural and structural aspects. Substantive rules specify the conditions that must be satisfied in order that liability be imposed. Procedural rules allocate the relevant burdens of proof, determine which questions are left for the jury, and so on. The structure of tort law provides the framework within which these substantive and procedural rules are implemented. To what extent does tort law, so conceived, implement or express a principle of corrective justice?

Our overarching ambition is to understand tort law within liberal political and legal theory. The kind of understanding we seek of tort law is provided by what Dworkin refers to as a constructive interpretation. In such an interpretation, tort law has a point or purpose that not only makes sense of it, but to use Dworkin's phrase, puts the practice in its best light. Seeing the practice in its best light requires that the principles the practice expresses and the goals to which it aspires "honor" the institution. The principles and goals would justify one's allegiance to it or would warrant the use of the state's coercive authority to sustain it. They are principles and goals agents adopting the internal point of view could rationally accept as binding upon them. At the very least, these principles and goals must provide grounds of action the state is authorized to pursue or implement.

We have three different questions to ask of corrective justice. Is the state authorized to implement corrective justice? Would a tort law based on corrective justice honor the institution? Is tort law ultimately a matter of corrective justice? Before we determine the extent to which current Anglo–American tort law implements corrective justice, we need to determine whether the state has the authority to enforce its demands.[1]

We must distinguish between two related questions: one concerns the attractiveness of corrective justice as a moral ideal; the other concerns the authority of the state to enforce corrective justice, however attractive a moral ideal it might be. The first raises matters in moral philosophy, the second in political philosophy. Corrective justice expresses demands of a private morality, a morality "between the parties." It *morally*, not legally, grounds a right to recover and a debt of repayment. Moral duties and rights do not give rise to legal liabilities and claims without the benefit of bridge principles. Bridge principles identify the nature and scope of a justified political authority. They determine which, if any, moral responsibilities are enforceable at law, and why. Not all moral duties should be enforceable by law. Why should those in corrective justice be? If the state can enforce reasons for acting under corrective justice, are there not other reasons, perhaps not in morality but in economics, with which the demands of corrective justice might conflict: grounds of action that might suggest a different sort of liability scheme, yet grounds upon which the state is authorized to act?

18.1 POLITICAL PHILOSOPHY

The nature and scope of the duties the state can create and enforce against individuals and groups depend on the relevant political, not moral, theory. Good character and virtuous action may be desirable, but the state may have only a limited authority to use its coercive powers to encourage either. Political philosophies differ with respect to the range of political coercion they sanction. A libertarian political philosophy, like Robert Nozick's,[2] may restrict the scope of political authority to remedying private rights violations. To the extent corrective justice requires that the losses resulting from private rights violations be repaired, the state may be authorized to enforce duties in corrective justice, but nothing more. In that case the state may be free to create a system of liability-for-loss based on the principle of corrective justice, but not one based on considerations of economic efficiency.

A utilitarian political theory may extend legitimate political authority much further. It may authorize the state to create and enforce a system of liability-for-loss that allocates accident costs in a way that minimizes them. Under such a scheme, whether a victim could recover for a loss would depend on whether doing so would be cost minimizing, not on whether he had a right in justice to repair. Similarly, whether an injurer or anyone else could be liable for another's costs would depend on whether imposing liability would be cost minimizing, not on whether he had a duty in justice to make good the loss.

In utilitarian political theory, the connection between injurer and victim is mediated not by corrective justice but by the relationship of each to the goal of reducing overall accident costs. The state would not be prevented from enforcing the demands of corrective justice, but it would not be required to do so either. Instead, it would do so only if linking injurers and victims in the way that corrective justice does is the most desirable or efficient way of bringing about the best overall consequences.

In a rational choice contractarian political philosophy, the state may be authorized to enforce both cost minimizing incentives and corrective justice between the parties. This is because in rational choice contractarianism the state is viewed as a solution to a market failure problem that has both distributive (including justice between the parties) and productive (cost minimization) dimensions.

The state will be authorized to implement corrective justice over a broad range of liberal political ideologies. Our concern is with corrective justice within the liberal political culture, and so we have reason for thinking that the sort of states we are interested in are authorized to implement corrective justice. Let's assume that the sort of political philosophy in countries like the United States, Canada, New Zealand, Australia, and the United Kingdom is, broadly speaking, liberal, not libertarian. That means that the state has the authority to create and enforce reasons for acting grounded in both considerations of corrective justice and efficiency. It can set up a tort system, a New Zealand-like no-fault plan, a first-party insurance plan or some mixture of these, and in doing so, it can offer as its justification that it is attempting to implement corrective justice, distributive justice, economic efficiency, or the like. It may be wrong. Perhaps, the New Zealand approach is not efficient; or maybe the tort system does not in fact adequately implement corrective justice. Whether the state's judgments are correct is independent of whether it has the authority to act on the basis of those judgments.

If we assume a liberal political theory, then the state will be authorized to enforce duties in corrective justice, but it may be equally free to create and enforce reasons for acting based on a range of other principles of political morality. Is this all there is to it? A liberal state can enforce the demands of corrective justice, but it need not? It can decide instead to ignore corrective justice in favor of economic efficiency? It can decide to have a tort system, but it need not? It can decide to have a tort system that does corrective justice, but it might just as well decide to have a tort system that creates incentives designed to minimize accident costs? Can the state legitimately ignore corrective justice? Can it justifiably set up a scheme of liability-for-loss that seeks instead to minimize accident costs or optimally spread risks? If it can, isn't the authority of the state at least constrained by corrective justice? That is, though the state may seek to minimize costs rather than enforce corrective justice, does not corrective justice function as a constraint on the state's ambitions to minimize or spread safety risks? We cannot determine whether corrective justice imposes constraints on the state's legitimate authority to implement other goals or principles or whether our current practices implement corrective justice until we settle on an account of what it means to implement corrective justice. That, in turn, depends on the demands of corrective justice.

18.2 THE DEMANDS OF CORRECTIVE JUSTICE

In the annulment thesis the point of corrective justice is simply to rectify or annul wrongful gains and losses. Implementing corrective justice means vindicating the underlying claims to repair. Understood in this way, corrective justice does not require a particular mode of rectification, though it constrains the set of modes of rectification compatible with it. Any way of annulling wrongful gains and losses is permissible provided it does not create other corrective injustices. In the annulment conception of it, doing corrective justice means annulling wrongful losses (and gains); corrective justice as a constraint means annulling wrongful gains in a way that does not create substantial additional wrongful gains and losses.

In the mixed view, individuals incur a duty to repair the wrongful losses for which they are responsible. The victim who has suffered a wrongful loss owing to another's agency has a right to recover and the individual whose agency is responsible for the loss has a duty to make the loss good. Doing corrective justice means imposing the victim's loss on the person who is responsible for it. Whereas doing corrective justice on the annulment thesis means seeing to it that wrongful gains and losses are annulled in ways that do not create wrongful gains and losses, doing corrective justice in the mixed view means imposing the victim's loss on that person who has a duty in justice to make it good, that is, the person who is responsible for it, usually, but not always, the injurer. The annulment thesis allows that a range of possible institutions can implement corrective justice; the mixed view denies this. Only those institutions that impose the victim's loss on the wrongdoer implement corrective justice.

The difference between the two is striking. In the annulment thesis it may be permissible as a way of doing corrective justice to put the victim's loss on that individual who is in the best position to spread or reduce risk (provided that doing so annuls the victim's loss without creating a substantial additional wrongful loss) whether or not the optimal risk spreader or reducer is the person responsible for the loss. In contrast, in the mixed view imposing the victim's loss on anyone other than the responsible party cannot count as implementing corrective justice, even if doing so can be a permissible on other grounds within the authority of the state to enforce.

The liberal state is free to implement corrective justice, but nothing we have said so far requires it to. If it chooses to enforce justice, then, in the annulment thesis, it can do virtually anything as long as it annuls the gains and losses that deserve to be annulled without creating substantial additional ones. Implementing corrective justice, according to the mixed view, means imposing liability on those agents who are responsible for creating wrongful losses. We have not argued that the state must implement corrective justice, only that if it does, this is what it must do. Indeed, my view is that the state need not implement corrective justice. I take up this argument in the next chapter. The state has the moral authority, but not the moral duty, to implement corrective justice. The question before us now is whether modern Anglo-American tort law in fact implements corrective justice. My view is that at its core, tort law is a matter of corrective justice. Nevertheless, not all of tort law implements corrective justice, and in subsequent chapters I will explore some of the ways in which modern accident law departs (often justifiably) from its corrective justice core. For now, I want to argue that the core of tort law implements corrective justice. I begin by exploring the extent to which the substantive rules of fault and strict liability express corrective justice.

18.3 CORRECTIVE JUSTICE AND FAULT LIABILITY

Negligence is the failure to take reasonable precautions. It is a departure from the norm of justifiable risk taking and is, therefore, a kind of wrongdoing in the sense developed in Chapter 17. Individuals who are injured as a result of negligence or fault generally are wrongfully harmed, their losses wrongful in the sense implicated by the principle of corrective justice. Under the mixed conception of corrective justice, the fact that the victim has suffered a wrongful loss is important because it grounds the injurer's duty to compensate him. Thus, corrective justice grounds the claim that faulty injurers have a duty to repair the losses their conduct occasions. The right of the victim to recover under the fault rule as well as the faulty injurer's duty to provide compensation are both matters of corrective justice.

Several cases that conventional wisdom treats as falling under the rule of strict liability might be usefully analyzed as involving the kind of fault implicated in the principle of corrective justice. *Rylands* v. *Fletcher* is an example.[3] In Rylands the defendant was held liable for the water that escaped from an above ground water reservoir. The water found its way down abandoned mine shafts and caused significant damage to adjacent property. There was no evidence introduced to suggest that the owner and operator of the reservoir was negligent in either its construction or maintenance. There was evidence that an engineer failed to locate or inform the defendant of potential dangers. There was no negligence in the ordinary sense on the part of the defendant, however. The court found the defendant liable in the absence of negligence, and that is why the case is normally taught under strict liability.

The grounds of liability in *Rylands* are of two sorts. First, the defendant is said to be liable because building reservoirs above the ground in England constitutes a nonnatural use of the land. One way of interpreting nonnatural use is as an unjustifiable use; it is a use that under other circumstances might pose permissible or reasonable risks, but under the extant circumstances imposes unreasonable ones. Rainfall in the United Kingdom is adequate for all reasonable uses, and so no matter how small the risk or well maintained the reservoir is, simply building a reservoir creates unnecessary, and therefore unreasonable risks. Thus, a nonnatural use is a faulty use. Such an account brings *Rylands* under the principle of fault liability.

The court also held that water is the sort of thing that, although perfectly safe when contained, is inherently dangerous, and should it escape, likely to cause substantial damage. This treats water (presumably as a function of its quantity) as an ultrahazardous commodity, and the keeping of it in reservoirs an ultrahazardous activity. Ultrahazardous activities are typically discussed under strict liability. But perhaps there is a fault liability story to be told here as well. We will need to distinguish between being at fault merely in virtue of engaging in an activity and being at fault in the way in which one engages in it. Ultrahazardous activities are inherently faulty. Someone is at fault merely for engaging in such activities whether or not one engages in the activity in a faulty manner. No feasible precautions are sufficient to reduce the risks associated with the activity to a non-negligent level. The negligence is not in the manner of doing, but in the very doing itself.

In the annulment thesis the fault of the injurer is relevant to two inquiries: Has the victim suffered a loss that is the concern of corrective justice to nullify – in other words, a wrongful loss? Has the injurer secured a gain that is the concern of corrective justice to nullify – in other words, a wrongful gain? In the annulment theory corrective justice requires annulling both wrongful gains and losses. In abandoning the annulment thesis for the mixed view, I have given up the claim that the point of corrective justice is to annul wrongful losses. I have also given up the view that corrective justice has anything at all to do with wrongful gains. In saying that, I do not mean to deny the existence of wrongful gains. They exist, and lots of them, too. Nor do I mean to deny their immorality. I mean only to deny that wrongful gains fall within the ambit of corrective justice. Why do wrongful losses count in corrective justice, whereas wrongful gains do not? Under what principle of justice do wrongful gains count?

In the mixed view the point of corrective justice is to provide agents with certain reasons for acting as a consequence of their conduct. If an actor's conduct gives rise to a wrongful loss, the actor has a reason for making repair, expressed as a duty to render compensation. This is the relationship between an agent and his actions as mediated by the principle of corrective justice. The duty to repair in corrective justice, in other words, does not depend on the wrongdoer's securing a (wrongful) gain as a result of his mischief.

What are the demands of justice in the event the injurer in fact secures a wrongful gain? Does his securing a wrongful gain give rise to a reason for acting in the same way that his being responsible for creating a wrongful loss does? If it does, is the reason best expressed as a duty to "disgorge" his gain? If the agent has a duty to disgorge his gain, who, if anyone, has a claim in justice to it? What principle of justice grounds both the right to the gains and the duty to disgorge them?

Suppose someone drives negligently. In doing so he imposes risks on a number of individuals. Let's suppose, however, that he hits only one person, a pedestrian. The negligent motorist saves the money or resources he would have had to expend in order to drive safely. This is his wrongful gain, a gain he secures at the expense of everyone who is put at risk as a result of his failure to take due care.

We can distinguish between two cases. In one case, the negligent motorist secures no additional gain as a consequence of his hitting the pedestrian. His only gain comes from his negligence. In the other case, the negligent motorist gains from both his negligence and his negligently harming the pedestrian. Let's consider the case in which the motorist secures a gain only through his negligence.[4]

If the wrongdoer has a duty in justice to disgorge his gain, each of those individuals he puts at risk has a claim in justice to part of it. He gains at their expense. He does so unjustifiably. His gain is wrongful and is causally connected to each pedestrian in a way that could ground a claim on behalf of each to a share of his benefit. The injured pedestrian is one such person. The pedestrian has an additional claim in justice, and that is to the repair of his loss occasioned by the motorist's negligence. Only this last claim, the one the pedestrian and no one else has, is a claim in corrective justice. Now consider the case in which the negligent motorist secures a gain as a consequence of his negligence and of his negligently harming the pedestrian. Everyone who is put at risk by virtue of the motorist's negligence has a claim in justice to part of the gain he secures thereby. Again, the injured pedestrian is one such person. The injured pedestrian, however, has two additional claims. The first is in corrective justice for repair of whatever loss he suffers as the victim of the motorist's negligence; the second is for that additional gain the motorist secures as a consequence of injuring him.

Wrongful loss is the concern of corrective justice; the relevant claim is for repair of a loss. Victims who press claims to an injurer's ill gotten gains are not seeking compensation for loss. Instead, they seek *restitution* for being wrongfully taken advantage of, used, or exploited. Their claims are grounded in *restitutionary* justice. Both forms of justice are relational. Corrective justice imposes the duty on the wrongdoer to compensate his victims for the costs his wrongdoing imposes on them. Restitutionary justice gives the victim the right to the wrongdoer's gains secured at her expense.

When the wrongful gains and losses exactly coincide, satisfying the demands of corrective justice suffices to satisfy the demands of restitutionary justice as well, and vice versa. Wrongful gains and losses need not coincide, however. Conduct that creates devastating losses can bring small advantage, whereas conduct that creates enormous gains can occasion minuscule losses. Tort law is the central institution for discharging the duty to repair wrongful losses; restitution is the legal remedy for repairing wrongful gains.

18.5 STRICT LIABILITY AND WRONGFUL LOSSES

Not every case in torts is adjudicated under the fault rule. Many are governed by the principle of strict liability. Can strict liability sometimes be a matter of corrective justice? Some cases of strict liability are covered by the principle of corrective justice because they are really cases of fault liability. What about cases of true strict liability? Sometimes innocent or justifiable conduct can be contrary to the constraints imposed by the rights of others. If it is, justifiable or innocent conduct can constitute a wrong, and when it does, the losses that result are wrongful in the sense necessary to impose on the injurer a duty to repair. This is how I understand *Vincent* v. *Lake Erie*, for example.[5]

In *Vincent* the dock owner had a right in contract to forbid the ship from being moored beyond the period of time specified in the contract. However, as the court noted, it would have been wrong for the dock owner to have exercised that right. I read this to mean that even though the dock owner had a right to exclude the ship from the use of his property, he would not have been justified in insisting on that right. It would have been wrongful of him to do what he had a right to do. Indeed, had he set the ship adrift to meet its fate, the court appears to have been ready to impose the ship's losses on the dock owner.[6] The fact that it would have been wrong of the dock owner to exclude the ship does not extinguish the right or the claims to which the right gives rise. Thus, by keeping the ship moored to the dock, the ship's captain infringes the dock owner's right, and commits, in that sense, a wrong. The damage that results is wrongful in the appropriate sense, and the victim is entitled to repair as a matter of justice, the injurer being duty bound to make good the loss.

The duty to repair in strict liability, therefore, is sometimes a matter of corrective justice, at least in cases like *Vincent*. It is a further question whether the injurer in these cases secures a wrongful gain at another's expense, and if he does, that gives the victim a right in restitution to it. There is no denying that injurers in cases like *Vincent*, the insulin case, and the backpacker case gain as a result of infringing the rights of others. But the gain is the result of conduct that is justifiable or permissible. In wronging the victim, each "injurer" does the right thing. His gains are therefore justifiable ones. He is enriched by his conduct, but not wrongfully or unjustifiably so.

Infringement cases are especially interesting, therefore. In them, the victim has a right in corrective justice to the repair of his wrongful loss. The injurer gains as a consequence of her creating a wrongful loss in others, but her gain is not a wrongful one. Therefore, she has no duty in justice to disgorge it, and no one has a claim in justice to it. If the injurer has a duty to his victims it is to repair, not to make restitution. The same conduct can create both gains and losses; the losses can be wrongful, the gains not.[7]

18.6 TORT LAW AND CORRECTIVE JUSTICE

We have outlined the ways in which the substantive claims to repair in torts can be grounded in the principle of corrective justice. In particular we have shown that the principle of fault liability expresses corrective justice; and we have argued that some areas of strict liability in which the retributive argument could not hope to apply also reflect the principle of corrective justice. Thus, we have met the challenge presented in Chapter 12 of finding a moral principle that underwrites important aspects of tort law, that makes sense of the distinction between fault and strict liability, and that does so within the confines of the state's authority. Or have we? Have we, in other words, established an interesting and robust sense in which tort law implements corrective justice?

I am inclined to the view that to this point we have not established that tort law implements the mixed conception of corrective justice. We have not in fact established any interesting relationship between tort law and corrective justice. To be sure, we have shown that several of the claims to repair in both fault and strict liability are consistent with this conception of corrective justice; they are claims to repair valid in corrective justice. But they are claims that are consistent with both the annulment conception of corrective justice and the mixed view. For all we have shown, they may well be consistent with other principles of justice or of economics. The fact that in torts victims are able to secure repair for wrongful losses underdetermines the principle that grounds liability and recovery in these cases. In order for tort law to implement corrective justice, it is not enough that the underlying claims to repair be consistent with corrective justice. If it is to implement corrective justice, tort law must impose liability on that individual who has the duty in corrective justice to make good the victim's loss. It must do so, moreover, because doing so is required by corrective justice. Thus, even if all the claims to repair recognized as enforceable in torts fully coincided with those that would be valid under the principle of corrective justice, it would not follow that tort law enforces, exemplifies or implements corrective justice. That is the argument we need to make. We begin by considering whether corrective justice provides the better account of the structure of tort law. The strategy is to show that when tort law's substantive rules and structure are seen as compatible and better explained by corrective justice than by any alternative, we would have done all we could to defend the claim that the core of tort law is a matter of corrective justice.

18.7 THE STRUCTURE OF TORT LAW

In the typical action tort suits bring victim-plaintiffs together with injurer-defendants, and only within this structure do questions regarding who should bear a particular accident's costs arise. That is, the goals of tort law are pursued only within a structure of case-by-case adjudication between individual victims and their respective injurers. It is not as if victims are free to bring suit against anybody. Normally, the victim is not free to argue that he should be compensated for his loss by someone simply because that person is a good risk spreader or reducer. Instead, the victim is usually required to show that the person he seeks to have held liable to him is responsible in the relevant way for his loss. Therefore, in a typical tort suit in which the victim has a legitimate claim to repair in justice, her loss is imposed on the individual responsible for the loss. And it is not part of the case for doing so that the responsible party is a good risk spreader or avoider. Instead, the injurer is held liable simply because she is responsible for the loss. She is the one who has the duty in corrective justice to make good the loss. To that extent, tort law appears to implement corrective justice in the sense expressed by the mixed view.[8]

The structure of tort law makes a kind of sense within the theory of corrective justice that it does not make within economic analysis. To see this compare the corrective justice understanding of the structure of tort law with the economic one. Whereas the structure of tort law is reasonably well fixed or stable, it remains, for the economist, a pliable instrument in the pursuit of optimal deterrence, optimal insurance, or both. Indeed, because determining who is the best insurer or cheapest cost-avoider is always an empirical inquiry, it is not obvious that injurers and their victims should invariably be included among the candidates for tort liability, let alone that the set of suitable candidates be restricted to them.

The problem with any form of economic explanation goes deeper, for the inadequacy of economic analysis is the result of its fundamentally *forward-looking* conception of liability running into a structure of litigation that embodies an essentially *backward-looking* theory of liability and recovery. This fundamentally backward looking dimension of existing tort law limits the extent to which economic goals can be pursued through it. Thus, tort law asks whether *A*, who allegedly injured *B*, should be liable to *B* in damages, or whether instead *B* should be made to shoulder his own costs. However that decision is made, it is structured in terms of *A* and *B*, two parties whose presence before the court is a consequence of a past event: namely, what *B* alleges *A* did. In contrast, the search for optimal insurers or cheapest cost avoiders is not similarly constrained by history. Accidents between *A* and *B* may in fact be most easily prevented by *C*. Consider automobile accidents. Whenever *A* rams his car into *B*, *B* brings suit against *A*. And on the economic analysis, we are then to decide whether *A* or *B* is the person who is in the best position to reduce accidents of this type. Yet the party best suited to optimize accident costs may well be the relevant car manufacturer(s), who is (are) party neither to the accident nor to the litigation.

On the face of it, considerations neither of optimal deterrence nor insurance require that litigation be structured so that only victims and their injurers are candidates for liability. Yet this structure of litigation is surely one of tort law's essential characteristics. Economic analysis can, therefore, only assume, but never explain, the structure of tort law.

375

18.8 THE ECONOMIC RESPONSE

The legal economist might make any of three different responses to this objection. First, he can simply deny that the injurer–victim structure of tort law is as sacred or central to tort law as this objection takes it to be. Second, he can accept the centrality of the injurer–victim structure, and offer an economic analysis of the terms victim and injurer, an analysis that might have the effect of infusing economics' forward-looking impetus into tort law's backward-looking structure. Or third, he can accept the centrality of the injurer–victim structure of litigation and our ordinary understanding of the key concepts, while providing an economic explanation of both.

Consider the last of these responses. Is there a compelling economic explanation of tort law's structuring of the problem of who pays? Tort law determines who pays by asking whether a particular victim or his respective injurer should. So the problem is framed by including injurers and victims but no one else. The challenge for the economist is to explain why the question of who pays is answered by including particular injurers and their victims and virtually no one else. We can begin by asking why structures for answering questions of liability for loss always include the victim?

One reason for making the victim party to the litigation is that by doing so we provide him with an incentive to bring an action. If the injured party does not initiate litigation, the court is not given the opportunity to pursue optimal risk reduction or spreading. In order to provide courts with the opportunity to seek efficient accident reduction, someone must initiate litigation. A victim will only do so if he stands to gain thereby. The possibility of securing compensation for his loss provides the requisite incentive. This is the private enforcement or private prosecutor argument we touched on in Chapter 17, that we will revisit in Chapter 19.

Once the victim is included, two questions remain: (1) Why include injurers? (2) Why include only victims and injurers? The obvious economic reason for including injurers is deterrence. If injurers are free from potential liability, their incentive to take precautions is dramatically reduced. Victims are included to give them incentive to litigate, to take precautions, or both; injurers are included to give them incentive to take precautions. No one else is included because the cost of searching for better risk reducers or spreaders from the populace at large is too high. Although other more plausible, even significantly better candidates for spreading or reducing risk may exist in individual cases, in categories of cases, or perhaps in all cases, the costs of identifying them and making them parties to actions are generally too high. Thus, the fact that in tort law the set of potentially liable parties is restricted to victims and their injurers can be given an explanation consistent with the general form of economic argument.

These are plausible economic arguments for restricting the liability decision to victims and their particular injurers. Thus, the objection that economics lacks an explanation of tort law's structure is unfounded. If in tort injurers are made to compensate their victims, there is a very good economic argument for their doing so. Victims recover to encourage private prosecution. In theory, they should be able to recover against whoever is the optimal risk reducer or spreader. The costs of searching for that person are often too high. Therefore, they recover against their particular injurers, who may in fact be the optimal risk reducers or spreaders, but, even if they are not, remain reasonably good choices given search costs.

18.9 THE LIMITS OF THE ECONOMIC EXPLANATION

There are two kinds of questions we might ask about economic analysis. The first is whether, even on its own terms, economic analysis provides a plausible account of tort law's structure. The second is whether the economic analysis provides a more persuasive account of tort law's structure than does the principle of corrective justice.

The private enforcement argument presupposes the necessity of at least some private enforcement as a prerequisite for optimal deterrence. If otherwise, no need would exist to present judges with the opportunity to use civil actions for this particular public end. Then, if civil actions initiated by victims were desirable, their desirability could not be explained by optimal deterrence. Were we able to reach injurers more effectively in some other way, victim instigated suits in torts would be inexplicable from an economic point of view. Also, it may not be true that if a victim fails to bring suit to recover damages, courts would be disabled from pursuing the private enforcement of public norms. We could simply give other parties incentive to litigate. Because including victims in the choice set is neither necessary nor sufficient for optimal enforcement, the private enforcement argument renders the role of the victim in tort law tenuous and contingent.

The deterrence argument, that injurers are included so that we are able to influence them to take precautions when that is economically sound and to avoid taking precautions when doing so would be inefficient, rests on the mistaken premise that being included in litigation is the only way to influence behavior. All sorts of individuals who are not themselves parties to civil or other actions alter their behavior as a consequence of legal rules. The truth of this claim is presupposed by all general deterrence arguments.

The private enforcement argument fails because one need not be a victim in order to be given incentive to litigate. The deterrence argument also fails because one need not be a party to litigation to be influenced by its outcome. If economic analysis explains the structure of tort law, it may do so in a way that renders it radically contingent and far too tenuous to explain its centrality to our actual practice.

Surely, the economist would agree. In principle, because the search for the cheapest cost avoider or best insurer requires empirical inquiry, there is no reason why the decision of who should bear the costs of particular accidents should be restricted to victims and injurers. However, considerations of *administrative efficiency* narrow the domain considerably, so that in most cases the decision is structured in terms of identifiable injurers and victims. It follows, of course, that there is nothing sacred about the structure. As the costs of identifying third parties better suited to avoid or to spread risks drops, we should expect alterations in the structure of litigation, or, in some cases, the abandonment of tort litigation entirely. That is, we would expect to find cheapest cost avoiders increasingly becoming parties to litigation even when they bear no causal or other responsibility for the harm of which the victim complains. Or we would expect to find a reduction in the form of resolution by litigation in favor of some other way of reaching the cheapest cost avoider, for example, regulation. The economist's explanation, moreover, has predictive implications: Changes in constraints or aims should yield alterations in structure.

The economist does not pretend that she can explain the necessity of the structure of litigation, only its plausibility. Given the costs of locating third parties, the victim-injurer structure of tort litigation provides a plausible framework within which the law can pursue the aims of optimal risk reduction and spreading. If the objection to economics is that such a structure is not simply a plausible way of securing the aims of tort law, but that it is a necessary feature of it, the economist's response would be to deny the objection's premise. The injurer-victim structure makes considerable economic sense. It may not, however, be central to tort law; surely it is not a necessary feature of it.

In sum, the economic argument is this: Theoretically, anyone can be a party to litigation. The victim usually is because she has an incentive to initiate litigation which is necessary to get the ball rolling. The set of individuals who fall within the net of liability is to be determined by entirely contingent matters: who are the cheapest cost avoiders and risk spreaders? The only constraint on the pursuit of potential risk reducers and spreaders is the extent of search and other administrative costs.

The economist has an explanation of the structure of litigation, but one that views it as subordinate to the law's substantive ambitions. Moreover, what corrective justice appears to treat as fixed and given, the economic analysis reveals to be fluid and derivative. Current trends in tort law expanding not only the scope of liability and recovery but the structure of litigation as well, lend further credence to the economist's position.

18.10 WHAT BRINGS INJURERS AND VICTIMS TOGETHER?

Ultimately, the problem with the economic interpretation of tort law is not that it has no explanation of the fact that litigation is restricted to injurers and their victims. Rather, the problem is that in economic analysis, the inclusion of injurers and victims is fundamentally contingent and does not in any way depend on their relationship to one another. The inclusion of victims depends on the efficiency of including them; the inclusion of injurers depends on the efficiency of including them; the exclusion of anyone else depends on the efficiency of exclusion. In economic analysis the relationship between injurers and victims is never really a relationship between particular injurers and victims but is, instead, a relationship between particular injurers and the goals of tort law *and* particular victims and the goals of tort law.

The legitimacy of a victim's claim to repair in economic analysis depends on the effects of compensation on his willingness to litigate or to take safety precautions, not on some connection between the injurer and him. The same is true of the injurer. The legitimacy of holding him liable depends on the economic consequences of doing so, not on some connection between the victim and him. His having done something to the victim may provide some evidence of his being someone who needs to take safety measures. It is not otherwise essential to the argument for holding him liable. Moreover, even where actual injury provides evidence that the injurer ought to be given a reason to act to reduce the probability of the harm's recurrence in the future, that evidence can be overcome by other evidence that someone else is in an even better position to reduce the risk than he is. The fundamental point is that in economic analysis, there are no principled reasons for connecting injurers and victims in the way in which tort law does. The mixture of policies, goals and the constraints imposed by search costs brings injurers and victims together; nothing about the relationship they bear to one another figures directly or fundamentally in the calculus of liability and recovery.

In tort law the victim and the injurer are typically brought together in ways that suggest a deeper connection, a connection between particular victims and injurers. Tort law brings injurers and victims together in a way that reflects their relationship to one another, rather than to the goals of tort law. Because it is a relational conception of justice, only corrective justice can reflect the relational structure of tort law.

The reason the victim brings his injurer to court, rather than someone else who might well be the cheapest cost-avoider, is that his claim to compensation as a matter of justice is analytically connected to some facts he seeks to establish about the injurer's conduct. In particular, his claim is valid only if (in most cases) he can show that his loss is the result of the injurer's fault or is otherwise the injurer's responsibility. The victim brings an action against his injurer because his (the victim's) claim to compensation as a matter of justice is based on his claims about what the injurer *did* to him, not on the fact that the injurer is better suited than he is to reduce accident costs. If it all of a sudden turned out that some third party were the cheapest cost avoider, there would be no reason in corrective justice for including him in the suit. Nothing about the cheapest cost avoider's prior behavior has anything at all to do with *B*'s claim to recompense being a matter of justice. On the other hand, when the goals of deterrence and insurance are no longer constrained by concerns to reduce administrative costs, there is no purely economic reason for preventing the victim from suing the cheapest cost avoider. Not only are the underlying claims at the core of accident law ones primarily of corrective justice, so, too, is its structure.

To the extent tort law is a forum for vindicating claims to

repair, the victim's connection to his injurer is fundamental and analytic, not tenuous or contingent. Thus, even if the current structure of tort litigation is consistent with economic analysis, it is better understood as embodying some conception of corrective justice. For as long as tort suits are so structured, we can understand that structure as embodying the ideal that in torts a victim seeks to show that the loss he has suffered is a wrongful one, one that requires recompense as a matter of right, not utility. The heart of the claim reflects a relationship in the world between injurers and victims. In general, the structure of tort law reflects that relationship.

18.11 REDEFINING ''INJURER''

The argument for corrective justice assumes that there exists some pre-theoretical conceptions of the terms victim, injurer, and causation, such that it makes sense to say that the injurer, who is not the cheapest cost avoider or best insurer, is responsible for the harm for which the victim rightly seeks redress. The economist denies that there are clear pretheoretical conceptions of these terms. The economist, after all, is simply an instrumentalist. Not only is tort law as a practice or institutional form infinitely pliable, but so are its basic concepts. Thus, the economist might respond by redefining terms like injurer in such a way as to infuse economic analysis's forward looking perspective into tort law's backward looking inquiry.

The concepts of injurer and causation can be given economic interpretations or meanings. For example, the ''injurer'' in any given case is not necessarily the chap who smashed the poor fellow over the head, but is instead that individual who could have prevented the head smashing incident at the lowest cost. The concept of causation is as empty as that of injurer. We are free, therefore, to give an economic rendering of it.

The objection that economic analysis cannot explain the backward-looking structure of tort litigation presupposes a non-economic meaning of the key terms: injurer, victim, fault and causation. All these terms can be given economic renderings, however. Once these concepts have been reconstructed from an economic point of view, the conflict between the backward-looking structure of tort litigation and the forward-looking aims of economic analysis evaporates. The sentence "The injurer wrongfully caused the victim's loss," which appears to express a proposition about past events that may only *contingently* be connected with the economic aims of cost avoidance, is, through the magic of economic reconstruction, *analytically* connected to it. The wrongful injurer is the cheapest cost avoider (by definition), and the causal connection between his act and the victim's loss is spelled out in terms of some statistical relationship whose normative significance is also a matter of economic policy.

The obvious problem with such an enterprise is that by reconstructing the key concepts of tort law in economic terms, economic analysis could hardly be said to be providing an explanation or interpretation of the practice as it finds it. Instead, it finds the practice void of content and constraint, remakes it in economic terms, and then quite unsurprisingly provides an economic analysis of what it finds. Nowhere is this intellectual practice more common than it is in the economic analysis of causation. If many legal theorists bemoan the Critical Legal Studies movement's fixation on law's indeterminacy, they have only the economists of law and other rampant reconstructionists to blame. For it was economic analysis, first, not Critical Legal Studies that treated legal concepts as if they could be remade at will in the light of one's preferred normative theory.

If we are to explain our social and legal practices we must assume that they have a content that is the object of explanation, a content that constrains what can count as an adequate explanation of it. Surely there will be aspects of a practice or a concept that will be contestable or controversial, that will require affirmative acts of interpretation.[9] These interpretations will aim to give structure and coherence to our practices, and in doing so, they may invoke normative premises. But it does not follow from the fact that a normative

383

theory is required to settle controversial cases, that the un-controversial cases or settled aspects of a practice impose no constraints whatsoever on the shape and substance interpretive theories can take. The fact that there are hard or controversial cases in which genuine doubt about the meaning of "injurer" or of "causation" exists provides no excuse for re-making the concepts entirely.

If controversy were to provide an invitation entirely to re-make concepts and practices by the lights of our normative or theoretical commitments, we could hardly be said, by in-voking those theories, to have explained those practices. For part of the argument for radical reconstruction is that, in a suitable sense, there is no practice to explain; there is no there, there. One literally cannot have it both ways.

To say that practices constrain their explanations or that concepts have content independent of normative theories is not to align oneself fully with the formalist. Practices and concepts have meaning. From that it does not follow that the meaning of the concepts are fixed or that they must constrain the form of the practice in the way in which the formalist believes they do. Thus, we need not agree with Weinrib that unless the institution of liability connects the concepts of in-jurer, wrongdoing and causation in a certain way, it cannot count as tort law. Some concepts, for example, responsibil-ity, victim and wrongdoer derive their meanings in part from the practices, including legal ones, in which they figure.

For the formalist, our ability to understand tort law as a unified whole depends on seeing tort law as a structure that uniquely reflects relationships between injurer and victim that occur in the world. The coherence of the structure, in turn, is given by the logic of the relevant concepts and the way they are expressed in the structure. For the instrumentalist-economist, institutional forms lack any inherent integrity. They are pliable instruments in the pursuit of abstract economic goals. Their integrity, if they have any, is bound up with their capacity ultimately to secure those goals. I have been advancing a different view. To understand tort law is to see it in part as a web of substantive and structural rules designed to enforce claims in corrective justice. On the other hand, there are substantive and structural features of the existing practice that cannot be usefully understood in terms of corrective justice. It is to those cases that we now turn.

Chapter 19

Justifiable departures from corrective justice

Nothing I have said so far could count as a logical demonstration of the claim that tort law implements corrective justice. Instead, I have argued that understanding it as implementing the mixed conception of corrective justice provides the best account of the core of accident law. The corrective justice interpretation of these cases is better than the economic analysis precisely because in the economic analysis, victims and injurers are not connected to one another as such. Instead, injurers and victims are separately connected to the goals of tort law. They are brought together in litigation by the fact that the costs of searching for others is too high. This contingent and tenuous connection between injurers and victims does not do justice to prevailing practice.

In fact, not every claim to repair enforceable in tort law is one that is, could or should be grounded in corrective justice. This has been a constant theme of this argument and, indeed of all my work in torts. Nothing I have argued to this point has been designed to suggest otherwise. This chapter considers three potentially justifiable ways of departing from the corrective justice core of tort law. In discussing these cases, I intend to develop further insights into the nature of corrective justice, the constraints it imposes on legal practices, and the way in which it can be constrained by social and other practices.

19.1 LIABILITY AND RECOVERY WITHOUT JUSTICE

Let's begin with an example of liability and recovery in torts that has nothing to do with corrective justice, yet may be defensible on other grounds. Suppose a manufacturer provides an ineffective (or inefficient) warning. It is inefficient because it fails fully or adequately to warn and, therefore, to deter. Someone uses the product and injures himself as a result. In order for his loss to be wrongful under corrective justice, the warning would have had to be ineffective; he would have had to have read it; had the warning been adequate it would have deterred him from using the product; he would have had to use the product believing that it was safe for him and so on. An optimal warning would have deterred him from using the product had he read it. The warning on the product would not have. In fact, our victim never read the warning. The warning is not optimal, but it does not in fact contribute to the victim's loss. Though there is no denying that the manufacturer is at fault, the victim's loss is not the manufacturer's fault. The victim has suffered a loss, but not one for which he has a claim in corrective justice to repair.

Nevertheless, a court might well impose liability on the product manufacturer for the purpose of encouraging more efficient warnings. The victim has no right to compensation. Compensation, however, provides him with an incentive to litigate. In litigation the victim acts as a private regulator. The manufacturer has a defective warning that needs to be improved. If part of the goal of the law is to encourage product manufacturers to provide optimal warnings, why should a court wait until a victim comes along who has a valid claim to repair in justice? The goal of encouraging efficient warnings does not discriminate among those victims who have suffered wrongful losses and those who have not.

To be sure, the "victim" in our example has no right to recover. Why should that matter? Presumably few among us would object if the state fined the manufacturer an amount equal to the damage that results from a defective warning.

Suppose the money from that fine were to go toward funding the relevant public regulatory scheme. On what grounds could one object to holding the product manufacturer liable for that amount to our "victim"? The victim is acting as a private prosecutor. The liability judgment works like a fine. Instead of funding the public regulatory scheme, it funds a private regulatory scheme.

The plausibility or desirability of the private prosecutor approach does not depend on the legitimacy of the underlying claim. Whether or not the victim has a right in corrective justice to repair, imposing his loss on the manufacturer can be defended on the grounds that it creates an attractive system of incentives. Whether or not the victim has a claim in justice to repair, we might view compensation as an incentive sufficient to encourage litigation, which, in turn, is necessary to put the appropriate incentives in place. Similarly, whether or not the defendant has a duty of repayment in corrective justice, we might view liability imposed on him as an incentive to increase his investment in safety.

Here, then, is a case in which the plaintiff recovers against a defendant, though they are not brought together by considerations of corrective justice. The defendant has acted wrongfully, but his wrongdoing is not responsible for the plaintiff's loss. The plaintiff has no right to repair in justice; the defendant has no duty either. This case differs from others in which the plaintiff has a right to repair in justice, but liability for his loss is imposed on someone other than the wrongdoer or injurer. Let's now consider such cases.

19.2 LIABILITY AND THE CHEAPEST COST-AVOIDER

In the case I am imagining, the victim has a claim in justice to repair, but the defendant does not have a duty in justice to him. The interesting feature of this case is that someone other than the defendant owes a duty of repair to the victim. Thus, there are the victim who has the sort of claim that would be valid under the principle of corrective justice, as well as an agent who has the duty to the victim because he is responsible for having created the loss, and some third party who the court is prepared to hold liable to the victim because he is the cheapest cost-avoider, though he is in no way responsible for the harm. Were the court to impose liability on the cheapest cost-avoider, it would be enforcing a claim valid in corrective justice, but it would not otherwise be implementing corrective justice. The question here is whether in imposing the victim's loss on the third party tort law violates corrective justice?

One reason for thinking that imposing the victim's loss on someone other than the individual who has the moral duty to repair is that the third party does not volunteer to have the loss imposed upon him; another is that the third party is an innocent individual. Neither of these reasons is persuasive.

In Chapter 16 we introduced the Donald Trump example. In that example Trump volunteers to pay all my debts of repair. If he does so, all claims against me are extinguished thereby; no injustice is done. The example suggests that someone other than the injurer can shoulder the victim's loss without violating corrective justice. In that example, however, Trump volunteers to bear my costs, and it is for that reason, one might say, that no violation of corrective justice occurs. Had my costs been imposed on him without his consent, our moral assessment of the situation would have been very different. This suggests that corrective justice is violated when the costs of accidents are imposed on someone who does not agree so to bind herself.

Involuntariness is not an adequate criterion of wrongfulness, however. There is no corrective injustice in imposing the victim's loss on the *wrongdoer*, though the wrongdoer does not agree to bear those costs. Similarly, a victim may sometimes be asked to bear his own costs (e.g., when no one else has an obligation in justice to shoulder them), though there is no reason to suppose that he agrees so to bind himself. Though it may sometimes be unjust to impose a loss on someone who has not agreed so to bind herself, the mere fact that someone does not volunteer to be liable is not sufficient to make imposing a loss upon her wrongful and a violation of corrective justice.

Neither the cheapest cost-avoider nor the wrongdoer agrees to bear the victim's costs. Though neither agrees to shoulder the relevant costs, there is an obvious difference between them; the cheapest cost-avoider is, ex hypothesi, innocent of mischief, the wrongdoer is not. This suggests that the reason that it is permissible to impose the victim's loss on the wrongdoer, but not on the cheapest cost-avoider, is that the latter is innocent of wrongdoing, whereas the former is not. The reason that imposing the victim's loss on the cheapest cost-avoider violates corrective justice, then, is that corrective justice prohibits imposing losses on innocent persons. Thus, imposing the loss on the wrongdoer is compatible with corrective justice (even required by it perhaps), but imposing the same loss on the cheapest cost-avoider violates justice.

In fact, imposing liability on someone innocent of wrongdoing need not constitute a corrective injustice. Innocent individuals can sometimes have a duty in corrective justice to repair. Far from being an offence to justice, imposing liability upon them may be required by it. An individual who justifiably infringes the right of another may have a duty in justice to repair, a duty grounded in the fact that his conduct constitutes a wrong to the person injured. We called these infringement cases. *Vincent* v. *Lake Erie* is a good example; so, too, is Feinberg's backpacker. Justifiably invading the rights of others may give rise to a duty to repair in justice. Being innocent of blame, indeed, being worthy of praise, is not a bar to liability in morality.

Because it is sometimes permissible to impose liability on the innocent and the unwilling, does it follow that imposing the loss on anyone, whether he or she is responsible for a loss or otherwise at fault, can be compatible with the demands of corrective justice? If it is permissible to impose a loss on anyone regardless of innocence or unwillingness to shoulder the costs, then a fortiori it is permissible to impose the loss on the cheapest cost-avoider.

By showing that it is not always impermissible to impose

a loss on an innocent and unwilling party, we have not shown that the state would always be justified in doing so. At the very least, the state must have some good reason for doing so. If it does, then imposing the loss on such a person may not violate corrective justice. We might suppose that creating a system of effective incentives to reduce the incidence of accidents could count as a good reason for imposing liability. In that case imposing the victim's loss on the cheapest cost-avoider would not violate corrective justice.

If the state is free to impose liability on the wrongdoer (under the auspices of corrective justice) or on the cheapest cost-avoider (under the auspices of efficiency consistent with corrective justice), then, provided the costs of searching out the best risk reducer are low enough, why would the state ever choose to implement corrective justice? In seeking to implement corrective justice, the state misses an opportunity to create a scheme of accident-cost-minimizing incentives. As long as devising such a scheme is compatible with corrective justice, why bother to implement the demands of corrective justice fully when there is no reason to do so and the opportunity costs are so high?

Does it really follow that imposing the loss on the cheapest cost-avoider will always be permissible, or that imposing it on anyone other than the individual who has the duty in corrective justice will be? Is the liberal state authorized to forgo implementing corrective justice when the opportunity to implement corrective justice presents itself? In other words, are there no other arguments in justice against imposing the loss on the innocent, but cheapest, cost-avoider?

Perhaps the problem with imposing liability on the cheapest cost-avoider is that the loss is imposed on an innocent individual when there is someone else who is a wrongdoer. The problem with this suggestion is that there are wrongdoers everywhere, all the time, most of whom are completely unconnected to the harm and to the goals of tort law. Imposing the loss on them would serve no obvious social policy or goal, other than the diffuse and not obviously defensible one of imposing burdens, even random ones, on

391

wrongdoers. At least imposing the loss on the cheapest cost-avoider has the effect of creating an attractive and valuable incentive.

We are getting closer, however. Perhaps the real problem with imposing the victim's loss on the cheapest cost avoider is that it is unjust to do so *when there is someone else who has the duty in corrective justice to make repair*. It may be permissible to impose a loss on the cheapest cost-avoider, even if that person is free of mischief and unwilling to bear the costs voluntarily – provided there is no individual who has a duty in justice to bear those costs. If there is such a person, as there is in our example, then imposing the loss on the cheapest cost avoider is wrongful for exactly that reason.

We might want to distinguish between two kinds of cases. In one, there is a wrongful loss, but there is no one who has a duty in corrective justice to repair it. In the other, there is a loss that someone has a duty in corrective justice to repair. The claim, then, is that although it may be permissible to impose liability on someone who is neither a wrongdoer nor otherwise responsible for the loss in the first case, provided there exists some other justification for doing so, it is impermissible to impose liability on someone other than the individual who has the duty in corrective justice in the latter case, whether or not there exists some other good reason for doing so.

This objection amounts to the claim that if the state has the opportunity to implement corrective justice in a particular case, then it must do so. To put the loss on anyone else, for whatever reason, is wrongful. And it is wrongful just because there is someone who has a duty to make repair in corrective justice. The fact that an opportunity exists for imposing liability in accord with corrective justice is, in effect, all that makes the imposition of liability on other grounds, however strong, wrongful. This conclusion follows only if corrective justice demands an absolute priority with respect to all other goals the state may legitimately pursue within a tort system. This conclusion cannot be sustained, however.

We might distinguish between two different ways in which

imposing liability on someone unconnected or otherwise not responsible for an accident's occurrence might be viewed as imposing a wrongful loss. In one case there are no good reasons whatsoever for imposing the loss upon her. She did not cause the harm; she was not negligent or otherwise at fault in any way; nor is she in a good position to reduce or spread risk. In this sense, the loss is imposed on her for no good reason connected to any plausible account of the point or purpose of accident law; it is imposed entirely without justification, and is wrongful in that sense. Liability, therefore, imposes a wrongful loss and violates the constraint of corrective justice. In this sense, there may have been nothing wrongful in imposing the loss had she been in an especially good position to reduce or spread risk, both legitimate goals of tort law that fall within the state's authority to implement. Thus, what makes the imposition of liability wrongful, and a violation of corrective justice in this sense, is that there exists no good reason or justification recognized within the relevant political morality for imposing the loss.

Suppose, instead, that there exists good reasons of the sort recognized as legitimate within the relevant political morality for imposing the loss. In the sense of wrongful just characterized, imposing liability would not be wrongful. However, we can imagine another sense of the term or criterion for its application that makes it wrongful to impose liability (even if there are good reasons of the sort the state is authorized to implement for doing so), that is, whenever liability could have been imposed on someone else who had the duty in corrective justice to make repair. Because there are good reasons for imposing the loss in some way other than that dictated by corrective justice, the only ground for holding that doing so is wrongful is that any such liability judgment forgoes the opportunity to do corrective justice. And that in turn can be wrongful only if doing corrective justice has some kind of absolute priority over other legitimate goals the state may pursue through its tort system.

I accept the first and reject the second way in which imposing losses on third parties can constitute a corrective injustice. The state must allocate costs for a reason that is within its authority to implement, and it must do so within the constraints of the relevant principles of justice and political morality. If it has no good reason of the relevant sort for imposing liability, it violates corrective justice, and, very likely, other principles of justice as well. On the other hand, if it acts on the basis of good reasons within the scope of its authority, it does not violate corrective justice, even though it does not implement it. Imposing the loss on an innocent third party may not be a good idea on other grounds, but it is not wrongful just because in doing so the state misses a chance to impose the loss on that person who has the duty in corrective justice. On the other hand, imposing the loss on a third party who is not a good risk reducer or spreader may create a wrongful loss, whether or not there is someone who has the duty in corrective justice to make repair, simply because there exists no justification for imposing the loss on him. The fact that someone has a duty to make repair in corrective justice has little, if anything, to do with the wrongfulness of imposing liability without a good reason for doing so.

In this account, corrective justice does not cancel or override reasons for acting the state may be otherwise authorized to implement. It has no absolute priority with respect to the state's other legitimate goals. I have not demonstrated just yet that mine is the proper conception of the role of corrective justice in political argument. I have not shown, in other words, that it is not wrongful to miss the opportunity to implement corrective justice whenever the opportunity to do so presents itself. Such a view depends on a political theory about the way in which considerations of corrective justice constrain other politically legitimate reasons for acting. In what follows, however, I want to show that far from constraining legal practices that might otherwise ignore its dictates, corrective justice, as a moral principle, is itself constrained by legal and other social practices. In other words, I want to defend the odd-sounding position that whether or not corrective justice imposes *moral* reasons for acting will depend on prevailing legal and social practices. If anything, the proponent of the view that it is unjust to forgo opportunities to implement corrective justice in legal practice whenever the opportunity presents itself has matters absolutely backwards.

19.3 LIMITING CORRECTIVE JUSTICE

It is one thing for a body of law to seek to achieve a particular goal or principle as its overarching ambition or purpose. It is quite another to devise a set of rules, guidelines, policies, and practices capable of actually implementing that ambition in practice. If I am correct, pursuing corrective justice is the point of the core, if not all, of our current tort practice. That was the argument of Chapter 18. Implementing corrective justice requires a set of substantive liability rules, for example, a rule of liability for negligence. In addition to substantive liability rules, implementing corrective justice requires administrative rules establishing burdens of proof and evidence. These rules are defensible because they provide the best chance of practically implementing corrective justice under less than ideal circumstances; and they do so within the relevant constraints of justice and the like. One consequence of applying these rules in particular cases is that there will be times when the outcome will not conform to corrective justice. The results of applying these rules under conditions of uncertainty, in other words, will be less than ideal. Therefore, we will have to be careful not to infer too much about the substantive goals of tort law from an examination of the cases.

Two cases famous in torts case books help to illustrate the relationship between administrative rules and the principles they are designed to implement. Consider first *Ybarra* v. *Spangard*.[1] In *Ybarra*, the plaintiff undergoes surgery, and, while under general anesthetic, is apparently mistreated. The plaintiff can establish neither negligence nor responsibility. He can prove that he suffered an injury. The court holds that the most plausible explanation of his injury suggests negligence on someone's part. The court applies the doctrine of ipso loquitur in order to shift the burden of proof to the defendants to show that no negligence transpired. In effect, the court holds that under the circumstances, each of the named parties within the operating room should have the burden of showing that he or she was not the responsible party. A defendant who cannot show that he or she was not responsible will remain subject to liability. And this will be true even if that defendant is not someone who has the duty in corrective justice to repair; even if, moreover, that person is not in a good position to reduce or spread the relevant risk.

Nevertheless, it is easy to see how such a rule for shifting the burden of proof could be thought of as constituting a plausible way of implementing corrective justice. In *Ybarra*, the best way for a defendant to free herself of the burden of liability is to identify the party who is responsible for the plaintiff's misfortune. Presumably, at least some of the defendants know who that person is. Being excused from liability provides each defendant with the incentive to reveal that information. If the information is revealed, then that person who is in fact responsible for the loss will be solely liable for it, and corrective justice will have been served.[2]

Summers v. *Tice*[3] can be given a similar rationale. In that case, two hunters negligently fire in the direction of a third. The plaintiff is hit by one bullet, but there is no way he can determine whose bullet is responsible for his injury. If, in order to recover, he had to identify the responsible party, he would be out of luck. Instead, the court allows the burden to be shifted to the defendants, both of whom acted negligently. Either could free himself of liability by showing that his bullet was not the effective one. In that case the other party whose bullet is responsible for the damage would be solely liable and corrective justice done. As it happens, the defendants are in no better position to identify the responsible bullet than is the plaintiff. Neither can free himself of liability. Both are liable to the plaintiff, when in fact only one has the duty in corrective justice to repair. Still, it is a mistake to infer that *Summers* marks a departure from corrective justice simply because someone other than the person who has the relevant duty must bear some of the costs. Rather, the outcome in *Summers* is a predictable consequence of applying evidentiary rules designed to implement corrective justice under conditions of uncertainty.

It is tempting to extend the rationale of *Summers* to modern torts cases like *Sindell*[4] and *Hymowitz*.[5] If *Summers* can be understood as an effort to extend the ambit of corrective justice, then *Sindell* and *Hymowitz* might be subject to a similar analysis. In each case plaintiffs had been injured as the result of diethylstilbesterol (DES) administered to their mothers during pregnancy as a miscarriage preventive, and the defendants were the manufacturers and marketers of the drug. During the period the defendants marketed DES, they knew or should have known that it causes cancerous or precancerous vaginal and cervical growths in the daughters of mothers who took it, but they failed to test for efficacy and safety or to warn of its potential danger. Because of the passage of time between ingestion of the drug by the mother and harm to the daughter, and the large number of manufacturers using the same drug formula, the plaintiffs in DES cases usually are not able to identify which defendant manufactured the drug ingested by their respective mothers.

Although the court in *Sindell* found inapplicable theories of "alternate liability," "concert of action" liability, and industry wide ("enterprise") liability, it adopted a "market share" theory in order to find for the plaintiffs. Under the court's market share formula, the plaintiff joins as defendant the manufacturers of a substantial share of the particular market of DES from which her mother might have taken. Damages are apportioned to each defendant's share of that particular market, and each defendant may cross-claim against other manufacturers or demonstrate that it, in fact, could not have produced the particular drug ingested by the plaintiff's mother.

While also adopting the market share theory, the *Hymowitz* court rejected the particular or appropriate market limitation, choosing instead to apportion damages based on each named defendant's share of the national market. Admitting that the national market share test fails to provide a reasonable link between liability and risk created by a particular defendant to a particular plaintiff, the court concluded that such apportionment corresponds to over-all culpability of each defendant measured by the risk created to the public at large. Given this overarching rationale, the court also rejected the idea in *Sindell* that a particular defendant could free itself of liability by showing that it could not have produced the particular drug ingested by the plaintiff's mother.

In the ideal *Sindell*-type case, all the wrongdoers and all the victims of wrongdoing are brought together in a consolidated litigation. Each victim is able to establish that she has suffered a wrongful loss caused by one or another of the defendants. Each defendant has been shown, moreover, to have fallen below the relevant standard of behavior. All that is left, according to corrective justice, is to link particular wrongdoers with their victims. If that could be done, then corrective justice could be achieved. But that is precisely what is missing and, worse, practically unobtainable. The absence of the relevant information, and the practical impossibility of obtaining it, make it impossible to link particular wrongdoers with their victims in the way required by corrective justice.

Following the line of reasoning in *Ybarra* and *Summers*, one could argue that the burden can be shifted legitimately to each of the many defendants to show that he is not responsible for anyone's wrongdoing. Indeed, that is part of the holding in *Sindell*. In other words, if a particular defendant can show that none of the drugs he manufactures is responsible for any of the harms suffered by members of the plaintiff class, he can free himself of liability. Because there is no practical way of determining which harms are the responsibility of those manufacturers who are not able to free themselves of liability, the court adopts the principle that each should be liable for that percentage of the total damages that corresponds to its share of the market. This is the principle of market share liability. If market share is a reasonable proxy for causal responsibility, then one can view *Sindell* as an extension of *Summers* and *Ybarra*, which in turn can be understood as efforts to pursue the overarching goal of corrective justice when facing substantial epistemic obstacles.

The problem with this, the standard interpretation of *Sindell*, is revealed by the ruling in *Hymowitz*. In *Hymowitz*, one of the defendants in fact establishes that his product is not causally responsible for any of the harms suffered by members of the plaintiff class. Under the *Sindell* formula, any defendant who can establish his freedom from causal responsibility is able to free himself of liability. The *Hymowitz* court, however, rejects this option, and allows the defendant liability reflecting his share of the national market.

One response to *Hymowitz* is to treat it as a mistake that does not conform to the administration of corrective justice story we have been weaving. Another alternative is to contend that *Hymowitz* in fact fits within the corrective justice account of tort law. This is Richard Wright's view.[6] According to Wright, *Hymowitz* establishes that the relevant *harm* for which people can be justly held liable in torts (in cases of this sort) is the *wrongful imposition of risk*. The defendant in *Hymowitz* cannot show that he did not impose unjustifiable risks. Indeed, he did. All he can show is that the risks he imposed did not mature into full blown harms of the relevant sort. Therefore, he can be held liable in corrective justice for the risks he creates. The degree of his liability reflects the degree of risk he imposes; his liability is for the harm he causes under the principle of corrective justice where the relevant harm is the unjustifiable risk created.

The problem with Wright's argument is that it is unmotivated and ad hoc. It is not helpful to say that *Hymowitz* introduces another category of harms particularly appropriate to cases of a certain sort (market share cases). Either the imposition of unjustifiable risk is the relevant harm in all cases, both those in which the risk matures and those in which it does not, or it is not. One cannot claim that in the uncomplicated torts case, the relevant harm is the injury the victim suffers, whereas in other cases in which this conception of the harm is problematic – those like *Hymowitz* – the relevant harm is the risk imposed. This is simply an ad hoc solution to a difficult problem.

This is not to suggest that one could not defend the view that the morally relevant harm in all torts cases is the unjustifiable imposition of risk. My trouble with Wright's solution is that he treats the imposition of risk as morally relevant in some cases and not in others. His solution lacks consistency and integrity. Let's take a moment to outline how one might go about defending the view that in all torts cases, complicated or not, the morally relevant harm is the imposition of unreasonable or unjustifiable risks. In the typical case in which the risk matures into injury, victims do not sue until they have suffered an injury because actual injury provides them with the best evidence that the wrongdoer has imposed unjustifiable risks. Actual harm is evidentiarily connected to the underlying wrong, which is the wrongful imposition of risk. In other cases, perhaps those of the DES variety, it may be possible to obtain evidence that the wrongdoer has wrongfully imposed risks on the plaintiff without the benefit of actual injury. In any case, actual harm provides no additional evidence of unjustifiable risk taking than that which is already available. Allowing a defendant to defeat liability by showing in fact that he caused no harm to anyone would undermine the possibility of holding him liable for what is the real harm for which he is responsible, namely, the wrongful imposition of risk. No doubt there will be problems in pursuing such a reconstruction of tort law. Still, such a project is needed if one wants to pursue the general line of interpretation of *Hymowitz* that the Wright argument suggests.

The standard interpretation rejects *Hymowitz* as a mistake, an unjustifiable departure from tort law's preoccupation with implementing corrective justice under the conditions of uncertainty bound to obtain. To his credit, Wright rejects this interpretation. His mistake is in thinking that *Hymowitz* can be defended as a form of corrective justice in which the relevant harm is the wrongful imposition of risk. The best interpretation of *Hymowitz*, however, does not view it as a mistake or as an attempt to implement corrective justice for a distinct category of harms. To understand *Hymowitz* and *Sindell*, we have to consider the principle of corrective justice once again.

Suppose that we all lived in New Zealand or that our community, wherever it was, decided to implement a New Zealand-like no-fault plan. Let's now set aside all questions about whether doing so would be a smart or otherwise desirable thing to do. The question we need to address is in what way does our having a New Zealand-like plan affect or otherwise relate to the principle of corrective justice? Suppose Carol negligently rams her automobile into Alan. Under corrective justice, Alan has a right to repair in corrective justice and Carol has a duty to provide it. In the world in which Carol, Alan, and the rest of us live, however, Alan recovers from the treasury, not from Carol. What do we want to say about this situation as regards its bearing on corrective justice? There are at least three alternatives.

The first thing we might say is that our New Zealand-like plan affronts corrective justice. Carol has the duty to compensate Alan, and any other scheme in which Alan secures compensation violates corrective justice. Note that this example simply generalizes the problem we began discussing in the last section when we asked whether imposing liability in a particular case on some third party would create a wrongful loss whenever there exists an individual who has the duty to repair in corrective justice. In that case, corrective justice is "ignored" on a case-by-case basis; here it is being ignored systematically. If it is wrong to impose liability on someone who is not responsible for a loss when there is someone who can be held liable and is responsible, then it is wrong to do so on a general basis. So one view we might hold about New Zealand plans is that they are impermissible departures from corrective justice. To ignore corrective justice, to decide on some other scheme for allocating accident costs, is, in effect to violate corrective justice.

The second thing we might say is that the New Zealand

plan has no bearing on the relationship between Alan and Carol with regard to corrective justice. Alan has a moral right to recover and Carol a moral duty to compensate, both derivable from corrective justice. That Alan has been compensated in some other way does not change that fact. The compensation scheme is a public or legal mechanism; the relationship between Alan and Carol under corrective justice is private and moral. The legal institution cannot affect the moral relationships. Thus, if Alan suffers a million dollars in damages as a result of Carol's mischief, Carol owes Alan a million dollars; and that does not change as a result of the existence of some public compensation scheme.

Both of these alternatives are implausible. The New Zealand plan neither affronts corrective justice, nor is its existence irrelevant to corrective justice. If Alan recovers from the treasury, he no longer has a moral right to recover from Carol. Some who accept this conclusion might argue that the reason he has no moral claim against Carol is that he forfeits or gives it up by accepting another form of compensation. Others might say that his claim against Carol is extinguished by the fact that he consents to some other compensation scheme, and so on. Whatever the underlying reason, the important point for our purposes is that in fact he has no claim in corrective justice to repair.

The reason he has no claim in corrective justice to repair is that there exists some other mechanism through which the costs of accidents are to be allocated. That means that whether or not corrective justice in fact imposes moral duties on particular individuals is *conditional* upon the existence of other institutions for making good victims' claims to repair. The capacity within a particular community of corrective justice to impose the relevant *moral* duties depends on the existence of certain *legal* or *political* institutions or social practices.

Even tort theorists like Ernest Weinrib, who deny that it is permissible to impose a loss on an innocent third party in a particular case, claim that it may be permissible to substitute a New Zealand no-fault plan for the tort system as a whole. The suggestion is that the state for a variety of presumably good reasons might choose to forgo implementing in law the demands of corrective justice. It can choose, for example, not to have a tort system, even if the tort system is itself the legal embodiment of the ideal of corrective justice. This claim is revealing in its own right, but does not go far enough.

The view I am suggesting is that whether or not corrective justice itself imposes moral duties on individuals in a community will depend on other practices that are in effect. The reason is this. Corrective justice links agents with losses. It provides individuals with agent-relative reasons for acting. These reasons for acting can be superseded by other practices that create reasons for acting, both agent-neutral and agent-relative. Such practices sever the relationship between agents and losses. The victim's wrongful loss may give her a right to recover. That right is part of the normative basis for imposing a duty of repair. The nature and scope of the duty depend on the practices in place. The content of the duty and the reasons for acting to which it gives rise do not follow logically from the nature of the right to repair, but from the normative practices in place within the community, practices that, in conjunction with the victim's right, give rise to specific obligations.

My view is not that other social and legal practices sever all of the relationships between wrongdoer and victim. After all, the wrongdoer may be responsible for the victim's loss. The question is to which duties does this relationship give rise. And my argument is that the nature and scope of the duties depend on the prevailing practices. Moreover, even if no-fault-like practices exist for handling accident costs, the injurer, and no one else, may have the duty to apologize, or the like.

The question before the state is not whether to forgo corrective justice; instead, it is, what ought to be done about losses including those that result from wrongful conduct. If there is a comprehensive plan put into effect for dealing with those losses by imposing them on everyone or on all those individuals who are at fault, whether or not their fault results in harm to others, then corrective justice itself imposes no duties within that community.[7] Thus, although corrective justice is private justice – justice between the parties – whether or not it imposes obligations between the parties depends on other social, political and legal practices. This, I take it, is a controversial, but I think inescapable truth about corrective justice. It may be true of other moral principles as well.

If corrective justice is conditional in this sense, then the state may choose to allocate accident costs in any number of ways. It may do so through a tort system that implements corrective justice; it may do so through a New Zealand no-fault scheme: it may do so through a generalized at fault plan; it may do so through a variety of localized or limited at fault plans. It may do so through a tort system that seeks to spread or minimize risk; or it may seek to do so through a tort system that seeks to do a combination of these things; and so on.

Suppose that instead of a New Zealand plan, our community had decided to implement an at fault pool for automobile accidents. The total costs of injuries suffered by the victims of car accidents over some period of time would be summed and then distributed among those drivers who are at fault in operating their vehicles whether or not their fault actually leads to any damage. If everyone were equally at fault and drove equally as often, then the likely solution would be to divide the costs among the class of drivers equally. If some drove more than others, then the division of the costs would likely reflect each driver's "market share."

Given the view of corrective justice I have just articulated, were such a scheme in place, Alan would have no claim in corrective justice against Carol, and she would have no duty to him. It would be a mistake, moreover, to view the at-fault pool itself as an effort to extend the ambit of corrective justice to the case of many injurers and victims. That argument would not be improved by claiming either that the at-fault pool merely shifts evidentiary or other burdens in an effort to implement corrective justice in a world of uncertainty or that it implements corrective justice in which the relevant harm for which one is entitled to recover is the unjustifiable imposition of risk. The at-fault pool cannot be reconstructed as an implementation or extension of corrective justice. It is simply an alternative means for allocating traffic accident costs, one, that if implemented and compatible with other demands of justice and morality, simply extinguishes all rights and duties under corrective justice.[8]

With this discussion in mind, let's return to the troubling cases of *Sindell* and *Hymowitz*. My suggestion is that we read the DES cases not as an effort to implement corrective justice in an imperfect world but as an effort to implement localized or constrained at-fault pools to deal with injuries caused by certain kinds of defective products. The losses are spread among those individuals who are at fault in creating unjustifiable risks of the sort that lead to the kinds of injuries that the members of the plaintiff class have suffered. If we assume that each manufacturer is equally at fault in producing a defective drug, the best approximation of the amount each should pay to the plaintiffs is given by the share of the market each has garnered. (The tort suit is used as a forum for implementing this plan simply because it uses the plaintiff class as private prosecutors and is presumably desirable on those grounds.)

The problem comes from trying to reconcile *Sindell* with *Hymowitz*. According to *Sindell*, although at fault, a defendant who could establish that his fault was not responsible for anyone's damage would free himself of liability. In *Hymowitz*, the absence of responsibility is inadequate to free the defendant of liability. *Hymowitz* is, in fact, the correct interpretation of the basic principles set forth in *Sindell*. *Sindell* is not an extension of corrective justice. Instead, it involves a localized at-fault plan. Under such a plan, whether or not one causes harm is irrelevant. Moreover, allowing a defendant who can show the absence of causal responsibility to free himself of liability will defeat the very point of allocating costs according to the fault of the agents.

To see this, return to our at fault plan for automobile accidents. The plan allocates accident costs among motorists according to the risks associated with their motoring. Now suppose that we add a wrinkle to our plan that allows each motorist to free himself of liability by showing that his negligence is harmless. That little wrinkle completely destroys the at-fault pool. That is precisely the point: One can have either a corrective justice scheme or an at fault pool. One cannot have both at the same time. For that reason, *Sindell* does not fully comprehend the underlying principles of liability that it creates. It is caught between two paradigms: corrective justice and at-fault liability. Perhaps, the Sindell court fails to see that the two cannot be reconciled; perhaps the court believes that imposing liability on the basis of fault or market share is at the heart of corrective justice, and that because it is, any defendant who can in fact show that he did not cause any harm should be able to free himself of liability. Whatever the reason, *Sindell* is torn between two conflicting approaches to allocating the relevant costs: one that imposes the duty in corrective justice; the other that imposes losses according to a localized at fault scheme. Therefore, rather than being an unjustifiable departure from the logic of *Sindell*, *Hymowitz* represents the correct understanding of *Sindell*'s underlying logic.

Chapter 20

Product liability

I have separated product liability law from the general discussion of accident law for several reasons. First, product liability law is among the most unsettled and unstable bodies of tort law. It would be difficult to try to extract its underlying normative commitments from a review of the doctrine, the doctrine itself being so unsettled. Second, a recent report of a committee of the American Law Institute asked to look into product liability reform suggests separating product liability law from the body of tort law. In the committee's view, product liability should be governed by distinct principles. This chapter, therefore, departs from the structure of the preceding chapters. Instead of trying to unpack product liability law in search of its underlying commitments, it seeks to provide a strategy of reform consistent with the arguments presented in both Parts II and III of the book. In doing so, it is committed to a certain view of the core of product liability, one which I recognize as controversial.

American manufacturers continue to grapple with the costly problem of products liability. The impact of the current system for compensating consumers for harm done by manufactured goods extends far beyond such celebrated cases as those facing cigarette manufacturers or asbestos suppliers. In 1985–6, nearly half (47 percent) of all product manufacturers in the United States removed product lines from the market place, 25 percent discontinued product research and 39 percent decided against introducing new products, all as the result of increased exposure to liability.[1] These are striking figures.

More importantly, in removing products already on the market, manufacturers are responding to continued changes in the rules governing liability for their products, changes they obviously did not predict. For had the manufacturers predicted that their products would have been deemed defective, either they would have altered the design earlier or simply not produced the product in the first place. Such radical changes in the availability of product lines cannot be a good thing either for manufacturers or consumers. On the other hand, it is certainly undesirable to allow dangerous products to remain in the market. What is undesirable about the current products liability system is its uncertainty. What the law will deem to be dangerous and the extent of responsibility are far less predictable than they should or could be.

Thus, it can come as no real surprise that two words capture the American manufacturer's concerns regarding liability for harms that result from the use of the products it places in the market place: *exposure* and *uncertainty*. These two concerns are connected. The manufacturer's concerns about exposure ranges over both *persons* and *time*. To whom can a manufacturer be liable? How far in time does the manufacturer's responsibility extend?

In 1979, the aviation industry produced over 17,000 aircraft. In 1987, it shipped only 1,085 a decrease of over 90%. Cessna, which produced 9,000 piston planes in 1979, produced *none* in 1987; Beech dropped from 1,214 in 1979 to 195 in 1987; and Piper's production for 1987 was 267. Teledyne Continental, a major engine manufacturer, saw its production drop from 11,000 to 400 in the same period. These figures do not represent a response to decreasing demand for the products generally, since the difference has been made up almost entirely by increased foreign production, especially by German companies. Rather, it reflects increased costs that make American products unattractive. Of these costs, product liability costs now constitute the largest single cost factor in the construction of a new piston aircraft. Industry officials allege that if actual product liability costs were added as an average cost per plane to each aircraft produced, it would increase the cost by $100,000 per aircraft.

The increase in product liability costs is not the result of increased accident rates. In fact, accident rates have steadily declined. Rather, price increases stem from the nature of product liability law itself. Though 85 percent of all accidents are due to pilot error, manufacturers, not pilots, are sued in well over 90 percent of cases involving fatalities or serious injury.

In 1977, the aviation industry paid $24 million dollars in claims; in 1985, it paid $210 million, though the number of suits remained relatively constant. There are, moreover, virtually no caps on recovery, and no meaningful time limitations. Once produced, manufacturers are liable for their products forever.

20.1 HOW DID WE GET HERE?

At one time product liability law was really a branch of the law of sales, risk was allocated by contract, and a manufacturer's liability was restricted by the doctrine of *privity* to those individuals who were the immediate purchasers of its products. As a result of privity, a car manufacturer might stand liable in the event of an injury to an employee of a car dealership resulting from a defective part. In contrast, were the very same defect to result in an injury to the ultimate purchaser of the car, the manufacturer could escape liability altogether. Privity insulated the product manufacturer from liability to the ultimate users of its products. Similarly, a manufacturer's potential liability would extend in time no longer than the period of ownership of the immediate purchaser, and often a good deal less.

Such a rule restricting the scope of liability over persons and time had two significant benefits for product manufacturers. First, it reduced significantly the costs of doing business. Many of the harms causally connected to the manufacturing process were not held to be the manufacturer's responsibility. Instead they were externalized, that is, imposed on third parties. As a consequence, manufacturers were not required to bear the full social costs of their activities. Second, the sales contract as a market mechanism of risk allocation enforceable at law provided manufacturers with a degree of *certainty* regarding at least one central element of the costs of production. With confidence and warrant, a manufacturer could estimate his exposure to liability and adjust its investments in safety accordingly.

The rule of risk allocation by contract gave rise to a dilemma – what was good for the producer was not necessarily best for society. It reduced uncertainty and exposure. In doing so, however, it too narrowly defined a manufacturer's responsibility, thereby allowing manufacturers to externalize certain costs. Thus, although manufacturers could rationally adjust their decisions about how much to invest in safety, the rule of liability itself may have encouraged them to underinvest.

The current problem is whether a rule of liability for products can provide both the predictability necessary for rational investment in safety and the incentives necessary for proper investment decisions. We have come a long way from a standard that allowed predictability but encouraged underinvestment to the present set of standards that, as the statistics cited dramatically indicate, magnifies uncertainty and, in doing so, undermines possibilities for rational investment in safety. The story of modern products liability law then is a tale of confused and failed attempts to bring concurrently both predictability and rationality to this body of law.

20.2 THE MODERN SOLUTION

It is obvious that the doctrine of privity as applied to defective products could not survive. For such a law did virtually nothing to protect the ultimate users of products – those individuals for whom the products were intended. The landmark case of *MacPherson* v. *Buick Motor Co.*[2] is widely credited with weakening the so-called privity limitation, thereby removing product liability from the law of sales while placing it within the law of *tort*.

The rejection of the sales contract as a vehicle for allocating risk, therefore, rests on two assumptions. The first is that the costs of contracting, of allocating risk by market forces, are too high, that, in effect, the market will allocate product safety risk inefficiently. In other words, if we left the allocation of risk to manufacturers and consumers we would either get too little or too much investment in safety. The usual intuition is that we will get too little investment in safety. The second assumption is that substituting externally imposed tort standards is more likely to lead to predictable, rational investments in safety.

Two questions naturally emerge. First, is the move from the contract to the tort solution warranted? Is there sufficient evidence that leaving risk allocation decisions to a market will be inefficient? Second, if courts were ultimately correct in abandoning contract for tort, has tort law provided the needed rationality and predictability. Let's take up these questions in reverse order.

20.3 RATIONALITY AND PREDICTABILITY

Modern product liability law is governed by a mixture of strict and negligence liability. The standard of liability in *Mac-Pherson* was negligence, and it was not until the 1960s that strict liability came to provide a basis for recovery. Like most developments in the law, the change from negligence to strict liability was slow and, in a way, tortured. The first significant movement from negligence to strict liability involved increasing reliance on the doctrine of res ipso loquitur. Under that procedural rule, the mere fact of an injury is taken to be presumptive evidence of negligence. Rather than a consumer having to show a manufacturer's negligence, a manufacturer would be forced to establish his innocence. Even a consumer's own negligence in using a product could become evidence of the manufacturer's negligence. For surely a manufacturer could foresee that sometimes products would be

411

misused. Failing to guard against foreseeable misuse would be further evidence of negligence. With no apparent way to defeat liability, manufacturers were held, in effect, strictly liable even though courts took pains to argue on negligence theories.

The turning point came in *Escola* v. *Coca Cola Bottling Co.*[3] The opinion of the court was written on a negligence theory, but a brilliant concurrence by Justice Traynor advanced the view that the real and correct standard of liability for products is strict. Traynor argued the view that the goals of tort law are primarily economic ones: deterrence and insurance. That is, rules of liability should be designed to minimize risk and to spread it maximally over persons and time. For Traynor, pursuing both goals dictated a strict liability standard. His argument has captured the imagination of judges and scholars alike for its elegance and coherence. Roughly the argument is this.

When neither manufacturer nor consumer is negligent, who should bear the costs? As between victims and manufacturers, the latter are better suited to obtain insurance at a lower cost and to spread those costs maximally over persons and time. In addition, manufacturers are better suited to invest in safety precautions or to determine which risks are worth taking. Consequently, or so Traynor argued, liability ought strictly to be imposed on manufacturers without regard to their negligence. Pursuing either end calls for a standard of strict liability.

As already noted, the widespread use of procedural devices aimed at easing the plaintiff's case for recovery under the negligence rule had reduced the availability and efficacy of the defense of contributory negligence. By the time the substantive rule of strict liability was openly imposed on manufacturers, the combination of forces yielded a rule very much like absolute liability: liability for all harms without regard to the negligence of the product user. In this regard, manufacturers were being asked to insure consumers for all safety-related risks. Tort law became, in effect, a vehicle by which public authorities, courts, created a private insurance scheme. Manufacturers insure product users – period.

In another sense, modern product liability law has maintained vestiges of negligence. In order to impose liability on a manufacturer some threshold requirement had to be met. This threshold was to be spelled out in terms of a manufacturer's failure to measure up to some standard of conduct either internally or externally imposed. These standards are represented by "manufacturing" and "design" defect requirements. A manufacturer's product is said to suffer a manufacturing defect if it fails to perform as the manufacturer represents it, that is, it falls below the manufacturer's own standards.

The negligence component is represented by design defect standards. And here lies the problem. For there is no one design defect test applicable in all jurisdictions, nor are any of the tests easy to administer. Most importantly, the results under these standards are not at all predictable.

Alan Schwartz has recently reviewed critically four separate design tests and finds them wanting.[4] These four tests are the expectation test, the Learned Hand test, the risk/benefit test, and the regulatory/compliance test. Under the expectation test, a manufacturer can be liable if its product is less safe than it is reasonable for a consumer to expect it to be. A manufacturer is liable under the Learned Hand test if it is negligent in the economic sense, that is, if the costs of taking precautions are less than the expected value of the harm. Liability under the risk/benefit test is more complex, since a firm's design is defective if, among all the feasible designs available, it fails to adopt the one that maximizes net benefits. In the regulatory compliance scheme the appropriate standards are set by a regulatory agency and the court's job is to enforce those standards. Failure to comply with the operative safety standard is negligent; compliance, however, is merely evidence of nonnegligence, *not* constitutive of it.

The expectation test is not helpful. In the absence of some other test that specifies the level of safety it is reasonable for consumers to expect, the test is empty. On the other hand, if there is such a test, *it*, and not the expectation test, does the relevant work. The Learned Hand test is merely the economic negligence test. It introduces all the administrative costs of gathering the relevant information about the benefit and damage schedules of manufacturers and consumers. These administrative problems are magnified under the general risk/ benefit test. How are juries to determine from among all possible feasible designs the one that maximizes social welfare? What do juries know about product design alternatives? The regulatory compliance test does not negate uncertainty because a manufacturer cannot know whether courts will consistently rule that regulatory compliance will free the firm from liability. Together the rule of strict liability in conjunction with the design defect tests have wreaked havoc within the manufacturing sector of the economy.

Strict liability, as Traynor noted, makes manufacturers insurers of consumers, though a manufacturer can theoretically recover these insurance costs in product prices. By adopting strict liability, tort law has created a system of *third party* insurance. First party insurance, for example, health insurance, the type consumers are most familiar with, is purchased to protest against something untoward happening to the purchaser. The problem with third party insurance is that it creates problems of "adverse selection" and "moral hazard" on excess of those created under a first party system.[5] People will be more inclined to pursue any hospital test or treatment as a result of an accident, regardless of cost, if someone else is paying for it. But if a person has to pay for the service or buy the relevant insurance, he or she would be inclined to consider undergoing only cost-justified treatments. Third party schemes are also much more expensive to administer. So great is the difference in cost between first and third party insurance that George Priest, America's leading insurance scholar, has argued that tort liability's imposition of a third party scheme to allocate product safety risks is the primary source of the recent insurance crisis.[6]

Finally, the design defect tests, which constitute a partial retreat from the rule of strict liability, turn out to be extremely costly to administer. These tests are so diverse in their requirements as to give little guidance to manufacturers seeking to determine the level of investment in safety they should make. When applied individually, design defect tests will result in wildly uncertain outcomes. In short, the modern solution has failed to provide what we seek, a principled, rational, and predictable body of law regulating product safety.

The absence of a predictable and rational legal standard is reflected in the insurance crunch. The greatest danger to an efficient insurance market is uncertainty, and that is precisely what the current regime has given us. The question then is whether there exists a set of policy recommendations that would add an element of rationality and certainty to the law governing product safety. In this regard, it is important to reconsider whether abandoning the contract mechanism for allocating risk was warranted in the first place.

20.4 CONTRACTS REVISITED

The most fundamental feature of modern products liability is the rejection of the market in favor of a tort solution. This rejection presupposes that the "contracts" between manufacturers and consumers do not or cannot adequately address issues of safety, and that a solution must be imposed in the form of a set of external standards. Another way of putting this is to say that the very idea of a tort or regulatory solution to the allocation of risks regarding product safety is predicated on a presumed fundamental market failure. That is to say, the contracts between manufacturers and consumers with regard to product safety are generally inefficient, thus a state-imposed (via tort or regulatory regimes) solution will produce efficiency gains in excess of costs.

The fact is that it is not at all obvious that the contract mechanism for allocating risk between manufacturers and consumers, that is, the market solution, would be grossly inefficient. Nor is it obvious that a general tort or regulatory

415

solution would produce relative net benefits as compared with the market alternative.

The usual argument in support of the market failure theory is that consumers have imperfect information regarding the rights and responsibilities made explicit in their contracts regarding risk allocation, the relative costs of various contracts, and the actual risks involved. First, contract clauses are difficult to read or comprehend, but the solution to this problem is not to reject contracts, but to enhance comprehensibility. Second, consumers probably do not search adequately for the best contracts, but there is no reason to believe that their failure to do so will necessarily lead to suboptimal contracts. It is just as likely that firms will provide the desired clauses, but exploit the low level of search by recapturing more than their marginal costs of providing these terms. Finally, consumers may under or overestimate risks, and if they do so systematically, contracts between consumers and manufacturers are unlikely to be efficient. However, it is not at all obvious that courts and juries are better positioned to make the appropriate risk/benefit calculations. Indeed, the information demands on courts and juries in applying any risk/benefit test are extraordinary. Even if systematic imperfect information threatens the efficiency of the market solution for allocating safety risks between consumers and producers, it is not obvious that the current approach can do better.

The market failure argument for rejecting contract in favor of tort is inadequately persuasive to support a total rejection of the market/contract as a risk allocation mechanism. One possible reform of the current law would be to consider ways of reintroducing the market as a central instrument in the allocation of safety-risks. This could be accomplished in either of two ways.

First, the tort approach would be eliminated entirely in favor of sales contracts. In other words, simply return to the sales contract as a vehicle for allocating safety as well as other risks, and forget about doing so through tort liability. The argument for doing so would be that the tort solution creates more problems than the contract approach, whatever its shortcomings. Contract, in other words, is the lesser of two evils. Such a change in the architecture of risk allocation mechanisms is at present infeasible. A second, more plausible solution would be to combine the contract and tort approaches. The sales contract can be reintroduced as an *option* in allocating risk by allowing parties to contract around tort rules. In this way, tort rules can apply as default provisions in the event contracting parties cannot efficiently or rationally allocate risk among themselves.

Any return to the contract model will increase predictability since the conditions under which a manufacturer is held liable are set out with some considerable degree of certainty in the contract. The rationality of the allocation and distribution of risk by contract, as we noted earlier, depends on the rationality and knowledge of consumers and producers. Consumers may be inadequately knowledgeable about the nature and scope of risk, and that is why we cannot rely entirely on markets. Rational actors will sometimes need to avail themselves of rules set by third parties: tort rules. So it is natural to mix contract with tort approaches. But if the current tort approach has led to crises, the problem will not be eliminated by the modest change of reintroducing contract as an option. Even if they are to apply only as default rules, something has to be done about the tort rules themselves. What should those rules be?

20.5 PRODUCT LIABILITY RULES

One argument for viewing product liability law on the model of the rational contract derives from a more general argument for treating all of torts in this way. As noted earlier, the law of tort, of which product liability law is a part, governs obligations regarding safety among strangers. Strangers are persons who, in this sense, lack a contractual relationship. They are not in contracting relationships because the transaction costs of contracting are too high.

For example, all auto drivers could in theory contract ex

417

ante with everyone who is put at risk by their operating an automobile. Such a contract would give the driver a right to put others at risk at some price acceptable to each person so endangered. The costs of finding and contracting with everyone who one might put at risk by driving are prohibitive, however, and no contracting occurs. Instead, a rule of liability is imposed in the event someone is injured by motoring.

What should this rule of liability be? One way of answering this question is to imagine that the relevant parties – motorists and pedestrians – could contract with one another at low cost. What contract would they agree to? When contracting or bargaining is too costly to be rational, we might adopt institutional arrangements that replicate what a contract between the parties would have produced. In effect, to determine what rules should apply among strangers we should ask ourselves, What rules would they have created contractually had transaction costs not made their doing so impossible?

Let's call the strategy that looks to the question, What would the parties have contracted to before any claim arose? the ex ante contract approach? The argument for applying the ex ante contract to the problem of product liability reform is that this is the approach that we should apply to all of tort law. If it should be applied to all of tort law, it should apply a fortiori to product liability law.

The argument is valid, but not sound. As I have argued, if one adopts an economic analysis of tort law, then it will be true that tort is just a general set of default provisions that arise in the absence of contracting. But one is not compelled to adopt the economic approach generally. I do not. One can argue that an economic approach to the bulk of tort law is not as illuminating as one based on corrective justice. That has been my argument to this point. Still, even if the economic or rational bargaining approaches miss something essentially about tort law generally, either might capture the essence of product liability. That is my view.

There seems to me to be a case for treating products liability on the contract model even if there isn't the same argument for treating all of tort law in that way. There is a sense in which we can treat product liability law as merely filling in the blanks in contracts between parties who are already in a contracting relationship with one another: producers and consumers. Auto accident law does not fill in contractual blanks; to treat auto accident law on the contract model is to create a framework of analysis that does not already exist. And there are arguments in favor and against doing so. On the other hand, in product liabilty law, to treat the relationship between consumers and producers with respect to the allocation of safety related risks on the contract model is not to create a new framework for analyzing their relationship; rather, it is to extend the framework in which they are already embedded. We may be driven to supplement through torts the "contract" between the parties, but it makes good sense that in doing so we create a tort law that conforms to the outcomes of a rational contracting process. If we do so, moreover, we will explain the sense in which strict product liability is both desirable and defensible.[7]

By analyzing potential rules of liability in a hypothetical contract model, we insure that the rules of tort used as default provisions in failed or incomplete contracts allocate risks in ways contract would. Thus, there is no discontinuity between the contract and tort approaches. Rather, the tort rules extend the contract approach, thereby enhancing the overall rationality and, as a consequence, the predictability of the scheme of risk allocation.

Suppose that Justice Traynor was right when he noted that manufacturers and consumers are concerned primarily with two aspects of the risks related to product safety. These are the reduction of risk, and its distribution. For convenience, the first of these is labeled deterrence and the second insurance. The questions are, How would rational actors distribute and seek to reduce product safety costs in an optimal contract? and How would adhering to that allocation scheme alleviate problems inherent in the current regime?

419

Rectifiable wrongs

20.6 THE INSURANCE FUNCTION OF PRODUCTS LIABILITY

To begin, recall that one advantage of strict liability is that it serves a private social insurance function. Manufacturers that are better situated to purchase insurance do so, then pass the costs to consumers, each of whom in effect buys insurance and pays a premium as part of a product's overall costs. This cost, presumably, is far less than what a consumer would have to pay to purchase insurance on his or her own, if in fact an individual could purchase sufficient insurance. Thus, in standard strict liability, risk is distributed in two steps. The cost of insuring against risk is imposed on the manufacturer. The manufacturer then passes those costs to consumers, spreading the costs over persons and time.

But does this procedure reflect how manufacturers and consumers would distribute the costs of insurance among one another if they could do so by contract? Yes and no. This may well be the way manufacturers and consumers would distribute insurance costs, but would consumers and manufacturers seek insurance against all risks? Under current law all risks are insured. But would rational consumers seek to insure against all risks? Consumers appear to insure against *pecuniary* losses, but are less likely to insure against *nonpecuniary* ones. What's the difference? The difference is usually explained, by economists at least, in terms of the marginal utility of the dollar. Individuals do not secure the same utility from each dollar they possess. If someone has a lot of money now, but expects to have very little in the future, some of his current dollars would be worth more to him later than they are worth now. Therefore, a rational agent will try to find a way to shift current dollars to the future when they will be worth more to him. One way of doing this is to save; another is to purchase insurance. It follows that rational people will consider purchasing insurance – move money from the present to the future – when those dollars will be worth more, when, in other words, the agent's marginal utility from the dollar will increase.

420

Pecuniary losses increase a persons' marginal utility of money. For example, if at some future point someone is unable to work as a result of an accident, that person's income drops and the value of each dollar relative to its current value may increase. To equalize expected utility, dollars are shifted from 'now' until 'later' by purchasing insurance. Rational, risk averse, actors will tend to buy insurance against pecuniary losses. Therefore, if one point of a tort liability rule imposed on product manufacturers is to provide insurance to consumers, then a rule that reflects the contract rational consumers would choose is one that provides full recovery for pecuniary losses. Nonpecuniary losses, in contrast, do not increase the marginal utility of money. For that reason rational actors are unlikely to insure against them. The problem is to identify which losses are nonpecuniary. Several commentators have suggested that "pain and suffering" awards fall into the category of recompense for a nonpecuniary loss, and that such damage awards should, therefore, be eliminated. In support of this claim, some have noted that insurance companies do not sell "pain and suffering" insurance on a first party basis. The absence of available coverage in a competitive industry suggests insufficient demands, which in turn supports the hypothesis that rational actors do not guard against nonpecuniary losses, as well as the intuition that pain and suffering constitute nonpecuniary costs. But the absence of a market for first party insurance for nonpecuniary losses does not demonstrate the absence of demand. Insurers may be disinclined to offer the insurance whatever the extent of demand because they fear fraudulent claims.

There are other examples of potential nonpecuniary losses. Suppose someone plays piano for recreation. An accident in which her fingers are severely injured may prevent recreational piano playing. That's a loss. But if she substitutes reading for piano playing, then the accident has, at least with respect to that loss, *not* increased her marginal utility of the dollar.

These considerations suggest that manufacturers should

not be required to provide coverage for nonpecuniary losses precisely because, in the absence of a tort law rule that provides it for them, rational consumers do not demand such protection. Thus, one additional suggestion for revision in current practice is drastically to reduce, or to eliminate entirely, recovery for nonpecuniary losses.[8]

20.7 THE RATIONAL CONTRACT AND RISK REDUCTION

Consumers are at least as interested in reducing risk, that is, increasing safety, as they are in insuring against it. How, then, do we reduce risks to consumers, and who should be responsible? Returning to *Escola*, the California Supreme Court argued that not only were manufacturers better suited to distribute risk (via insurance) but that, as between them and consumers, producers were better suited to reduce risk or to decide which risks were worth reducing. Manufacturers can better reduce risk, but how much risk reduction do consumers want? Consumers do not want to purchase more safety than is rational. In other words, consumers want to increase expenditures on safety until the point at which additional safety costs more than the expected value of the harm it is designed to guard against. If it cost $90 to prevent $100 damage, then that is money a consumer would want to spend. But consumers would not spend $110 to prevent the same damage. If safety prevention costs are accurately reflected in product prices, that is, passed on to consumers as they would be in a contract, they will want manufacturers to engage in optimal safety prevention activities.

The consumer's demand for efficient investment in safety can be met by a variety of very different tort liability rules. As we noted in Chapter 12, both negligence and strict liability with the defense of plaintiff's contributory negligence are efficient in the relevant sense. Either a negligence rule or a strict liability rule can, in theory, produce efficient investments in safety. As an example, consider the $100 accident. Spending $50 successfully to prevent it would be rational;

spending $200 would not be. We would want a potential injurer to spend anything up to $99 to prevent the harm, but nothing above $100. Both negligence and strict liability give us that result.[9] Under negligence, an injurer will be negligent if he doesn't spend $99 to prevent $100 of damage. If he doesn't spend $99, he will be liable for $100, and therefore he will pay $100. But it will make sense for him to pay $99 rather than $100, and he will do so. Under strict liability he will be required to pay the $100 no matter what. But if he can prevent it for $99, he will do so. In that case if causing the harm is a product of a course of conduct worth less than $100 to him, he simply will not engage in it. Thus, we get the same result. On the other hand, if it costs $150 to prevent the harm, then under negligence, we will not want an agent to prevent it. And so the $100 accident occurs. The same is true under strict liability. The injurer will bear the $100 costs no matter what. But if the activity that causes it is worth $150 to him, he will go ahead and do it and create $100 of damages. The incentives for safety – at least with respect to injurers – are the same under both rules. Thus, a liability regime seeking to provide the safety consumers would have bargained for by contract can choose either strict or negligence liability.

As noted, modern products liability is a mixture of strict and negligence liability with that distinction reflected by the difference between manufacturing and design defect tests. The manufacturing defect test is a form of strict liability. Manufacturers are liable if their products fail to measure up to their own standards. Liability that is strict in this sense is desirable on several grounds, not the least of which are its concreteness and predictability. To choose only a manufacturer defect test is to choose strict liability; to choose a design defect test is to take the negligence approach to safety.

The greatest degree of uncertainty and unpredictability arises in the application of design defect standards. Consumers want safety at reasonable cost and manufacturers want predictability. Both can be attained by jettisoning *all* design defect tests in favor of a simple rule of strict liability that allows defendants to defeat claims against them by establishing the contributory negligence of product users. Manufacturers will then be liable for all harms their products cause unless the injuries result from product misuse or inadequate care by the consumers. Such a rule is efficient, knowable and far easier to administer than any of the alternatives for assessing design defect.

Not only does this rule replicate the ideal contract, it is also "fair," for unlike the current regime, it allows manufacturers to escape or to reduce liability when injuries are wholly or partly the fault of victims. The current practice, in contrast, is weighted toward getting questions to a jury and framing those questions in ways that unduly burden manufacturers. For example, instead of asking – as the strict liability alternative would – whether the *victim* took inadequate care in maintaining or using a product, the current system asks whether the manufacturer could have *foreseen* that a consumer might misuse or negligently use a product. Under the negligence rule, a victim's negligence has the perverse effect of enhancing rather than defeating his case for recovery. The design defect tests may well have reduced rather than increased the consumer's incentive to take care.

20.8 NONPECUNIARY COSTS

Justice Traynor held the view that deterrence and insurance goals can be pursued coherently and simultaneously, and he thought strict liability was the appropriate mechanism for doing both. But the argument presented here may raise doubts about this assumption. If we start with the contract model, as I have suggested we should, then consumers should not be compensated by manufacturers for nonpecuniary losses. If manufacturers are not required fully to compensate consumers, then they will not have to bear the full social costs of their conduct. Thus, they will be led to underinvest in safety.

There is, at least in theory, a solution to this dilemma. I have argued on several occasions that questions of liability can be separated from questions about recovery. This distinction between reasons for holding someone liable and reasons for compensating someone helps us see our way clear of the dilemma. Manufacturers can be required to compensate victims for all pecuniary costs, but deny victims recovery for nonpecuniary ones. At the same time *fines* can be imposed on manufacturers *equal to the nonpecuniary costs* caused by their products. The imposition of fines moves the proceeding away from the law of tort as we know it, creating a role for a regulatory or administrative agency. Thus, we may be able to pursue both the insurance and deterrence goals but not with only one institution, that is, tort law.

This solution may strike some as controversial and odd. Why should manufacturer's pay fines to regulatory agencies that are not victims of defective products? Why not just compensate the true victims? Moreover, if we allow victims to recover both pecuniary and nonpecuniary damages through the courts, we do not create a need for a regulatory intervention in the process. This would create an additional savings in administrative costs.

In general the problem is this: To achieve deterrence, we must make manufacturers liable for the *full* costs of their conduct, and that includes both pecuniary and nonpecuniary costs. We can simply allow victims to recover both. Moreover, if the victims are not compensated for their losses – at least on a lump sum basis – they will overinvest in safety. That is to say, they will have an additional incentive to take precautions that are unconnected to the role their conduct plays in reducing the incidence of harm, an incentive created by incomplete compensation. On the other hand, if we decide that victims should not be allowed to recover nonpecuniary losses since it would be irrational to compensate them for losses they would not insure against, then we have to find some other way of making manufacturers pay the difference. We are, I believe, torn in two directions. On the one hand, victims should be compensated for their losses – all their losses, including nonpecuniary ones. On the other hand, why should consumers secure insurance through product liability for losses they would not themselves ordinarily insure against? If we begin by viewing manufacturer's liability on the market model, then we simply must reject victim recovery for nonpecuniary loss. The argument for allowing consumers to recover nonpecuniary losses requires the formulation of a different basis for product liability, perhaps one grounded in principles of corrective justice. Or does it?

Consumers pay a certain premium as part of the price of a product in return for a reduction in the probability of harm. Harms can occur nevertheless and losses result as a consequence. These losses can be either pecuniary or nonpecuniary. Rational individuals do not in general insure against nonpecuniary losses, and so they would not buy a special premium to reduce the probability of their suffering such losses. This suggests that in products liability victims should not recover nonpecuniary losses. On the other hand, just because rational individuals do not insure against a loss, it does not follow that the loss can never be wrongful. Losses can be both wrongful and not rational to insure against. If the principle of corrective justice is the right way to think about recovery, then the victims of such harms should be compensated for their losses. On the other hand, individuals should not recover for nonpecuniary losses if they would not insure against these losses generally. Corrective justice holds that nonpecuniary costs, even those which are not insured against, can be wrongful; and when they are, the duty to annul them falls to the product manufacturer. The theory of rational bargaining appears to claim that such losses ought not be compensated because the victim would not require the producer to insure against them.

In fact, the rational bargaining approach to defective product liability does not always prohibit recovery for nonpecuniary losses. Suppose the probability of injury associated with a particular product is .10, which we can (with some license) interpret as meaning that one of every ten products will cause an injury. This level of risk is, let us assume, unacceptable to consumers. Consumers will bargain with producers to reduce the risk to the desired level in return for which consumers are willing to pay a price. Let's say that the efficient probability of harm is .01, which is to say that one of one hundred products will cause harm. Consumers in other words will pay to guard against harm, but they will not buy down the probability of harm to zero, since ex hypothesi, doing so is not worth its costs. There is some chance, therefore, that each consumer will be injured when using the product: roughly a one in one-hundred chance. If the consumer is risk averse, he will buy insurance against that possibility. The amount of insurance each purchases would presumably reflect, among other things, expected pecuniary, but not nonpecuniary, costs.

Now imagine two possibilities. In one case, the manufacturer abides by the terms of the "new contract," reduces the probability of harm to the desired level, that is, .01, but the product injures poor Guido. Under the terms of the contract, the manufacturer was in no sense negligent or in non-compliance. Still, the contract calls for strict liability. Guido's costs will be shifted to the manufacturer. However, there is no sense in which Guido's loss is a wrongful one. The manufacturer did not act wrongfully, nor did it invade any right of Guido's. Like every other consumer, Guido has a "contractual" right that the manufacturer reduce the probability of harm to .01, which the manufacturer does. If Guido is prevented from securing recovery for nonpecuniary losses, it is no way incompatible with the theory of corrective justice. For neither his nonpecuniary losses nor his other losses are wrongful.

In the second case, the manufacturer has failed to comply with the term's of the contract and has succeeded in reducing the probability of the harm to .05 only. Thus, the manufacturer, whether or not through any fault of its own, has failed to meet the terms of the contract. The manufacturer has created in Guido a claim in justice to the rectification of wrongful losses, given the analysis presented here. The losses are wrongful because they are the result of conduct invasive of his right to be exposed to a probability of harm not greater than .01. Here considerations of corrective justice apply and Guido is entitled to rectification of both his pecuniary and nonpecuniary losses. It may always be irrational to purchase insurance for nonpecuniary losses, and so a rational consumer cannot demand compensation for such losses as part of a contractual relationship with producers to reduce the probability of harm to a specified level. However, in the event the manufacturer fails to reduce the risk to the contractually agreed upon level, the fact that the consumer cannot contractually demand recompense for nonpecuniary costs no longer is relevant. The contract has been violated by the manufacturer; the consumer has been wronged. As a wronged party, she is entitled to the repair of her wrongful losses; and losses can be wrongful even if they are ones against which a rational party would not have insured.

In other words, strict product liability modeled on a rational bargain between consumers and producers is not incompatible with corrective justice. When manufacturers satisfy the terms of the contract, victims recover strictly but not for nonpecuniary costs. This is compatible with both models. The contract does not impose the burden of insuring against such costs on manufacturers. The losses result from action in compliance with the rights and duties under the contract and so the losses that result are not wrongful under corrective justice. When manufacturers fail to meet the terms of the contract, their liability is strict, but their conduct is also wrongful. Thus recovery for nonpecuniary costs is defensible on grounds of corrective justice and not incompatible with the contract model.[10]

This completes the account of tort law in which I have focused primarily on accident law. My argument has been that the core of tort law implements corrective justice, but that it is a mistake to hold that tort law as a whole is a matter of corrective justice. Indeed, I have argued in Chapters 19 and 20 that tort law allows for significant departures from its corrective justice core, and, more importantly, that its doing so is defensible. Tort law is a mixture of markets and morals.[11]

What I have failed to do is argue for boundaries on tort law, confines within which it must remain if it is to have integrity and coherence. Although I do not believe that tort law can pursue any goals or implement any principles, it remains for me to develop the relevant theory of institutional competence that will provide tort law its normative boundaries. Happily that is a task I must save for another occasion. What I cannot save for another occasion is the responsibliity of trying to tie together the arguments in Parts I, II, and III of this book. It is to that task that I now turn.

Chapter 21

Liberalism revisited

We can distinguish between backward and forward looking approaches to the allocation of accident costs. A forward looking approach evaluates allocation or liability decisions in terms of their incentive effects. Good liability decisions are those that create desirable incentives. Economic analysis is paradigmatically forward looking in this regard. From this perspective, it really does not matter whether accident costs are imposed because the conduct is wrongful or otherwise unjustified. Wrongdoing or mischief matters only insofar as it can have an effect on the way in which individuals respond to the imposition of liability. Liability imposed ex post is to be evaluated in the light of its ability to contribute to future efficient coordination.

This book has rejected the forward looking perspective as a way of understanding the core of tort law. Instead, it has argued that tort law imposes liability to reflect a judgment regarding preexisting claims litigating parties press against one another. These claims depend on facts about the relationship between the parties, in particular, that the party held liable is responsible for having created the victim's wrongful loss. It is no part of the victim's case that the injurer is a better risk reducer or spreader; or, if it is part of her case, it is secondary to the backward looking considerations just mentioned.

Although this book explicitly rejects the forward looking approach to tort law, it openly embraces that perspective on the practice of contracting. Therein lies an apparent tension that I feel needs to be addressed. Surely, part of the implicit claim in Part III is that however enlightening the forward looking perspective might be in helping us to appreciate tort law's coordinating function, focusing on tort law's coordination function will lead us to misunderstand, misrepresent, or miss entirely, essential aspects of the practice. The same is not necessarily true of contract.

Contract is about coordination for mutual advantage. The norms are designed to govern a relationship among individuals who have expressed or have an interest in cooperating with one another. The possibility of securing mutual gain brings the parties together. The rules of contract help them determine if mutual gains are available, and, if they are, how they might be secured.

In contrast, harm, not advantage, is what brings individuals together (at least in the first instance) in tort. Of course, liability decisions can be framed to aid in coordination, but it is the unilateral imposition of cost that creates the very reason for tort law.

Remove the damage remedy for contractual breach and the law of contracts still makes sense as norms designed to encourage coordination among individuals who have declared themselves to be pursuing mutually advantageous interaction. Take away the damage remedy of liability for wrongful loss and tort law loses both its content and its point.

In the typical tort case, the backward looking property of harming or wronging brings the parties together, and it is between the parties that the allocation decision about who should hear the loss is to be resolved. Normally, factors pertaining to the event that brings the parties together in litigation provide the reasons for imposing liability. These are the core features of accident law. They are missed or grossly misunderstood by any entirely forward-looking theory of torts, including an economic one, in much the same way the core elements of the criminal law are misconstrued by similar accounts of it.

There is a good argument for adopting a forward looking approach to contracting that does not apply to tort law. A backward looking approach to tort and a forward looking approach to contract may illuminate both institutions in which applying either a forward or a backward looking approach to both would not. The tension between the two approaches is more apparent than real.

21.1 CORRECTIVE JUSTICE AGAIN

We can distinguish among a variety of different backward-looking accounts of tort or accident law. Some, like retributivism, will point to the moral wrongness of the injurer's conduct as the reason for imposing liability. These accounts will fail to explain tort practice, however. Retributive accounts simply can not explain the centrality of the victim or plaintiff, why, in other words, he is compensated by the injurer. Retributivism, after all, requires exacting a penalty or cost; it does not require the wrongdoer to compensate anyone, let alone the victim. Moreover, the sort of wrongdoing exemplified in tortious conduct often fails to be blameworthy in the sense required by the retributive view.

Other backward looking accounts of tort law, including corrective justice, might share with retributivism the view that the point of imposing liability is redress. They might differ from one another in specifying the object and means of redress, and the grounds for it. Ernest Weinrib, for one, holds that the object of redress is the *wrong* itself. The means of redress is compensation. The grounds for redress and the duty to provide it arise from the conjunction of wrong and causation. In contrast, George Fletcher holds that the object of redress is the *loss*, and that the imposition of nonreciprocal risks grounds the duty to redress. Richard Epstein appears also to identify the object of redress with loss, compensation with the mode of redress, but, for him, the grounds of redress are provided by causation. In my view, the object of redress is *wrongful loss*. Compensation is its mode. And it is the fact that one party is responsible for the wrongful loss that grounds the duty to provide it.

Each of these accounts provides the basics of a conception

432

of corrective justice, an exemplification of the social practice of individuals identifying "messes," those "whose mess it is," and in virtue of this relationship, ascribing duties of repair. They differ from one another in the content they give to the various components of corrective justice, and, perhaps, with respect to the method by which that content is determined.

With respect to this last point, Ernest Weinrib, for example, claims to have derived the content of corrective justice from a more abstract Kantian or Hegelian conception of free agency. My approach could not be more different. My conception of corrective justice is constructed from the social practice described above and spelled out in somewhat more detail in Chapter 16.[1] My conception of corrective is an interpretation, or a way of understanding, a prevalent social practice. The argument for my conception makes no mention of a particular liberal moral or political theory, nor does my argument for it require any specific version political morality. It attempts no derivation from more abstract commitments, either moral or metaphysical. This is part of what I mean by calling the account a constructive interpretation. It derives from the practice, not from abstract principle.

The analytical structure of corrective justice, so conceived, no doubt reflects liberal values of equality, respect for persons, and their well-being, as well as responsibility for the consequences of one's actions. These values do not strictly entail the conception of corrective justice I defend, but it would be disingenuous to claim that the account I give is uninformed by the fact that the social practice from which I draw this conception is itself located in a political morality and culture of a certain kind.

Different conceptions of corrective justice will appear to be exemplified to greater or lesser extent in legal practice depending upon the details of the conception. In Part III I have defended my conception of corrective justice against alternatives (including one that I previously advanced), and I have argued that the core of tort law exemplifies corrective justice so conceived.

Wrongful losses, like losses more generally, are interferences with human welfare or well-being. In liberal political theory, human well-being is a ground for action, individual and collective, private and public. It provides agents with reasons for acting. Promoting well-being is a good thing and individuals often have both agent-neutral and agent-relative reasons for doing so. By the same token, setbacks to well-being can be reason-giving. The core idea behind corrective justice is that being responsible (in a suitable sense) for an unjustified setback to a person's well-being can provide one with an agent-relative reason for acting, for making good the loss for which one is responsible.

This way of attaching agents to losses for the purposes of repairing the losses is not a necessary social practice, even among moral people. It is a practice, however attractive, that can be superseded by other practices creating other reasons for acting, practices that can have the effect of severing the connection between agents and losses under corrective justice. A community might decide to allocate accident costs through the tax coffers. In that case no duties in corrective justice would exist. Under such conditions, the prevailing social practice might be reflected in remarks like "There's a mess that you created; *we* have to do something about repairing it."

The existence of a supervening social practice could extinguish duties that would otherwise arise under corrective justice – there would be in that community no practice of corrective justice – but it might not extinguish other duties wrongdoers owe their victims, including the duty to apologize.

This account of the relationship among social practices means that I am unwilling to treat departures from corrective justice in tort law as mistakes in need of reform. Instead, other parts of tort law may reflect alternative approaches to allocating losses, both wrongful and other, in ways that sever the relationship between agent and loss under corrective justice.

My reluctance to treat departures from corrective justice as

mistakes is both a virtue and a vice of Part III. The virtue is
modesty. The vice is more interesting. Because I fail to identify mistakes in tort law, Part III lacks a set of constraints on
the goals and principles tort or accident law can legitimately
pursue. The institution appears to lack integrity. Or better, I
impose no internal or external constraints upon it. Ultimately, the argument requires a theory of institutional competence. I have none. Given my account of the social dimensions of corrective justice, that principle cannot provide the
constraints we seek.

21.2 LIBERALISM, STABILITY, AND THE MORALITY OF FREEDOM

I said at the outset that one could read my enterprise in several different ways. At one level, it is an effort to explore the
limits of rational choice liberal political theory as a possible
account of important institutions of private law. At another
level, the book provides three very distinct theses: one about
rational choice liberalism, another regarding contract law as
encouraging local cooperation, and a third about the moral
dimensions of tort law.

Of these themes, the arguments that matter most to me
are those in Part I designed to show the impossibility of employing the market to explain or justify forms of constrained
interaction, and those designed to develop the importance of
the market to liberal political cultures like our own. Liberalism is committed to markets, not to efficiency as such. Contemporary proponents of law and economics have favored
efficiency over markets, but their doing so robs the legal
practices they study of a powerful normative grounding. In
Part II, the central arguments are those that grow out of
viewing contracting as a scheme of local cooperation, and
those that suggest the view of default provisions as ways of
conserving endogenous transaction resources. The latter is
not the prevailing view among contract theorists. In Part III,
the heart of the argument concerns the social nature of corrective justice, the ways in which it constrains the set of norms

it can constrain, and the way in which it can be constrained by other social practices.

Foolishly, perhaps, this book makes more ambitious claims about the relationships among its constituent parts. Here is where the second major tension in the book emerges. The foundational view developed in Part I is deployed in Part II, but appears to play no role in Part III. The middle-level theory developed in Part III, moreover, appears incompatible with the foundational view of Parts I and II. Should we conclude that there is a deep normative divide between torts and contracts? Must different legal domains reflect different liberal political theories? I do not think so. I believe that the arguments in Parts I, II, and III can be reconciled. I want to close this book by reconceiving the political theory of Part I in a way that renders it sufficiently rich to embrace the economic analysis of Part II and the moral concerns expressed in Part III.

The key is the claim that markets are rational for agents in liberal political cultures because under conditions that normally exist in large heterogenous communities markets can contribute to social stability. Members of such communities typically have different conceptions of the good, what counts as a good life for each, and so on. Stability is rational for such agents primarily because stable social practices or institutions are a prerequisite of individuals being free to pursue their projects, plans and goals against a background of value pluralism. If Joseph Raz is right, value pluralism is essential to human autonomy.[2] The liberal conception of autonomy requires both diversity or value pluralism, a range of possible ways of life, and social stability, a stable framework within which individuals can construct and pursue their projects, plans and goals. Markets help to create the stable framework within the context of value pluralism. Stability of the sort outlined in Part I is important to the liberal because it is a practical requirement of political freedom.

The arguments in Part III emphasize the relationship of corrective justice to responsible human agency and well-being. It is worth noting, however, that the argument in Chapter 17 suggests that corrective justice sustains norms that coordinate the expectations, understandings and behavior of members of the community. These conventions arise to give expression to a local understanding of reasonable risk taking behavior. Acting in compliance with these norms provides coordination. The conventions sustained by corrective justice need not be efficient in the technical sense nor need they conform ideally to the demands of justice. The stability they provide is valuable in the way I have outlined whether or not the norms that give rise to reasons for acting are fully just or efficient.

The argument in Chapter 17 also emphasizes the role of corrective justice in enforcing property rights against all incursions, justifiable or not. This practice allows members of communities governed by such conventions to form stable expectations about the behavior of others with whom they interact. In addition to sustaining norms in a way that is necessary for the meaningful exercise of political freedom, corrective justice expresses liberal ideals of responsibility for the consequences of one's actions, the flip side, as it were, of autonomous choice.

To this point we have focused on two ways in which corrective justice contributes to political freedom and autonomy: first, by stabilizing a set of norms that provide the background against which agents can pursue their projects and goals; second, by imposing liability for the untoward consequences of one's wrongful conduct. I want to close by considering a third, equally important way in which corrective justice in tort law exemplifies the liberal conception of autonomy. The focus of my discussion is the ordinary damage remedy.

The typical damage remedy in torts is compensatory relief. In a recent article, advocates of an economic approach to torts have advocated eliminating the damage remedy in a large class of cases in favor of a system of "contracts-for-care."[3] The idea is that in many cases in which victims suffer serious injury, the victims require a range of health, educational, and social services. This need often lasts a long time, sometimes

437

the course of their lives. Conventional lump sum damage awards may inadequately respond to these needs. Victims may spend their resources unwisely and find themselves unable to purchase the care they need. The authors suggest that instead of a compensatory award, victims should receive a package of long term contracts providing them with the services they will need. The content of the package is to be determined by negotiation between the plaintiff and defendant attorneys, and, in the event negotiations fail, arbitration.

Whatever its merits as an option victims might be free to avail themselves of, this form of remedy is fundamentally discontinuous with the liberal underpinnings of tort law. Part of our liberalism is our acceptance of the view that individuals have a constrained (by law, convention and morality) control over their resources. Each individual can put those resources to use in executing his projects and plans, in pursuing his goals. The law provides a reasonably stable framework (and hopefully a fair one as well) in which agents can act on the reasons these goals provide. Law enables individuals to turn interest into action, aspiration into reality.

When someone is injured by the wrongful behavior of another, why should we think that the agent has lost thereby the moral autonomy over his resources? But this is what imposing a system of contracts-for-care entails, and it is precisely what the conventional damage remedy denies.

Compensating a victim involves making him whole in more than one way. It involves the rather complex idea of leaving him indifferent in welfare or utility terms between his positions ex ante and ex post. It expresses as well the morally complex and important idea that the liberal conception of autonomy is not extinguished by the misfortune or injustice of injury and accident. Compensating resources are awarded to put the victim back to where he would have been had the accident not occurred, both morally and otherwise. Resources are provided for his use in the light of his projects, plans and goals, projects and goals that may have been altered by his injury, but ones which are nevertheless his to formulate and to execute.

This way of understanding the damage remedy in torts further instantiates the interplay between stability and autonomy at the heart of the overarching liberal political theory that informs all our private law practices. Any other damage remedy, applied broadly, would do little more than add institutional insult to personal injury.[4]

In sum: Though the political theory outlined in Part I emphasizes the importance of stability in heterogenous societies, both stability and heterogeneity are important to the liberal because of their connection to political freedom. The freedom worth having requires both the kinds of options reflected in heterogeneous communities and stability within which individuals can advance their well-being through projects, plans and goals. By the same token, even if it appears at first glance to emphasize liberal conceptions of freedom, responsibility and equality, accident law is not oblivious to the importance of stability. Corrective justice sustains norms that encourage coordination and sustain important social institutions. These norms provide part of the stable framework within which free and equal individuals pursue the projects and goals they believe contribute to their well-being. The liberal political theory that grounds the private law of contract and tort links human freedom with stable institutions in ways I have only outlined here.

Notes

INTRODUCTION

1. David Gauthier, "Jules and the tortist," *Harvard Journal of Law and Public Policy*, forthcoming.
2. Middle-level theory is in many ways both the least and the most satisfying kind of enterprise. It is most satisfying, at least philosophically, because it fully engages the practice, and it does so, not at the microlevel of cases, but at the macrolevel of trying to understand it as a practice, as a dimension of social life, in its relationship to other practices. On the other hand, middle-level theory lacks even the promise of resolution one can secure by engaging in microlevel, predictive social science. Some theories are, at that level, likely to be better predictors than are others, and that's all there is to it. Middle-level theory also lacks the power that being committed to a foundational view has. If I believed, for example, that utilitarianism was the correct political theory, then I would have a tool I could bring to the practices I hoped to understand and endorse. It would give me a kind of power that one who does middle-level theory simply does not possess.

On the other hand, to be engaged in middle-level theory is to be engaged fully in a practice. And it is not to ignore completely the possibility of pursuing either foundational or predictive inquiries. Indeed, at some level, in order for one's middle-level account of a practice ultimately to be fully satisfying and complete, the theorist must argue that the norms he identifies in the practice could be accepted by reasonable individuals engaged within the practice – or he must indicate the direction an argument for that conclusion would take.

441

CHAPTER 1

1. Redistribution has an insurance dimension, which might make it rational for *risk-averse* agents. Pure redistribution would not be rational for a group of *risk-neutral* agents, however.
2. In Chapter 5, I offer concession rationality as a particular conception of bargaining rationality.
3. A divisible P.D. has more than one mutually advantageous cooperative outcome. Thus, the players must agree to cooperate (rather than to defect) and to a particular mutually advantageous contract. The divisible P.D. is developed in Chapter 5.
4. Michael Taylor, *The Possibility of Cooperation* (Cambridge University Press, 1987). Rev. ed. of *Anarchy and Cooperation* (1976).
5. Robert Axelrod, *The Evolution of Cooperation* (New York: Basic Books, 1984).
6. Michael Taylor, *Community, Anarchy, and Liberty* (Cambridge University Press, 1982).
7. The sources of contract failure and their relationship to creating and sustaining markets is developed in Part II.
8. The argument in this section requires that we modify some of the claims made earlier. Commitment to the principle of rational choice does not itself yield a form of contractarianism, for one may be inclined to interpret the political and moral domains as conventions that evolve among rational agents in something like the way Hume thought they did. Alternatively, one can reject the contract model on the grounds that interaction among individuals is iterated in a way that makes the vision of a once-and-for-all-time choice unhelpful or unilluminating. Instead, one might model cooperation, not as a one-shot divisible P.D. but as an iterated P.D. In that case the division problem drops out and the compliance problem takes center stage. But the extent of that problem is reduced, presumably, by the fact that agents are repeat players.
9. Jody S. Kraus and Jules L. Coleman, "Morality and the theory of rational choice," 97 *Ethics* 715 (1987).
10. Unless they are viewed entirely as insurance mechanisms among risk-averse agents.
11. For a fuller discussion of the vagueness of "market failure" and an account of its many sources, see Chapter 4.

CHAPTER 2

1. One might have in mind the claim that legal and moral practices are social facts that need to be understood and appreciated, not justified, their roles in the lives of members of the community complex and fundamental, but so internal to the very conception of the person as to render justification either impossible or question-begging. Perhaps this objection to the rational-choice approach means to draw our attention to the important social fact that members of a community understand themselves in the light of their membership in the community, and that the community itself is defined in terms of relevant social, political, legal, and moral norms. These norms are essential to one's self-understanding; and to that extent, it is misleading to think of them as requiring a justification external to the role they play in self-understanding.

Put another way: Justification is essentially external to a practice, whereas moral norms are constitutive of the practice and of persons who participate in it. These individuals are in no position to require that the norms be justifiable to them, for that presupposes an important distinction between the person and the norms, a distinction that simply does not exist. To be is to be embedded in a practice or a tradition of some sort. Like the community as a whole, the self is constituted by the norms, and so it is impossible to demand that the norms be justifiable to the "self."

There are two ways of understanding this objection. The first is that the norms constitutive of a community require no justification at all. The second is that such norms are justifiable only internally, not externally. That is, there are no norms external to the practice that individuals engaging in the practice can call upon to justify the norms themselves.

It does not follow from the fact that practices or communities are "defined" by certain norms that the norms require no justification. There can be partially or wholly unjust and unjustifiable practices. The more interesting question is whether individuals who are themselves participants in the practice require that the norms be justified to them. One reason they might not is that the norms are partially constitutive of the persons who participate in practices. But this does not mean that the norms cannot be justified or that individuals who participate in the practice would not require them to be justifiable. To adopt the internal point of view is not to adopt a position of reflective incapacity. As long as the norms are coercive, individuals subject to their force have sufficient reason to require that they be justifiable to them.

2. Edward F. McClennen, *Rationality and Dynamic Choice* (University Press, 1990).
3. *Morals by Agreement* (Oxford: Clarendon Press, 1986).
4. McClennen, *Rationality and Dynamic Choice.*
5. David Schmidtz, "Rationality Within Reason," *Journal of Philosophy,* forthcoming.
6. This approach to reading Gauthier was suggested to me by Jean Hampton.
7. Because the market paradigm countenances no substantive principles of fairness that cannot be derived from rationality, this principle of fairness is in a relatively precarious position. We cannot take it as given or defensible on other grounds. If instead we define or characterize it as the outcome of a process of rational decision or bargaining, then it may fail to provide an independent criterion by which the outcomes of rational bargains are to be assessed.
8. I am not describing a strategy of reflective equilibrium between fairness on the one hand and rationality on the other in which we seek a conceptual compromise between the two. There are no compromises here. The principle of rationality is given; only the conception of fairness is revisable. If it turns out that the process of rational bargaining leads to grossly unfair outcomes as judged by the revisable, but pretheoretic, criterion of fairness, then we may find ourselves having to give up the idea of deriving morality from the theory of rational bargaining altogether. For to alter the theory of rational bargaining in the light of the principle of fairness is to accept fairness as a constraint outside the domain of rational choice, a move the market paradigm does not permit. On the other hand, suppose that the process of rational bargaining produces outcomes that are fair in the intuitive sense. Then we have the mutually reinforcing result that suggests both the plausibility of the intuitive conception and the soundness of the methodological approach.
9. Recall that earlier I noted that one of the consequences of adopting a rational-choice approach to political justification is that it ties together the *substantive* component of the theory with the

motivational aspect of it. A set of political or moral principles that fails to motivate, or whose demands reach beyond the capacities of those who would otherwise be motivated to act in accord with its dictates, is not likely to emerge as the outcome of an agreement among rational actors. Gauthier's arguments for the claim that rational bargaining will be fair and will not begin from unfair initial allocations exploit the relationship between the stability of compliance and the constraints that imposes on the character of the substantive principles.

10. In Chapter 6 I emphasize epistemic obstacles to cooperation. I show how a variety of factors exacerbate uncertainty, thereby leading to breakdown in cooperation; I also show how various social practices reduce uncertainty, thereby increasing cooperation.

11. Kraus and Coleman, "Morality and the theory of rational choice."

12. We can imagine two general dispositions toward compliance a rational agent might adopt, both of which are sufficient to permit the agent (under certain conditions) to enjoy the fruits of cooperative activities in a state of nature. These are: (1) a disposition to comply with the outcomes of all rational bargains and (2) a disposition to comply only with the outcomes of fair rational bargains. Following Gauthier we may call the first disposition *broad* compliance and the second, *narrow* compliance. If fairness creates stability in the state of nature, then Gauthier's burden is to show that the disposition to be narrowly compliant is uniquely rational.

Broad, but not narrow, compliance, is compatible with pre-bargaining predation. Broad compliance does not, therefore, preclude unfair outcomes of rational bargains. Only narrow compliance precludes unfair outcomes. If Gauthier accepts fairness as a constraint on justifiable political moralities, then his claim that rational-choice theory can accommodate it ultimately turns on his ability to show not just that it is rational to dispose oneself to comply with the agreements one makes, but that it is rational to dispose oneself to comply only with those of one's agreements that are fair. It is, in other words, uniquely rational to be narrowly compliant.

In "Morality and the theory of rational choice," Kraus and I argue that Gauthier does not succeed in forging the convergence between fairness and rationality, a convergence he believes is necessary if the theory of rational bargaining is to ground the substantive demands of morality.

13. Graphically, the problem can be illustrated as follows:

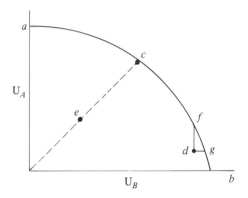

Let $U_A = A$'s utility.
Let $U_B = B$'s utility.
Then ab is the Pareto frontier.
Let d = the predatory outcome.
Let c = the cooperative outcome had neither A nor B acted in a predatory fashion.
Let e = the noncooperative, nonpredatory inefficient equilibrium.
Let fg = contract curve given d.

Although c is Pareto preferable to e for both A and B, c is not preferable to d for B. Thus, although A and B have an incentive to cooperate if they are at points e or d, B has no incentive to avoid predation if doing so means c will obtain. His noncooperative holdings at d are better than he can expect to receive by cooperation if others will cooperate with him only if he gives up predation. He's better off giving up cooperation.

14. It may also be possible to bring the results of a process of rational bargaining in line with fairness by imposing constraints on our characterization of the choice problem. When this happens, we have to remind ourselves of what it is that is doing the work. Perhaps we shall find that apparently innocent assumptions – like zero transaction costs – can have enormous normative consequences. See, for example, Kraus and Coleman, "Morality and the theory of rational choice."

15. Jules L. Coleman, "Competition and cooperation," 98 *Ethics* 76 (1987).
16. The point I am making generally about producers as a class has been made in other contexts with respect, for example, to cartels. Cartels face a divisible prisoner's dilemma, one that we hope they are unable to solve. Competition among them emerges only if they are unable to solve their cooperation problem.
17. See, especially, Chapter 6 regarding factors influencing uncertainty. This is one of the reasons I claim that markets are easiest to create and enforce when they are least necessary, and most difficult to sustain when they are most needed.
18. This is how I read the central argument in Michael Taylor, *Community, Anarchy, and Liberty*.
19. The argument for the market in liberal political theory that I have emphasized is *not* based on a *moral skepticism* about value, namely, the view that either we cannot know what is good or that there is nothing that is intrinsically good. In the case of a skeptic, the market is a desirable means of organization because it allows us to interact in ways that do not depend on knowledge of the good or on the existence of it. In the skeptic's argument, the market is the best way of organizing economic-allocation decisions and (analogously) democracy the best way of making political choices, because such institutions treat each person's preferences as equally sound *when there are no objective grounds for treating them otherwise*. There is no right or wrong about the good, no valid or invalid claims to knowledge of it. One apparent implication of the skeptic's position, however, is that if there were a uniquely defensible conception of the good or a mechanism for determining it, markets and democratic collective-choice mechanisms might well lose their appeal, for there would no longer be reason enough to treat each person's preference equally in the ways in which markets and democratic collective decision rules do – unless, of course, the market (very unlikely) or the democratic decision processes (more plausibly) were the instruments through which a community came to identify or to construct the good.

The argument I am advancing is compatible with skepticism but does not require it. For disputes among citizens about fundamental values may in fact have a correct resolution, but as long as people disagree about what the truth is, a scheme of

447

cooperation that requires agreement on that truth as a condition of social intercourse may well be ineffective and undesirable. It is not so much a moral skepticism that justifies the market within the form of rational-choice liberalism I am exploring as much as it is the concern for stable social practices.

20. I am not alone among reformed rational choice theorists in abandoning the reductionist aspirations of rational-choice theory. In a recent paper, one of the field's high priests – and my coauthor – John Ferejohn, argues that in order to provide an interpretation of any interesting social practice, rational-choice methods have to be supplemented with various "thick descriptions" of prevailing culture, history, and the like. Ferejohn appears to reject the possibility of deriving substantive conclusions from rational-choice premises because he accepts the so-called folk theorem. According to the folk theorem, any outcome can be sustained as an equilibrium in repeat play. Therefore we can never explain, on purely rational-choice grounds, why one rather than another outcome emerges. To do so, we must appeal to particular facts about a community, its culture, history and the like. This is very similar to the view expressed here, but my argument does not rely on the folk theorem. Rather it relies on the impossibility of taking competition as prior to cooperation. It, therefore, suggests that both competition and cooperation are, at a deeper level, expressions of cooperation. Which form of cooperation will depend on the sorts of empirical facts Ferejohn points to. See John Ferejohn, "Rationality and interpretation: Parliamentary elections in early Stuart England," in *Economic Approach to Politics*, ed. Kristine Monroe (New York: Harper, Collins, 1991).

21. The exception, I believe, is Frank Knight.

22. See Part II for a development of this thesis.

23. The defense of the market is consistent with both liberalism and the theory of rational choice. The market is particularly attractive to the liberal because of its capacity to maximize social interaction among individuals pursuing diverse conceptions of the good. Questions that shape and sharpen collective identity, that explore the range of fundamental values and commitments, are raised by and explored through public debate, not private transaction. Legal norms, especially Constitutional principles, are sometimes thought to give expression to these values and commitments. Political and moral debate

about the commodification of various resources and relationships, for example, are issues about the scope of markets; they
are not issues that arise *within* markets. This conception of the
market is consistent with rational theory in that the market, so
conceived, is a rational form of *cooperation* for individuals under certain sets of empirical, including historical and cultural,
conditions.

CHAPTER 3

1. Of course, some theorists have disagreed. Professor Anthony
   Kronman, for example, has argued that a scheme of contract
   law is minimally defensible only if it expresses a particular conception of distributive justice – a form of Paretianism – and
   Judge Richard Posner has defended an economic interpretation of the United States Constitution. See Anthony Kronman,
   "Contract law and distributive justice," 89 *Yale Law Journal* 472
   (1980).
2. For a different view, see Chapters 15–18.
3. Guido Calabresi, "Torts – the law of the mixed society," 56
   Texas Law Review 519 (1978).
4. Before we explore any strategy of this sort, we should note
   from the outset that the arguments we are about to consider
   work, if they work at all, only for theorists like myself who
   accept an economic conception of contracting. The argument
   is a nonstarter for those who reject an economic theory of contracting.
5. Guido Calabresi and Douglas Melamed, "Property rules, liability rules, and inalienability: One view of the cathedral," 85
   Harvard Law Review 1089 (1972).
6. Jules L. Coleman and Jody Kraus, "Rethinking the theory of
   legal rights," 95 *Yale Law Journal,* 1335 (1986). For a fuller discussion, see Chapter 17.
7. See Chapter 4 for a fuller discussion.
8. See Chapter 8 for a fuller discussion.

CHAPTER 4

1.

Ms. Give

Give   Keep

		Give	Keep
Mr.	Give	Exchange	Theft
Take	Keep	Theft (keep, give)	No exchange (keep, keep)

Since, over all other outcomes, both Give and Take prefer to keep their own goods while taking that of their "trading partner," no exchange will occur. In other words, the defection payoff is individually rational for both of them. Thus, no exchange occurs. In fact, exchanges do occur as does cooperation more generally. In Part II, we explain how this can be given the P.D. structure of both.

2. For a more complete discussion, see Jules Coleman, "The foundations of constitutional economics," in *Markets, Morals, and the Law* (Cambridge University Press, 1988), p. 133.
3. I adopt and develop a related view in Chapter 6.
4. For a discussion of whether force and fraud can be assumed to be part of any and all frameworks of exchange, or whether, instead, such prohibitions help to define some, but not all, such frameworks, see Coleman, "Constitutional economics."
5. Jules Coleman, "Constitutional contractarianism," in 1(2) *Constitutional Political Economy*, 135–46, 1990.
6. Coleman, "Unanimity," in *Markets, Morals, and the Law*, p. 277.
7. Coleman, "Market Contractarianism," in *Markets, Morals, and the Law*, p. 243.
8. James M. Buchanan and Gordon Tullock, *The Calculus of Consent* (Ann Arbor: University of Michigan Press, 1962).
9. Although I think it is very important to have a theory that distinguishes market from political failures for just the reasons I mentioned, I have no such theory, and do not want to pretend otherwise. Moreover, none of the arguments in this book (I believe) depend on my having such a theory. And so we will drop

the matter for now, and return to the problem of constructing a theory of success against which market failure is to be measured, and to that of differentiating between market failure and inefficiency. Nothing I say about these problems is decisive against alternative views. Still, the problems strike me as of central importance to the overall enterprise in which I am engaged, and I need to present some plausible account of them.

10. This is perfectly analogous to the point I made in Chapter 2 against the view that rational agents will always prefer to cooperate than to act noncooperatively.

CHAPTER 5

1. I want to clarify several dimensions and assumptions of this project before embarking upon it. First, it is not my view that the account I am developing will provide a comprehensive understanding of contract law. Very likely, there will be aspects of the practice that require a different account. Liberal contract law is likely to serve liberal ideals other than those that are identified with the foundational theory developed in Chapter 2. But it does seem to me that there is much to be said on behalf of the importance of stability in liberal theory, and the account of contract law I offer may enable us to rethink contract practices in ways that may not otherwise have occurred to us.

Second, the approach to contract that I am taking is what I called in the Introduction a top-down approach. It assumes the defensibility of a particular normative theory, then asks how a practice might be illuminated by understanding it as embodying the principles of that theory. There must be a bridge principle that makes application of the more abstract principles plausible in the case of a particular instance. In the case of this argument, I have claimed that the liberal theory developed in Part I holds out a special place for markets and that contracting is important to the idea of the market. On the other hand, I am not claiming that the theory I employ to explore contract law is the only plausible top-down political or legal theory one might employ, nor do I claim that it is the only plausible top-down theory that one can apply consistently with the argument in Part I. A classical liberal may bring an entirely different normative framework with him as might a rational-choice contractarian. Either of these frameworks might prove exceptionally illuminating, and for those who accept the underlying normative principles, normatively powerful as well. Moreover, as I suggested in Chapter 2, rational-choice contractarianism can also be defended as consistent with the argument in Part I. A libertarian might look at contract law doctrine in the hopes of finding reliance upon rational autonomous will as a condition of contractual obligation; he might look to other doctrines to discover the extent, if any, to which they foster free choice, and so on. No doubt, he will find his share of mistakes as well. The rational-choice contractarian will look at contract law to determine the extent to which its doctrines "enable individuals to replicate at the microlevel the macrolevel structure of their interpersonal relationships." He too will locate his share of mistakes.

Because I am conceiving of contracting as a "local scheme of cooperation for mutual advantage," I will be employing the divisible prisoner's dilemma as the model of interaction between the parties. This model is being employed largely as a heuristic device. For a variety of reasons, formal game theorists do not use the prisoner's dilemma to model contracting. One reason for their reluctance to do so is that the prisoner's dilemma is a game of perfect information, whereas contracts typically involve agents with less than full information. On the other hand, formal game theorists do not analyze contracting from the perspective of the state of nature, whereas, for reasons that this chapter makes clear, I do. I have different goals in mind than do the formal theorists. Also, I will continue to speak of division, or concession, rationality as a separate dimension of the problem of rational choice, though Ariel Rubenstein has recently proposed a noncooperative bargaining theory that rejects the claim that there is a separate principle of division rationality. His arguments are powerful, but remain controversial. My goal throughout is not to generate theorems or predictions or to enter into a debate with theorists of formal noncooperative bargaining theory. I am using the prisoner's dilemma as a heuristic device to generate insights, not as a formal device to generate results.

One final clarification. I will use rather informal bargaining theory to help elucidate the contract as a local scheme of rational cooperation. This model emphasizes division problems in a way in which conventional economic analysis does not. I am not *defending* rational-bargaining theory as the correct form of economic analysis, as the form of it that follows from the argument in Part I. What follows from the argument in Part I is the importance of markets to liberal political theory. Given that, I then suggest that we treat markets as sets of discrete transactions, and that we think of each discrete transaction as a local scheme of cooperation. My claim about bargaining theory is that it provides us with the best model of local cooperation in the absence of law, not that it is a normatively attractive form of economic analysis. In other words, if you were to ask me how I might want to model the very idea of cooperating in a state of nature, I would answer that I think the problem is best captured as a bargaining game in a P.D. structure. In saying that, I would not be defending bargaining theory as a normatively attractive ideal. I would simply be trying to convey the idea that bargaining theory captures more aspects of the nature of the problem than does conventional economic analysis. For all I would have said, I might still find both approaches normatively indefensible.

With these preliminaries and disclaimers out of the way, the task that remains is to present the account of contracting as rational cooperation and see if it bears fruit.

2. Anthony T. Kronman, "Contract law and the state of nature," 1 *Journal of Law, Economics and Organization* 5 (1985).

3. Janet Landa and Bernard Grofman, "Games of breach and the role of contract law in protecting the expectation interest," 3 *Research in Law and Economics* (Greenwood, Conn.: JAI Press, 1981).

4. For the sake of the exposition, we treat each phase in temporal progression and as distinct from the others. In fact, a rational bargainer may treat concerns arising in different phases of the process at the same time or in the reverse order we suggest. Ours is an analytic device in which the phases of contracting progress in logical space–time.

5. Just think of the Coase Theorem and the long line of Chicago-style law and economics that sees itself driven by Coase's insight that, when transaction costs are low, individuals contract around inefficiencies. Thus the identification of contract with low transaction costs. Coase himself did not commit the mistake of identifying contracting with low transaction costs.

6. Daniel Farber, "Contract law and modern economic theory," 78 *Northwestern University Law Review* 2 (April, 1983).

7. Gary McClelland and John Rohrbaugh, "Who accepts the Pareto Axiom? The role of utility and equity in arbitration decisions," 23 *Behavioral Science* (1978).

8. Robert Cooter, "The cost of Coase," 11 *Journal of Legal Studies* 1 (1982); Jules Coleman, "Unanimity" and "Democracy and social choice," in *Markets, Morals and the Law*, pp. 243 and 277.

9. Whereas mixtures between contracts 1 and 2 are assumed to be feasible in this game (hence, the C_1C_2 line), mixtures between other outcomes of this game are assumed not to be feasible. We adopt this convention to simplify the analysis.

10. Daniel Kahneman, Jack Knetsch, and Richard Thaler, "Fairness as a constraint on profit seeking: Entitlements in the market," 76 *American Economic Review* 4 (1986); Norman Frohlich, Joe Oppenheimer, and Cheryl Eavy, "Choices of principles of distributive justice in experimental groups," 31 *American Journal of Political Science* 606 (1986).

11. Elizabeth Hoffman and Matthew Spitzer, "Entitlements, rights, and fairness: An experimental examination of subjects' concepts of distributive justice," 14 *Journal of Legal Studies* 2 (1985).

12. Daniel Kahneman, Jack Knetsch, and Richard Thaler, "Fairness as a constraint on profit seeking: Entitlements in the market," 76 *American Economic Review* 4 (1986); Norman Frohlich, Joe Oppenheimer, and Cheryl Eavy, "Choices of principles of distributive justice in experimental groups," 31 *American Journal of Political Science* 606 (1986).

13. Formal theoretic accounts of bargaining have been proposed by economists, game theorists, social psychologists, and strategic analysts. See Oran Young, *Bargaining: Formal Theories of Negotiation* (Urbana: University of Illinois Press, 1975); John Harsanyi, *Rational Behavior and Bargaining Equilibrium in Games and Social Situations* (Cambridge University Press, 1977); Alvin Roth, *Game-Theoretic Models of Bargaining* (Cambridge University Press, 1985); Ken Binmore, Ariel Rubinstein, and Asher Wolinsky, "The Nash bargaining solution in economic modeling," 17 *Rand Journal of Economics* 176 (1986).

14. Cooter, "The cost of Coase."

15. Samuel Bacharach and Edward Lawler, *Bargaining Power, Tactics, and Outcomes* (San Francisco: Josey-Bass, 1981).

16. Douglas Heckathorn, "A formal theory of social exchange: Process and outcome," in *Current Perspectives in Social Theory*, v. 5, ed. Scott McNall (Greenwich, Conn.: JAI Press, 1984).

17. This is also David Gauthier's view; see *Morals by Agreement*.
18. At least in the case of cooperating to produce a public good, which can be studied as a prisoner's dilemma game, experimental evidence reveals cooperation rates significantly better when people expect an agreement to be enforceable as compared to when they receive money-back guarantees that they will be no worse off than when they started if the group effort fails. See Robin Dawes, John Orbell, Randy Simmons, and Alphonse Van de Kragt, "Organizing groups for collective action," 80 *American Political Science Review* 4 (December, 1986).
19. Heckathorn, "Formal theory of social exchange."
20. Harsanyi, *Rational Behavior and Bargaining Equilibrium*.
21. The conclusions reached here also hold in the n-person cases and in the dynamic context. We use the static one to simplify the analysis. See Heckathorn, "Formal theory of social exchange."

CHAPTER 6

1. Kraus and Coleman, "Morality and the theory of rational choice."
2. The comparisons here, as with those involved in making concessions, entails no invalid interpersonal comparisons of utility. The calculus for creating safeguards follows the calculus of resistance theory, in which people are comparing concessions normalized with respect to each individual's stake in the game. Since the mathematical expressions take the form of the ratio of two utility differences, resistances are validly comparable across individuals. In this way, resistance theory captures a prominent feature of actual bargaining and actual equity judgments.
3. Jean Tirole, "Procurement and renegotiation," 92 *Journal of Political Economy* 2 (1986).
4. This generalizes a formulation found in Guido Calabresi, *The Costs of Accidents* (New Haven, Conn.: Yale University Press, 1970) and implied in Cooter's analysis of Coasian versus Hobbesian perspectives on assigning liability, a seminal application of bargaining theory to legal issues (Cooter, "The cost of Coase"). The Coasian perspective supposes the obstacle to cooperation is the cost of communicating, so courts need only enforce private agreements; Cooter recognizes that the strategic nature of the situation and the absence of a division rule

may preclude cooperation, even when communication costs are zero, evoking a more-intrusive court. However, Cooter's perspective does not count the cost of concessions as part of the strategic problem to which a court might attend. The Hobbesian perspective supposes that bargainers increase their demands on each other at every opportunity, defeating cooperation unless a third party exists to dictate the terms of a contract. Cooter recognizes that people may adapt their strategies to achieve an agreement, evoking a less-intrusive court. Cooter concludes that institutions such as markets serve efficiency without an extraordinarily intrusive state because a market eliminates the power of parties to threaten each other. But the proper standard of efficiency is generating optimal threats, not eliminating threats. Our analysis joins the Coasian and Hobbesian treatments of law, making the court's role contingent on contextual features of social relationships that defeat cooperation.

5. Mancur Olson, *The Logic of Collective Action* (Cambridge, Mass.: Harvard University Press, 1965).
6. Axelrod, *The Evolution of Cooperation*.
7. Kronman, "Contract law and the state of nature."
8. Randy Barnett, "Pursuing justice in a free society: Part one – power vs. liberty," *Criminal Justice Ethics*, Summer/Fall, 1985.
9. Marc Galanter, Justice in many rooms: Courts, private ordering, and indigenous law, 19 *Journal of Legal Pluralism* 1 (1981).
10. The axes and frontier correspond in part to a classification system described in Robert Ellickson, "A critique of economic and sociological theories of social control," XVI *Journal of Legal Studies* 1 (1987). Ellickson sees administering positive and negative sanctions as involving rules that divide human behavior into three categories: (1) good behavior that triggers rewards; that can have something to do with doctrines encouraging concession making as well as trust; (2) bad behavior that triggers punishment; his concern here is clearly with doctrines discouraging defection; and (3) ordinary behavior that warrants no judicial response; this corresponds to our type 1 situation in which parties have sufficient endogenous resources. As he put it, "The prevalence of tripartite systems is a clue that rulemakers are attuned to an overarching goal of minimizing costs, including administrative costs." Ibid., p. 71.

11. Arthur Corbin, *Corbin on Contracts* (St. Paul, Minn.: West Publishing Co., 1952), p. 124.
12. "One of the parties must carry the risk of loss and inconvenience. We need a definite rule; but we must choose one. We can put the risk on either party; but we must not leave it in doubt. The party not carrying the risk can then act promptly and with confidence in reliance on the contract; the party carrying the risk can insure against it if he so desires. The business community could no doubt adjust itself to either rule; but the rule throwing the risk on the offeror has the merit of closing the deal more quickly and enabling the performance more promptly."
13. Farber, "Contract law and modern economic theory."
14. Clare Dalton, "An essay in the deconstruction of contract doctrine," 94 *Yale Law Journal* (1985).
15. Morris Cohen, *Law and the Social Order* (New York: Archon Books, 1967).
16. See the essays in Anthony Kronman and Richard Posner, *The Economics of Contract Law* (Boston: Little, Brown, 1979).

CHAPTER 7

1. This last point is important, as we shall see when we turn our attention to torts. In torts, the parties involved, injurers and victims, are not generally repeat players, nor is the so-called forced exchange created by liability rules embedded in a market. Indeed, in the economic theory, torts is a *nonmarket* exchange relationship designed to rectify market failure. For these reasons the distributional aspects of liability rules may be significantly more important in torts than they are in contracts.
2. *Laidlaw* v. *Organ*, 15 U.S. (2 Wheat.) 178 (1817).
3. Anthony Kronman, "Mistake, disclosure, information, and the law of contracts," 11 *Journal of Legal Studies* 1 (1978).
4. Ibid., p. 18.
5. Jack Hirshleifer, "The private and social value of information and the reward to inventive activity," 61 *American Economic Review* 651 (1977).
6. Ibid., p. 570.
7. Kronman, "Mistake, disclosure, information," p. 17, note 46.
8. Hirshleifer, "Private and social value of information," p. 573.

9. Kronman, "Mistake, disclosure, information," p. 17.
10. Ibid., p. 14.
11. Ibid., p. 190.
12. This is not quite true. The frontier will be displaced slightly toward the origin whenever costs are incurred to litigate the uncertainty. Still, the general point is correct. Mistakes in division are largely redistributive, and although they impose costs, are very likely still to leave the relevant parties better off than they were prior to pursuing a cooperative strategy.
13. See R. Hastie, S. Penrod, and N. Pennington, *Inside the Jury* (1983); Kaye "And then there were twelve: Statistical reasoning, the Supreme Court, and the size of the Jury," 68 *California Law Review* 1004 (1980).
14. ". . . *speculation* in grain, for example, by setting aside a certain class of persons to assume the risks of trade, has the effect of reducing these risks by putting them in the hands of those who have most knowledge, for, as we have seen, risk varies inversely with knowledge." Irving Fisher, The *Theory of Interest* (New York: Macmillan, 1930), pp. 221. See also Sarkis Khoury, *Speculative Markets* (New York: Macmillan, 1984), 169–70.
15. Although two parties invest in crafting contractual safeguards when allocating risk, it is particularly difficult to craft a force of agreement that will ensure compliance when, as here, the contract entails the small risk of a large loss. Laidlaw lost big. The facts ex post created a circumstance in which reclaiming the tobacco made sense, even accounting for possible legal action by Organ and disapprobation from the community. Whatever privately enforced norms existed among commodity brokers in New Orleans, Laidlaw, who appeared to be performing in accord with the contract long after news of the treaty circulated, no doubt had to confront his client, a New York merchant who might not have had a stake in those norms. Indeed, whether in the absence of legal action, reputation effects would have ultimately punished Laidlaw or Organ for violating a norm could well have been unclear. Given the immediate stakes, each party had ample incentive to seek authoritative affirmation of his view.
16. Robert C. Ellickson, *Order Without Law: How Neighbors Settle Disputes* (Cambridge University Press, 1991). Ellickson argues that the members of the community remain ignorant of the prevailing legal rules and develop social conventions as alternatives to them. Legal rules provide salience and enable par-

ties to coordinate, but in some contexts, individuals are able to develop conventions endogenously, a practice they invariably prefer for a variety of reasons of the sort we have already touched upon.

1. Alan Schwartz, "Proposals for products liability reform: A theoretical synthesis," 97(3) *Yale Law Journal* (1988), in which the tort problem of specifying the conditions of liability for defective products is recast as a contracts problem, that is, the terms of liability should be those the parties would have agreed to ex ante.
2. I am using the term "default rule" to cover both gap-filling and default rules. Both have become the subject of a large, although recent, body of literature. The difference between them is this. Gap-filling rules complete incompletely specified contracts. Default rules are the background rules within which contracting occurs. They can be of two sorts. Some default rules can be contracted around. Others cannot be. For the purposes of our discussion, there is no important difference between gap-filling rules and default rules that the parties are free to contract around. In a more complete work, I would need to develop a fuller account of all default and gap-filling rules. My purpose here is only to reflect on the extent to which contract theories generally rely upon the theory of rational bargaining in specifying the terms of gap-filling rules. For a more complete discussion of default provisions, see Richard Craswell, "Contract law, default rules, and the philosophy of promising," 88 *Michigan Law Review* 489 (1989); Ian Ayres and Robert Gertner, "Filling gaps in incomplete contracts: An economic theory of default rules," 99 *Yale Law Journal* 87 (1989).
3. This is, of course, not the only gap-filling rule a judge can apply. One alternative might be: Wherever the contract is silent, the court should assign rights and responsibilities according to a principle of social justice, wealth redistribution, or insurance.
4. My claim is not that every form of economic analysis makes use of the ex ante contract as a default rule. Alan Schwartz's work on products liability is a clear example of a form of economic analysis that does rely on the ex ante contract; Ayres and Gertner on default rules is a good example of an account

that does not. The puzzle is why would any form of economic analysis be attracted to a rational bargaining approach. The question is not, why is every form of economic analysis attracted to it.

5. See Coleman, "Efficiency, utility, and wealth maximization," in *Markets, Morals, and the Law*, p. 95.

6. 1910, 100 Minn. 456, N.W. 221.

7. Posner has argued that by accepting compensation ex post someone gives consent, which in this case means that in spite of his protestations to the contrary, the dock owner consented to the captain's decision by accepting compensation. Surely this is seriously confused; first, because people often demand compensation not to give their consent to being harmed, but as redress for a wrong done to them; second, because if to accept compensation is to give consent, then the only way not to consent is to refuse compensation, which, of course, would ordinarily count as giving consent. The argument that compensation constitutes consent has things absolutely backward.

8. Schwartz, "Proposals for products liability reform." We will have occasion to return both to the problems of product liability and to Professor Schwartz's views on products liability in Chapter 20. My purpose in referring to Schwartz's work in this context is his liberal use of the rational bargaining model as a way of specifying the requirements of a defensible products liability law.

9. This is our first concrete example of the way in which economic analysis naturally views tort law as designed to correct market inefficiencies arising within contract.

10. Whether or not it is inconsistent will depend on whether some decisions that impose inefficient outcomes in a particular case create incentives that can lead to efficient outcomes over the long term.

11. The default rule guarantees at the very least that the agreement imposed in default of explicit bargaining will be no more unfair than the outcome the parties would have secured had they pressed their initial advantages.

CHAPTER 9

1. If no compensation is required, then the incentive to take is greatest, and even those individuals who are lower value users

will be inclined to take what they have no right to. If compensation is required, but if the amount of compensation is set too low, a similar result will occur. If the amount of compensation is set too high, some higher value users will be discouraged from taking. Only if compensation is set somewhere between the value of the entitlement to the right holder and its value to the "taker" will liability rules induce efficient transfers. (Moreover, in the same way that high ex ante transaction costs can discourage efficient voluntary transfers, high compensation costs ex post can discourage efficient forced transfers. Liability rules are only partial solutions to high transaction costs, and it may be that in at least some circumstances the costs of compensating ex post will exceed the costs of transacting ex ante.

2. Chapters 16 and 17 also clarify the distinctions among "wrong," "wrongdoing," and "wrongful loss," terms that I have lumped together in this chapter to distinguish the moral approach from the economic one.

CHAPTER 10

1. See Chapter 19 for examples of each.
2. Ernest J. Weinrib, "Understanding tort law," 23 *Valparaiso Law Review* 485 (1989).
3. Ibid., pp. 493–4.
4. Ibid., pp. 510–24.
5. We have an analogy between two views of the market discussed in Chapter 2. In one view, nonmarket institutions are responses to market failure, justifiable only to the extent that they mimic the outcome of the market. On the other hand, these institutions are genuine alternatives to the market that arise in part to articulate the underlying norms of a community through which a community's identity is forged. The same be said of the relationship between torts and contracts. Precisely because considerations of collective justice may be inappropriate in private bargaining, to the extent tort law is concerned with justice, it may be an appropriate vehicle for allocating risk even when rational contracting is possible.
6. Robert Nozick, *Anarchy, State and Utopia* (New York: Basic books, 1974).
7. Calabresi, *The Costs of Accidents*.
8. See, for example, R. A. Duff, *Trials and Punishments*.

461

9. O. W. Homes, Jr., *The Common Law* (Boston: Little, Brown, 1881).
10. Kronman, "Contract law and distributive justice."

CHAPTER 11

1. These are reasonably unsophisticated characterizations of the distinctions between fault and strict liability. They serve the purposes for which they are employed in this discussion, however.
2. The latin phrase means "the thing speaks for itself." See *Byrne* v. *Boadle*, 2 H.&C. 722, 159 Eng. Rep. 299 (Exch. 1863); *Larson* v. *St. Francis Hotel*, 83 Cal. App. 2d 210, 188 P.2d 513 (1948).
3. 3.33 Cal. 2d 80, 199 P.2d 1 (1948).
4. This cannot be a sufficient condition for generally shifting the epistemic burden. Shifting the burden of proof simply because the alleged injurer might have better or more reliable information would often involve a substantial invasion of privacy.
5. I discuss an alternative interpretation of *Summers* in Chapter 19.
6. Unlike defenses of privilege, which negate the tortious nature of a defendant's act, defenses of immunity are available despite admission of a defendant's tortious act. Defenses of immunity are based on public policy rationales, and include: interspousal immunity, parental–child immunity, charitable immunity, and governmental immunity. Each form of immunity has been increasingly limited in recent years.
7. I am going to do very little to remedy that situation here. Instead, I will discuss liability rules and the reasons they express, which are taken as adequate to shift losses from victims to injurers. I will have something to say, from time to time, about positive defenses, especially in the context of products liability law, but I do not pretend to be offering anything like a general theory of them. See Richard A. Epstein, "Defenses and subsequent pleas in a system of strict liability," 3 *Journal of Legal Studies* 165 (1974).
8. See *Vosberg* v. *Putney*, 80 Wis. 523, 50 N.W. 403 (1891).
9. Henry Terry, "Negligence," 29 *Harvard Law Review* 40 (1915).
10. See *Vaughn* v. *Menlove*, 3 Bing. (N.C.) 468, 132, Eng. Rep. 490 (1837).
11. Chapter 13 distinguishes among three ways in which excuses can figure in tort liability.

12. Tort theorists capture this by saying that the standard of negligence is objective or external.
13. See H. L. A. Hart, "Prolegomenon to the principles of punishment," in *Punishment and Responsibility* (Oxford: Oxford University Press, 1968), p. 1.
14. Liability, whatever else it may be, imposes a cost on individuals. Increasing the cost of engaging in an activity reduces the extent to which individual engage in it. If that were not true, the entire subject matter of economics would be empty. Demand would not fluctuate conversely with price. Anything that reduces an activity's attractiveness discourages it. If it is wrong or otherwise inappropriate to discourage justifiable conduct, how is it that tort law has missed or chosen to ignore this obvious truth?
15. Perhaps I am just confusing two different kinds of costs. One kind of cost is the cost that the defendant's conduct imposes on the victim. The other is the cost associated with being punished or incarcerated. If the defendant is not suited to suffer the latter costs, no one else, least of all the victim, must. But what of those other costs; the costs the defendant's conduct imposes on the victim?

   Well, what of them? Not every criminal offence requires a victim, so there may be no costs of this sort that the criminal's offence imposes on a particular victim. Crimes are violations of certain rules, and in violating at least some rules, for example, conspiracy to commit a crime, no one need be victimized. We can ignore this nicety, however, and allow that every defendant imposes costs on his victims, and that every crime has a victim. Suppose that the defendant is found guilty and is sent off to prison. None of the costs he endures does anything to annul or to rectify the costs he has imposed on the victim. The criminal law does not annul or shift those losses. It imposes *additional* costs on defendants. And it is not part of the law's justification for doing so that the imposition of the additional cost does anything to annul the victim's loss. The victim continues to bear those costs.
16. There are sometimes punitive costs in torts, but these are added to compensatory awards and are not a substitute for them.
17. In Chapter 12 we consider in more detail the claim that strict liability actually discourages reasonable activities. Even reasonable activities can be engaged in at unreasonable levels. Strict

liability often has the effect of insuring that reasonable activities are engaged in at reasonable levels.
18. See Calabresi, *The Costs of Accidents*.
19. For a fuller discussion, see Chapter 20.
20. There are, of course, other positive defenses. For example, in the case of products liability there is the defense of product misuse as opposed to negligent (but proper type of) use.
21. Here, for convenience, we are ignoring defenses that might be available. We'll be more accurate later, when it matters.
22. For a more complex view see, Chapters 15–18.

CHAPTER 12

1. See Jules Coleman, "On the moral argument for the fault system," 71 *Journal of Philosophy* 473–90 (1974).
2. Moreover, even if it were sound, the retributive argument would only justify imposing liability on the faulty injurer; it would not justify the strict victim liability aspect of the fault principle.
3. George Fletcher, "Fairness and utility in tort theory," 85 *Harvard Law Review* 537 (1972).
4. Richard A. Epstein, "A theory of strict liability," 2 *Journal of Legal Studies* 151 (1973); Richard A. Epstein, "The unintended revolution in product liability law," 10 *Cardozo Law Review* 2193 (1989); Richard A. Epstein, "Causation – in context: An afterword," 63 *Chicago–Kent Law Review* 653 (1987); Richard A. Epstein, Michael J. Trebilcock, and Samuel A. Rea, Jr., "Products liability as an insurance market," 14 *Journal of Legal Studies* 645 (1985); Richard A. Epstein, "Nuisance law: Corrective justice and its utilitarian constraints," 8 *Journal of Legal Studies* 49 (1979); Judith Jarvis Thomson, "Causality and rights: Some preliminaries," 63 *Chicago–Kent Law Review* 497 (1987); Richard W. Wright, "Causation in Tort Law," 73 *California Law Review* 1735 (1985).
5. But see Chapters 15 through 18 for a different view.
6. *United States* v. *Carroll Towing Co.*, 159 F.2d 169, 173 (2d Cir. 1947) (liability for negligent act based on whether cost of adequate precautions is less than the cost of the harm multiplied by the probability of the harm).
7. But see Chapter 17, note 18, for the distinction between acting *rationally* and acting *reasonably*.
8. See Chapter 17 for a more detailed discussion of this point.

9. The distinction between the analytic and normative dimensions of the theory is important for another, but related, reason. The same analysis of fault may well be compatible with very different normative theories. An economic analysis of the concept of fault may be compatible with both an economic and a corrective justice account of the *grounds* for imposing liability on the basis of fault. It is both important and unsurprising that different theories can generate a defense of the same practice: in this case, the practice of imposing liability on the basis of fault. Convergence of judgment may well be essential both for the plausibility of the theory and for the defensibility of the practice. For we would hardly find a theory about the nature of a well-entrenched social practice plausible if it failed to give us explanations, predictions, and, where appropriate, normative judgments fundamentally similar to the answers given by other plausible theories. And it would be troubling if our social practices could be understood or defended within one or two normative frameworks, but not within a variety of frameworks that are otherwise expressed in other prevailing social practices. Practices that endure normally secure the allegiance of individuals motivated in different ways, some by self-interest, others by a sense of benevolence, and others still by a conception of personal duty. It would be surprising if institutional practices, like the practice of imposing liability for harms, could not be plausibly defended on a variety of very different grounds that reflect the variety of motivations people have for compliance with their norms.
10. At least in the case of "one-party" accidents.
11. Guido Calabresi and Jon Hirschoff, "Toward a test for strict liability in torts," 71 *Yale Law Journal* 1055 (1972).
12. See, for example, Steven Shavell, *Economic Analysis of Accident Law* (Cambridge, Mass.: Harvard University Press, 1987), pp. 73–104; Calabresi, *The Costs of Accidents*, pp. 286–7.
13. Jules L. Coleman and Charles Silver, "Justice in settlements," in *Markets, Morals, and the Law*, p. 202.
14. George L. Priest, "The current insurance crisis and modern tort law," 96 *Yale Law Journal* 1521 (1987); George L. Priest, "The invention of enterprise liability: A critical theory of the intellectual foundations of modern tort law," 14 *Journal of Legal Studies* 461 (1985); George L. Priest, "A theory of the consumer product warranty," 90 *Yale Law Journal* 1297 (1981).

15. Suppose you are injured in an accident that is no one's fault, but under the prevailing rule of strict liability, will turn out to be your injurer's responsibility. Now you are choosing among medical treatments you might take to relieve your pain. If the costs are fully covered by your injurer's insurance company, you will be inclined to pursue expensive treatments, even though they have a low probability of success, if your only other option is to find a way to cope with the pain. Sometimes pursuing such treatments is the appropriate thing to do, and we would want to encourage you to do so. Sometimes pursuing them makes no sense and we would like to discourage you from doing so. But your costs are being taken care of; what incentive have you to act reasonably? Unfortunately, the answer is none.

   Economists urge us to look at how different your approach would be in choosing among treatments if you were required to shoulder the full costs of your treatments, or if you had to shoulder the insurance costs. You would be led to consider only reasonable responses to your painful condition, and would be led away from inefficient expenditures. Reduction in ex post moral hazard reduces overall accident costs and is accomplished better through a system of first, not third-party, insurance. And that suggests the desirability of a fault to a strict liability regime.

16. The goal of this chapter has not been to defend economic analysis of torts or to offer original insights into its nature or structure. I had in mind two rather more modest ambitions. First, many readers of this book, especially philosophers, will be unfamiliar with the economic approach to torts. This chapter provides an introduction for them to the kind of analysis economists engage in. Second, here and in Chapters 13–14, I explore theories of torts that purport to unify it under a single principle. I reject this idea and develop my alternative later. Economic analysis, however, is one such theory, and I wanted to give the reader a sense of its claim for comprehensiveness as well as an appreciation of its elegance and underlying simplicity, both sources of its great appeal.

CHAPTER 13

1. Fletcher, "Fairness and utility in tort theory."
2. Ibid., pp. 551–6.
3. Ibid., p. 542.
4. Ibid., pp. 543–51.
5. 159 Eng. Rep. 737, 3 H. & C. 774, (Exch. 1865), reversed, L.R. 1 Ex. 265 (1866), affirmed, L.R. 3 H.L. 330 (1868).
6. In fact, the principle of reciprocity of risk goes beyond considerations of the relationship between injurers and victims. In particular, it relies on the notion of a "community of risk takers" to define the relevant background of risk. For a discussion of the relational aspect of reciprocity of risk, see Catharine Pierce Wells, "Tort law as corrective justice: A pragmatic justification for jury adjudication," 88 *Michigan Law Review* 2348 (1990); Jules L. Coleman, "Justice and reciprocity in tort theory," 14 *Western Ontario Law Review* 105 (1975).
7. The thesis I will offer in defense of Fletcher's insistence on excusing conditions is, I believe, compatible with his overall account. On the other hand, I am not sure that Fletcher would himself endorse it. It is, however, an argument that is central to my own thesis, and I am, therefore, prepared to defend it on its own terms.
8. It will sometimes be a matter of controversy whether something counts as an action. Still, wherever we draw the line, we allow a category of excuses that defeat liability, not by showing the absence of culpability, but by showing the absence of agency instead.

   Even the earliest cases under the old writ system of Trespass and Case recognized this distinction between excuses that defeat blame and those that defeat action. To see this, consider the famous dicta in *Weaver v. Ward:*

   [N]o man shall be excused of a tresspass . . . except [as] it may be judged utterly without his fault. As if a man by force take my hand and strike you, or if here the defendant had said, that the plaintiff ran cross his piece when it was discharging, or had set forth the case with the circumstances, so as it had appeared to the Court that it had been inevitable, and that the defendant had committed no negligence to give occasion to the hurt. Hobart 134, 80 Eng. Rep 284 (K.B. 1616)

The proper analysis of this section of the opinion is controversial, and the diversity of examples used to illustrate what is
meant by the phrase "utterly without fault" is not fully clarifying. My reading is this: An individual is utterly without fault
for a harm's occurrence if the harm occurred through no action
of her own. Thus, B is not liable to C if she hit C as a result of
A's hurling her into C. An individual is also utterly without
fault for a harm's occurrence if the action, though it contributed to the harm's occurrence, is not in fact the *cause* of it.
Thus, if B shoots his rifle in the air and C runs in front of it,
then it is C's running in front of the rifle shot that is the cause
of the harm, and B is utterly without fault. Failure to act, or, if
one acts, the failure of one's action to be the real cause of the
harm, renders one "utterly without fault" and therefore free
from liability.

9. Recently I have been convinced by Steven Shute and John
Gardner that an individual can incur duties to others as a result
of his bodily movements even if those movements fail to meet
the minimum standards of human action. According to Shute
and Gardner, we might divide the duties we have to others
into those requiring compensation for loss and others that require apology and other forms of aid. Their speculation is that
in the case of all duties of the latter sort, the relevant conventions do not require human agency. Untoward consequences
that result from twitches and other bodily movements that fall
short of actions can ground the relevant duty. If I twitch and
knock you down, then I may have a duty (or at least, a moral
reason) to pick you up, though your being knocked down was
not a result of any action of mine. In the case of the duty to
compensate, human agency is required, but it is never itself
enough to ground the moral duty. So, for example, if I knock
you down and thereby cause you $100 in damages, then whether
or not I owe you compensation under the relevant principle
(say, corrective justice) depends on whether my knocking you
down is somehow otherwise at fault. So "action" by itself is
too weak to ground a moral duty to compensate, and not necessary to ground the full range of other duties we might owe
others we "injure."

10. Calabresi, "Optimal deterrence and accidents."

11. We ought not conclude that Jane can have no duties to Joe that
Joe would not have to himself simply because neither of them

"acted." Jane may have a duty to apologize or to come to Joe's aid in some other way. It's just that there is no better reason based on considerations of agency for holding her liable for his costs than there is for holding him liable for them. In other words, if the absence of agency defeats liability, it defeats it in the case of both Joe and Jane. On the other hand, the absence of agency may not defeat other duties one might incur to others as a result of what one is involved in "doing" to them. See note 9.

12. For further discussion of this, see Chapters 16 and 17.
13. See Fletcher, "Fairness and utility in tort theory," pp. 550-2 and notes 50 and 57.
14. Ibid., p. 550.

CHAPTER 14

1. Exceptions include Epstein, "A theory of strict liability"; Wright, "Causation in tort law"; H. L. A. Hart and Tony Honoré, *Causation in the Law* (2nd ed.) (Oxford: Clarendon Press, 1985); A. M. Honoré, "Responsibility and Luck," 104 *Law Quarterly Review* 530 (1988); A. M. Honoré, "Ownership," in *Oxford Essays in Jurisprudence*, ed. Anthony Gordon Guest (Oxford: Oxford University Press, 1961), p. 107.
2. As will become apparent, corrective justice requires a theory of responsibility. Though responsibility is not, I will argue, coextensive with causation, the notion of "causal power" is an important component of any satisfactory account of responsibility.
3. Epstein, "A theory of strict liability."
4. Compare Wright, "Causation in tort law"; Richard W. Wright, "Causation, responsibility, risk, probability, naked statistics, and proof: Pruning the bramble bush by clarifying concepts," 73 *Iowa Law Review* 1001 (1988).
5. Epstein, "A theory of strict liability."
6. Richard A. Epstein, "The utilitarian foundations of natural law," 12 *Harvard Journal of Law and Public Policy* 713 (1989).
7. Like Fletcher, Epstein is committed to tort law's allowing defendants to introduce excuses that defeat agency. In Epstein's case, excuses are relevant because they bear on an individual's responsibility, and responsibility is a condition of liability.
8. The most common response to objections of this sort relies on

the claim that the accident would not have occurred but for your failure to shovel the snow. Therefore, your failure to shovel, your not shoveling the snow, is the *cause* of the harm. In this sense, causation is at the heart of responsibility and necessary for it.

This response makes the mistake of treating an individual's omitting to do something as a kind of doing. In this case, failing to shovel the snow is the relevant omission that counts as a kind of doing. But causal relations exist between events, states of affairs, or, for the small group of theorists who believe in so-called agent-causation, between states of affairs or events and agents. An omission is not an event; it is the absence of an event. The reason the snow fails to be shoveled is not that you are engaged in the act of not shoveling the snow. This is not to suggest that no omissions can be events, actions, or causes; whether an omission is a cause may depend on whether it is an intentional refraining from doing something.

Individuals can be responsible for the consequences of their failures to act, but their failures to act, other than intentional refrainings, are not causes in the metaphysical sense. Maybe that's the problem. The notion of causation that is relevant to responsibililty is not the metaphysical one. Instead, the relevant concept is something like *moral causation*. When we ask, who or what is the cause of an event within the framework of an institution designed to serve normative ends, the metaphysics of the matter are of little moment. We want to know whose conduct or which agent we should focus on, given the avowedly normative character of our inquiry. In this sense of causation, it makes perfectly good sense to focus on an individual's failure to shovel the snow as the cause of the neighbor's injury.

The problem here is that this notion of moral causation is either mysterious, superfluous, or question-begging. It is question-begging if it just turns out that something is the moral cause if and only if it is that to which (on whatever grounds) we ascribe responsibility. It is superfluous if it fails to provide any grounds different from those grounds upon which our judgment of responsibility is based. In other words, if, in the snow-shoveling example, we want to hold liable the person who failed to clear the walk, because doing so will encourage a change in behavior, or because it will rectify a wrongful loss, then we have all the reasons we would need for holding that person liable. There is nothing gained from either the moral or the explanatory point of view by claiming that the individual who failed to shovel the snow is being held liable because the failure to shovel is the moral cause of the injury. Worse, the claim that the failure to shovel the snow is the moral cause of the injury is likely to be no more than a conclusion of the very same argument whose premises provide us with the grounds for imposing liability in the first place.

9. See Chapter 17 for a discussion of just how complex this issue really is.

10. For a more complete and satisfactory account of wrong, see Chapter 17.

11. There are two kinds of questions we can ask about the relationship between normative and epistemic expectations. The first is whether one's right to recover depends on the normative or the epistemic conception of expectations. The second concerns the extent to which one's normative expectations themselves depend on epistemic expectations. My view is that normative expectations give rise to claims to repair, but that epistemic expectations play some role in determining the range and scope of normative expectations. Actually, epistemic expectations do not play a role in deriving normative expectations. Rather, they provide reliable barometers of what those expectations are. They can serve this function because often they have the same causal basis as normative expectations do. To see this, consider cases in which normative expectations are established by conventions within an industry or social group. In these cases, the relevant standard of liability – what one can normatively expect from others – is sometimes set by "customary practice." In addition to establishing the parameters of normative expectations, customary practices provide the basis for epistemic expectations. Thus, epistemic expectations are reliably connected to normative expectations. Both, in certain contexts at least, derive from customary practices.

12. See Chapter 15 for a fuller discussion of this kind of necessity case.

13. This is a good time to summarize our arguments on behalf of strict liability. The goal of the argument is to find a theory of liability that is both strict and just. We began, as Epstein does, by focusing on the causal condition alone, attempting to ground it either in a more general theory of responsibility or in a form

471

of equilibrium theory. These attempts fail. Not every way of causing another person a loss provides a basis either for liability or for recovery.

We then considered ways of distinguishing among ways of causing losses to see if we could hit on one that explains and justifies our practices of imposing liability and providing compensation that does not rely on the concept of fault. The key to these arguments is the concept of harm. The claim is that to cause someone a loss by harming her is to create in oneself an obligation to repair that loss and to create in the victim a right to recover. We considered two accounts of harm, neither of which ultimately does the trick. In the first, to harm someone is to set back a legitimate interest of hers. There are, however, all sorts of perfectly legitimate reasons for harming people in this sense, and there is no reason, moreover, why legitimate interests should be secured or protected by compensation whenever they suffer a setback. According to the second analysis, to harm someone is to frustrate a legitimate expectation of hers. This argument requires a distinction between normatively and epistemically legitimate expectations. The legitimacy of a claim to repair rests on normatively, not epistemically, legitimate expectations. The theory of legitimate expectations presupposes a theory of relevant norms, that is, the norms that give rise to the warranted expectations. If the norms require that individuals not impose unreasonable risks on one another, then the legitimate expectations one has is that others not be at fault. That expectation can be frustrated if and only if someone is at fault. Thus, rather than avoiding reliance on fault, it depends crucially on it.

In our search to provide a full theory of strict liability, we then turned our attention to a possible analysis of harm as action contrary to an individual's right. To harm someone is either to infringe or to violate a right of hers. Infringements are justifiable or permissible invasions; violations are wrongful invasions. If compensation is due for losses consequent on infringements, the case for compensation depends on the existence of the right, not on any purported wrongdoing in the agent's conduct. If the existence of a rights invasion is sufficient to warrant compensation in the case of an infringement, it should also be sufficient in the case of a wrongful invasion, namely a violation. In every case in which liability and recovery are warranted, it is because a right has been invaded.

CHAPTER 15

1. Unsurprisingly, the history of tort law reveals a tension between strict and fault liability, a tension that reflects the difficulty of choosing between faultless victims and blameless injurers. At times, the dominant standard has been strict liability. At other times, it has been fault liability. These principles differ largely with respect to which category of litigants – victims or injurers – are required to bear the costs of faultlessly occasioned accidents, on the assumption that members of either the victim or the injurer class must bear them. When we answer both the questions of liability and recovery at the same time, as our current practice requires us to do, we can adopt the perspective of the interests and claims of either victims or injurers, but not both. Whose perspective should be adopted? Whose interests should we be especially sensitive to: faultless victims or faultless injurers? And on which grounds should we choose between them?

In saying that there is an underlying tension in tort law, I am not saying that there is a deep contradiction between strict and fault liability that makes tort law incomprehensible. Instead, my view is that tort law is altogether comprehensible, and that understanding it depends in part on identifying the institutional features that create this tension in it. Perhaps this tension exists because tort law disables us from treating the claims of victims and injurers separately and differently. We can avoid the tension if we avail ourselves in practice of the theoretical distinction between victim recovery and injurer liability. If we pursue this distinction in practice as well as in theory, we may no longer find it necessary to adopt either the perspective of the injurer or the victim; we can adopt both perspectives, each to enable us to answer a different question. In doing so, however, we give up tort law as we know it. For it is an essential feature of tort law that these two questions – does the victim have a claim to repair? Has the injurer done anything for which he should be liable? – are answered simultaneously. Before we give up on tort law, however, we should explore whether a case in justice can be made for it.

2. In that case, we might say that because justice permits and requires us to impose costs on the injurer equal to, but no less nor greater than, the wrongful gain she secures, imposing costs in excess of those gains creates an additional wrongful loss, a loss that justice demands be rectified. If corrective justice requires that no more nor less than the injurer's wrongful gain and the victim's wrongful loss be annulled, then tort law, which more often than not imposes costs on injurers in excess of the gains they secure by their mischief, will be indefensible as a matter of justice. These issues are taken up again in Chapter 18 in the discussion of the difference between corrective and restitutionary justice.

3. Of course, it is controversial whether individuals will insure against nonpecuniary losses. However, for the sake of this argument we can simplify the problem as follows. Let's define pecuniary costs, like lost wages due to accident, as those against which rational agents will insure, and nonpecuniary costs, like emotional distress or pain and suffering, as those against which rational agents would not insure. Then it will be an important and controversial question to determine which costs fall into which category.

4. The distinction between pecuniary and nonpecuniary costs raises the general problem of identifying the class of compensable losses. How can we determine which losses that an individual suffers should be compensated for as a matter of justice? The losses that one suffers, for example, because a valued friend betrays a friendship by breaching a confidence may be painful, extensive, and wrongfully imposed. Does justice require that they be annulled, however? Are they damages, however real, that ought to be compensated for in some way? Are they the sorts of damages, moreover, that legal institutions should be designed to deal with?

Defining the class of compensable losses is ultimately necessary to any account of liability and recovery for loss, but I confess that I have no account of the requisite sort, nor, for that matter, does anyone else. One possibility is that we limit the class of compensable losses to those that rational individuals would insure against. This limits the class of compensable losses, but it merely re-creates rather than resolves the problem we noted above. For a loss that one would not have guarded against by insurance may nevertheless be a wrongful one, one that justice requires to be annulled.

5. Joel Feinberg, "Voluntary euthanasia and the inalienable right to life," 7 *Philosophy & Public Affairs* 93 (1978).

6. 109 Minn. 456, 124 N.W. 221 (1910).

7. Of all the arguments in this book, I am least satisfied with those I have been able to muster in support of my treatment of necessity cases. It's not that I am convinced that other solutions are superior to the one in the text. To see this, let's consider a few alternatives and problems with them.

One approach I did not consider holds that the victim's property right is well defined in that it entitles her both to exclusion and to compensation. Necessity overcomes or temporarily extinguishes the power to exclude, but not the power to demand compensation. While it alters the content of rights in some respects, necessity does not extinguish all claims associated with rights ownership, including the right to fair value, whether determined ex ante or ex post.

In this account the claim to repair is grounded in the right, but not in the fact that action is *contrary* to the right. Part of the problem with this approach is that if the injurer is justified in what he does, then why should he have to pay compensation? The answer is that the victim is entitled to it as part of her right. But the content of her right can not be given a priori. The claim to repair in it does not derive from what it *means* to have a right. After all, it is hardly incoherent to have a system of property rights in which right holders are given powers to exclude and alienate, backed up by a mixture of criminal sanctions and disapprobation, in which failures to abide by the constraints imposed by property rights do *not* give rise to claims to repair against anyone. Instead, it would be up to the property owner to secure his interest by first-party insurance. It is not part of the meaning of property rights that there are such claims to repair in them. Any argument for giving rights that content must be *normative*. It must provide us with good grounds for conferring that claim upon rights holders. The general problem arises if we accept the Feinberg–Thomson account of these cases. That account holds that the reason the injurer's conduct in necessity cases gives rise to claims to repair is that, though permissible, the injurer's conduct infringes the victim's right; it is "action contrary to the vic-

475

tim's right." Problems arise in specifying the sense in which the conduct that is morally permissible may nevertheless be "contrary to" or "infringing upon" the right. If necessity alters the content of the victim's right by extinguishing the power to exclude, then it is hard to identify any sense in which what the injurer does is action contrary to the victim's right. If you cannot exclude me, then what did I do that was wrong, that would require me to compensate you?

We might hold that I did something wrong precisely because I did not secure your consent. This is the thesis of the text. Necessity does *not* alter the content of the right. It does not extinguish the power to exclude. Though the sense in which the right is wronged is made clear by this approach, it fails to give a plausible reason for treating justifiable appropriations in which liability lies differently from innocent ones in which it does not. Necessity is a justification, but justified conduct can infringe a right, and if it does, a claim in justice to repair can arise. So if Hal takes Carla's insulin to stay alive, he owes her repair. But what of innocent infringements? If instead of taking Carla's insulin to keep from lapsing into a coma, Hal had quite innocently lost or destroyed some of it, we might feel that he owed Carla nothing, however regrettable her loss might be. If innocent infringements were to give rise to claims in justice to repair, we would be left with the core of the theory of strict liability, a thesis I rejected in the previous chapter. In general, the innocent or reasonable imposition of risk does not give rise to a claim to repair even if, in the end, the risk matures to harm. Why would an *intentional* but justifiable appropriation ground a claim to repair, whereas an innocent and unintentional one would not? Do not both set back the relevant interest, invade the relevant right, or fail to respect adequately the victim's power to exclude? If so, there are no principled grounds for treating them differently.

We need an account of the power to exclude. In one account, exclusions are powers with respect to the intentional actions of others, not the unintended consequences of intentional acts. This might help us understand why the justifiable but intentional appropriation is action "contrary to" the right, whereas the unintentional and innocent conduct is not. I simply do not know how helpful or convincing such an approach would ultimately turn out to be. Another alternative, suggested by Stephen Perry, invites us to treat justifiable but intentional appropriation of property as, in an appropriate sense, "fault-like." In this approach, the power to exclude might be extinguished by necessity, but the injurer's conduct is in a sense faulty, nevertheless. Thus, the claim to repair derives not from the victim's right being invaded, but from the fact that his legitimate interest is "faultily" set back. This would place necessity cases, and justification cases more generally, in the first category of cases. Then justification would be treated like innocence. If there is no fault in the doing, in either the paradigmatic or attenuated fault-like sense, there can be no right to repair, no moral duty to provide it. My problem with this approach rests on the widespread belief that even if it is in a sense regrettable, justifiable conduct is not at fault in any way. That's what it means for it to be justifiable.

The concept of a rights infringement rests on the claim that we can assess separately the quality of the injurer's conduct and the content of the victim's right. Perhaps this assumption is simply false. Perhaps the notion of a right infringement is empty or, worse, incoherent. It may not be possible to assess separately the justifiability of an injurer's conduct and the content of the victim's right. This line of argument is suggested by Joseph Raz's account of rights. According to Raz, rights are primarily normative grounds of duties. If the injurer is justified in what he does, he has no duty not to do it. If he has no duty to forbear, there simply can be no right that, by doing what he has no duty not to do, he violates. It does not follow that the victim has no right to repair, only that the right to repair cannot be grounded in the victim's right (however understood) that is invaded or infringed by the injurer. One consequence of pursuing this line would be to put the necessity cases either into the first or third categories. If they go into the first category, then justification is not fault-like and there is no liability. If they go into the third category, then even though the conduct is not at fault, there is a duty to repair, and the problem of identifying its source will remain. We might want to distinguish more carefully than we have among cases that fall into the third category. Some will involve compensation as a condition of legitimate transfer in which compensation rights what in its absence would be wrong. Necessity cases would not be of this sort, however. In the typical necessity case, we want to encourage people to do what necessity requires of them, or at least we would not mean to dis-

courage them. That means that we do not think that what they
do is wrong. If this is right, holding them to a duty to repair
simply cannot be understood as righting what in its absence
would be wrong. There is no wrong to right. Compensation
might then be justified instrumentally. It helps secure expectations that grow up around property rights and encourages justified appropriations only. In the typical case, compensation
would be the victim's right, but its basis would not be corrective
justice.

For the remainder of the book, I adopt the solution outlined
in this chapter. If one of these other accounts or some other
account proves more compelling, it may restrict the scope of
corrective justice as an account of tort law. If either Perry or Raz
is right, although the distinction between wrongs and wrongdoing developed in Chapter 17 will remain intact, it will no longer
help us understand infringement cases.

CHAPTER 16

1. In what follows, I present a particular conception of corrective
justice. Like any conception, this one will be controversial and
contestable. One of the central questions the reader will no doubt
want answered is, by what criteria are competing conceptions
of corrective justice to be evaluated? This is an especially important question, since even among tort theorists who advance the
view that to some extent at least tort law is a matter of corrective
justice, there is virtually no agreement about just what corrective justice requires. In the argument that follows, I will try to
say something useful in defense of my version of corrective justice and something about how various conceptions are to be
evaluated. Ultimately, no defense of a conception of corrective
justice will be satisfactory in the absence of a foundation for it.
Of course, there will be different views about what counts as an
appropriate foundation for a principle of justice; there will even
be differences of opinion about whether foundational arguments are possible. On these matters, I am partial to the wisdom of my teacher, Joel Feinberg, that progress can be made on
the penultimate questions in philosophy even as the ultimate
ones remain unresolved.

My account of corrective justice grounds in it social practice
in a way I want to make clear. In the first place, I am not trying

to derive the content of corrective justice from some more-abstract normative theory of persons, agency, equality, or the like. That is Ernest Weinrib's project, not mine. Rather, I look first at our informal moral practices to note that people often say to one another something like: "There is a mess that you are responsible for, and because you are, you are going to have to do something about it." This practice of identifying "messes," "agents responsible for them," and ascribing "reasons for acting" as a result of the link between the two is widespread and important. It is the practice that exemplifies what I am calling corrective justice. In developing a conception of corrective justice, it is this practice I hope to give structure, content, and coherence to. In doing so, my account begins with the social practice, but it is not content merely to describe the practice. Mine is an *analysis* of the practice, one that must offer a theory of "messes," of "responsibility for messes," and an account of the ways in which these two come together to create reasons for acting. Importantly, it will also provide an account of the ways in which related practices might limit the scope of the reason-giving dimension of this practice. (See Chapter 19 on the limitations on corrective justice.) My ultimate goal is to determine if this practice, conceptualized in a particular way, or one similar to it, exists or is exemplified in tort law.

Tort law (and law generally) is a practice. For the purposes of my enterprise, it would be question-begging to develop the conception of corrective justice by reference to legal practice generally or tort law in particular. After all, I want to see if law exemplifies a moral practice of corrective justice. So I cannot appeal to the legal practice in order to give content to the moral practice. On the other hand, if tort law does exemplify the social practice, then the law itself will be a source from which a richer or fuller conception of corrective justice can be drawn.

The strategy is to develop the relevant conception of corrective justice, identify salient features of law, and then ask whether, and to what extent, we can see the law as an institutional embodiment of this practice. The view I come to is that corrective justice is at the core of tort law. It is not everywhere in tort, however; we should not be hasty in labeling as mistakes departures from the core. Rather, in part because of the theory developed in Chapter 19, limitations on the applicability and scope of corrective justice are perfectly defensible, provided certain conditions are satisfied. Thus modesty, rather than demands for reforms, inform this enterprise.

Two other remarks are in order. First, although I try to develop the conception of corrective justice independent of legal practice and what I know of it, I want to make it clear that part of what *motivates* this exercise is my knowledge of the law, my belief that such a practice of liability for the losses for which one is responsible is embedded within it, and the belief that other understandings of law, especially economic ones, miss entirely or badly misunderstand or misrepresent these features of law. This is my research, or working, hypothesis.

On the other hand, I entered into this project open-minded about the conclusions, about where the argument would take me. Maybe tort law exemplifies corrective justice more than I think it does, maybe less, maybe not at all. Given the project as a whole, no sympathetic reader can believe that this is an enterprise of trying to fit the law into a preconceived framework. I have a working hypothesis, but I am prepared to follow the argument wherever it will go, even if that means revising or abandoning my initial assumptions.

Second, the strategy here is to identify and develop a conception of corrective justice, identify key institutional features of tort law, and then ask whether the law, or some important part of it, can be seen as exemplifying corrective justice so conceived. This strategy presupposes that one can identify tort law's features, substantive and structural, *independent* of a theory of the law. This sort of enterprise would be especially difficult for someone who has an overall jurisprudence according to which the law at any given time just is the best normative interpretation of it. That kind of connection between law and the best normative interpretation of it makes it hard to imagine how one might ask whether the law (independent of a normative interpretation of it) exemplifies corrective justice so conceived. I'm a legal positivist. I believe that even if we need a normative theory to solve hard cases, we can still identify central features of the law independent of a normative theory of law. In short, then, my enterprise depends on the truth of certain jurisprudential and metaethical claims, the former about the nature of law, the latter about the social dimension of moral practices. Neither of these assumptions is defended here.

2. The view of corrective justice I put forward is partially moti-

vated by two pretheoretical commitments that I am prepared ultimately to abandon, but which can be abandoned only at some cost to the plausibility of one's theory. These are: (1) the belief that your claim to compensation in the case I have constructed can be a matter of justice as well as efficiency, and (2) the New Zealand plan for allocating accident costs may be wrongheaded, unworkable, maybe even inefficient, but it does not constitute one gigantic affront to the principle of corrective justice. We will have more to say about the New Zealand plan and liability schemes like it when we turn our attention to institutional embodiments of the principle of corrective justice. For now, I want to confine the discussion to the principle of corrective justice itself.

3. See Chapter 17 for important modifications of the claim that corrective justice can sustain distributively unjust states of the world.

4. This is the conception of corrective justice I have defended until now. The most complete statement of it appears in "Tort law and the demands of corrective justice," *Indiana Law Journal* 349 (1992).

5. Several limitations on this principle need to set out. Two of these are especially important. First, not every loss, however wrongfully created, is the concern of corrective justice. Let's suppose that losses are wrongful if they are the result of negligent or wrongful interference with a person's legitimate interests. Then whenever a person has suffered a wrongful loss in this sense he will have the makings of a claim in corrective justice to repair. But, there are many losses that an individual suffers at the hands of others, which, although they may fall within the ambit of morality, are nevertheless outside the scope of corrective justice. That theory will not itself be part of corrective justice, but will instead set the boundaries of it. The analogous problem in torts is the problem of specifying the range of compensable harms. Even when we know what the principles and standards of recovery in torts are, we may still have questions about the sorts of losses for which victims can seek repair, or the kinds of interests the law seeks to protect.

The second qualification is that corrective justice is concerned with the losses that one person causes another. I suppose it is possible to wrong oneself and therefore to impose wrongful losses upon oneself. Similarly, it may be possible to secure wrongful gains at no one's expense. These gains and losses are not primarily the concern of corrective justice, though there may be no reason to exclude them entirely from its ambit.

6. David Lyons, "Utility and rights," 24 *Nomos* 107 (1982).

7. See especially, his essay "Comment on Coleman: Corrective justice," 67 *Indiana Law Journal* 381 (1992).

8. In effect, I am suggesting that public-goods or market-failure arguments can lead to much more "liberal" conceptions of the scope of legitimate political authority than is usually believed.

9. Given the discussion in note 1, we might understand Stephen Perry's objection to the annulment view of corrective justice as follows: If we look at our informal moral practices, what we do not see is people making statements of the following sort, "There's a mess that you are responsible for; *we* have a problem, and there's something we have to do ."

10. If we inquire further, and want to know why responsibility or causal power is necessary to impose a duty to repair, the answer is even more tentative. It is through the exercise of the powers of autonomous agency that individuals make their mark in the world. It is through their actions that we come to understand individuals, and, more importantly, it is through our actions that we come to our self-understandings.

CHAPTER 17

1. In sum: Though nonlegitimate interests can be protected by rights to repair when they are injured, compensation cannot be a matter of corrective justice. Legitimate interests can be protected by rights to repair for similar reasons. However, when those interests are harmed unjustifiably or wrongly, the claim to repair is a matter of corrective justice. When rights are invaded, losses that result are wrongful, and worthy of repair in justice whether or not the conduct invasive of the right is otherwise wrongful.

2. *Vosburg* v. *Putney*, 80 Wis. 523, 50 N.W. 403 (1891).

3. The sense in which corrective justice relies on community norms or conventions is developed in section 17.12.

4. Though hurricanes and other natural disasters can cause enormous damage and suffering, only human agents can wrong one another or engage in wrongdoing of one kind or another.

There is a difference between misfortune and injustice, and part of the difference is the role of human agency.

5. Recall the distinction between two reasons for countenancing excuses that defeat agency. In one case, excuses that defeat agency are relevant because it is wrong to hold someone liable for events that are not the consequence of his doing. In the other case, excuses that defeat agency are relevant because they demonstrate that the victim has no right in corrective justice to repair. In discussing Fletcher's claim that tort law exemplifies an ideal of risk reciprocity, I defended this last conception of the role of excuses that defeat agency. In other words, my view is that culpability-defeating excuses are irrelevant to tort law, whereas agency-defeating excuses are relevant precisely because, if valid, they undermine the victim's claim to repair in justice. The argument in Chapter 13 explored the role of excuses in a defensible theory of *tort liability*. Our concern here is slightly different. We want to understand the role of excuses in the proper conception of *corrective justice.*

6. The responsibility relationship is important in corrective justice in a way in which it is not in tort law. The reason is that in corrective justice the question is whether a duty ought to be imposed on a particular person, whereas in tort law it is whether a loss ought to be allocated to one or the other litigant – when the loss must fall to one of them. Establishing that an injurer is without responsibility for the loss may mean that there are no grounds in corrective justice for holding him liable for it. But that is not enough to conclude that there are no grounds at all for holding him liable. After all, the same may well be true of the victim. She, too, may not be responsible in the sense required by corrective justice for the loss. Tort law requires a different inquiry.

Because tort law requires a different kind of inquiry, it does not follow that if the victim has no claim in corrective justice to repair, the loss must be hers to shoulder. Other principles of justice may then come into play to determine whether the loss should fall to the victim or the injurer, neither of whom has a reason in corrective justice to bear the loss. All we can say is that if the injurer has an agency-defeating excuse, then there is no reason in corrective justice for making repair. There can be other reasons, based on other principles and policies, for requiring him to make good the victim's loss. Similar remarks bear on the case in which the victim is left to shoulder her costs. There may often be no reason in corrective justice for imposing liability upon her. But there are other principles and policies that do not require agency relevant to allocating risk. Because there are such principles and policies, there are grounds that create reasons for acting on the basis of considerations other than corrective justice.

7. Jules L. Coleman and Jody Kraus, "Rethinking the theory of legal rights," 95 *Yale Law Journal* 1335 (1986).
8. Ronald Dworkin, *Taking Rights Seriously* (Cambridge, Mass.: Harvard University Press, 1978).
9. Joseph Raz, *The Morality of Freedom* (Oxford: Clarendon Press, 1986), pp. 165–92.
10. Joel Feinberg, *Social Philosophy* (Englewood Cliffs, N.J.: Prentice-Hall, 1973).
11. In the case of rights whose content is given by property rules only, failure to comply with those terms is a wrong, but in the absence of a liability rule, the right that is wronged provides no grounds for compensation. We might protect such rights by the criminal sanction, punishing transactional wrongs. There are two problems with adopting this kind of approach to rights invasions. First, some wrongs, like Hal's taking Carla's insulin without her consent, can be justifiable, and do not warrant punishment. Indeed, in Hal's case, we may believe that he owes Carla compensation, not that he should be punished. Second, in the absence of a liability rule, we would leave the right holder, the wronged party, without a claim to compensatory redress, even if we found punishing the invader desirable. Punishing Hal would do Carla no good. Thus, it would not be unusual for the content of rights to be specified by the conjunction of property and liability rules.
12. The failure to seek or to secure consent as a condition of transfer may or may not be justifiable. Thus, wrongs against these rights need not be wrongdoings. In either case, compensation is for wrong done.
13. Again, we can imagine cases in which such failure is permissible or excusable. In all such cases, however, it constitutes a wrong in the appropriate sense, and should damage occur, it can create wrongful losses in the sense required by corrective justice.
14. The distinction is important. If the content of a right is speci-

fied by a liability rule only, then compensation is required in order to satisfy the constraints rights ownership imposes. If the content of a right is specified by the conjunction of property and liability rules in which the former provides the conditions of legitimate transfer, then compensation is owed because the conditions of legitimate transfer have not been adequately respected. Thus, we cannot determine from the fact that compensation is paid whether it serves to legitimate a transfer consistent with the demands imposed by the victim's rights, or whether, instead, it is owed because a wrong has been done, a right invaded. Compensation can be owed both as a way of respecting rights and as a way of redressing a wrong. We cannot know which role compensation plays in a particular case until we know what the content of the relevant right is. That depends on the transaction rule applied, and that, in turn, depends on the underlying normative theory.

15. In his first formulations of the theory of strict liability, Richard Epstein did not emphasize the role of rights in the justification of compensation and liability. Instead, his concern was primarily to downplay fault and to upgrade the importance of causation. His early work sought to embed strict liability in a theory of personal responsibility, rather than in a theory of rights. Eventually, the theory of strict liability has come to hold that the source of the victim's claim to repair is the fact that a right of hers has been invaded. In this version of the theory, causation is relevant to the concept of a rights invasion. Causation is the means by which injurers transgress or invade victims' rights. The causal condition does not provide the grounds of liability or recovery; rights invasions do that. Causation provides the appropriate theory of invasion.

16. The difference between economic analysis and the theory of strict liability, then, is just the difference between whether the content of rights is to be given the *disjunction* of property and liability rules (economic analysis) or by the *conjunction* of property and liability rules (the theory of strict liability). And this is the difference between whether liability rules specify terms of legitimate transfer (economic analysis) or ground claims to repair in the event the conditions of legitimate transfer are not followed (the theory of strict liability). And this is all the difference in the world.

In the economic analysis, all rights are really guarantees to streams or levels of welfare or utility. It is this fact about them that makes compensation by injurers a way of legitimately compelling transfers within the constraints imposed by rights. For similar reasons, the content of rights is given by the disjunction of property and liability rules. Within the classical liberal theory of strict liability, rights secure a domain of autonomy or control. It is this fact about them that makes compensation by injurers a matter of moral duty owed because a right has been invaded. Any nonconsensual taking is a wrong, whether justified or not; liability will be strict, independent of the motivation or care of the injurer. Thus, within the classical liberal theory of strict liability, the content of rights is given by the conjunction of property and liability rules.

17. This conclusion depends on the argument first presented in Chapter 15 regarding necessity cases to the effect that a rights infringement does not require fault on the injurer's behalf. Some might argue against this view that there is a kind of fault in the doing in the infringement cases, that is, even if the injurer's conduct is justifiable or permissible on balance. The fault may consist in the intentional taking of another's holdings without his consent, even though doing so can be justified. If these critics are correct, then the theory of responsibility that covers cases of wrongdoing should apply in these cases as well. One theory of responsibility would cover all cases because, although there may be causation without fault, there is no responsibility without fault (in the doing).

18. Having said that, we should ask whether economic analysis provides the best interpretation of wrongdoing in torts. The form of economic analysis offered by Learned Hand in *U.S. v. Caroll Towing*, 159 F. 2d 169, 173 (1947), is an account of objective negligence. Whereas many of the cases adjudicated under the fault rule involve negligence, fault in torts encompasses other forms of wrongdoing as well, including recklessness and intentional wrongdoing. There may well be a moral shortcoming or fault in wrongdoing of this sort that is not reducible entirely to inefficiency.

Let's focus on negligence, in which the economic argument or interpretation is apparently strongest. The Hand formula for negligence holds that a person is negligent if she fails to take rational or cost-justified precautions. The standard of care is the standard of rational care. The principle of negligence in torts, however, is based on departure from the requirement of reasonable risk taking. The difference is important. To see it we have to make use of both the Coasian strategy of argument and Thomas Nagel's distinction between the personal and impersonal points of view. (See *The Possibility of Altruism* [Oxford: Clarendon Press, 1970]).

Against which risks ought rational social policy guard? The Coasian approach to answering this question begins by assuming that the same person owns all the relevant activities. Then we would ask which accidents that person would prevent. Of course, he would prevent the cost-justified ones. Those are the ones for which the costs of precaution are less than the expected costs of the harm. On the assumption that he is a risk-neutral expected-utility maximizer, that is what it would be rational for him to do. Notice that the Hand formula is simply an application of this general form of argument. If it is rational for one person who owns both activities to take precautions that are cost justified, then we would want our liability rules to encourage injurers to take the same precautions: the rational or efficient ones. And that is precisely what the Hand formula for negligence requires each individual to do.

The strategy makes a good deal of sense – up to a point. Let's now introduce the distinction between the personal and the impersonal points of view. To view matters from the personal point of view is to see them from your perspective, given your interests, weighed as you would weigh them. To view matters from the impersonal point of view is to "take the you out of it." From this perspective, no one person's interests count any more than anyone else's.

In the case in which one individual is presumed to own or engage in both activities, the personal and impersonal points of view converge. All the costs are personal, and so no special weighing of conflicting interests or points of view is appropriate. The impersonal is the personal and vice versa. On the other hand, things change when we imagine that the activities are owned by different people. The requirement of collective rationality that the injurer should impose the same risks, take the same precautions he would have taken had he owned both activities, forces all parties whose behavior is governed by the reasonable-person standard to take the impersonal point of view. It forces each to treat the costs and benefits without regard to their distribution. It requires each agent to act as utilitarianism requires: as someone occupying the impersonal point of view only, concerned to maximize an impersonal good.

But agents occupy the personal as well as the impersonal standpoint, and their doing so, moreover, can be reasonable. From the personal point of view, investments in safety worth taking when one owns both activities may no longer seem reasonable or appropriate when the injurer and victim are different individuals. We do not normally hold that it is reasonable to act only from the impersonal point of view; we do not always fault individuals for taking into account personal interests, the effects of their actions on friends and family. We might follow Rawls in saying that the demand to act on the basis of the way we see the world from the impersonal point of view imposes undue "strains of commitment." It asks too much of us. Instead, we expect of one another that we will act reasonably; and reasonable action is a coherent and defensible compromise struck between the personal and the impersonal points of view. If negligence is the failure to take all cost-justified precautions in the case of *single* ownership of two activities – the deep insight behind the Coase Theorem – it does not follow that negligence imposes the same burden in the typical accident case in which reasonable risk taking reflects the personal as well as the impersonal points of view.

19. I am especially indebted to Joseph Raz and Frances Kamm for discussions that helped clarify my thinking about the issues I take up in the following section.

20. This requirement applies over a set of rights, not over individual rights. It can also be strengthened. For example, instead of saying that the state can reallocate without giving rise to demands for compensation only if it implements that system of rights required by the best theory of justice, we might allow the state to substitute any system of entitlements better than the current one, and so on. I prefer the formulation in the text for illustrative purposes.

21. There may be no moral reason for making repair based on justice, but even in these cases there may be moral reasons for acting that grow out of respect for civil relationships and well-entrenched expectations. Injustice, after all, does not exhaust the domain of morality and of the reasons for acting morally creates and sustains.

22. This is the status of property rights that I assume is true for the remainder of this book.

23. In my previous work, I argued for two theses that are incompatible with the argument presented here. First, I held the view that corrective justice was compatible with any underlying distribution, whether just or not. In part, I was anxious to defend the view, repeated here, that corrective justice is compatible with an economic theory of wrong and wrongdoing. In part, my previous argument relied on the second postulate I now reject, namely, that corrective justice is transactional in the narrow sense; it does not reach the justice of the underlying entitlements. When I held these positions I also defended the annulment conception of corrective justice. In abandoning that conception, I argue that corrective justice imposes agent-relative reasons for acting. These are moral reasons. Thus, corrective justice constrains the set of underlying entitlements sustainable by it to the set compatible with this fact about it. The view defended here is that corrective justice is not compatible with every possible set of entitlements, regardless of their justice, and corrective justice is not transactional in the narrow sense; it reaches the underlying entitlements. If those entitlements fail to satisfy the minimal condition set out in the text, then there can be no reason in corrective justice for sustaining them by imposing a duty of repair. It does not follow, however, that there are no good reasons for sustaining those entitlements any more than it would follow that there are no good reasons for enforcing the relevant transaction norms. For example, suppose that the minimal condition is not met and that you have what you have no right to. If I take it from you without justification, all that follows is that you have no right in corrective justice to its return or to compensation for its loss and that I have no duty to make repair to you. It does not follow that I have a right to keep what I have taken. I may have a duty to turn it over to the relevant officials or to make payment into a general fund, etc. There is a difference, after all, between the claim that you have no right to X and the claim that I am within my rights to take X from you.

24. My argument is that the principle of distributive justice is itself inadequately local to be the source of claims based on corrective justice. Principles of distributive justice may *ground* or *justify* a set of concrete rights and duties among individuals of a

community. When there are such rights and duties, a claim in corrective justice may follow from my having done something wrong to you, not from the fact that the principle of distributive justice has been thwarted.

25. This point is analogous to H. L. A. Hart's distinction between primary and secondary rules. Secondary rules specify the formulas individuals must pursue if they are to create primary rules to regulate the relationships among them.

CHAPTER 18

1. It may seem odd that we need to ask questions of justification prior to ones of explanation. After all, one might argue, even if the state is not authorized to enforce the demands of corrective justice, our current practice may well do so. And if it does, that would show that the state was doing what it had no right to do. However, a normative interpretation requires that we see if there is an understanding of our practice that would make the state's use of its coercive powers prima facie defensible. That would require us to look again at the practice of tort law and see if it might also be understood as enforcing another ideal the state can legitimately pursue, perhaps a particular conception of distributive justice or economic efficiency. In the case in which the state is not justified in imposing the demands of corrective justice, then even though corrective justice might fit the current practice, it could not count as the sort of interpretation of it that we seek. Often, this is the sort of objection to economic analysis people have in mind. Even if it appears to fit the practice, it does not provide an interpretation of it that sees it in its best light because the state may not have the authority to use the courts (though it may have the authority to use legislative bodies) to pursue collective aims of that sort. It may turn out that no principle or set of consistent principles both fit a practice and help us to see it in a way that makes the exercise of authority prima facie defensible. In that case, there may be all sorts of explanations of the practice, political and causal, but no normative or constructive interpretation of it in the sense in which I am using the term here.

We can also distinguish two kinds of legal reform. In one case reform is urged because no interpretation in this sense is available of a practice. This is external reform. Alternatively, a practice might only incompletely conform to a set of principles that could count as an interpretation of it. This interpretation might then function as an internal criterion of criticism and reform, something at which to aim more steadfastly and wholeheartedly than the practice at any time actually does. Legal philosophers like myself are often internal reformers at bottom. We seek to identify the logic of a body of law that makes sense of it by bringing coherence to it but that does not try to fit all of it under independently justifiable principles. Instead, we want to illustrate what at its best an institution of law might be, so that we might more adequately and accurately exemplify those ideals or achieve those goals in the future. Of course, the interpretive enterprise may lead even the most optimistic internal reformer to reject a current practice as beyond repair, leaving only external reform a viable option.

2. Robert Nozick, *Anarchy, State and Utopia* (New York: Basic Books, 1974).

3. 159 Eng. Rep. 737, 3 H. & C. 774 (Exch. 1865), reversed, L.R. 1 Ex. 265 (1866), affirmed, L.R. 3 H.L. 330 (1868).

4. I have held different positions on the question of whether a negligent driver gains as a consequence of his negligence alone. First, in articles defending no-fault automobile insurance, I denied that negligent drivers gain as a consequence. Often, I argued, they are as likely to be injured in an accident as are their victims. Then Richard Posner pointed out to me that negligence involves an unjustified savings in precautions, and therefore a kind of wrongful gain – always and necessarily. I accepted Posner's objection, but not the conclusion he wanted me to draw from it – namely, that there is always wrongful gain sufficient to impose liability in corrective justice on the injurer. Recently, I have come to a different view. I was wrong to suppose that negligent driving, for example, cannot constitute a wrongful gain for the wrongdoer. It surely can. On the other hand, it need not. Sometimes, individuals who lack adequate cognitive skills may invest far more in safety than would have been necessary for them to have invested optimally. It's just that they get it wrong; they make the wrong investments. The Posner view that wrongdoers always gain treats wrongdoing like defection in a prisoner's dilemma. The wrongdoer refuses to incur the oppor-

tunity costs of compliance. In fact, however, the wrongdoer may be no defector at all, just an incompetent do-gooder.

5. 109 Minn. 456, 124 N.W. 221 (1910).

6. See ibid., 124 N.W. 222.

7. I have said all along that although many cases in torts could be seen as expressing an ideal of corrective justice, there are claims to repair recognized in torts that are not grounded in corrective justice at all. In many of these cases, the claim to compensation is not based on wrong done or right invaded, but on the conditions of legitimate transfer within rights. The most interesting of these cases involve liability for products. I take up products liability in Chapter 20.

8. It follows that I take the following elements to make up the core of tort law: the substantive rule of fault liability; the structural implementation of that rule in which liability is imposed on a case-by-case basis (the plaintiff brings suit against the person he alleges to be responsible for his loss, and if the victim's claim is vindicated, he recovers against the person responsible for his loss). This is a contestable conception of the core. It claims that fault liability is more important conceptually to tort law than is strict liability. It recognizes that sometimes victims sue individuals other than those whom they view as responsible for their losses and that sometimes liability is imposed on parties who are not in the sense developed in Chapter 17 responsible for the loss for which they are held liable. It treats these as departures from the core. Others may have a different view of tort law's core. But the core is not defined by the majority of cases or even by the direction the law is taking. Instead, the core is that part of the practice that we identify essentially with tort law. So understood, the core is not immutable. Our reflective conception of what is at the heart of tort law may change. It probably will. This is a claim about modern Anglo–American tort law, but it is one, I recognize, that may be falsified within my lifetime.

9. Ronald Dworkin. *Law's Empire* (Cambridge, Mass.: Belknap Press, 1986).

CHAPTER 19

1. *Ybarra* v. *Spangard*, 25 Cal. 2d 486, 154 P.2d 687 (1944).

2. It is a further question whether such a burden-shifting rule will

actually prove effective. The point here is simply to illustrate how various rules can still be interpreted as part of a general plan to implement an ideal, say, of corrective justice, even if the results the rules generate in particular cases do not fully correspond to the results corrective justice would require.

3. *Summers* v. *Tice*, 33 Cal. 2d 80, 199 P.2d 1 (1948).

4. *Sindell* v. *Abott Laboratories*, 26 Cal. 3d 588, 607 P.2d 924, 163 Cal. Rptr. 132 (1980).

5. *Hymowitz* v. *Eli Lilly and Co.*, 73 N.Y. 2d 487, 539 N.E. 2d 941 (1989), cert. denied sub nom. *Rexall Drug Co.* v. *Tigue*, 110 S. Ct. 350 (1989).

6. Wright, "Causation, responsibility, risk, probability, naked statistics, and proof."

7. There are some conditions that must be satisfied before this is valid. First, the victims must be fully compensated under the alternative plan, or they must be as fully compensated under the alternative as they would be under a scheme that implements corrective justice. Second, the alternative must accomplish some additional goals not secured by a corrective-justice plan. Third, the alternative must conform to the relevant demands of justice and morality.

In my earlier work, I claimed that the duties in corrective justice could be discharged by parties other than those who are responsible for creating wrongful losses. Thus, my claim was that no-fault plans were ways of discharging duties in corrective justice (provided other conditions like those mentioned above were met). I still accept the claim that it is possible for someone other than the wrongdoer to discharge the wrongdoer's obligations (otherwise insurance would be unthinkable), but I reject the idea that no-fault plans are ways of meeting the demands of corrective justice. Instead, certain practices simply mean that no duties in corrective justice arise in a particular community. Thus, it is not as if New Zealand has an unusual approach to meeting the demands of corrective justice with respect to accident-related losses. Rather, in New Zealand, there is no practice of corrective justice with respect to such losses. After all, in corrective justice, the faulty injurer has a duty to repair, and under the plans we are talking about, there simply is no agent-relative duty of any sort. The victim's right grounds a duty, but the duty it grounds depends on the practice. The practice of corrective justice imposes that duty on the faulty injurer. Other practices or social conventions might well impose different duties.

Whereas I used to say that other practices can *discharge* the wrongdoer's duty, I now say that such practices either *extinguish* duties in corrective justice that would otherwise arise or that duties in corrective justice simply do not arise. The difference between the latter two approaches is important. In one view, corrective justice is like a default rule. If no other practices of the appropriate sort exist, then corrective justice does, and it imposes duties of a certain agent-relative kind. In the other, if there is no practice of corrective justice, there are no duties of corrective justice, whatever other practices may exist. I have not settled on a view about which of these alternatives is correct, but everything I have said so far is compatible with both interpretations.

8. It follows that even if the state is authorized to act on the basis of corrective justice, it is not required to do so. It may simply ignore corrective justice, though it may not be free to ignore the plight of the victims of wrongdoing altogether. See note 7 for a further development of this idea.

CHAPTER 20

1. Report of the United States Conference Board, 1987.
2. *MacPherson* v. *Buick Motor Co.*, 217 N.Y. 382. The defendant is a manufacturer of automobiles. It sold an automobile to a retail dealer, who resold to the plaintiff. While the plaintiff was in the car, it suddenly collapsed, and he was thrown out and injured. One of the wheels was made of defective wood, and its spokes crumbled into fragments. The wheel was not made by the defendant; it was bought from another manufacturer. There is evidence, however, that its defects could have been discovered by reasonable inspection, and that inspection was omitted. There is no claim that the defendant knew of the defect and willfully concealed it. The charge is one, not of fraud, but of negligence. The question to be determined is whether the defendant owed a duty of care and vigilance to anyone but the immediate purchaser.
3. *Escola* v. *Coca-Cola Bottling Co.*, 24 Cal 2C 453, 150 P.2d 436 (1944). The plaintiff was a waitress. While on her job, she was putting into the restaurant's refrigerator bottles of Coca-Cola that had

been delivered to the restaurant at least 36 hours earlier. As she was putting the fourth bottle into the refrigerator, it exploded in her hand, causing severe injuries. The plaintiff alleged that the defendant had been negligent in selling "bottles containing said beverage which on account of excessive pressure of gas or by reason of some defect in the bottle was dangerous . . . and likely to explode." The plaintiff, however, could not show any specific acts of negligence on the part of the defendant.

4. Alan Schwartz, "Proposals for products liability reform: A theoretical synthesis," 97(3) *Yale Law Journal* (1988).

5. With respect to insurance, problems of adverse selection and moral hazard can be explained by example. Moral hazard is the effect of the existence of insurance itself on the level of insurance claims made. Ex ante moral hazard is the phenomenon of reduced prevention simply because insurance is available. Ex post moral hazard is the increase in claims after the fact, and, as the example in the text illustrates, is partially a function of who pays. The adverse-selection problem is a function of the variance in expected risks in a pool. As the variance becomes too great, the low-risk members no longer find insurance attractive and drop out, leaving only higher-risk members, thereby making it unattractive for an insurance company to provide insurance against that risk.

6. George Priest, "The current insurance crisis," 96 *Yale Law Journal* (1987).

7. Admittedly, this line of argument will not apply to third-party products liability.

8. This proposal is interesting because it shows the tension in all reform proposals as well as the difficulty inherent in any proposal. Nonpecuniary losses are imposed by the manufacturer. Why shouldn't the manufacturer pay for those costs? He caused them! If we start with the premise that tort law should impose the costs of accidents on those who cause them, then as long as nonpecuniary losses are costs (and they are), manufacturers should bear those costs. On the other hand, if we start out with the premise that tort law should reflect the terms of a bargain between consumers and manufacturers, then consumers should not demand that manufacturers compensate their nonpecuniary losses. How we resolve the question of who bears the risks of nonpecuniary losses depends, then, on how we think we ought to think about tort law generally. On the one hand, if we start

out with one kind of premise, namely, that people should be liable for all the losses they *cause*, it looks like manufacturers should bear those risks. On the other hand, if we start with the premise that the tort rules emerge only because the market fails and that a sensible tort scheme should reflect an ideal market solution, then because consumers would not insure against nonpecuniary losses, it follows that manufacturers should not be required to provide that insurance for them.

9. Cf. Steven Shavell, *Economic Analysis of Accident Law*, (Cambridge, Mass.: Harvard University Press, 1987).

10. I am grateful to Alan Schwartz for helping me develop this argument.

11. I want to resolve the apparent conflict between my unwillingness to use the hypothetical contract as a way of fleshing out tort law generally, and my willingness to employ this model in the case of product safety law. This conflict is more apparent than real. First, I nowhere claim that it is in general inappropriate or otherwise impermissible to employ the hypothetical rational bargain as a model of tort law. I argue instead that even if such a model were the best account of contract law, it would not *follow* that it is the uniquely appropriate model of tort liability. The view I have consistently expressed is that the law of torts emphasizes wrongfulness in ways that the hypothetical, rational bargain does not in general illuminate and that the theory of corrective justice does. Corrective justice is the best interpretation of that significant aspect of tort law.

However, there are parts of the law of torts that are appropriately modeled as hypothetical rational bargains, in part because they do not emphasize the wrongfulness of conduct. Rather, they emphasize the role compensation ex post plays in completing after the fact a full contract that, for one or another reason, cannot be fully articulated ex ante. I have argued as well that products liability law falls within the category of conduct in which the typical claim to compensation is not a matter of justice, but is instead a matter of creating efficient transfers. Manufacturing is a risky activity that is worth its risks, but which must shoulder its social costs. My view is that the model of the hypothetical rational bargain is a particularly helpful way of understanding the relationship between product manufacturer and consumer.

CHAPTER 21

1. See, especially, Chapter 16, note 1.
2. Raz, *Morality of Freedom.*
3. James F. Blumstein, Randall R. Bovberg, and Frank A. Sloan, "Beyond tort reform: Developing better tools for assigning damages for personal injury," 8(1) *Yale Journal on Regulation* (1991).
4. Jules L. Coleman, "Adding institutional insult to personal injury," 8(1) *Yale Journal on Regulation* (1991).

Index

accident costs
  allocation of, 430
  choosing between strict and fault
    liability for, 10–11
  one-party vs. two party, 247
  reducing, 466 n.15
  two aspects of primary, 205
accident law
  backward-looking accounts of,
    432
  best account of the core of, 386
accidents
  at-fault pool for automobile, 404
  one- and two-party, 244–7
  tort law and victims of, 209, 375–
    6
activity levels, 247–8
actus reus requirement, 222
agency
  excuses that defeat, 335, 469 n.7,
    483 n.5
  incurred duties and, 468 n.11
agency, liability without, 261–6
agreement
  enforceable, 115
  threat of defection and, 33
annulment thesis
  corrective justice and, 307–11,
    312, 314–16, 318–19, 365–6
autonomy
  liberal conception of, 436
  rights and, 342–4

Axelrod, Robert, 35, 38

bargaining
  aspiration level and, 114
  contracting and, 31–3, 141
  theories, 113–14, 121
  well-defined property rights
    and, 160
  see also rational bargaining
bargaining theory, 121
  as model of local cooperation in
    the absence of law, 441 n.1
Buchanan, James, 91–3, 94, 95–7,
  98, 177

Calabresi, Guido, 74–5, 77, 84–5,
  183, 204, 245, 261, 336–9
causal paradigms, 271–2
causation, 270
  but-for and proximate, 270–1
  responsibility and, 273–4
civil action for public end, 378
Coase theorem, 113
collective action problem, 3
common pool, private property
  and, 293–4
communication costs, 128
community norms, failure to abide
  by, 334
compensation
  consent and, 460 n.7
  and the incentive to "take,"
    460 n.1

Index

efficiency, 92–4
  default rules and, 173–5
  legal institutions and, 2
  rational bargains and, 175–8
  rationality and consent and, 180–2
  relative nature of, 91–3
  strict liability and, 240–3
  voluntary choice and, 94–6
  see also Kaldor–Hicks efficiency
Ellickson, Robert, 456 n.10, 458 n.16
endogenous resources, preference for, 134–6
epistemic burdens, liability rules and, 213–15
Epstein, Richard, 216, 271–3, 315–16, 432, 485 n.15
equilibrium, causation and, 275–7
error costs, defections and, 154–7
Escola v. *Coca Cola Bottling Co.*, 24 Cal 2C, 453, 150 P.2d 436 (1944), 412, 422, 494 n.3
exchange, comparing frameworks of, 96–7
excuses
  agency-defeating, 335, 469 n.7, 483 n.5
  culpability-defeating, 334–5
  fault and justice and, 224–6
  reciprocity and, 259–61
  tort liability and, 224
  wrongdoing and, 333–5
expectations, relationship between normative and epistemic, 471 n.11

fairness
  as a constraint on bargaining, 53–7
  solving the problem of, 57–9
fault liability
  corrective justice and, 367–9
  cost of administering a system of, 226

the fault in, 217–19
  and justice and excuses, 224–6
  meaning and grounds of, 239–40
  retributivism and, 234–6
  strict liability and, 226–8, 256–8
  as strict victim liability, 229
  tort law and, 219
fault rule, 229
Ferejohn, John, 448 n.20
First Fundamental Theorem of Welfare Economics, 4
  basic implication of, 40
  see also Fundamental Theorems of Welfare Economics
Fletcher, George, 236, 253, 259, 266, 432
force of agreement, 119
forced transfers, 183
  compensation to legitimate, 190
formalism, 200
Fundamental Theorems of Welfare Economics
  standard proof of, 60
  see also First Fundamental Theorem of Welfare Economics

gap-filling rules, 181, 459 n.2, 459 n.3
  contracts and, 187
Gauthier, David, 3, 10, 48, 53–6, 445 n.12
grounds of recovery
  liability and, 285, 287
  modes of recovery and, 287
group size in contracting
  heterogeneity of principal parties and, 127
  spatial dispersion and, 128

harm
  concept of, 472 n.13
  strict liability and, 277–9
Hart, H. L. A., 220
Hirshleifer, Jack, 151–2
Holmes, O. W., 209, 212

502

Index

Hymowitz v. Eli Lilly and Co., 73
N.Y. 2d 487, 539 N. E. 2d 941
(1989), 397, 399–401, 405, 406
ideal contracts
nonideal agents and, 178–9
inalienability rules, 77, 336
individual rationality, 31, 126
inefficiencies, low transaction costs
and, 453 n.5
information
contract failure and incomplete,
130
coordination and private, 157–63
distinction between technological and distributive dimensions of, 151–4
effects of, 149–54
hazards from imperfect, 111
property rights and, 148–9, 153
transaction costs and, 125–6
see also private information
information requirements, litigation costs and, 248–9
initial liability rules, 212
injurer, redefining, 382–5
injustice, difference between misfortune and, 483 n.4
instability, transaction resources
and, 129
instrumentalism, forms of, 203–4
insurance, 205–9, 250–1

justice
between parties, 354–60
and fault and excuses, 224–6
reciprocity and, 266–8

Kahneman, Daniel, 112
Kaldor–Hicks efficiency, 167
Kaldor, Nicholas, 168
Knetsch, Jack, 112
Kronman, Anthony, 105, 148, 149–
50, 152–3, 449 n.1

Laidlaw v. Organ, 15 U. S. (2
Wheat.) 178 (1817), 148–63

law
economics and, 2
economic theories of, 102
instrumentalist account of, 200
local cooperation in the absence
of, 451 n.1
market failure and, 3
legal rules, social conventions as
alternatives to, 458 n.16
legitimate expectations, strict liability and, 279–81
legitimate interests, 278, 284
as rights, 331
liability
assigning, 455 n.4
on the basis of culpability, 263
cheapest cost-avoider and, 388–
95
distinction between criminal and
tort, 225
distinction between grounds of
recovery and, 285, 287
excuses that defeat, 467 n.8
grounds and scope of, 288–91
nature of strict and fault, 229–30
recovery and, 253–4, 285–7
tension between strict and fault,
473 n.1
without agency, 261–6
see also product liability; strict liability
liability decisions
economic arguments for restricting to victims and their particular injurers, 377
distributive dimensions of, 248
liability rules, 77, 78–80, 82, 83,
336–7
activity levels and, 247–8
compensation under, 189–90
conjunction with property rules,
340
epistemic burdens and, 213–15
property rules and, 183–4, 188–
90, 339–40, 341

Index

Index